Basic Ship Theory

K. J. Rawson
R.C.N.C., C.Eng., F.R.I.N.A., Wh.Sch.

E. C. Tupper
B.Sc., R.C.N.C., C.Eng., F.R.I.N.A., Wh.Sch.

2nd. Edition in two volumes
Volume 1
Chapters 1 to 9
Hydrostatics and Strength

Longman London and New York

LONGMAN GROUP LIMITED
London and New York
Associated companies, branches and representatives throughout the world

Published in the United States of America by
Longman Inc., New York

© *K. J. Rawson and E. C. Tupper* 1968 *and* 1976

All rights reserved. No part of this publication may be reproduced, stored in a retrieval system, or transmitted in any form or by any means, electronic, mechanical, photocopying, recording, or otherwise, without the prior permission of the Copyright owner.

First published 1968
Second edition 1976 (in two volumes)
Second impression 1977
Third impression 1978
Volume 1 ISBN 0 582 44523 X
Volume 2 ISBN 0 582 44524 8

Set in Times New Roman
and Printed in Hong Kong by Wing King Tong Company Limited

Contents

Preface to Second Edition   v

Foreword to the First Edition   vi

Introduction   vii
Units — Examples — **References and further reading**

Symbols and nomenclature   xvi
General — Geometry of ship — Propeller geometry — Resistance and propulsion — Seakeeping — Manoeuvrability — Strength — Notes

1 Art or Science?   1
History   Naval architecture today — Ships **Authorities**   Classification societies — Government bodies — International bodies — Learned bodies **References**

2 Some tools   7
Basic geometric concepts   Properties of irregular shapes   Plane shapes — Three-dimensional shapes — Metacentre — Hollow shapes — Symbols and conventions **Approximate integration**   Trapezoidal rule — Simpson's rules — Newton–Cotes' rules — Tchebycheff's rules — Gauss rules **Machines**   Planimeter — Integraph — Integrator — Analogue computers and simulators — Digital computers **Approximate formulae and rules**   Normand's formula — Weight conventions **Statistics**   Probability — Probability curve **Worked examples** *Problems* **References**

3 Flotation and trim   55
Flotation   Properties of fluids — Archimedes' principle — Vertical movement **Trim**   Changes of draught with trim-moment causing trim — Addition of weight — Large weight additions — Determination of design trim — Change of water density **Hydrostatic data**   Hydrostatic curves — Calculation of hydrostatic data — Metacentric diagram **Worked examples** *Problems*

4 Stability   93
Initial stability   Adjustment of transverse metacentric height by small changes of dimensions — Effect of mass density — Effect of free surfaces of liquids — Effect of freely suspended weights — The wall-sided formula **Complete stability**   Cross curves of stability — Derivation of cross curves of stability — Accuracy of stability calculations — Curves of statical stability — Main features of the $\overline{GZ}$ curve — Effect of free liquid surfaces on stability at large angles of inclination — Surfaces of B, M, F, and Z — Influence of ship form on stability — Stability of a completely submerged body **Dynamical stability**   **Stability assessment**   Stability standards — The inclining experiment *Problems* **References**

5 Hazards and protection   146
Flooding and collision   Watertight subdivision — Flotation calculations — Damaged stability calculations — Damage safety margins — Loss of stability on grounding — Berthing and ice navigation **Safety of life at sea**   Fire — Life-saving equipment — Anchoring — Damage control — Uncomfortable cargoes — Nuclear machinery **Other hazards**   Mechanical shock — Ship signatures — Enemy action — **Vulnerability** — Environmental pollution *Problems* **References**

iv *Contents*

6 The ship girder   175

The standard calculation The wave — Weight distribution — Buoyancy and balance — Loading — Shearing force and bending moment — Second moment of area — Bending stresses — Shear stresses **Extensions to the standard calculation** Influence lines — Changes to section modulus — Slopes and deflections — Horizontal flexure — Behaviour of a hollow box girder — Wave pressure correction — Strip theory — Structural dynamics — Longitudinal strength standards by rule **Criterion of failure** Full-scale trials — The nature of failure — Structural reliability — Statistical determination of loading **Discontinuities** Theory — Built-in stress concentrations — Brittle fracture — Discontinuities in structural design — Superstructures and deckhouses **Conclusions** *Problems* **References**

7 Structural design and analysis   226

Loading and failure — Structural units of a ship **Stiffened plating** Simple beams — Grillages — Swedged plating **Panels of plating** Behaviour of panels under lateral loading — Available results for flat plates under lateral pressure — Buckling of panels **Frameworks** Methods of analysis — Elastic stability of a frame — End constraint **Fittings** Control surfaces — Shaft brackets **Finite element techniques** *Problems* **References**

8 Launching and docking   275

Launching Launching curves — Construction of launching curves — Groundways — The dynamics of launching — Strength and stability — Sideways launching **Docking** Load distribution — Block behaviour — Strength of floating docks — Stability during docking *Problems* **References**

9 The ship environment   291

The external environment The sea Water properties — The sea surface **Waves** Trochoidal waves — Sinusoidal waves — Irregular wave patterns — Histograms and probability distributions — Wave spectra — Sea state code — ITTC Spectra — Wave amplitudes — Extreme wave amplitudes — Other means of defining an irregular wave system **Climate** The wind — Ambient air — Climatic extremes **Physical limitations The internal environment Ship motions The air Lighting Vibration and noise** Excitation — Responses — Cures — Calculations — Noise — **Ice** *Problems* **References**

Answers to problems   xxi

Index   xxv

Volume 2

10 Powering of ships—general principles

11 Powering of ships—application

12 Seakeeping

13 Manoeuvrability

14 Major ship design features

15 Ship design

16 Special ship types

Answers to problems

Index

Preface to the Second Edition

Knowledge and practice advances today with such speed that textbooks must be updated with increasing regularity. Basic Ship Theory was first published at a time when SI units were to be introduced but before any clear guidance upon preferred units or values had been prepared—indeed, debate upon this subject is far from dead. Fortunately, we were able to anticipate correctly how the profession would move and changes in the second edition on this score are few. We have extended the use of metric SI but have felt that it is not yet time to abandon the old units totally; consequently, old and new units have been retained—a state of affairs which practising naval architects will have to face for many years yet. Ships and shipping are, after all, international and enduring!

It is a good deal more difficult to incorporate in a book of this type the very rapid advances in theory which have been encouraged by the development of the digital computer. So many of these advances depend upon a mathematical technique which cannot reasonably be yet expected in students at this stage of their learning. Yet the exclusion of this basic work would render the book incomplete. The authors have therefore incorporated a superficial description of such material as strip theory, finite element technique, structural dynamics, computing techniques, etc., so that the students will be aware of its existence and the way in which they are forced to rely upon an increasing array of specialists until they are themselves able to study these topics in detail.

It has been decided to issue the second edition in two volumes, the first volume dealing with statics, structure and environment and the second dealing with hydrodynamics, ship dynamics and design. In this way, it is hoped that the swelling number of people, inspired perhaps by the challenge of offshore engineering and maritime affairs, will be encouraged to establish their interest in the sea with some basic knowledge of its technology and science.

September 1974

                                                                                                    K J R   E C T

Foreword to the First Edition

*By Sir Alfred J. Sims, K.C.B., O.B.E., D.Sc., R.C.N.C.,
formerly Director General Ships, Ministry of Defence,
Principal Technical Adviser to the Navy Board
and President of the Royal Institution of
Naval Architects*

The textbooks available in theoretical naval architecture are few. The one with which I have had some association in later years—Attwood's *Theoretical Naval Architecture*—has stood the profession in good stead since the beginning of this century.

For some time I have looked forward to a new book in this field, encompassing the many important developments in the subject and the modern aids to good ship design.

Now, two members of the Royal Corps of Naval Constructors have undertaken this task with enthusiasm and competence. Both authors have recently been in the forefront of the design of complex warships. Both are well able to expound the latest theories and to be able to select the most useful material for students of all ages.

The authors have taken care to cover the merchant ship field as well as warships and the book will have wide appeal throughout the profession on this account.

To new students, I commend the book in the confidence that it will be helpful and stimulating. To those already in the profession, or well advanced in their studies, I commend the work as a valuable book of reference.

December 1966   ALFRED J. SIMS

Introduction

Naval architecture is a rapidly developing subject. Advances in other scientific and technical subjects, development of new design techniques and the ubiquitous computer all enable the ship designer to carry out his work with greater precision and confidence. New ideas and methods are complementing or replacing old concepts.

Not unnaturally the major changes are taking place at the more advanced levels. Nevertheless, they influence the method of presentation of the more basic ideas and the emphasis placed on various aspects of the subject. At the same time, in common with other professions, it is desirable that students be presented with concepts more advanced than have been available in general textbooks to date. This is in keeping with the Chapman Report (Reference 1) which presented the shipbuilding and shipping industries with a challenge that must be met.

Only in this way can the shipping and shipbuilding industries cope with the ever changing technologies with which they interface.

This book aims at providing an introduction to ship theory—a term embracing theoretical naval architecture and other specialized theory used by those whose work is associated with ships. Besides extending the scope of earlier textbooks in this way, the conventional bounds of the subject have been extended. Care has been taken to avoid duplicating, as far as possible, work the student will be doing in other subjects as part of his degree or engineering or technician courses; indeed, it is necessary to assume that his knowledge in all subjects advances with his progress through this book. It is hoped that this book will encourage more people to interest themselves and advance their knowledge in ships. Reference 1 concludes that the number of graduates and those with HNC qualifications employed in shipbuilding should be more than doubled in each instance. It also notes that, at present, a loss of interest and enthusiasm often occurs in the early stages of training. The authors have tried to stimulate and hold the interest of the student by a careful arrangement of the subject matter of the book. Chapter 1 and the opening paragraphs of each succeeding chapter have been presented in somewhat lyrical terms in the hope that the authors will convey to the students some of the enthusiasm which they feel themselves for this fascinating subject. Naval architects need never fear that they will have, during their careers, to face the same problems day after day. Before they reach the Board Room to direct basic thought and policy, they will spend many years on as wide a variety of sciences as are touched upon by any profession.

Before embarking on the book proper it is necessary to comment on the units employed, and the use made of examples and references.

UNITS

In May 1965, the Government announced its view that British Industry should move to the use of the metric system. In addition, at the present time, a newly rationalized set of metric units is coming into international use following endorsement by the International Organization for Standardization. It is the Système International d'Unités (SI)—and the UK is able to adopt it from the outset. It replaces also the British Standard Specification 1991 for symbols and terminology.

The adoption of SI units has been patchy in many countries while some have yet to change from their traditional positions. A change from inches to metres is simple and has been widely effected; the rejection of tonf in favour of MegaNewton has proceeded slowly. One of the reasons for this is the retention of kg as the unit of mass and its ready—and erroneous—acceptance by trade and industry as the unit of force because weighing devices are dependent upon springs which respond to force. Neither does moment of a mass have meaning. Students beware!

In the following notes, the SI system of units is presented briefly; a fuller treatment appears in Ref. 2. To assist the change to the metric system in the United Kingdom and to meet the needs of the readers in other countries, this book has been written in terms of British and metric units. Examples in both British and metric units are included both as worked examples and set problems and, wherever appropriate, basic data is presented in terms of both sets of units.

The SI is a rationalized selection of units in the metric system. It is a coherent system, i.e. the product or quotient of any two unit quantities in the system is the unit of the resultant quantity. The six basic units are as follows:

Quantity	Name of unit	Unit symbol
Length	metre	m
Mass	kilogramme	kg
Time	second	s
Electric current	ampere	A
Thermodynamic temperature	degree Kelvin	°K
Luminous intensity	candela	cd

Special names have been adopted for some of the derived SI units and these are listed below together with their unit symbols:

Physical quantity	SI unit	Unit symbol
Force	newton	$N = kg\,m/s^2$
Work, energy	joule	$J = N\,m$
Power	watt	$W = J/s$
Electric charge	coulomb	$C = A\,s$
Electric potential	volt	$V = W/A$
Electric capacitance	farad	$F = A\,s/V$
Electric resistance	ohm	$\Omega = V/A$
Frequency	hertz	$Hz = s^{-1}$
Illumination	lux	$lx = lm/m^2$

In the following two tables are listed other derived units and the equivalent values of some UK units respectively:

Physical quantity	SI unit	Unit symbol
Area	square metre	m^2
Volume	cubic metre	m^3
Density	kilogramme per cubic metre	kg/m^3
Velocity	metre per second	m/s
Angular velocity	radian per second	rad/s
Acceleration	metre per second squared	m/s^2
Angular acceleration	radian per second squared	rad/s^2
Pressure, Stress	newton per square metre	N/m^2
Surface tension	newton per metre	N/m
Dynamic viscosity	newton second per metre squared	$N\,s/m^2$
Kinematic viscosity	metre squared per second	m^2/s
Thermal conductivity	watt per metre degree Kelvin	$W/(m\,°K)$

(Note: N/m^2 is known also as a pascal. 10^5 N/m^2 is also known as a bar.)

Quantity	UK unit	Equivalent SI units
Length	1 yd	0·9144 m
	1 ft	0·3048 m
	1 in	0·0254 m
	1 mile	1609·344 m
	1 nautical mile (UK)	1853·18 m
	1 nautical mile (International)	1852 m
Area	1 in^2	$645·16 \times 10^{-6}\,m^2$
	1 ft^2	0·092903 m^2
	1 yd^2	0·836127 m^2
	1 mile^2	$2·58999 \times 10^6\,m^2$
Volume	1 in^3	$16·3871 \times 10^{-6}\,m^3$
	1 ft^3	0·0283168 m^3
	1 UK gal	0·004546092 m^3

(*continued on p. xii*)

(continued from p. xi)

Velocity	1 ft/s	0·3048 m/s
	1 mile/hr	0·44704 m/s; 1·60934 km/hr
	1 knot (UK)	0·51477 m/s; 1·85318 km/hr
	1 knot (International)	0·51444 m/s; 1·852 km/hr
Standard acceleration, g	32·174 ft/s^2	9·80665 m/s^2
Mass	1 lb	0·45359237 kg
	1 ton	1016·05 kg
Mass density	1 lb/in^3	27·6799 × 10^3 kg/m^3
	1 lb/ft^3	16·0185 kg/m^3
Force	1 pdl	0·138255 N
	1 lbf	4·44822 N
Pressure	1 lbf/in^2	6894·76 N/m^2
Stress	1 tonf/in^2	15·4443 × 10^6 N/m^2
Energy	1 ft pdl	0·0421401 J
	1 ft lbf	1·35582 J
	1 cal	4·1868 J
	1 Btu	1055·06 J
Power	1 hp	745·700 W
Temperature	1 Rankine unit	5/9 Kelvin unit
	1 Fahrenheit unit	5/9 Celsius unit

Prefixes to denote multiples and sub-multiples to be affixed to the names of units are:

Factor by which the unit is multiplied	Prefix	Symbol
1 000 000 000 000 = 10^{12}	tera	T
1 000 000 000 = 10^9	giga	G
1 000 000 = 10^6	mega	M
1 000 = 10^3	kilo	k
100 = 10^2	hecto	h
10 = 10^1	deca	da
0·1 = 10^{-1}	deci	d
0·01 = 10^{-2}	centi	c
0·001 = 10^{-3}	milli	m
0·000 001 = 10^{-6}	micro	μ
0·000 000 001 = 10^{-9}	nano	n
0·000 000 000 001 = 10^{-12}	pico	p
0·000 000 000 000 001 = 10^{-15}	femto	f
0·000 000 000 000 000 001 = 10^{-18}	atto	a

We list, finally, some proposed metric values (values proposed for density of fresh and salt water are based on a temperature of 15°C (59°F).)

Item	Accepted British figure	Direct metric equivalent	Preferred SI value
Gravity, g	32·17 ft/s^2	9·80665 m/s^2	9·807 m/s^2
Mass density salt water	64 lb/ft^3 35 ft^3/ton	1·0252 tonne/m^3 0·9754 m^3/tonne	1·025 tonne/m^3 0·975 m^3/tonne
Mass density fresh water	62·2 lb/ft^3 36 ft^3/ton	0·9964 tonne/m^3 1·0033 m^3/tonne	1·0 tonne/m^3 1·0 m^3/tonne
Young's modulus, E	13,500 tonf/in^2	2·0855 × 10^7 N/cm^2	209 GN/m^2
Atmospheric pressure	14·7 lbf/in^2	101,353 N/m^2 10·1353 N/cm^2	10^5 N/m^2 or Pa or 1·0 bar
TPI (salt water)	$\dfrac{A_w}{420}$ tonf/in	1·025 A_w (tonnef/m)	1·025 A_w tonnef/m
TPM NPM	A_w (ft^2)	100·52 A_w (N/cm) 10,052 A_w (N/m)	10^4 A_w (N/m)
MCT 1″ (salt water) (Units of tonf and feet)	$\dfrac{\Delta \overline{GM_L}}{12L}$ $\dfrac{\text{tonf ft}}{\text{in}}$	$\dfrac{\Delta \overline{GM_L}}{L}\left(\dfrac{\text{MN m}}{\text{m}}\right)$	$\dfrac{\Delta \overline{GM_L}}{L}\left(\dfrac{\text{MN m}}{\text{m}}\right)$
One metre trim moment, (Δ in MN or $\dfrac{\text{tonnef m}}{\text{m}}$, Δ in tonnef)			
Force displacement Δ 1 tonf		1·01605 tonnef 9964·02 N	1·016 tonnef 9964 N
Mass displacement Σ 1 ton		1·01605 tonne	1·016 tonne
Weight density: Salt water Fresh water			0·01 MN/m^3 0·0098 MN/m^3
Specific volume: Salt water Fresh water			99·5 m^3/MN 102·0 m^3/MN

Of particular significance to the naval architect are the units used for displacement, density and stress. The force displacement Δ, under the SI scheme must be expressed in terms of newtons. In practice the meganewton (MN) is a more convenient unit and 1 MN is approximately equivalent to 100 tonf (100·44 more exactly). This new unit will eliminate any confusion between the displacement and tonnage of a ship but, to assist students in making the change from one system of units to another, the authors have additionally introduced the tonnef (and, correspondingly, the tonne for mass measurement) as explained more fully in Chapter 3.

Many preferred values are used by naval architects, e.g. 36 for the number of cubic feet in a ton of fresh water, although the precise figure is slightly different. Conversion to the metric system will involve the adoption of new preferred values which are not precisely equivalent to the old. The authors have adopted those shown in the table immediately above.

EXAMPLES

A number of worked examples has been included in the text of most chapters to illustrate the application of the principles enunciated therein. Some are relatively short but others involve lengthy computations. They have been deliberately chosen to help educate the student in the subject of naval architecture, and the authors have not been unduly influenced by the thought that examination questions often involve about 30 minutes' work.

In the problems set at the end of each chapter, the aim has been adequately to cover the subject matter, avoiding, as far as possible, examples involving mere arithmetic substitution in standard formulae. The opportunity has also been taken to extend the scope of the chapter in some instances. Many of these are or are based closely on actual examination questions. Others have been introduced to lead to a better understanding of the subject without direct concern for time of execution. All have been made as realistic as possible.

Where actual examination questions have been used acknowledgement is made according to the following list:

RNC	Royal Naval College, Greenwich
RNATE	Formerly R.N. Artificer Training Establishment
AP & S	Attwood, E. L., and Pengelly, H. S. revised by Sims, A. J., *Theoretical Naval Architecture* Longmans, 1953.
HMDTC	H.M. Dockyard Technical Colleges.

REFERENCES

References are listed at the end of each chapter in order to acknowledge the source of information presented and to enable the student to study in more detail any particular aspect of the subject. The references are not exhaustive but most provide further guidance on recommended reading. Where information has been presented or used in more than one paper or book an attempt has been made to select the one most likely to be accessible to the student. A large number of references have been made to the transactions of the Royal Institution of Naval Architects as these are widely available. The authors apologize if this should, in any instance, appear to credit a development to anyone other than the true originator but would point out that some students may not have as ready access to scientific journals as research workers often enjoy.

The authors also seek indulgence where limitations in the space available in or scope of this volume have meant that the arguments of other authors have not been fully covered. Indeed, in some cases, it has been necessary to forsake mathematical precision in order to present the essential elements of an idea without confusing the student with the many qualifying conditions often involved.

The following abbreviations have been used in the references:

RINA   Royal Institution of Naval Architects (INA prior to 1960).

SNAME   The Society of Naval Architects and Marine Engineers.
SNAJ   Society of Naval Architects of Japan.
NEC   North East Coast Institution of Engineers and Shipbuilders.
IESS   Institution of Engineers and Shipbuilders of Scotland.
IMarE   Institution of Marine Engineers.
IMechE   Institution of Mechanical Engineers.
HMSO   Her Majesty's Stationery Office.
BSI   British Standards Institution.
DTMB   David Taylor Model Basin, Washington.

The letter T before a set of the above initials represents the transactions, and the letter J the journal, of that body.

ACKNOWLEDGEMENTS

The authors are grateful to Sir Alfred J. Sims, formerly the DG Ships, Ministry of Defence, for the original suggestion that this work should be undertaken and for his continued interest and encouragement during the progress of the work.

In addition to the acknowledgements made in the first edition, the authors are grateful for the constructive comments made by readers and by their colleagues in industry, the universities, colleges, schools and in the Ministries and by friends at home and abroad. With their help, the few errors that crept inevitably into the first edition are, hopefully, eradicated.

The book is published with the permission of the Ministry of Defence but the responsibility for any statements of fact or opinion rests solely with the authors.

References and further reading

1. *The Higher Education and Training of Naval Architects.* Report to the Council of the Royal Institution of Naval Architects by J. H. B. Chapman, 1966.
2. Paffett, J. A. H. Metrication in ship research and design, *TRINA*, 1971.
3. Baxter, B. N. Qualifications in shipbuilding, *TRINA*, 1971.
4. British Standards Institution BS 3763 (1970) and PD 5685 (1972).
5. *Guides to the preparation of papers*, RINA and I.Mech.E.

Symbols and Nomenclature

GENERAL

a	linear acceleration
A	area in general
B	breadth in general
D, d	diameter in general
E	energy in general
F	force in general
g	acceleration due to gravity
h	depth or pressure head in general
h_w, ζ_w	height of wave, crest to trough
H	total head, Bernoulli
L	length in general
L_w, λ	wave-length
m	mass
n	rate of revolution
p	pressure intensity
p_v	vapour pressure of water
p_∞	ambient pressure at infinity
P	power in general
q	stagnation pressure
Q	rate of flow
r, R	radius in general
s	length along path
t	time in general
$t°$	temperature in general
T	period of time for a complete cycle
u	reciprocal weight density, specific volume,
u, v, w	velocity components in direction of x-, y-, z-axes
U, V	linear velocity
w	weight density
W	weight in general
x, y, z	body axes and Cartesian co-ordinates
	Right-hand system fixed in the body, z-axis vertically down, x-axis forward. Origin at c.g.
x_0, y_0, z_0	fixed axes
	Right-hand orthogonal system nominally fixed in space, z_0-axis vertically down, x_0-axis in the general direction of the initial motion.
α	angular acceleration
γ	specific gravity
Γ	circulation
δ	thickness of boundary layer in general
θ	angle of pitch
μ	coefficient of dynamic viscosity
ν	coefficient of kinematic viscosity
ρ	mass density
ϕ	angle of roll, heel or list
χ	angle of yaw
ω	angular velocity or circular frequency
∇	volume in general

GEOMETRY OF SHIP

A_M	midship section area
A_W	waterplane area
A_X	maximum transverse section area
B	beam or moulded breadth
$\overline{BM}$	metacentre above centre of buoyancy
C_B	block coefficient
C_M	midship section coefficient
C_P	longitudinal prismatic coefficient
C_{VP}	vertical prismatic coefficient
C_{WP}	coefficient of fineness of waterplane
D	depth of ship
F	freeboard
$\overline{GM}$	transverse metacentric height
$\overline{GM}_L$	longitudinal metacentric height
I_L	longitudinal moment of inertia of waterplane about CF
I_P	polar moment of inertia
I_T	transverse moment of inertia
L	length of ship—generally between perps
L_{OA}	length overall
L_{PP}	length between perps
L_{WL}	length of waterline in general
S	wetted surface
T	draught
Δ	**displacement force**
λ	scale ratio—ship/model dimension
∇	**displacement volume**
Σ	**displacement mass**

PROPELLER GEOMETRY

A_D	developed blade area
A_E	expanded area
A_O	disc area
A_P	projected blade area
b	span of aerofoil or hydrofoil
c	chord length
d	boss or hub diameter
D	diameter of propeller
f_M	camber
P	propeller pitch in general
R	propeller radius
t	thickness of aerofoil
Z	number of blades of propeller
α	angle of attack
ϕ	pitch angle of screw propeller

RESISTANCE AND PROPULSION

a	resistance augment fraction
C_D	drag coeff.
C_L	lift coeff.
C_T	specific total resistance coeff.
C_W	specific wave-making resistance coeff.
D	drag force
F_n	Froude number
I	idle resistance
J	advance number of propeller
K_Q	torque coeff.
K_T	thrust coeff.
L	lift force

P_D	delivered power at propeller
P_E	effective power
P_I	indicated power
P_S	shaft power
P_T	thrust power
Q	torque
R	resistance in general
R_n	Reynolds' number
R_F	frictional resistance
R_R	residuary resistance
R_T	total resistance
R_W	wave-making resistance
s_A	apparent slip ratio
t	thrust deduction fraction
T	thrust
U	velocity of a fluid
U_∞	velocity of an undisturbed flow
V	speed of ship
V_A	speed of advance of propeller
w	Taylor wake fraction in general
w_F	Froude wake fraction
W_n	Weber number
β	appendage scale effect factor
β	advance angle of a propeller blade section
δ	Taylor's advance coeff.
η	efficiency in general
η_B	propeller efficiency behind ship
η_D	quasi propulsive coefficient
η_H	hull eff.
η_O	propeller eff. in open water
η_R	relative rotative efficiency
σ	cavitation number

SEAKEEPING

c	wave velocity
f	frequency
f_E	frequency of encounter
I_{xx}, I_{yy}, I_{zz}	real moments of inertia
I_{xy}, I_{xz}, I_{yz}	real products of inertia
k	radius of gyration
m_n	spectrum moment where n is an integer
M_L	horizontal wave bending moment
M_T	torsional wave bending moment
M_V	vertical wave bending moment
s	relative vertical motion of bow with respect to wave surface
$S_\zeta(\omega), S_\theta(\omega)$, etc.	one-dimensional spectral density
$S_\zeta(\omega, \mu), S_\theta(\omega, \mu)$, etc.	two-dimensional spectral density
T	wave period
T_E	period of encounter
T_z	natural period in smooth water for heaving
T_θ	natural period in smooth water for pitching
T_ϕ	natural period in smooth water for rolling
$Y_{\theta\zeta}(\omega)$	response amplitude operator—pitch
$Y_{\phi\zeta}(\omega)$	response amplitude operator—roll
$Y_{\chi\zeta}(\omega)$	response amplitude operator—yaw
β	leeway or drift angle
δ_R	rudder angle
ε	phase angle between any two harmonic motions
ζ	instantaneous wave elevation
ζ_A	wave amplitude

ζ_w	wave height, crest to trough
θ	pitch angle
θ_A	pitch amplitude
κ	wave number
ω_E	frequency of encounter
Λ	tuning factor

MANOEUVRABILITY

A_C	area under cut-up
A_R	area of rudder
b	span of hydrofoil
c	chord of hydrofoil
K, M, N	moment components on body relative to body axes
O	origin of body axes
p, q, r	components of angular velocity relative to body axes
X, Y, Z	force components on body
α	angle of attack
β	drift angle
δ_R	rudder angle
χ	heading angle
ω_C	steady rate of turn

STRENGTH

a	length of plate
b	breadth of plate
C	modulus of rigidity
ε	linear strain
E	modulus of elasticity, Young's modulus
σ	direct stress
σ_y	yield stress
g	acceleration due to gravity
I	planar second moment of area
J	polar second moment of area
j	stress concentration factor
k	radius of gyration
K	bulk modulus
l	length of member
L	length
M	bending moment
M_p	plastic moment
M_{AB}	bending moment at A in member AB
m	mass
P	direct load, externally applied
P_E	Euler collapse load
p	distributed direct load (area distribution), pressure
p'	distributed direct load (line distribution)
τ	shear stress
r	radius
S	internal shear force
s	distance along a curve
T	applied torque
t	thickness, time
U	strain energy
W	weight, external load
y	lever in bending
δ	deflection, permanent set, elemental (when associated with element of breadth, e.g. δb)
ρ	mass density
ν	Poisson's ratio
θ	slope

NOTES

(a) A distance between two points is represented by a bar over the letters defining the two points, e.g. $\overline{GM}$ is the distance between G and M.

(b) When a quantity is to be expressed in non-dimensional form is it denoted by the use of the prime '. Unless otherwise specified, the non-dimensionalising factor is a function of ρ, L and V, e.g. $m' = m/\frac{1}{2}\rho L^3$, $x' = x/\frac{1}{2}\rho L^2 V^2$, $L' = L/\frac{1}{2}\rho L^3 V^2$.

(c) A lower case subscript is used to denote the denominator of a partial derivative, e.g. $Y_u = \partial Y/\partial u$.

(d) For derivatives with respect to time the dot notation is used, e.g. $\dot{x} = dx/dt$.

1 Art or Science?

Many thousands of years ago when man became intelligent and adventurous, those tribes who lived near the sea ventured on to it. They built rafts or hollowed out tree trunks and soon experienced the thrill of moving across the water, propelled by tide or wind or device. They experienced, too, the first sea disasters; their boats sank or broke, capsized or rotted and lives were lost. It was natural that those builders of boats which were adjudged more successful than others, received the acclaim of their fellow men and were soon regarded as craftsmen. The intelligent craftsman observed perhaps, that capsizing was less frequent when using two trunks joined together or when an outrigger was fixed, or that he could manoeuvre better with a rudder in a suitable position. His tools were trial and error and his stimulus was the pride in his craft. He was the first naval architect.

The craftsmen's expertize developed as it was passed down the generations: the Greeks built their triremes and the Romans their galleys; the Vikings produced their beautiful craft to carry soldiers through heavy seas and on to the beaches. Several hundred years later, the craftsmen were designing and building great square rigged ships for trade and war and relying still on knowledge passed down through the generations and guarded by extreme secrecy. Still, they learned by trial and error because they had yet no other tools and the disasters at sea persisted.

The need for a scientific approach must have been felt many hundreds of years before it was possible and it was not possible until relatively recently, despite the corner stone laid by Archimedes two thousand years ago. Until the middle of the eighteenth century the design and building of ships was wholly a craft and it was not, in Britain, until the second half of the nineteenth century that science affected ships appreciably.

Isaac Newton and other great mathematicians of the seventeenth century laid the foundations for so many sciences and naval architecture was no exception. Without any doubt, however, the father of naval architecture was Pierre Bouguer who published in 1746, *Traité du Navire* (Ref. 1). In this book, Bouguer laid the foundations of many aspects of naval architecture which were developed later in the eighteenth century by Bernoulli, Euler and Santacilla (Ref. 2). Lagrange and many others made contributions but the other outstanding figure of this century was the Swede, Frederick Chapman who pioneered work on ship resistance which led up to the great work of William Froude a hundred years later. A scientific approach to naval architecture was encouraged more on the continent than in Britain where it remained until the 1850's, a craft surrounded by pride and secrecy. On 19 May 1666, Samuel Pepys wrote of a Mr Deane,

And then he fell to explain to me his manner of casting the draught of water which a ship will draw before-hand; which is a secret the King and all admire in him, and he is the first that hath come to any certainty before-hand of foretelling the draught of water of a ship before she be launched. (Ref. 3.)

The second half of the nineteenth century, however, produced Scott Russell, Rankine and Froude and the development of the science, and dissemination of knowledge in Britain was rapid. This development in Britain is described in Ref. 4.

NAVAL ARCHITECTURE TODAY

It would be quite wrong to say that the art and craft built up over many thousands of years has been wholly replaced by a science. The need for a scientific approach was felt, first, because the art had proved inadequate to halt the disasters at sea or to guarantee to the merchant that he was getting the best for his money. Science has contributed much to alleviate these shortcomings but it continues to require the injection of experience of successful practice. Science produces the correct basis for comparison of ships but the exact value of the criteria which determine their performances must, as in other branches of engineering, continue to be dictated by previous successful practice, i.e. like most engineering, this is largely a comparative science. Where the scientific tool is less precise than one could wish, it must be heavily overlaid with craft; where a precise tool is developed, the craft must be discarded. Because complex problems encourage dogma, this has not always been easy.

The question, 'Art or Science?' is therefore loaded since it presupposes a choice. Naval architecture is art and science.

Basically, naval architecture is concerned with ship safety, ship performance and ship geometry, although these are not exclusive divisions.

With ship safety, the naval architect is concerned that the ship does not capsize in a seaway, or when damaged or even when maltreated. He must ensure that the ship is sufficiently strong so that it does not break up or fracture locally to let the water in. He must ensure that the crew has a good chance of survival if the ship does let water in through accident or enemy action.

The performance of the ship is dictated by the needs of trade or war. The required amount of cargo must be carried to the places which the owner specifies in the right condition and in the most economical manner; the warship must carry the maximum hitting power of the right sort and an efficient crew to the remote parts of the world. Size, tonnage, deadweight, endurance, speed, life, resistance, methods of propulsion, manoeuvrability and many other features must be matched to provide the right primary performance at the right cost.

Ship geometry concerns the correct interrelation of compartments which the architect of a house considers on a smaller scale. In an aircraft carrier, the naval architect has 2000 rooms to relate, one with another. He must provide up to fifty different piping and ducting systems to all parts of the ship. He must provide comfort for the crew and facilities to enable each member to perform his correct function. The ship must load and unload in harbour with the utmost speed and perhaps replenish at sea. The architecture of the ship must be such that it can be economically built, and the production arrangements for the ship are an important consideration. Finally, the geometry must be arranged, in so far as is possible, to be aesthetically pleasing; a merchant ship must appeal to its potential customers, while a warship must appear formidable to a potential enemy.

It must be clear that naval architecture involves complex compromises of many of these features. The art is, perhaps, the blending in the right proportions. There can be few other pursuits which draw on such a variety of sciences to blend them into an acceptable whole. There can be few pursuits as fascinating. This book attempts to isolate many of the basic calculations and considerations applicable to all ships.

SHIPS

Ships are designed to meet the requirements of owners or of war and their features are dictated by these requirements. The purpose of a merchant ship has been described (Ref. 5) as conveying passengers or cargo from one port to another in the most efficient manner. This was interpreted by the owners of *Cutty Sark* as the conveying of relatively small quantities of tea in the shortest possible time, because this was what the tea market demanded at that time. The market might well have required twice the quantity of tea per voyage in a voyage of twice the length of time, when a fundamentally different design of ship would have resulted. The economics of any particular market have a profound effect on merchant ship design. Thus, the change in the oil market following the second world war resulted in the disappearance of the 12,000 ton deadweight tankers and the appearance of the 400,000 ton deadweight supertankers. The economics of the trading of the ship itself have an effect on its design; the desire, for example, for small tonnage (and therefore small harbour dues) with large cargo-carrying capacity brought about the three island and shelter deck ships where cargo could be stowed in spaces not counted towards the tonnage on which insurance rates and harbour dues are based. Such trends have not always been compatible with safety and requirements of safety now also vitally influence ship design. Specialized demands of trade have produced the great passenger liners and bulk carriers, the natural-gas carriers, the trawlers and many other interesting ships. Indeed, the trend is towards more and more specialization in merchant ship design.

Specialization applies equally to warships. Basically, the warship is designed to meet a country's defence policy. Because the design and building of warships takes several years, it is an advantage if a particular defence policy persists for at least ten years and the task of long term defence planning is an onerous and responsible one. The Defence Staff interprets the general Government policy into the needs for meeting particular threats in particular parts of the world and the scientists and technologists produce weapons for defensive and offensive use. The naval architect then designs ships to carry the weapons and the men to use them to the correct part of the world. Thus, nations, like Britain and the USA with commitments the other side of the world, would be expected to expend more of the available space in their ships on facilities for getting the weapons and crew in a satisfactory state to a remote, perhaps hot, area than a nation which expects to make short harrying excursions from its home ports. It is important, therefore, to regard the ship as a complete weapon system and weapon and ship designers must work in the closest possible contact.

Nowhere, probably, is this more important than in the aircraft carrier. The type of aircraft carried so vitally affects an aircraft carrier that the ship is virtually designed around it; only by exceeding all the minimum demands of an aircraft and producing monster carriers, can any appreciable degree of flexibility be introduced. The guided missile destroyer results directly from the Defence Staff's assessment of likely enemy aircraft and guided weapons and their concept of how and where they would be used; submarine design is profoundly affected by diving depth and weapon systems which are determined by offensive and defensive considerations. The invention of the torpedo led to the motor torpedo boat which in turn led to the torpedo boat destroyer; the submarine, as an alternative carrier of the torpedo, led to the design of the anti-submarine frigate; the missile carrying nuclear submarine led to the hunter killer nuclear submarine. Thus, the particular demand of war, as is natural, produces a particular warship. Reference 6 gives a valuable historical survey while the host of specialized warships that arose from the second world war are described in Ref. 7.

Particular demands of the sea have resulted in many other interesting and important ships: the self-righting lifeboats, the ground effect machines, mulberry harbours, cargo drones, hydrofoil craft and a host of others. All are governed by the basic rules and tools of naval architecture which this book seeks to explore. Precision in the use of these tools must continue to be inspired by knowledge of sea disasters; the first Liberty ships of the second world war (Ref. 8), the loss of the *Royal George*, the loss of HMS *Captain* (Ref. 9), and the loss of the *Vasa*:

> In 1628, the *Vasa* set out on a maiden voyage which lasted little more than two hours. She sank in good weather through capsizing while still in view of the people of Stockholm. (Ref. 10.)

Authorities

CLASSIFICATION SOCIETIES

The authorities with the most profound influence on shipbuilding, merchant ship design and ship safety are the classification societies. Among the most important are Lloyd's Register of Shipping, det Norske Veritas, the American Bureau of Shipping, Bureau Veritas, Registro Italiano, Germanische Lloyd and Nippon Kaiji Kyokai. Lloyd's Register, combined since 1949 with the British Corporation is the largest and most influential.

It is odd that the two most influential bodies in the shipbuilding and shipping industries should both derive their names from the same owner of a coffee shop, Edward Lloyd, at the end of the seventeenth century. Yet the two organizations are entirely independent with quite separate histories. Lloyd's Insurance

Corporation is concerned with mercantile and other insurance. Lloyd's Register of Shipping is concerned with the maintenance of proper technical standards in ship construction and the classification of ships, i.e. the record of all relevant technical details and the assurance that these meet the required standards. Vessels so registered with Lloyd's Register are said to be classed with the Society and may be awarded the classification ✠ 100 A1. The cross denotes that the ship has been built under the supervision of surveyors from Lloyd's Register while 100 A shows that the vessel is built in accordance with the recommended standards. The final 1 indicates that the safety equipment, anchors and cables are as required. Other provisos to the classification are often added.

The maintenance of these standards is an important function of Lloyd's Register who require surveys of a specified thoroughness at stated intervals by the Society's surveyors. Failure to conform may result in removal of the ship from class and a consequent reduction in its value. The total impartiality of the Society is its great strength. It is also empowered to allot load line (see Chapter 5) certificates to ships, to ensure that they are adhered to and, as agents for certain foreign governments, to assess tonnage measurement and to ensure compliance with safety regulations. Over 1000 surveyors, scattered all over the world, carry out the required surveys, reporting to headquarters in London or other national centres where the classification of the ships are considered.

The standards to which the ships must be built and maintained are laid down in the first of the two major publications of Lloyd's Register, *Rules and Regulations for the Construction and Classification of Steel Ships*. This is issued annually and kept up to date to meet new demands. The other major publication is the *Register Book* in several volumes, which lists every known ship, whether classed with the Society or not, together with all of its important technical particulars. Separate books appear for the building and classification of yachts and there are many other publications to assist surveyors.

GOVERNMENT BODIES

The Department of Trade (formerly the Board of Trade) is the United Kingdom Government's authority for declaring the standards of safety for merchant ships, related to damage, collision, subdivision, life-saving equipment, loading, stability, fire protection, navigation, carriage of dangerous goods, load line standards and many allied subjects. This department is also the authority on tonnage measurement standards. It is responsible for seeing that the safety standards, many of which are governed by international agreements, are maintained and for enquiring into sea disasters. Ship surveyors in the Marine Division and similar national authorities in other countries, like the US Coastguards, carry, thus, an enormous responsibility.

The Ship Department of the Ministry of Defence (formerly the Admiralty) is responsible for the design, construction and repair of its own ships. This highly specialized task is performed by members of the Royal Corps of Naval Constructors, a civilian body formed in 1883 for these purposes. The need for such a body arises from the different design philosophy associated with merchant ships and warships. The owner of the merchant ship wants to make money from his capital investment and requires therefore a short building time, the minimum of maintenance, the maximum time at sea and simplicity of design. These factors render the construction of robust, simple ships possible by rule. The nation, however, gets no return for *its* capital investment save protection from potential enemies. While attempting to keep costs within reason, the constructor's prime task is to produce an efficient maintainable ship-weapon system, neglecting no aspect which might put the warship at a disadvantage in the face of an enemy. This means that each warship has to be tailor made.

INTERNATIONAL BODIES

The Inter-Governmental Maritime Consultative Organization (IMCO), represents almost 100 of the major maritime nations of the world. The organization sponsors international action with a view to improving and standardizing questions relating to ship safety and measurement. It sponsored the International Conferences on Safety of Life at Sea in 1960 which agreed to the application of new standards of safety (Ref. 11). The same organization sponsors, also, international conferences on the load line and standardizing action on tonnage measurement and many other maritime problems (Refs. 12, 13).

LEARNED BODIES

The Institution of Naval Architects was formed in 1860 when interest in the subject in Britain quickened and it has contributed much to the development of naval architecture (Ref. 4). It became the Royal Institution of Naval Architects in 1960. The North East Coast Institution of Engineers and Shipbuilders and the Institution of Engineers and Shipbuilders in Scotland are two other learned bodies in Britain where naval architecture is discussed and developed. Abroad, among the many societies worthy of mention are the Association Technique Maritime et Aèronautique in France and the Society of Naval Architects and Marine Engineers in the USA.

References
1. Stoot, W. F. Some aspects of naval architecture in the eighteenth century, *TINA*, 1959.
2. Stoot, W. F. Ideas and personalities in the development of naval architecture, *TINA*, 1959
3. Wheatley, H. B. (Ed.). *The diary of Samuel Pepys*, Bell, 1952.
4. Barnaby, K. C. *The Institution of Naval Architects—an historical survey*, Allen and Unwin, 1960.
5. Murray, J. M. Merchant Ships 1860–1960, *TRINA*, 1960.
6. Sims, A. J. Warships 1860–1960, *TRINA*, 1960.
7. Various papers, *TINA*, 1947.
8. Hodgson, J. and Boyd, G. M. Brittle fracture is welded ships, *TINA*, 1958.
9. Hawkey, A. *HMS Captain*, Bell, 1963.
10. Bengt, Ohrelius. *Vasa, the King's ship*. Translated by M. Michael, Cassell, 1962.
11. International conference on safety of life at sea, Published for IMCO by HMSO, 1960.
12. Wilson, E. The 1969 international conference on tonnage measurement, *TRINA*, 1970.
13. Murray Smith, D. R. The 1966 international conference on loadlines in ships, *TRINA*, 1969.
14. Corlett, E. C. B. The steamship *Great Britain*, *TRINA*, 1971.

2 Some tools

No occupation can be properly developed without tools, whether it be gardening or naval architecture or astro-navigation. Many tools needed for the study of naval architecture are already to hand, provided by mathematics, applied mechanics and physics and it will be necessary to assume as the book progresses that knowledge in all allied subjects has also progressed. Knowledge, for example, of elementary differential and integral calculus is assumed to be developing concurrently with this chapter. Moreover, the tools need to be sharp; definitions must be precise, while the devices adopted from mathematics must be pointed in such a way as to bear directly on ship shapes and problems. As a means of examining this science, these are the tools.

It is convenient too, to adopt a terminology or particular language and a shorthand for many of the devices to be used. In this chapter, which lays a firm foundation from which to build up the subject, some of the machines of use to the naval architect are examined. Finally, there are short notes on statistics and approximate formulae.

Basic geometric concepts

The main parts of a typical ship together with the terms applied to the principal parts are illustrated in Fig. 2.1. Because, at first, they are of little interest or influence, superstructures and deckhouses are ignored and the hull of the ship is considered as a hollow body curved in all directions, surmounted by a watertight deck. Most ships have only one plane of symmetry, called the *middle line plane* which becomes the principal plane of reference. The shape of the ship cut by this plane is known as the sheer plan or profile. The *design waterplane* is a plane perpendicular to the middle line plane, chosen as a plane of reference at

Fig. 2.1

8   Basic ship theory

or near the horizontal; it may or may not be parallel to the keel. Planes perpendicular to both the middle line plane and the design waterplane are called *transverse planes* and a transverse section of the ship does, normally, exhibit symmetry about the middle line. Planes at right angles to the middle line plane, and parallel to the design waterplane are called *waterplanes*, whether they are in the water or not, and they are usually symmetrical about the middle line. Waterplanes are not necessarily parallel to the keel. Thus, the curved shape of a ship is best conveyed to our minds by its sections cut by orthogonal planes. Figure 2.2 illustrates these planes.

Fig. 2.2

Transverse sections laid one on top of the other form a *body plan* which, by convention, because the sections are symmetrical, shows only half sections, the forward half sections on the right-hand side of the middle line and the after half sections on the left. Half waterplanes placed one on top of the other form a *half breadth plan*. Waterplanes looked at edge on in the sheer or body plan are called *waterlines*. The sheer, the body plan and the half breadth collectively are called the *lines plan* or *sheer drawing* and the three constituents are clearly related. (See Fig. 2.3.)

Fig. 2.3 Lines plan

It is convenient if the waterplanes and the transverse planes are equally spaced and datum points are needed to start from. That waterplane to which the ship is being designed is called the *load waterplane* (LWP) or *design waterplane* and additional waterplanes for examining the ship's shape are drawn above it and below it, equally spaced, usually leaving an uneven slice near the keel which is best examined separately.

A reference point at the fore end of the ship is provided by the intersection of the load waterline and the stem contour and the line perpendicular to the LWP through this point is called the *fore perpendicular* (FP). It does not matter where the perpendiculars are, provided that they are precise and fixed for the ship's life, that they embrace most of the underwater portion and that there are no serious discontinuities between them. The *after perpendicular* (AP) is frequently taken through the axis of the rudder stock or the intersection of the LWL and transom profile. If the point is sharp enough, it is sometimes better taken at the after cut up or at a place in the vicinity where there is a discontinuity in the ship's shape. The distance between these two convenient reference lines is called the *length between perpendiculars* (LBP or L_{PP}). Two other lengths which will be referred to and which need no further explanation are the *length overall* and the *length on the waterline*.

The distance between perpendiculars is divided into a convenient number of equal spaces, often twenty, to give, including the FP and the AP, twenty-one evenly spaced ordinates. These ordinates are, of course, the edges of transverse planes looked at in the sheer or half breadth and have the shapes half shown in the body plan. Ordinates can also define any set of evenly spaced reference lines drawn on an irregular shape. The distance from the middle line plane along an ordinate in the half breadth is called an *offset* and this distance appears again in the body plan where it is viewed from a different direction. All such distances for all waterplanes and all ordinates form a *table of offsets* which defines the shape of the hull and from which a lines plan can be drawn. A simple table of offsets is used in Fig. 3.30 to calculate the geometric particulars of the form.

A reference plane is needed about mid-length of the ship and, not unnaturally, the transverse plane midway between the perpendiculars is chosen. It is called *amidships* or *midships* and the section of the ship by this plane is the midship section. It may not be the largest section and it should have no significance other than its position halfway between the perpendiculars. Its position is usually defined by the symbol ⊕.

The shape, lines, offsets and dimensions of primary interest to the theory of naval architecture are those which are wetted by the sea and are called *displacement* lines, ordinates, offsets, etc. Unless otherwise stated, this book refers normally to displacement dimensions. Those which are of interest to the shipbuilder are the lines of the frames which differ from the displacement lines by the thickness of hull plating or more, according to how the ship is built. These are called *moulded* dimensions. Definitions of displacement dimensions are similar to those which follow but will differ by plating thicknesses.

The *moulded draught* is the perpendicular distance in a transverse plane from the top of the flat keel to the design waterline. If unspecified, it refers to

Fig. 2.4 *Moulded and displacement lines*

Fig. 2.5

amidships. The draught amidships is the mean draught unless the mean draught is referred directly to draught mark readings.

The *moulded depth* is the perpendicular distance in a transverse plane from the top of the flat keel to the underside of deck plating at the ship's side. If unspecified, it refers to this dimension amidships.

Freeboard is the difference between moulded depth at side and moulded draught. It is the perpendicular distance in a transverse plane from the waterline to the upperside of the deck plating at side.

The *moulded breadth extreme* is the maximum horizontal breadth of any frame section. The terms breadth and beam are synonymous.

Certain other geometric concepts of varying precision will be found useful in defining the shape of the hull. *Rise of floor* is the distance above the keel that a tangent to the bottom at or near the keel cuts the line of maximum beam amidships. See Fig. 2.6.

Fig. 2.6

Tumble home is the tendency of a section to fall in towards the middle line plane from the vertical as it approaches the deck edge. The opposite tendency is called *flare*. See Fig. 2.6.

Deck camber or *round down* is the curve applied to a deck transversely. It is normally concave downwards, a parabolic or circular curve, and measured as x inches in y feet.

Sheer is the tendency of a deck to rise above the horizontal in profile.

Rake is the departure from the vertical of any conspicuous line in profile such as a funnel, mast, stem contour, superstructure, etc. (Fig. 2.7).

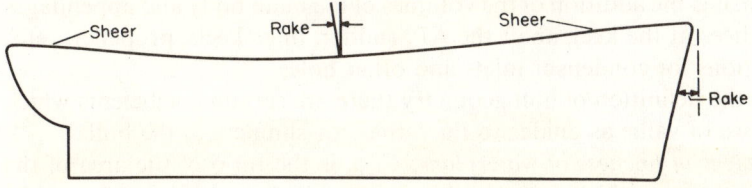

Fig. 2.7

There are special words applied to the angular movements of the whole ship from equilibrium conditions. Angular bodily movement from the vertical in a transverse plane is called *heel*. Angular bodily movement in the middle line plane is called *trim*. Angular disturbance from the mean course of a ship in the horizontal plane is called *yaw* or *drift*. Note that these are all angles and not rates, which are considered in later chapters.

There are two curves which can be derived from the offsets which define the shape of the hull by areas instead of distances which will later prove of great value. By erecting a height proportional to the area of each ordinate up to the LWP at each ordinate station on a horizontal axis, a curve is obtained known as the *curve of areas*. Figure 2.8 shows such a curve with number 4 ordinate, taken as an example. The height of the curve of areas at number 4 ordinate represents the area of number 4 ordinate section; the height at number 5 is proportional to the area of number 5 section and so on. A second type of area curve can be obtained by examining each ordinate section. Figure 2.8 again takes 4 ordinate

Fig. 2.8

section as an example. Plotting outwards from a vertical axis, distances corresponding to the areas of a section up to each waterline, a curve known as a *Bonjean curve* is obtained. Thus, the distance outwards at the LWL is proportional to the area of the section up to the LWL, the distance outwards at 1WL is proportional to the area of section up to 1WL and so on. Clearly, a Bonjean curve can be drawn for each section and a set produced.

The *volume of displacement*, ∇, is the total volume of fluid displaced by the ship. It is best conceived by imagining the fluid to be wax and the ship removed from it; it is then the volume of the impression left by the hull. For convenience of calculation, it is the addition of the volumes of the main body and appendages such as the slices at the keel, abaft the AP, rudder, bilge keels, propellers, etc., with subtractions for condensor inlets and other holes.

Finally, in the definition of hull geometry there are certain coefficients which will later prove of value as guides to the fatness or slimness of the hull.

The *coefficient of fineness of waterplane*, C_{WP}, is the ratio of the area of the waterplane to the area of its circumscribing rectangle. It varies from about 0·70 for ships with unusually fine ends to about 0·90 for ships with much parallel middle body.

$$C_{WP} = \frac{A_W}{L_{WL}B}$$

The *midship section coefficient*, C_M, is the ratio of the midship section area to the area of a rectangle whose sides are equal to the draught and the breadth extreme amidships. Its value usually exceeds 0·85 for ships other than yachts.

$$C_M = \frac{A_M}{BT}$$

The *block coefficient*, C_B, is the ratio of the volume of displacement to the volume of a rectangular block whose sides are equal to the breadth extreme, the mean draught and the length between perpendiculars.

$$C_B = \frac{\nabla}{BTL_{PP}}$$

Fig. 2.9 Waterplane coefficient

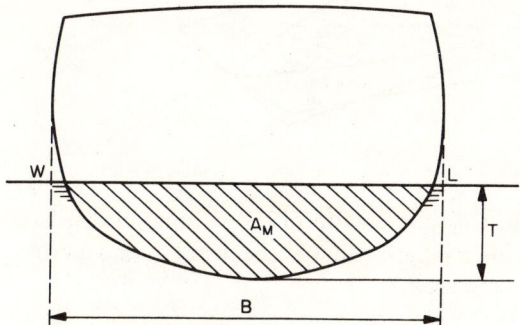

Fig. 2.10 Midship coefficient

Mean values of block coefficient might be 0·88 for a large oil tanker, 0·60 for an aircraft carrier and 0·50 for a yacht form.

The *longitudinal prismatic coefficient*, C_P, or simply *prismatic coefficient* is the ratio of the volume of displacement to the volume of a prism having a length equal to the length between perpendiculars and a cross-sectional area equal to the midship sectional area. Expected values generally exceed 0·55.

$$C_P = \frac{\nabla}{A_M L_{PP}}$$

Fig. 2.11 Block coefficient

14 Basic ship theory

Fig. 2.12 Longitudinal prismatic coefficient

The *vertical prismatic coefficient*, C_{VP} is the ratio of the volume of displacement to the volume of a prism having a length equal to the draught and a cross-sectional area equal to the waterplane area.

$$C_{VP} = \frac{\nabla}{A_w T}$$

Before leaving these coefficients for the time being, it should be observed that the definitions above have used displacement and not moulded dimensions because it is generally in the very early stages of design that these are of interest. Practice in this respect varies a good deal. Where the difference is significant, as for example in the structural design of tankers by Lloyd's Rules, care should be taken to check the definition in use. It should also be noted that the values of the various coefficients depend on the positions adopted for the perpendiculars.

Properties of irregular shapes

Now that the geometry of the ship has been defined, it is necessary to anticipate what properties of these shapes are going to be useful and find out how to calculate them.

PLANE SHAPES

Waterplanes, transverse sections, flat decks, bulkheads, the curve of areas and expansions of curved surfaces are some of the plane shapes whose properties are of interest. The area of a surface in the plane of Oxy defined in Cartesian coordinates, is

$$A = \int y \, dx$$

in which all strips of length y and width δx are summed over the total extent of x. Because y is rarely, with ship shapes, a precise mathematical function of x the integration must be carried out by an approximate method which will presently be deduced.

Fig. 2.13

There are first moments of area about each axis. (For the figures shown in Fig. 2.14, x_1 and y_1 are lengths and x and y are co-ordinates.)

$$M_{yy} = \int xy_1\,dx \quad \text{and} \quad M_{xx} = \int x_1 y\,dy$$

Fig. 2.14

Dividing each expression by the area gives the co-ordinates of the centre of area, $(\bar{x}, \bar{y})$:

$$\bar{x} = \frac{1}{A}\int xy_1\,dx \quad \text{and} \quad \bar{y} = \frac{1}{A}\int x_1 y\,dy$$

For the particular case of a figure bounded on one edge by the x-axis

$$M_y^* = \int \frac{1}{2}y^2\,dx \quad \text{and} \quad \bar{y} = \frac{1}{2A}\int y_1^2\,dx$$

For a plane figure placed symmetrically about the x-axis such as a waterplane, $M_{xx} = \int x_1 y\,dy = 0$ and the distance of the centre of area, called in the particular case of a waterplane, the *centre of flotation* (CF), from the y-axis is given by

$$\bar{x} = \frac{M_{yy}}{A} = \frac{\int xy_1\,dx}{\int y_1\,dx}$$

Fig. 2.15

* Note that $M_y \equiv M_{xx}$.

It is convenient to examine such a symmetrical figure in relation to the second moment of area, since it is normally possible to simplify work by choosing one symmetrical axis for ship shapes. The second moments of area or moments of inertia about the two axes for the waterplane shown in Fig. 2.15 are given by

$$I_T = \frac{1}{3} \int y_1^3 \, dx \quad \text{about } Ox \text{ for each half}$$

$$I_{yy} = \int x^2 y_1 \, dx \quad \text{about } Oy \text{ for each half}$$

The parallel axis theorem shows that the second moment of area of a plane figure about any axis, Q, of a set of parallel axes is least when that axis passes through the centre of area and that the second moment of area about any other axis, R, parallel to Q and at a distance h from it is given by (Fig. 2.16),

$$I_R = I_Q + Ah^2$$

Fig. 2.16

From this, it follows that the least longitudinal second moment of area of a waterplane is that about an axis through the centre of flotation and given by (Fig. 2.17)

$$I_L = I_{yy} - A\bar{x}^2$$

i.e.

$$I_L = \int x^2 y_1 \, dx - A\bar{x}^2$$

Fig. 2.17

THREE-DIMENSIONAL SHAPES

It has already been shown how to represent the three-dimensional shape of the ship by a plane shape, the curve of areas, by representing each section area by a

Some tools 17

length (Fig. 2.8). This is one convenient way to represent the three-dimensional shape of the main underwater form (less appendages). The volume of displacement is given by

$$\nabla = \int_{x_1}^{x_2} A \, dx$$

i.e. it is the sum of all such slices of cross-sectional area A over the total extent of x (Fig. 2.18).

Fig. 2.18

The shape of the ship can equally be represented by a curve of waterplane areas on a vertical axis (Fig. 2.19), the breadth of the curve at any height, z, above the keel representing the area of the waterplane at that draught. The volume of displacement is again the sum of all such slices of cross-sectional area A_w, over the total extent of z from zero to draught T,

$$\nabla = \int_0^T A_w \, dz$$

Fig. 2.19

The first moments of volume in the longitudinal direction about Oz and in the vertical direction about the keel are given by

$$M_L = \int Ax \, dx \quad \text{and} \quad M_V = \int_0^T A_w z \, dz$$

Dividing by the volume in each case gives the co-ordinates of the centre of volume. The centre of volume of fluid displaced by a ship is known as the *centre of buoyancy*; its projections in the plan and in section are known as the longitudinal centre of buoyancy (LCB) and the vertical centre of buoyancy (VCB)

$$\text{LCB from } Oy = \frac{1}{\nabla} \int Ax \, dx$$

$$\text{VCB above keel} = \frac{1}{\nabla} \int A_w z \, dz$$

Fig. 2.20 *Centre of buoyancy projections*

Should the ship not be symmetrical below the waterline, the centre of buoyancy will not lie in the middle line plane. Its projection in plan may then be referred to as the transverse centre of buoyancy (TCB). Had z been taken as the distance below the waterline, the second expression would, of course, represent the position of the VCB below the waterline. Defining it formally, the *centre of buoyancy* of a floating body is the centre of volume of the displaced fluid in which the body is floating. The first moment of volume about the centre of volume is zero.

The *weight* of a body is the total of the weights of all of its constituent parts. First moments of the weights about particular axes divided by the total weight, define the co-ordinates of the centre of weight or centre of gravity (CG) relative to those axes. Projections of the centre of gravity of a ship in plan and in section are known as the longitudinal centre of gravity (LCG) and vertical centre of gravity (VCG) and transverse centre of gravity (TCG).

$$\text{LCG from } Oy = \frac{1}{W} \int x \, dW$$

$$\text{VCG above keel} = \frac{1}{W} \int z \, dW$$

$$\text{TCG from middle line plane} = \frac{1}{W} \int y \, dW$$

Defining it formally, the *centre of gravity* of a body is that point through which, for statical considerations, the whole weight of the body may be assumed to act. The first moment of weight about the centre of gravity is zero.

Fig. 2.21 Centre of gravity projections

METACENTRE

Consider any body floating upright and freely at waterline WL, whose centre of buoyancy is at B. Let the body now be rotated through a small angle in the plane of the paper without altering the volume of displacement (it is more convenient to draw if the body is assumed fixed and the waterline rotated to $W_1 L_1$). The centre of buoyancy for this new immersed shape is at B_1. Lines through B and B_1 normal to their respective waterlines intersect at M which is known as the *metacentre* since it appears as if the body rotates about it for small angles of rotation. The *metacentre* is the point of intersection of the normal to a slightly

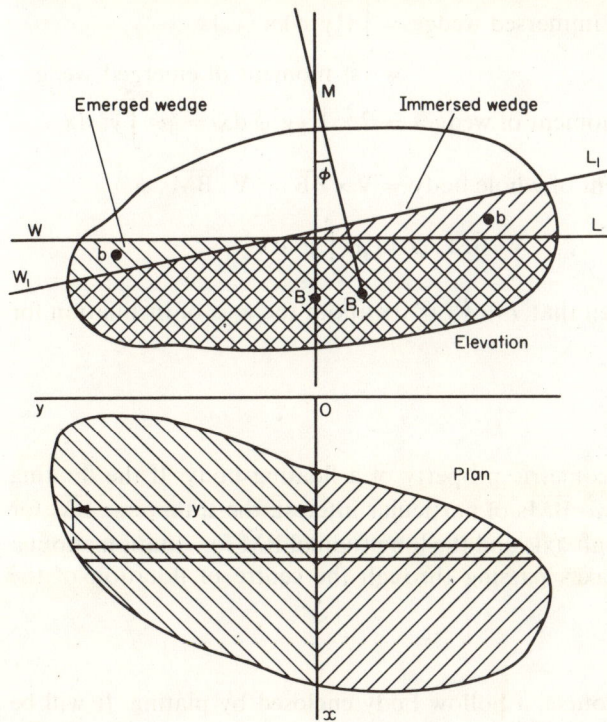

Fig. 2.22

inclined waterplane of a body, rotated without change of displacement, through the centre of buoyancy pertaining to that waterplane and the vertical plane through the centre of buoyancy pertaining to the upright condition. The term metacentre is reserved for small inclinations from an upright condition. The point of intersection of normals through the centres of buoyancy pertaining to successive waterplanes of a body rotated infinitesimally at any angle of inclination without change of displacement, is called the *pro-metacentre*.

If the body is rotated without change of displacement, the volume of the immersed wedge must be equal to the volume of the emerged wedge. Furthermore, the transfer of this volume from the emerged to the immersed side must be responsible for the movement of the centre of buoyancy of the whole body from B to B_1; from this we conclude:

(a) that the volumes of the two wedges must be equal
(b) that the first moments of the two wedges about their line of intersection must, for equilibrium, be equal and
(c) that the transfer of first moment of the wedges must equal the change in first moment of the whole body.

Writing down these observations in mathematical symbols,

$$\text{Volume of immersed wedge} = \int y \times \tfrac{1}{2} y \phi \, dx$$

$$= \text{Volume of emerged wedge}$$

$$\text{1st moment of immersed wedge} = \int (\tfrac{1}{2} y^2 \phi) \times \tfrac{2}{3} y \, dx$$

$$= \text{1st moment of emerged wedge}$$

$$\text{Transfer of 1st moment of wedges} = 2 \times \int \tfrac{1}{3} y^3 \phi \, dx = \tfrac{2}{3} \phi \int y^3 \, dx$$

$$\text{Transfer of 1st moment of whole body} = \nabla \times \overline{BB'} = \nabla \cdot \overline{BM} \cdot \phi$$

$$\therefore \quad \nabla \cdot \overline{BM} \cdot \phi = \tfrac{2}{3} \phi \int y^3 \, dx$$

But we have already seen that $I = \tfrac{2}{3} \int y^3 \, dx$ about the axis of inclination for both half waterplanes

$$\therefore \quad \overline{BM} = \frac{I}{\nabla}$$

This is an important geometric property of a floating body. If the floating body is a ship there are two $\overline{BM}$s of particular interest, the transverse $\overline{BM}$ for rotation about a fore-and-aft axis and the longitudinal $\overline{BM}$ for rotation about a transverse axis, the two axes passing through the centre of flotation of the waterplane.

HOLLOW SHAPES

The hull of a ship is, of course, a hollow body enclosed by plating. It will be necessary to find the weight and positions of the centre of gravity of such shapes.

A pseudo-expansion of the shape is first obtained by a method described fully in a textbook on laying off. Briefly, the girths of section are plotted at each ordinate and increased in height by a factor to allow for the difference between projected and slant distances in plan. A mean value of this factor is found for each ordinate.

It is now necessary to apply to each ordinate a mean plating thickness which must be found by examining the plating thicknesses (or weights per unit area, sometimes called poundages) along the girth at each ordinate (Fig. 2.23). The variation is usually not great in girth and an arithmetic mean t' will be given by dividing the sum of each plate width × plate thickness by the girth. If the weight density of the material is w, the weight of the bottom plating is thus given by $W = w \int g't' \, dx$ and the position of the LCG is given by

$$\bar{x} = \frac{w}{W} \int g't'x \, dx$$

Fig. 2.23 Bottom plating

To find the position of the VCG, it is necessary to return to the sections and to find the position by drawing. Each section is divided by trial and error, into four lengths of equal weight. The mid-points of two adjacent sections are joined and the mid-points of these lines are joined. The mid-point of the resulting line is the required position of the c.g. and its height h above the keel measured. For the whole body, then, the position of the VCG above the keel is given by

$$\bar{h} = \frac{w}{W} \int g't'h \, dx$$

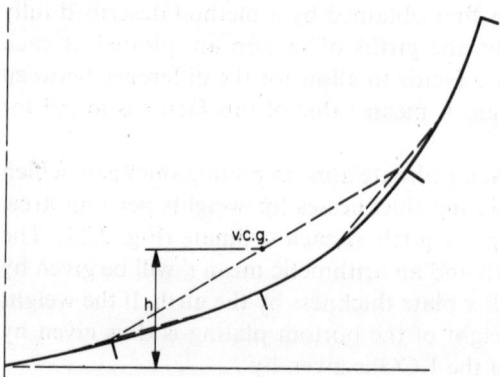

Fig. 2.24 VCG of bottom plating

Various factors can be applied to the weight density figure to account for different methods of construction. An allowance for the additional weight of laps, if the plating is raised and sunken or clinker, can be made; an addition can be made for rivet heads. It is unwise to apply any general rule and these factors must be calculated for each case.

SYMBOLS AND CONVENTIONS

It would be simpler if everyone used the same symbols for the same things. Various international bodies attempt to promote this and the symbols used in this book, listed at the beginning, follow the general agreements. As explained in the Introduction, industry, following a declaration of intent by the Government, is in the process of changing from the units given in British Standards 1991 to SI metric units. Force, for example, which by BS 1991 might be expressed in tonf will, by SI, be expressed in newtons or meganewtons. Industry will take time to adjust and this book uses both sets of units with a view to encouraging a facility in both. The symbols and units associated with hydrodynamics are those agreed by the International Towing Tank Conference.

Approximate integration

A number of different properties of particular interest to the naval architect have been expressed as simple integrals because this is a convenient form of shorthand. It is not necessary to be familiar with the integral calculus, however, beyond understanding that the elongated S sign, $\int$, means the sum of all such typical parts that follow the sign over the extent of whatever follows d. Some textbooks at this stage would use the symbol Σ which is simply the Greek letter S. It is now necessary to adopt various rules for calculating these integrals. The obvious way to calculate $A = \int y \, dx$ is to plot the curve on squared paper and then count up all the small squares. This could be extended to calculate the first moment, $M = \int xy \, dx$, in which the number of squares in a column, y, is multiplied by the number of squares from the origin, x, and this added for all of the columns that go to make up the shape. Clearly, this soon becomes laborious

Some tools 23

Fig. 2.25 The squared paper approach

and other means of determining the value of an integral must be found. The integral calculus will be used to deduce some of the rules but those who are not yet sufficiently familiar with that subject—and indeed, by those who are—they should be regarded merely as tools for calculating the various expressions shown above in mathematical shorthand.

THE TRAPEZOIDAL RULE

A trapezoid is a plane four-sided figure having two sides parallel. If the lengths of these sides are y_1 and y_2 and they are h apart, the area of the trapezoid is given by

$$A = \tfrac{1}{2}h(y_1 + y_2)$$

Fig. 2.26 A trapezoid

A curvilinear figure can be divided into a number of approximate trapezoids by covering it with n equally spaced ordinates, h apart, the breadths at the ordinates in order being $y_1, y_2, y_3, \ldots, y_n$.

Commencing with the left-hand trapezoid, the areas of each trapezoid are given by

$\tfrac{1}{2}h(y_1 + y_2)$

$\tfrac{1}{2}h(y_2 + y_3)$

$\tfrac{1}{2}h(y_3 + y_4) \ldots$

Fig. 2.27 Curvilinear figure represented by trapezoids

By addition, the total area A of the figure is given by

$$A = \tfrac{1}{2}h(y_1 + 2y_2 + 2y_3 + \ldots + y_n)$$
$$= h(\tfrac{1}{2}y_1 + y_2 + y_3 + \ldots + \tfrac{1}{2}y_n)$$

This is termed the *Trapezoidal Rule*. Clearly, the more numerous the ordinates, the more accurate will be the answer. Thus, to evaluate the expression $A = \int y\,dx$ the shape is divided into evenly spaced sections h apart, the ordinates measured and substituted in the rule given above. If the ordinates represent cross-sectional areas of a solid, then the integration gives the volume of that solid, $V = \int A\,dx$.

Expressions can be deduced for moments, but these are not as convenient to use as those that follow.

SIMPSON'S RULES

Generally known as Simpson's rules, these rules for approximate integration were, in fact, deduced by other mathematicians many years previously. They are a special case of the Newton–Cotes' rules. Let us deduce a rule for integrating a curve y over the extent of x. It will be convenient to choose the origin to be in the middle of the base $2h$ long, having ordinates y_1, y_2 and y_3. The choice of origin in no way affects the results as the student should verify for himself.

Assume that the curve can be represented by an equation of the third order,

$$y = a_0 + a_1 x + a_2 x^2 + a_3 x^3$$

The area under the curve is given by

$$A = \int_{-h}^{h} y\,dx = \int_{-h}^{h} (a_0 + a_1 x + a_2 x^2 + a_3 x^3)\,dx$$

$$= \left[a_0 x + a_1 \frac{x^2}{2} + a_2 \frac{x^3}{3} + a_3 \frac{x^4}{4} \right]_{-h}^{+h} = 2a_0 h + \tfrac{2}{3}a_2 h^3 \qquad \text{Equation (i)}$$

Assume now that the area can be given by the expression

$$A = L y_1 + M y_2 + N y_3 \qquad \text{Equation (ii)}$$

Fig. 2.28

Now

$$y_1 = a_0 - a_1 h + a_2 h^2 - a_3 h^3$$
$$y_2 = a_0$$
$$y_3 = a_0 + a_1 h + a_2 h^2 + a_3 h^3$$

Substituting in Equation (ii)

$$A = (L+M+N)a_0 - (L-N)a_1 h + (L+N)a_2 h^2 - (L-N)a_3 h^3$$

Equation (iii)

Equating the coefficients of a in equations (i) and (iii)

$$\left. \begin{array}{l} L+M+N = 2h \\ L-N = 0 \\ L+N = \tfrac{2}{3}h \end{array} \right\} \quad \therefore \quad L = N = \tfrac{1}{3}h \quad \text{and} \quad M = \tfrac{4}{3}h$$

The area *can* be represented by Equation (ii), therefore, provided that the coefficients are those deduced and

$$A = \tfrac{1}{3}hy_1 + \tfrac{4}{3}hy_2 + \tfrac{1}{3}hy_3 = \tfrac{1}{3}h(y_1 + 4y_2 + y_3)$$

This is known as *Simpson's First Rule* or *3 Ordinate Rule*. A curved figure can be divided by any uneven number of equally spaced ordinates h apart. The area within ordinates numbers 1 and 3 is

$$A_1 = \tfrac{1}{3}h(y_1 + 4y_2 + y_3)$$

within 3 and 5 ordinates

$$A_2 = \tfrac{1}{3}h(y_3 + 4y_4 + y_5)$$

within 5 and 7 ordinates

$$A_3 = \tfrac{1}{3}h(y_5 + 4y_6 + y_7)$$

and so on.

Fig. 2.29

The total area is therefore given by

$$A = \tfrac{1}{3}h(y_1 + 4y_2 + 2y_3 + 4y_4 + 2y_5 + 4y_6 + 2y_7 + \ldots + y_n)$$

i.e.

$$A = \tfrac{2}{3}h(\tfrac{1}{2}y_1 + 2y_2 + y_3 + 2y_4 + y_5 + 2y_6 + y_7 + \ldots + \tfrac{1}{2}y_n)$$

This is the generalized form of the first rule applied to areas. The common multiplier is $\tfrac{1}{3} \times$ the common interval h and the individual multipliers are 1, 4, 2, 4, 2, 4, ..., 2, 4, 1.

The rule is one for evaluating an integral. While it has been deduced using area as an example, it is equally applicable to any integration using Cartesian or polar co-ordinates. To evaluate the integral $M_x = \int xy\,dx$, for example, instead of multiplying the value of y at each ordinate by the appropriate Simpson multiplier, the value of xy is so treated. Similarly, to evaluate $I_x = \int x^2 y\,dx$, the value of $x^2 y$ at each ordinate is multiplied by the appropriate Simpson multiplier. All of these operations are best performed in a methodical fashion as shown in the following example and more fully in worked examples later in the chapter. Students should develop a facility in the use of Simpson's rules by practice.

EXAMPLE 1. Calculate the value of the integral $\int P\,dv$ between the values of v equal to 7 and 15. The values of P at equal intervals of v are as follows:

v	7	9	11	13	15
P	9	27	36	39	37

Solution: The common interval, i.e. the distance between successive values of v, is 2. Setting out Simpson's rule in tabular form,

v	P	Simpson's multipliers	Functions of $\int P\,dv$
7	9 × 1		9
9	27 × 4		108
11	36 × 2		72
13	39 × 4		156
15	37 × 1		37
			382

$\int P\,dv = \tfrac{1}{3} \times 2 \times 382 = 254{\cdot}7$

The units are, of course, those appropriate to $P \times v$.

To apply the trapezoidal rule to a curvilinear shape, we had to assume that the relationship between successive ordinates was linear. In applying Simpson's first rule, we have assumed the relationship to be bounded by an expression of the third order. Much greater accuracy is therefore to be expected and for most functions in naval architecture the accuracy so obtained is quite sufficient. Where there is known to be a rapid change of form, it is wise to put in an intermediate ordinate and the rule can be adapted to do this. Suppose that the rapid change is known to be between ordinates 3 and 4 (Fig. 2.30)

Fig. 2.30

Area between 1 and 3 ords. = $\frac{1}{3}h(y_1+4y_2+y_3)$

Area between 3 and 4 ords. = $\frac{1}{3}\frac{h}{2}(y_3+4y_{3\frac{1}{2}}+y_4) = \frac{1}{3}h(\frac{1}{2}y_3+2y_{3\frac{1}{2}}+\frac{1}{2}y_4)$

Area between 4 and 6 ords. = $\frac{1}{3}h(y_4+4y_5+y_6)$

Total area = $\frac{1}{3}h(y_1+4y_2+1\frac{1}{2}y_3+2y_{3\frac{1}{2}}+1\frac{1}{2}y_4+4y_5$
$+2y_6+ \ldots +y_n)$

Note that, unless a second half ordinate is inserted, n must now be even.

Rules can be deduced, in a similar manner, for figures bounded by unevenly spaced ordinates or different numbers of evenly spaced ordinates. For four evenly spaced ordinates the rule becomes

$A = \frac{3}{8}h(y_1+3y_2+3y_3+y_4)$

Fig. 2.31

This is known as *Simpson's Second Rule*. Extended for a large number of ordinates, it becomes

$$A = \tfrac{3}{8}h(y_1 + 3y_2 + 3y_3 + 2y_4 + 3y_5 + 3y_6 + 2y_7 + \ldots + y_n)$$

Thus, the common multiplier in this case is $\tfrac{3}{8}$ times the common interval and the individual multipliers, 1, 3, 3, 2, 3, 3, 2, 3, 3, 2, ..., 3, 3, 1. It is suitable for 4, 7, 10, 13, 16, etc., ordinates. It can be proved in a manner exactly similar to that employed for the first rule, assuming a third order curve, and it can be used like the first rule to integrate any continuous function.

Another particular Simpson's rule which will be useful is that which gives the area between two ordinates when three are known. The area between ordinates 1 and 2 is given by

$$A_1 = \tfrac{1}{12}h(5y_1 + 8y_2 - y_3)$$

Fig. 2.32

This rule cannot be used for moments. The first moment of area of that portion between ordinates 1 and 2 about number 1 ordinate is

$$M_x = \tfrac{1}{24}h^2(3y_1 + 10y_2 - y_3)$$

These two rules are known loosely as the 5,8 *minus one Rule* and the 3,10 *minus one Rule*. They are somewhat less accurate than the first two rules. Incidentally, applying the 5,8 minus one rule backwards, the unshaded area of Fig. 2.32 is

$$A_2 = \tfrac{1}{12}h(-y_1 + 8y_2 + 5y_3)$$

and adding this to the expression for A_1, the total area is

$$A = \tfrac{1}{3}h(y_1 + 4y_2 + y_3)$$

If the common multiplier has been forgotten, the student can quickly deduce it by applying the particular rule to a rectangle.

Rules can be combined one with another just as the unit for each rule is combined in series to deal with many ordinates. It is important that any discontinuity in a curve falls at the end of a unit, e.g. on the 2 multiplier for the first and second rules; if this is so, the rules can be used on curves with discontinuities. In general, because of differences in the common interval necessary each side of a discontinuity, it will be convenient to deal with the two parts separately.

The first rule deals with functions bounded by 3, 5, 7, 9, 11, 13, etc., ordinates and the second rule with 4, 7, 10, 13, etc., ordinates. Let us deduce a rule for six ordinates

Fig. 2.33

Area between 1 and 2 ords. $= \frac{1}{12}h(5y_1+8y_2-y_3) = h(\frac{5}{12}y_1+\frac{8}{12}y_2-\frac{1}{12}y_3)$

Area between 2 and 5 ords. $= \frac{3}{8}h(y_2+3y_3+3y_4+y_5)$
$= h(\frac{3}{8}y_2+\frac{9}{8}y_3+\frac{9}{8}y_4+\frac{3}{8}y_5)$

Area between 5 and 6 ords. $= \frac{1}{12}h(-y_4+8y_5+5y_6)$
$= h(-\frac{1}{12}y_4+\frac{8}{12}y_5+\frac{5}{12}y_6)$

Total area

$$A = h(\frac{5}{12}y_1+\frac{25}{24}y_2+\frac{25}{24}y_3+\frac{25}{24}y_4+\frac{25}{24}y_5+\frac{5}{12}y_6)$$
$$= \frac{25}{24}h(0{\cdot}4y_1+y_2+y_3+y_4+y_5+0{\cdot}4y_6)$$

These few Simpson's rules, applied in a repetitive manner, have been found satisfactory for hand computation for many years. The digital computer makes somewhat different demands and the more generalized Newton–Cotes' rules, summarized in Table 2.1 from Ref. 1, may be found more suitable for some purposes.

Table 2.1
Newton–Cotes' rules

Number of ordinates	Multipliers for ordinates numbers				
	1	2	3	4	5
2	$\frac{1}{2}$	$\frac{1}{2}$			
3	$\frac{1}{6}$	$\frac{4}{6}$	$\frac{1}{6}$		
4	$\frac{1}{8}$	$\frac{3}{8}$	$\frac{3}{8}$	$\frac{1}{8}$	
5	$\frac{7}{90}$	$\frac{32}{90}$	$\frac{12}{90}$	$\frac{32}{90}$	$\frac{7}{90}$
6	$\frac{19}{288}$	$\frac{75}{288}$	$\frac{50}{288}$	$\frac{50}{288}$	$\frac{75}{288}$	...

30 Basic ship theory

Table 2.1 (continued)
Newton-Cotes' rules

Number of ordinates	Multipliers for ordinates numbers				
	1	2	3	4	5
7	$\dfrac{41}{840}$	$\dfrac{216}{840}$	$\dfrac{27}{840}$	$\dfrac{272}{840}$	$\dfrac{27}{840}$ ...
8	$\dfrac{751}{17280}$	$\dfrac{3577}{17280}$	$\dfrac{1323}{17280}$	$\dfrac{2989}{17280}$	$\dfrac{2989}{17280}$ ...
9	$\dfrac{989}{28350}$	$\dfrac{5888}{28350}$	$\dfrac{928}{28350}$	$\dfrac{10496}{28350}$	$\dfrac{4540}{28350}$ ....

Area = $L \times \Sigma$ (Multiplier $\times$ ordinate)

Ordinates are equally spaced with end ordinates coinciding with ends of curve. Multipliers are always symmetrical and are indicated by dots.

TCHEBYCHEFF'S RULES

Returning to Equation (ii) on p. 24, the rule required was forced to take the form of the sum of equally spaced ordinates, each multiplied by a coefficient. The rule could have been forced to take many forms, most of them inconvenient.

Fig. 2.34

One form which does yield a convenient rule results from assuming that the area can be represented by the sum of ordinates placed a special distance x (which may be zero) from the origin, all multiplied by the same coefficient, i.e. instead of assuming the form as before, assume that the area can be represented by

$$A = p(y_1 + y_2 + y_3), \quad y_2 \text{ being at the origin}$$

Now
$$y_1 = a_0 - a_1 x + a_2 x^2 - a_3 x^3$$
$$y_2 = a_0$$
$$y_3 = a_0 + a_1 x + a_2 x^2 + a_3 x^3$$
adding:
$$A = p(3a_0 + 2a_2 x^2)$$
equating coefficients of a above with those of Equation (i) on p. 24
$$3p = 2h \quad \therefore \quad p = \tfrac{2}{3}h$$
and
$$2px^2 = \tfrac{2}{3}h^3 = ph^2$$
$$\therefore \quad x = \frac{1}{\sqrt{2}}h = 0.7071h$$

The total shaded area in Fig. 2.34 can therefore be calculated by erecting ordinates equal to 0·7071 of the half length from the mid-point, measuring their heights and that of the mid-ordinate, adding the three heights together and multiplying the total by two-thirds of the half length.

$$A = \tfrac{2}{3}h(y_1 + y_2 + y_3)$$

where y_1 and y_3 are 0·7071 of the half length h, from the mid-point.

This is Tchebycheff's rule for three ordinates. Similar rules can be deduced for 2, 3, 4, 5, 6, 7 and 9 ordinates when spacings become:

Table 2.2
Tchebycheff's rule spacings

Number of ordinates, n	Spacing each side of mid-ordinate as a factor of the half length h					Degree of curve
2	0·57735					3
3	0	0·70711				3
4	0·18759	0·79465				5
5	0	0·37454	0·83250			5
6	0·26664	0·42252	0·86625			7
7	0	0·32391	0·52966	0·88386		7
8	0·10268	0·40620	0·59380	0·89733		5
9	0	0·16791	0·52876	0·60102	0·91159	9
10	0·08375	0·31273	0·50000	0·68727	0·91625	5

The eight and ten ordinate rule spacings have been deduced by applying the four and five ordinate rules each side of the mid-point of the half length. The common multiplier for all rules is the whole length $2h$ divided by n, the number of ordinates used, $2h/n$.

Tchebycheff's rules are used not infrequently, particularly the ten ordinate rule, for calculating displacement from a 'Tchebycheff body plan', i.e. a body plan drawn with ordinate positions to correspond to the Tchebycheff spacings. Areas of the sections are calculated by Simpson's rules or by other convenient means, merely added together and multiplied by $2h/n$ to give volume of displacement. Lines are, in fact, often faired on a Tchebycheff body plan to avoid the more prolonged calculation by Simpson's rules with each iteration. Since fairing is basically to a curve or areas, this assumes the use of Tchebycheff ordinates to define the body plan.

GAUSS RULES

It has been seen that the Simpson rules and Newton–Cotes' rules employ equally spaced ordinates with unequal multipliers and the Tchebycheff rules use constant multipliers with unequal ordinate spacing. A third set of rules, the Gauss rules, uses unequal spacing of ordinates and unequal multipliers as shown in Table 2.3.

Table 2.3
Gauss' rules

Number of ordinates	Spacing each side of mid-ordinate as a factor of the half length. Multiplier		
2	Spacing 0·57735 Multiplier 0·50000		
3	Position 0 0·77460 Multiplier 0·44444 0·27778		
4	Position 0·33998 0·86114 Multiplier 0·32607 0·17393		
5	Position 0 0·53847 0·90618 Multiplier 0·28445 0·23931 0·11846		
	Integral = Sum of products × whole base		

The Gauss rules have the merit of being more accurate than either the Simpson or Tchebycheff rules, but their application involves more tedious calculation when manual methods are used. For this reason, they have been largely neglected by naval architects in the past. When an electronic computer is used, it is as easy and quick to manipulate the more complicated multipliers and the basic calculations are similar for all three rules. By using Gauss rules, the naval architect can either obtain greater accuracy by using the same number of ordinates or he can obtain the same accuracy with fewer ordinates and in less time.

The relative accuracy obtainable with the three rules is discussed in Ref. 1. It is shown that:

(*a*) a Simpson rule with an even number of ordinates is only marginally more accurate than the next lower odd ordinate rule; odd ordinate Simpson rules are therefore to be preferred,

(b) a Tchebycheff rule with an even number of ordinates gives the same accuracy as the next highest odd ordinate rule. Even ordinate Tchebycheff rules are therefore to be preferred,
(c) a Tchebycheff rule with an even number of ordinates gives an accuracy rather better than the next highest odd ordinate Simpson rule, i.e. the two-ordinate Tchebycheff rule is more accurate than the three-ordinate Simpson rule,
(d) The five-ordinate Gauss rule gives an accuracy comparable with that achieved with nine-ordinate Simpson or Tchebycheff rules.

EXAMPLE 2. Integrate $y = \tan x$ from $x = 0$ to $x = \pi/3$ by the five ordinate rules of (a) Simpson, (b) Newton–Cotes, (c) Tchebycheff, (d) Gauss.

Solution: The precise solution is

$$\int_0^{\pi/3} \tan x = [-\log \cos x]_0^{\pi/3}$$

$$= 0.69315$$

$$= 0.22064\pi$$

(a) Simpson

x	y	SM	$f(A)$
0	0	$\frac{1}{2}$	0
$\pi/12$	0·26795	2	0·53590
$\pi/6$	0·57735	1	0·57735
$\pi/4$	1·00000	2	2·00000
$\pi/3$	1·73205	$\frac{1}{2}$	0·86603
			3·97928

$$\text{Area} = \frac{2}{3} \times \frac{\pi}{12} \times 3.97928 = 0.22107\pi$$

(b) Newton–Cotes

x	y	M	$f(A)$
0	0	7	0
$\pi/12$	0·26795	32	8·57440
$\pi/6$	0·57735	12	6·92820
$\pi/4$	1·00000	32	32·00000
$\pi/3$	1·73205	7	12·12435
			59·62695

$$\text{Area} = \frac{1}{90} \times \frac{\pi}{3} \times 59.62695 = 0.22084\pi$$

(c) Tchebycheff

x	y
$\pi/6(1-0\cdot83250) = 5\cdot025°$	0·08793
$\pi/6(1-0\cdot37454) = 18\cdot764°$	0·33972
$\pi/6 = 30°$	0·57735
$\pi/6(1+0\cdot37454) = 41\cdot236°$	0·87655
$\pi/6(1+0\cdot83250) = 54\cdot975°$	1·42674
	3·30829

$$\text{Area} = \frac{\pi}{15} \times 3\cdot30829 = 0\cdot22055\pi$$

(d) Gauss

x	y	M	f(A)
$\pi/6(1-0\cdot90618) = 2\cdot815°$	0·04918	0·11846	0·00583
$\pi/6(1-0\cdot53847) = 13\cdot846°$	0·24647	0·23931	0·05898
$\pi/6 = 30°$	0·57735	0·28445	0·16423
$\pi/6(1+0\cdot53847) = 46\cdot154°$	1·04114	0·23931	0·24916
$\pi/6(1+0\cdot90618) = 57\cdot185°$	1·55090	0·11846	0·18372
			0·66192

$$\text{Area} = \frac{\pi}{3} \times 0\cdot66192 = 0\cdot22064\pi$$

Machines

There are several machines which are of particular use to the naval architect, especially suitable for the geometry of ship shapes and the associated computation. The slide rule will already be sufficiently familiar and the adding and more refined calculating machines need no explanation. Certain ingenious mechanisms exist for measuring some of the interesting properties of plane figures and no naval architect can work efficiently these days without using computers.

PLANIMETER

A planimeter is a machine for measuring the area enclosed by a closed plane figure. It comprises two bars. The first bar has a weighted pin at one end, which is stuck into the paper and a hinge at the other end which mates with a hinge towards the end of the second bar. At one end of the second or floating bar is a rest and a pointer which is taken completely round the closed curve whose area is required. At the other end of the floating bar is a disc which slides edge on to the paper and is able to rotate about the bar as axis. It is the rotation of the disc that measures the area circumnavigated by the pointer and the rotation is recorded by a worm drive and vernier scales attached to the disc and to the bar. As the disc is dragged in the direction of its axis it does not rotate at all; dragged in any other direction, a component causes rotation. It is important therefore with this and the two machines described next that the paper be clean and even, that the discs have been preserved in perfect condition and the instrument be so positioned that the disc slides a minimum amount.

Fig. 2.35 The planimeter

INTEGRAPH

The integraph is a machine for drawing the integral curve of any given curve. If $y = f(x)$ is the original curve, the ordinate of the integral curve $a = \int y \, dx$. A Bonjean curve is the integral curve of a transverse section of a ship.

The sliding axle of the machine has a large heavy roller on each end permitting movement of the machine only in a direction parallel to the reference axis. Two slides on the axle control the pointer for the curve to be integrated and the pen tracing the integral curve. At the middle of the axle is mounted a rotating slide through which the directing arm passes. The directing arm joins the pointer to a mechanism which ensures that the guide wheel for the pen remains always parallel to the directing arm. The sharp rim of the guide wheel keeps the path of the pen parallel to the directing arm.

The essential feature of the machine is the inclination of the director arm, θ proportional to the ordinate y of the curve to be integrated,

$$\tan \theta = \frac{y}{c}$$

Fig. 2.36 *The integraph*

But the mechanism makes the pen trace a curve at any moment parallel to the directing arm so that

$$\tan \theta = \frac{da}{dx}$$

$$\therefore \quad a = \frac{1}{c} \int y \, dx$$

The constant of the machine is set by adjusting the length of the arm, c.

INTEGRATOR

The integrator is a machine for obtaining the area and the first and second moments of area about a datum line of any closed plane figure. It comprises essentially a framework constrained to move along a grooved bar which ensures

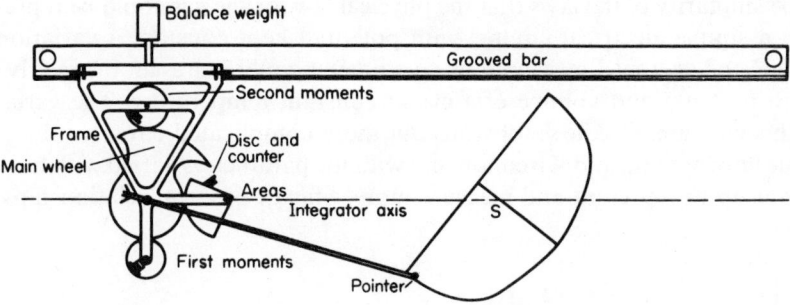

Fig. 2.37 The integrator

that the axle of a single central horizontal toothed wheel moves along a prescribed axis. Fixed radially to this main wheel is a long arm OP at the other end of which is a rest and pointer that circumnavigates the closed curve under investigation. Two smaller toothed wheels mesh with the main wheel each with discs whose edges are in contact with the paper and whose axes pass through the axles of the smaller toothed wheels. The discs drive vernier scales which give readings proportional to area, first moment of area and to area plus second moment.

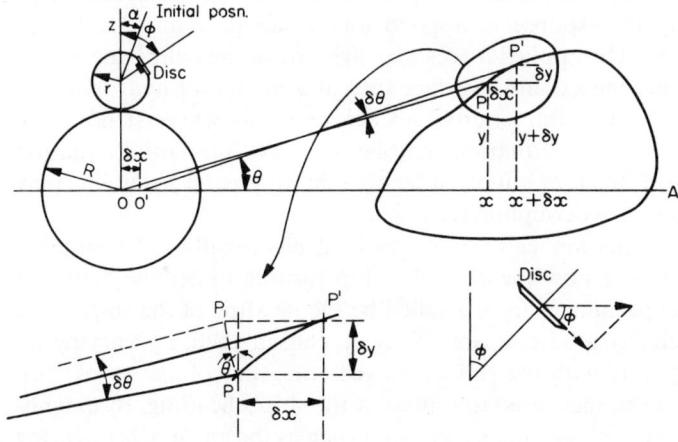

Fig. 2.38

The essential features of the integrator are shown in Fig. 2.38.

ANALOGUE COMPUTERS AND SIMULATORS

The physical laws connecting pressure, volume and absolute temperature of a gas and connecting electrical potential, resistance and current of a simple circuit are respectively:

$$\frac{P \times V}{T} = \text{Constant} \quad \text{and} \quad \frac{I \times R}{E} = \text{Constant}$$

Such is the similarity of the laws that the physical law for the gas could be represented by a simple electrical circuit; with potential kept constant a variation applied to R and current I measured by an ammeter could represent the relative changes to pressure and volume of a gas at constant temperature. The variations in this case are, of course, obvious but more complicated circuits subject to the basic laws of Ohm and Kirchhoff and with the parameters varied with time can be built up to represent and measure more difficult physical relationships.

Fig. 2.39

This is the basis of the *analogue computer*. Let us anticipate some of the work of Chapter 13 to demonstrate a particular application of the electrical analogue. The motion of a ship in response to applied forces can be represented by a mathematical equation. The applied forces may arise from the deliberate action of those on board in moving a control surface such as a rudder (or hydroplane in the case of a submarine) or from external agencies such as waves striking the ship. In its simplest form, the equation may be a linear differential equation involving one degree of freedom but, in order to achieve greater accuracy, may include non-linear and cross-coupling terms.

The same form of equation can be represented electrically by a suitably contrived circuit. Consider now the case of a ship turning under the action of the rudder and let the parameter to be studied be the heading of the ship. If the components of the electrical circuit are correctly chosen then, by varying an input signal in conformity with the rudder movements, the voltage across two points of the circuit can be measured to represent the ship's heading. By extending the circuitry, more variables can be measured such as the angle of heel during turn, drift angle, etc.

Clearly, a difficulty arises in determining the correct values of the electrical components to suit a particular ship. These may have to be computed by theoretical means, or measured by model or full scale trials. Having determined them, however, the circuit will represent faithfully the ship's behaviour. That is to say, it will 'simulate' the ship's behaviour. It can be made to do this in real time, e.g. the ship's head can be made to vary at the same rate as in the full scale ship in real life.

The realism can be heightened by mounting the computer on a platform which can turn, heel and pitch in response to signals from the computer and the input can be derived from a steering wheel so that the operator gains the impression of actually being on board a ship. The complete system is referred to as a *simulator* and such devices are used extensively for training personnel particularly in the aircraft and guided missile spheres. The famous Link trainer used for the ground training of fighter pilots in the second world war is a good example.

It will be realized from the above that the analogue computer is a specialized tool. It can be made reasonably flexible by permitting adjustment of the electrical constants over a wide range. In this way, the same computer can be adjusted to represent different ships or to study another problem provided that the problem can be represented by the same basic equations. Compared, however, with the digital computer, described below, it is much less versatile.

One big advantage of being able to work in real time is that it is often possible to introduce into the electrical circuit actual components of the real system. If the behaviour of a particular hydraulic control system is difficult to represent mathematically, (it may be non-linear in a complex manner, for example) it can itself be built into the simulator. This would be impossible with a digital computer.

DIGITAL COMPUTERS

In essence, a digital computer is an electronic device capable of holding large amounts of data and of performing simple arithmetical computations at high speed. The ship designer need not know in detail how it works but he should understand its basic characteristics, its strengths and its weaknesses if he is to use it effectively. Only then can he appreciate the full significance of the data he extracts from the computer and the relevance to specific problems of particular programs.

Any computer system includes the following elements:

(*a*) input units which accept information in a suitably coded form. These may be simple tape readers, teletypes, document readers or light pens;
(*b*) storage or memory units for holding instructions, one for immediate access and one as a back-up store. Typically, storage will be on discs, tapes or drums;
(*c*) a calculation unit by which data is manipulated;
(*d*) output units for presenting answers to enquiries or results of calculations. These may be printers, graph plotters or visual display units (VDUs). The immediate output may be a magnetic tape which can be decoded later on separate print-out devices. Sometimes the output tape is used directly to control a machine tool or automatic draughting equipment;
(*e*) a power unit.

Often the input and output units are remote from the computer itself, providing a number of outstations with access to a large central computer.

As with any other form of communication, that between the designer and the computer must be conducted in a language understood by both. There are several such languages such as Fortran, Algol and Cobol suitable for scientific, engineering and commercial work. Modern computer languages resemble stilted English. The machine itself translates the words into the more complex machine language through a compiler.

Increasingly, teletypes and VDUs are being made interactive, enabling a designer to engage in a dialogue with the computer. He can, for example, feed in one set of data, ask the machine to perform a program upon it and report the result. Depending upon the answer he can proceed to the next program or start again with new data. The computer can store intermediate results so that if the designer has, for instance, used it to fair the hull form (Ref. 2) he can recall it to proceed with a later task like the calculations on stability. For a lengthy calculation a computer can be programmed to ask for data at various times so minimizing the expertise demanded of the user of the system.

It does not follow that because a computer can be used to provide a service it should be so used. A well-designed computer system is expensive to set up both in terms of money and time. It is particularly difficult to replace the versatility of the human brain.

For what work then is a computer suitable? To answer this its special abilities must be considered. It can:

(a) carry out repetitive calculations accurately and rapidly, e.g. solve multiple differential equations;
(b) store large quantities of data, updating and retrieving it rapidly on demand;
(c) manipulate stored data, sorting it and causing it to be printed in a variety of formats.

The ship designer can therefore use it to:

(a) provide a large library of accurate and up to date facts, e.g. data on performances, size, weight, cost, reliability, delivery times, etc. This data may be accessed through direct interrogation by an on-line terminal or by means of catalogues printed out regularly to some agreed format;
(b) carry out calculations either as discrete activities or as part of an integrated suite of design calculations. Data may be fed in separately for each calculation or be called up by the computer from its own memory;
(c) analyse data on achievement of planned dates, cash flow or manpower usage, monitoring the achievement with the plan of work.

Applications of especial interest are considered in the following paragraphs.
Computer-aided design. Systems by which the designer can use a terminal to assist in the design process by giving him immediate access to the data stored and to a complete suite of design programs are being developed for many industries. Several systems have been developed for ship design, some concentrating on the initial design phase and others on the detailed design process and its interaction with production. The aim is to obtain the right balance between man and machine using the strengths of one to complement the other.
Automated draughting equipment. This equipment has been available for some years. Typically, a reader and keyboard are used by an operator to record from a general arrangement drawing of an equipment all relevant information needed to define its components. By feeding the tape so generated into a plotter the

Fig. 2.40

detail drawings of all components can be generated automatically. In association with a VDU the equipment can be used to generate a new drawing or to develop a rough sketch into a full working drawing. Where a symbol or component is repeated many times over the operator can generate it once, store it in the computer and recall it as an entity as many times as required. Very successful applications of this have been achieved in the design of printed circuit boards and in the structural design of supertankers.

Simulation modelling. Provided that the factors governing a real life situation are understood, it may be possible to represent it by a set of mathematical relationships. In other words it can be *modelled* and the model used to study the effects of changing some of the factors much more quickly, cheaply and safely than could be achieved with full scale experimentation. Consider tankers arriving at a terminal. Factors influencing the smooth operation are numbers of ships, arrival intervals, ship size, discharge rate and storage capacities. A simulation model could be produced to study the problem, reduce the queueing time and to see the effects of additional berths and different discharge rates and ship size. The economics of such procedures is also conducive to this type of modelling.

Approximate formulae and rules

Approximate formulae and rules grew up with the craftsman approach to naval architecture and were encouraged by the secrecy that surrounded it. Many were bad and most have now been discarded. There remains a need, however, for coarse approximations during the early, iterative processes of ship design. Usually, the need is met by referring to a similar, previous design and correcting the required figure according to the dimensions of new and old, e.g. supposing an estimate for the transverse $\overline{BM} = I_T/\nabla$ is required, the transverse second moment of area I_T is proportional to $L \times B^3$ and ∇ is proportional to $L \times B \times T$

$$\therefore \quad \overline{BM} \propto \frac{LB^3}{LBT} = \frac{B^2}{T}$$

$$\therefore \quad \overline{BM} = \frac{B^2}{KT}$$

where K is a constant for geometrically similar ships.

or
$$\frac{\overline{BM}_1}{\overline{BM}_2} = \frac{B_1^2}{B_2^2} \times \frac{T_2}{T_1}$$

This presumes that the forms are similar. This formula is one that may suffice for a check; K varies between 10 and 15 for ship shapes. More important, it shows how ship dimensions affect this geometric property, viz. that the beam contributes as its square, the draught inversely and the length not at all. The effects of changes to dimensions can, therefore, be assessed.

An approximate formula for the longitudinal $\overline{BM}$ is

$$\overline{BM}_L = \frac{3A_W^2 L}{40 B \nabla}$$

NORMAND'S FORMULA

This is known also as Morrish's rule. It gives the distance of the centre of buoyancy of a ship-like form below the waterline.

$$\text{Distance of VCB below waterline} = \frac{1}{3}\left(\frac{T}{2} + \frac{\nabla}{A_W}\right)$$

The formula is remarkably accurate for conventional ship forms and is used frequently in the early design stages.

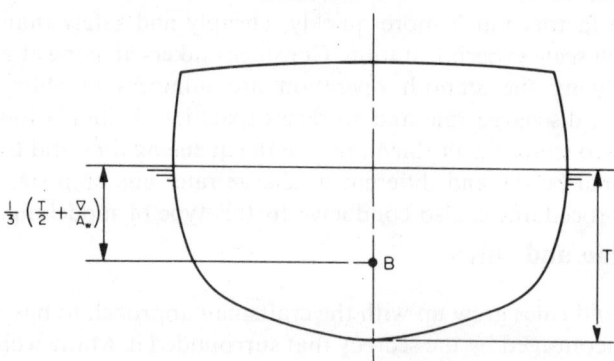

Fig. 2.41

WEIGHT CONVENTIONS

Plating thickness in ships is usually specified in decimals of an inch or in millimetres. In warship practice, thickness used to be specified as a weight per square foot of surface. Since steel weighs about 480 lbf/ft^3, plating one inch thick weighs about 40 lbf/ft^2.

Sections used in ship construction are also specified in different ways. The sections commonly used in merchant ships have varying web thicknesses and are specified in the dimensions of depth × flange × flange × web thickness, e.g. $10 \times 3\frac{1}{2} \times 3\frac{1}{2} \times 0.50$ channel has a depth of 10 in., flanges $3\frac{1}{2}$ in. wide and a web

0·50 in. thick. Reference to standard tables would show that its flange thickness is 0·56 in. Nowadays, sections are defined almost exclusively in millimetres, web × table × thickness with a mass per metre in kg/m.

Statistics

A feature of present day naval architecture, as in other engineering disciplines, is the increasing use made of statistics by the practising naval architect. This is not because the subject itself has changed but rather that the necessary mathematical methods have been developed to the stage where they can be applied to the subject.

It will be concluded, for example in Chapter 6, that the hull girder stress level accepted from the standard calculation should reflect the naval architect's opinion as to the probability of exceeding the standard assumed loading during the life of the ship. Again, in the study of ship motions the extreme amplitudes of motion used in calculations must be associated with the probability of their occurrence and probabilities of exceeding lesser amplitudes are also of considerable importance.

It is not appropriate in a book of this nature to develop in detail the statistical approach to the various aspects of naval architecture. As an introduction to the mathematics of statistics Ref. 3 can be read. However, use is made in several chapters of certain general concepts of which the following are important.

PROBABILITY

Consider an aggregate of n experimental results (e.g. amplitudes of pitch from a ship motion trial) of which m have the result R and $(n-m)$ do not have this result. Then, the probability of obtaining the result R is $p = m/n$. The probability that R will not occur is $1-p$. If an event is impossible its probability is zero. If an event is a certainty its probability is unity.

PROBABILITY CURVE

When a large amount of information is available, it can be presented graphically by a curve. The information is plotted in such a way that the area under the curve is unity and the probability of the experimental result lying between say R and $R + \delta R$ is represented by the area under the curve between these values of the abscissa. There are a number of features about this probability curve which may best be defined and understood by an example.

Consider the following example of experimental data.

EXAMPLE 3. Successive amplitudes of pitch to the nearest half degree recorded during a trial are:

4, 2, $3\frac{1}{2}$, $2\frac{1}{2}$, 3, 2, $3\frac{1}{2}$, $1\frac{1}{2}$, 3, 1, $3\frac{1}{2}$, $\frac{1}{2}$, 2, 1, $1\frac{1}{2}$, 1, 2, $1\frac{1}{2}$, $1\frac{1}{2}$, 4, $2\frac{1}{2}$, $3\frac{1}{2}$, 3, $2\frac{1}{2}$, 2, $2\frac{1}{2}$, $2\frac{1}{2}$, 3, 2, $1\frac{1}{2}$.

Solution: As a string of figures these values have little significance to the casual reader. Using the concepts given above however, the occurrence of specific pitch amplitudes is given in columns (1) and (2) below:

(1) Pitch amplitude	(2) Number of occurrences	(3) (1)×(2)	(4) (1)−μ	(5) (4)²	(6) (5)×(2)
$\frac{1}{2}$	1	$\frac{1}{2}$	−1·82	3·312	3·31
1	3	3	−1·32	1·741	5·23
$1\frac{1}{2}$	5	$7\frac{1}{2}$	−0·82	0·672	3·36
2	6	12	−0·32	0·102	0·61
$2\frac{1}{2}$	5	$12\frac{1}{2}$	+0·18	0·032	0·16
3	4	12	0·68	0·462	1·85
$3\frac{1}{2}$	4	14	1·18	1·392	5·57
4	2	8	1·68	2·822	5·64
	30	$69\frac{1}{2}$			25·73

Selecting the information from this table,

ARITHMETIC MEAN $= \mu = \dfrac{69\frac{1}{2}}{30} = 2\cdot32$ deg

MEDIAN is the mid measurement of the 30 which occurs midway between 2 and $2\frac{1}{2} = 2\cdot25$ deg. The median bisects the area

MODE $= 2$ deg. The mode is the most common value

RANGE $= 4 - \frac{1}{2} = 3\frac{1}{2}$ deg. The range is the difference of extreme values of variate

STANDARD DEVIATION $= \sigma = \sqrt{\left(\dfrac{25\cdot73}{30}\right)} = 0\cdot926$ deg

VARIANCE $= \sigma^2 = 0\cdot858$ (deg)²

These values provide a much clearer physical picture of the motion being measured than does the original test data. The significance of these various features of the probability curve will be clear to the student with some knowledge of statistics.

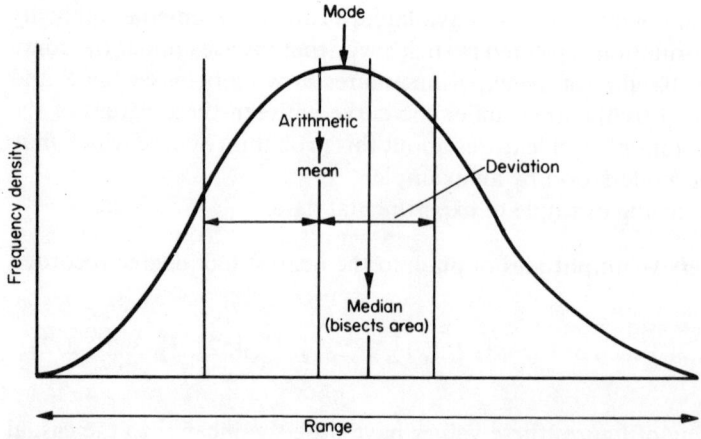

Fig. 2.42

Worked examples

EXAMPLE 4. Calculate the area, position of the centre of flotation and the second moments of area about the two principal axes of the waterplane defined by the following ordinates, numbered from forward. It is 220 m long.

Ordinate number	1	2	3	4	5	6	7	8	9	10	11
½ Ord. (m)	0·2	2·4	4·6	6·7	8·1	9·0	9·4	9·2	8·6	6·3	0·0

Solution:

Fig. 2.43

Ord. no.	½ Ord. y	S.M.	Func. of y	Lever x	Func. of xy	Lever x	Func. of x^2y	½ Ord.^{3} y^3	Func. of y^3
1	0·2	½	0·1	5	0·5	5	2·5	0·0	0·0
2	2·4	2	4·8	4	19·2	4	76·8	13·8	27·6
3	4·6	1	4·6	3	13·8	3	41·4	97·3	97·3
4	6·7	2	13·4	2	26·8	2	53·6	300·8	601·6
5	8·1	1	8·1	1	8·1	1	8·1	531·4	531·4
6	9·0	2	18·0	0	68·4	0	0·0	729·0	1458·0
7	9·4	1	9·4	−1	−9·4	−1	9·4	830·6	830·6
8	9·2	2	18·4	−2	−36·8	−2	73·6	778·7	1557·4
9	8·6	1	8·6	−3	−25·8	−3	77·4	636·1	636·1
10	6·3	2	12·6	−4	−50·4	−4	201·6	250·0	500·0
11	0·0	½	0·0	−5	0·0	−5	0·0	0·0	0·0
			98·0		−122·4		544·4		6240·0
					68·4				
					−54·0				

$$\text{Area} = \int y\,dx \text{ for each half}$$

There are eleven ordinates and therefore ten spaces, $\frac{220}{10} = 22$ m apart. The total of the $f(y)$ column must be multiplied by $\frac{2}{3}$ times 22, the common interval, to complete the integration and by 2, for both sides of the waterplane.

$$\text{Total area} = 2 \times \tfrac{2}{3} \times 22 \times 98\cdot0 = 2{,}874\cdot7 \text{ m}^2$$

$$\text{1st moment} = \int xy\,dx \text{ for each half}$$

Instead of multiplying each ordinate by its actual distance from Oy, we have made the levers the number of ordinate distances to simplify the arithmetic so that the total must be multiplied by a lever factor 22. We have also chosen Oy as number 6, the mid-ordinate as being somewhere near the centre of area, to ease the arithmetic; it may well transpire that number 7 ordinate would have been closer. The moments each side are in opposition and must be subtracted to find the out-of-balance moment. First moment about number 6 ordinate, $M_x = 2 \times \tfrac{2}{3} \times 22 \times 22 \times 54\cdot0$.

Now the distance of the centre of area from $Oy = M_x/A$; three of the multipliers are common to both and cancel out, leaving,

$$\text{CF abaft 6 ord. } \bar{x} = 22 \times \frac{f(xy)}{f(y)} = \frac{22 \times 54}{98} = 12 \cdot 1 \text{ m}$$

$$\text{2nd Moment about } Oy = \int x^2 y \, dx \text{ for each half}$$

We have twice multiplied by the number of ordinate spacings instead of the actual distances so that the lever factor this time is 22×22. The second moments all act together (x is squared and therefore always positive) and must be added

$$\therefore \quad I \text{ about 6 ord.} = 2 \times \tfrac{2}{3} \times 22 \times 22 \times 22 \times 544 \cdot 4 = 7{,}729{,}000 \text{ m}^4$$

Now this is not the least I and is not of much interest; the least is always that about an axis through the centre of area and is found from the parallel axis theorem

$$I_L = I - A\bar{x}^2 = 7{,}729{,}000 - 2874 \cdot 7 \times (12 \cdot 1)^2 = 7{,}309{,}000 \text{ m}^4$$

$$\text{2nd Moment about } Ox = \tfrac{1}{3} \int y^3 \, dx \text{ for each half}$$

To integrate y^3, $f(y)^3$ must be multiplied by $\tfrac{2}{3}$ times the common interval.

$$I_T = 2 \times \tfrac{1}{3} \times \tfrac{2}{3} \times 22 \times 6240 \cdot 0 = 61{,}000 \text{ m}^4$$

This time, the axis already passes through the centre of area.

EXAMPLE 5. A ship has a main body defined by the waterplane areas given below. The waterlines are 1 ft 3 in. apart. In addition, there is an appendage having a volume of displacement of 330 ft³ with a centre of volume $3\tfrac{1}{2}$ in. below No. 4 WL.

What are the volume of displacement and the position of the VCB?

Waterline	1	2	3	4
Area (ft²)	1230	1100	870	480

Solution:

WL	Area A	S.M.	$f(A)$	Lever, y	$f(Ay)$
1	1230	1	1230	0	0
2	1100	3	3300	1	3300
3	870	3	2610	2	5220
4	480	1	480	3	1440
			7620		9960

$$\text{Volume of displacement for main body} = \tfrac{3}{8} \times 1 \cdot 25 \times 7620 = 3572 \text{ ft}^3$$

$$\text{VCB below 1 WL for main body} = \frac{9960}{7620} \times 1 \cdot 25 = 1 \cdot 63 \text{ ft}$$

Some tools 47

Fig. 2.44

Adding volumes and moments for main body and appendage:

    Main body volume = 3572 ft^3
    Appendage volume =   330 ft^3
      Total volume = 3902 ft^3
    Main body moment below 1 WL = $3572 \times 1\cdot63$ = 5830 ft^4
    Appendage moment below 1 WL = $330(3\cdot75+0\cdot29)$ = $\underline{1333}$ ft^4
                                                                  7163 ft^4

$$\text{Whole body VCB below 1 WL} = \frac{7163}{3902} = 1\cdot84 \text{ ft}$$

The value of a sketch, however simple, cannot be over-emphasized in working through examples.

All of these examples are worked out by slide rule. The number of digits worked to in any number should be pruned to be compatible with this level of accuracy.

EXAMPLE 6. Calculate by the trapezoidal rule the area of a transverse half section of a tanker bounded by the following waterline offsets. Waterlines are 3 m apart:

WL	1	2	3	4	5	6
Offset (m)	24·4	24·2	23·7	22·3	19·1	3·0

Compare this with the areas given by Simpson's rules,

(a) with six ordinates
(b) with five and a half ordinate equal to 16·0 m

Calculate for (b) also the vertical position of the centre of area.

Solution:

WL	Offset, y	Trap. mult.	$f_1(y)$	Simp. mult.	$f_2(y)$
1	24·4	$\frac{1}{2}$	12·2	0·4	9·8
2	24·2	1	24·2	1	24·2
3	23·7	1	23·7	1	23·7
4	22·3	1	22·3	1	22·3
5	19·1	1	19·1	1	19·1
6	3·0	$\frac{1}{2}$	1·5	0·4	1·2
			103·0		100·3

48 Basic ship theory

Fig. 2.45

Area by trapezoidal rule = $3 \times 103\cdot 0 = 309\cdot 0 \text{ m}^2$

Area by Simpson's rule = $\frac{25}{24} \times 3 \times 100\cdot 3 = 313\cdot 4 \text{ m}^2$

WL	Offset, y	S.M.	$f(y)$	Lever, x	$f(xy)$
1	24·4	1	24·4	0	0
2	24·2	4	96·8	1	96·8
3	23·7	2	47·4	2	94·8
4	22·3	4	89·2	3	267·6
5	19·1	1½	28·65	4	114·6
5½	16·0	2	32·0	4½	144·0
6	3·0	½	1·5	5	7·5
			319·95		725·3

Area = $\frac{1}{3} \times 3 \times 319\cdot 95 = 319\cdot 95 \text{ m}^2$

Centre of area below 1 WL = $\dfrac{725\cdot 3}{319\cdot 95} \times 3\cdot 0 = 6\cdot 80 \text{ m}$

EXAMPLE 7. An appendage to the curve of areas abaft the after perpendicular, ordinate 21, is fair with the main body curve and is defined as follows:

Ordinate	20	21	22
Area (ft²)	114·6	110·0	15·0

The ordinates are equally spaced 18 ft apart. Calculate the volume of the appendage and the longitudinal position of its centre of buoyancy.

Solution:

Ord. no.	Area, A	S.M.	$f(A)$	S.M.	$f_M(A)$
20	114·6	−1	−114·6	−1	−114·6
21	110·0	8	880·0	10	1100·0
22	15·0	5	75·0	3	45·0
			840·4		1030·4

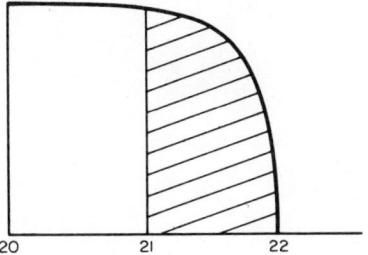

Fig. 2.46

Volume of appendage $= \frac{1}{12} \times 18 \times 840\cdot 4 = 1260\cdot 6 \text{ ft}^3$

c.b. from 22 ordinate $= \frac{1}{24} \times 18^2 \times 1030\cdot 4 \times \dfrac{12}{18 \times 840\cdot 8}$

$$= \frac{18 \times 1030\cdot 4}{2 \times 840\cdot 8} = 11\cdot 03 \text{ ft}$$

c.b. abaft the AP $= 18\cdot 0 - 11\cdot 03 = 6\cdot 97 \text{ ft}$

EXAMPLE 8. It is necessary to calculate the volume of a wedge of fluid immersed by the rotation of a vessel through 20 degrees. The areas and distances of the centres of areas from the axis of rotation of the immersed half waterplanes have been calculated at 5 degree intervals as follows:

Angle of inclination (deg)	0	5	10	15	20
Area (m²)	650	710	920	1030	1810
Centre of area from axis (m)	3·1	3·2	3·8	4·8	6·0

Calculate the volume of the immersed wedge.

Solution: The Theorem of Pappus Guldinus states that the volume of a solid of revolution is given by the area of the plane of revolution multiplied by the distance moved by its centre of area. If r is the distance of the centre of area of a typical plane from the axis, for a rotation $\delta\theta$, it moves a distance $r\,\delta\theta$ and the volume traced out by the area A is

$$\delta V = Ar\,\delta\theta \quad (\theta \text{ in radians})$$

The total volume is therefore given by

$$V = \int Ar\,\mathrm{d}\theta$$

This time, therefore, an approximate integration has to be performed on Ar over the range of θ.

50 Basic ship theory

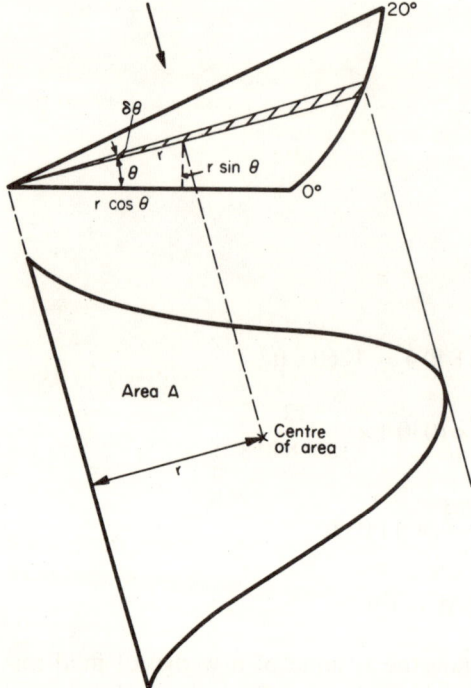

Fig. 2.47

Ord.	A	r	Ar	S.M.	f(Ar)
0	650	3·1	2015	1	2015
5	710	3·2	2272	4	9088
10	920	3·8	3496	2	6992
15	1030	4·8	4944	4	19776
20	1810	6·0	10860	1	10860
					48731

$$\text{Volume} = \tfrac{1}{3} \times 5 \times \frac{\pi}{180} \times 48731 = 1420 \text{ m}^3$$

Had we been required to find the position of the centre of volume in Cartesian co-ordinates, we would simply have evaluated the integrals for the moments

$$M_V = \int Ar^2 \sin\theta \, d\theta$$

and

$$M_H = \int Ar^2 \cos\theta \, d\theta$$

in exactly the same manner, by preparing columns of ($Ar^2 \sin\theta$) and ($Ar^2 \cos\theta$) and applying Simpson's rule to these values.

Some tools 51

Problems

1. A ship, 200 m between perpendiculars, has a beam of 22 m and a draught of 7 m. If the prismatic coefficient is 0·75 the area of the waterplane 3500 m² and mass displacement in salt water is 23,000 tonnes, estimate

   (a) block coefficient
   (b) waterplane coefficient
   (c) midship section coefficient and
   (d) the distance of the centre of buoyancy above the keel.

   (HMDTC)

2. The length, beam and mean draught of a ship are respectively 115, 15·65 and 7·15 m. Its midship section coefficient is 0·921 and its block coefficient is 0·665. Find

   (a) displacement in tonnef and newtons in salt water
   (b) area of immersed midship section
   (c) prismatic coefficient of displacement.

3. Two similar right circular cones are joined at their bases. Each cone has a height equal to the diameter of its base. The composite body floats so that both apexes are in the water surface. Calculate

   (a) the midship section coefficient
   (b) the prismatic coefficient
   (c) the waterplane coefficient. (HMDTC)

4. A curve has the following ordinates, spaced 1·68 m apart: 10·86, 13·53, 14·58, 15·05, 15·24, 15·28, 15·22 m. Calculate the area by Simpson's first rule and compare it with the area given by the trapezoidal rule. What is the ratio of the two solutions?

5. The half ordinates of the load waterplane of a vessel are 1·2, 4·6, 8·4, 11·0, 12·0, 11·7, 10·3, 7·5 and 3·0 ft respectively and the overall length is 120 ft. What is its area?

6. A curvilinear figure has the following ordinates at equidistant intervals: 12·4, 27·6, 43·8, 52·8, 44·7, 29·4 and 14·7. Calculate the percentage difference from the area found by Simpson's first rule when finding the area by (a) the trapezoidal rule, (b) Simpson's second rule.

7. The effective girths of the outer bottom plating of a ship, 27·5 m between perpendiculars, are given below, together with the mean thickness of plating at each ordinate. Calculate the volume of the plating. If the plating is of steel of mass density 7700 kg/m³, calculate the weight in meganewtons.

Ord. No.	AP	10	9	8	7	6	5	4	3	2	FP
Girth (m)	14·4	22·8	29·4	34·2	37·0	37·4	36·8	28·6	24·2	22·6	23·2
Thickness (mm)	10·2	10·4	10·6	11·4	13·6	13·6	12·8	10·4	10·1	10·1	14·2

8. The half ordinates of a vessel, 144 m between perpendiculars, are given below.

Ord. No.	AP	8	7	6	5	4	3	2	FP
½ Ord. (m)	17·0	20·8	22·4	22·6	21·6	18·6	12·8	5·6	0·0

52 Basic ship theory

In addition, there is an appendage, 21·6 m long, abaft the AP, whose half ordinates are:

Ord. No.   12   11   10   AP
½ Ord. (m)   0·0   9·6   14·0   17·0

Find the area and position of the centre of area of the complete waterplane.

(RNATE)

9. The loads per foot due to flooding, at equally spaced positions on a transverse bulkhead are given below. The bulkhead is 45 ft deep. Calculate the total load on the bulkhead and the position of the centre of pressure

Ord. No.   1   2   3   4   5   6   7   8   9   10
Load (tonf/ft)   0   15   30   44   54   63   69   73   75   74

(RNATE)

10. A tank is 8 m deep throughout its length and 20 m long and its top is flat and horizontal. The sections forward, in the middle and at the after end are all triangular, apex down and the widths of the triangles at the tank top are respectively 15, 12 and 8 m.

Draw the calibration curve for the tank in tonnes of fuel against depth and state the capacity when the depth of oil is 5·50 m. SG of oil fuel = 0·90. Only five points on the curve need be obtained. (HMDTC)

11. Areas of waterplanes, 2·5 m apart, of a tanker are given below.

Calculate the volume of displacement and the position of the VCB. Compare the latter with the figure obtained from Normand's (or Morrish's) rule.

Waterplane   1   2   3   4   5   5½   6
Area (m²)   4010   4000   3800   3100   1700   700   200

12. The waterline of a ship is 70 m long. Its half ordinates, which are equally spaced, are given below. Calculate the least second moment of area about each of the two principal axes in the waterplane.

Ord. No.   1   2   3   4   5   6   7   7½   8
½ Ord. (m)   0·0   3·1   6·0   8·4   10·0   10·1   8·6   6·4   0·0

13. The half ordinates of the waterplane of a ship, 440 ft between perpendiculars, are given below. There is, in addition, an appendage abaft the AP with a half area of 90 ft² whose centre of area is 8 ft from the AP; the moment of inertia of the appendage about its own centre of area is negligible.

Calculate the least longitudinal moment of inertia of the waterplane.

Section   AP   10   9   8   7   6   5   4   3   2   FP
½ Ord. (ft)   6·2   16·2   22·5   26·0   27·5   27·4   23·7   19·2   14·5   8·0   0·0

(HMDTC)

14. The half breadths of the 16 ft waterline of a ship which displaces 18,930 tonf in salt water are given below. In addition, there is an appendage abaft the AP, 30 ft long, approximately rectangular with a half breadth of 35·0 ft. The length BP is 660 ft.

Calculate the transverse $\overline{BM}$ and the approximate value of $\overline{KM}$.

Station	FP	2	3	4	5	6	7	8	9	10	AP
½ Breadth (ft)	0·0	21·0	32·0	37·0	40·6	43·0	43·8	43·6	43·0	40·0	37·0

15. The shape of a flat, between bulkheads, is defined by the ordinates, spaced 4 ft apart, given below. If the plating weighs 7 lbf per square foot of surface area, calculate the weight of the plating and the distance of the c.g. from No. 1 ordinate.

Ord. No.	1	2	3	4	5	6
Breadth (ft)	53·0	50·0	45·0	38·0	30·0	14·0

16. Each of the two hulls of a catamaran has the following dimensions.

Ord. No.	1	2	3	4	5	5½	6
½ Ord. (in.)	0·0	4·0	6·2	7·2	6·4	4·9	0·0

The length and volume of displacement of each hull are respectively 18 ft and 5·3 ft³. The hull centre lines are 6 ft apart. Calculate the transverse $\overline{BM}$ of the boat. (HMDTC)

17. Compare the areas given by Simpson's rules and the trapezoidal rule for the portions of the curve defined below:
   (a) between ordinates 1 and 4
   (b) between ordinates 1 and 2

Ord. No.	1	2	3	4
Ord. (m)	39·0	19·0	12·6	10·0

The distance between ordinates is 10 m.

18. Apply Normand's (or Morrish's) rule to a right circular cylinder floating with a diameter in the waterplane. Express the error from the true position of the VCB as a percentage of the draught.

19. Deduce a trapezoidal rule for calculating longitudinal moments of area.

20. Deduce the five ordinate rules of (a) Newton–Cotes, (b) Tchebycheff.

21. Compare with the correct solution to five decimal places $\int_0^\pi \sin x \, dx$ by the three ordinate rules of (a) Simpson, (b) Tchebycheff, (c) Gauss.

22. A quadrant of 16 m radius is divided by means of ordinates parallel to one radius and at the following distances: 4, 8, 10, 12, 13, 14 and 15 m. The lengths of these ordinates are respectively: 15·49, 13·86, 12·49, 10·58, 9·33, 7·75 and 5·57 m. Find:

   (a) the area to two decimal places by trigonometry
   (b) the area using only ordinates 4 m apart by Simpson's rule
   (c) the area using also the half ordinates
   (d) the area using all the ordinates given
   (e) the area using all the ordinates except 12·49. (AP & S)

23. Calculate, using five figure tables, the area of a semicircle of 10 m radius by the four ordinate rules of (a) Simpson, (b) Tchebycheff, (c) Gauss and compare them with the correct solution.

24. Show that $\overline{KB}$ is approximately $T/6(5 - 2C_{VP})$.

25. From strains recorded in a ship during a passage, the following table was deduced for the occurrence of stress maxima due to ship motion. Calculate for this data (a) the mean value, (b) the standard deviation.

Max. stress (MN/m^2)	10	20	30	40	50	60
Occurrences	852	1335	772	331	140	42

26. Construct a probability curve from the following data of maximum roll angle from the vertical which occurred in a ship crossing the Atlantic. What are (a) the mean value, (b) the variance, (c) the probability of exceeding a roll of 11 degrees

Max. roll angle, deg.	1	3	5	7	9	11	13	15	17
Occurrences	13,400	20,550	16,600	9720	4420	1690	510	106	8

References

1. Miller, N. S. The accuracy of numerical integration in ship calculations, *TIESS*, 1963–4.
2. Kuo, C. *Computer methods for ship surface design*, Longman, 1971.
3. Moroney, M. J. Facts from figures, Pelican,
4. Lambe, C. G. *Elements of statistics*, Longman, 1962.
5. Snaith, G. R. and Parker, M. N. Ship design with computer aids, *TNEC*, 1972.

3 Flotation and trim

A ship, like any other three-dimensional body, has six degrees of freedom. That is to say, any movement can be resolved into movements related to three orthogonal axes, three translations and three rotations. With a knowledge of each of these six movements, any combination movement of the ship can be assessed. The three principal axes have already been defined in Chapter 2. This chapter will be confined to an examination of two movements
(a) behaviour along a vertical axis, Oz in the plane Oxz
(b) rotation in the plane Oxz about a transverse horizontal axis, Oy.

Fig. 3.1

Attention will be confined to static behaviour, i.e. conditions applying when the ship is still. Generally, it is the change from one static condition to another that will be of interest and so it is convenient to imagine any movement occurring very slowly. Dynamic behaviour, involving time, motion and momentum will be dealt with in later chapters.

Flotation

PROPERTIES OF FLUIDS

The *mass density* of a fluid ρ, is the mass of the fluid per unit volume. The *weight density w*, of a fluid is the weight of the fluid per unit volume. In SI units, $w = \rho g$ so that, if ρ is in kg/m^3, w is in newtons/m^3. In British units, $w = \rho(g/g)$ so that, if ρ is in lb/ft^3, w has the same numerical value in lbf/ft^3. Similarly, in old metric units, w has the same numerical value in tonnef/m^3 as ρ has in tonne/m^3. Since they vary with pressure and temperature, the values must be related to a standard condition of pressure and temperature. The former is normally taken to be one atmosphere, 14·7 lbf/in² (10^5 Pa = 1 Bar) and the latter sometimes 15°C (59°F), and for water sometimes 4°C (39°F) when its density is a maximum.

The ratio of the density of a solid or a liquid to the density of pure water is the *specific gravity*, γ. Since it is the basic reference for all such materials, the weight properties of pure distilled water are reproduced in Fig. 9.1.

The inverse of the weight density is called the *reciprocal weight density u*, or *specific volume*. The standard value assumed in British units for salt water is 35 ft^3/tonf and it is for this value that hydrostatic data for the ship are normally compiled; the SI equivalent to 35 ft^3/tonf is 0·975 m^3/tonnef or 99·5 m^3/MN. Corrections are applied for variations of reciprocal weight density from this value. Table 3.1 gives values of mass density for common fluids and for steel, air and mahogany.

Table 3.1
Properties of some common materials

Material	Mass density, ρ (lb/ft^3)	(kg/m^3)	Reciprocal mass density (ft^3/ton)	(m^3/Mg)	Specific gravity, γ
Fresh water (standard)	62·4	1000	35·9*	1·00	1·00
Fresh water (British preferred value)	62·2	996*	36·0	1·00	1·00
Salt water	64·0	1025	35·0	0·975	1·03
Furnace fuel oil	59·1	947	37·8	1·05	0·95
Diesel oil	52·5	841	42·6	1·19	0·84
Petrol	43·5	697	51·5	1·44	0·70
Steel	480	7689	4·7	0·13	7·70
Mahogany	53	849	42·3	1·18	0·85
Air	0·0807	1·293	27,800	774·775	—

* Not used; these are for comparison only.

The reciprocal weight density is found merely by inverting the weight density and adjusting the units; for example, the weight density w lbf/ft^3 results in a reciprocal weight density u ft^3/tonf as follows:

$$u \, \text{ft}^3/\text{tonf} = \frac{1}{w} \frac{\text{ft}^3}{\text{lbf}} \times \frac{2240 \, \text{lbf}}{1 \, \text{tonf}}$$

Thus, 35 ft^3/tonf corresponds to 64 lbf/ft^3 and 62·2 lbf/ft^3 to 36 ft^3/tonf. With SI units, the reciprocal weight density u must be expressed in m^3/MN which involves g. Hence, weight density reciprocal

$$u = \frac{1}{\rho} \frac{\text{m}^3}{\text{kg}} \frac{\text{s}^2}{9·807 \, \text{m}} \frac{\text{kg m}}{\text{s}^2 \, \text{newton}} \frac{10^6 \text{N}}{\text{MN}}$$

$$= \frac{10^6}{9·807\rho} \text{m}^3/\text{MN} \quad \text{with } \rho \text{ in kg/m}^3$$

for steel, for example,

$$u = \frac{10^6}{9·807 \times 7689} = 13·26 \, \text{m}^3/\text{MN}$$

The student is advised always to write in the units in his calculation to ensure that they cancel to the required dimensions.

ARCHIMEDES' PRINCIPLE

This states that when a solid is immersed in a liquid, it experiences an upthrust equal to the weight of the fluid displaced.

Thus, the tension in a piece of string by which a body is suspended, is reduced when the body is immersed in fluid by an amount equal to the volume of the body times the weight density of the fluid; a diver finds an article heavier to lift out of water than under it, by an amount equal to its volume times the weight density of water. This upthrust is called the buoyancy of the object. If, by chance, the body has the same weight density as the fluid, the upthrust when it was totally immersed would be equal to its weight; the string would just go limp and the diver would find the object to be apparently weightless. If the body were to have a smaller weight density than the fluid, only sufficient of the body to cause an upthrust equal to its weight could be immersed without force; if the body is pushed further down the buoyancy exceeds the weight and it bobs up, like a beach ball released from below its natural position in the sea.

This leads to a corollary of Archimedes' principle known as the *Law of Flotation*. When a body is floating freely in a fluid, the weight of the body equals the buoyancy, which is the weight of the fluid displaced.

The *buoyancy* of a body immersed in a fluid is the vertical upthrust it experiences due to displacement of the fluid (Fig. 3.2). The body, in fact, experiences all of the hydrostatic pressures which obtained before it displaced the fluid.

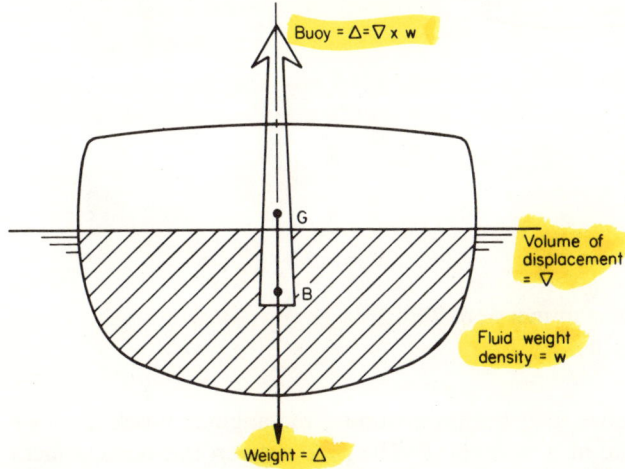

Fig. 3.2

The buoyancy is the resultant of all of the forces due to hydrostatic pressure on elements of the underwater portion (Fig. 3.3). Now, the hydrostatic pressure at a point in a fluid is equal to the depth of the point times the weight density of the fluid, i.e. it is the weight of a column of the fluid having unit cross-section and

58 Basic ship theory

Fig. 3.3

Fig. 3.4 Hydrostatic pressure at a point

length equal to the depth of immersion, T

$p = Tw$

Let us examine the pressure distribution around a rectangular block $a \times b \times c$ floating squarely in a fluid at a draught T. The pressures on the vertical faces of the block all cancel out and contribute nothing to the vertical resultant; the hydrostatic pressure at the bottom face is Tw and so the total vertical upthrust is this pressure multiplied by the area:

upthrust $= (Tw)ab$

But this is the displaced volume, abT, times the weight density of the fluid, w, which is in accordance with the law of flotation. Worked example 3 is relevant.

Flotation and trim 59

Fig. 3.5

In the general case, imagine a body floating freely in a fluid as shown in Fig. 3.3. The body is supported by the summation of all the pressure forces acting on small elements of the surface area of the body. Now imagine the body removed and replaced by a thin film of material with the same surface shape, and further imagine that the interior volume created by this film is filled with the same fluid as that in which the body is floating. If the film has negligible weight, a state of equilibrium will be produced when the level of fluid reaches the outside level. Thus, the forces acting on the film from the outside just support those acting on the film from the inside, i.e. the weight of fluid displaced by the body.

Buoyancy is plainly a force. It is the upthrust caused by displacement of fluid. For very many years naval architects have used the terms *buoyancy* and *displacement* interchangeably and the latter has become an alternative word for the upthrust of the fluid upon a floating vessel. Both weight and buoyancy vary in the same way with gravity so that anywhere in the world, the ship will float at exactly the same waterline in water of the same density. For static considerations we are interested wholly in forces and weights and so the concept of a *force displacement* Δ identical to buoyancy is satisfactory and convenient and is retained in this book.

The same is not quite true for the study of dynamic behaviour of a vessel which depends upon mass rather than weight. It is necessary to introduce the concept of *mass displacement* Σ. However it is force which causes change and normally the single word displacement refers to a force and is defined by the symbol Δ. Thus:

$$\Delta = g\Sigma = \varrho g \nabla = w\nabla$$

Retention of the metric tonneforce (tonnef) seems likely for many years yet in rule-of-thumb practice, although students should find no difficulty in dealing with displacement in terms of newtons. The tonnef is the force due to gravity acting on a mass of one tonne and has the merit of being numerically identical to the tonne and quite close to the old British tonf:

1 tonf = 1·016 tonnef = 9964 newtons (1 tonnef = 9807 newtons)

It is convenient thus to work in terms of the mass of a ship $\Sigma = n$ tonnes which, under gravity leads to a force displacement, $\Delta = \Sigma g = n \times g = n$ tonnef

60 *Basic ship theory*

With an understanding of the relationship of buoyancy and weight, the wonder at why steel objects can float diminishes. It is natural to expect a laden cargo ship to wallow deeply and a light ballasted ship to tower high, and we now know that the difference in buoyancy is exactly equal to the difference in loading. An important and interesting example is the submarine; on the surface, it has a **buoyancy equal to its weight** like any other floating body. When submerged, sufficient water must have been admitted to make weight and buoyancy approximately equal, a small out-of-balance force being provided by the control surfaces. A ground effect machine, or cushion craft obeys Archimedes' principle when it hovers over the sea; the indentation of the water beneath the machine has a volume which, multiplied by the weight density of the sea, exactly equals the weight of the craft.

The watertight volume of a ship above the water line is called the *reserve of buoyancy*. It is clearly one measure of the ship's ability to withstand the effects of flooding following damage and is usually expressed as a percentage of the load displacement.

Fig. 3.6 *Reserve of buoyancy*

VERTICAL MOVEMENT

Figure 3.2 shows the forces acting upon a floating body which are

(*a*) the weight, vertically downwards, which may be taken for static considerations as acting as if it were all concentrated at the centre of gravity, as for any rigid body;
(*b*) The buoyancy, vertically upwards, which may be assumed concentrated at the centre of buoyancy, which is the centre of volume of the underwater shape.

It must be made clear that when the ship is still, the weight and buoyancy forces must act in the same straight line BG, otherwise a couple would act upon the ship, causing it to change its attitude. What happens when a small weight is placed on the vertical line through BG? (Strictly speaking, over the centre of flotation, as will become clear later.) Clearly the vessel sinks—not completely but by an amount so that the additional buoyancy equals the additional weight and vertical equilibrium is again restored. The ship undergoes a parallel sinkage having a buoyancy W and the centre of buoyancy B moves towards the addition by an amount $\overline{BB'}$. Taking moments about B

$$W\overline{Bb} = (\Delta + W)\overline{BB'}$$
$$\therefore \overline{BB'} = \frac{W\overline{Bb}}{\Delta + W} \qquad \text{Equation (i)}$$

Thus, the new buoyancy $(\Delta + W)$ acts now through the new centre of buoyancy B', whose position has just been found. It has been assumed that there is no trim; when there is, Fig. 3.7 shows the projections on to a transverse plane and the same result holds.

Fig. 3.7   Fig. 3.8

In the same way, the ship has a new centre of gravity. Taking moments about G (see Fig. 3.8)

$$W\overline{Gg} = (\Delta + W)\overline{GG'}$$

$$\therefore \quad \overline{GG'} = \frac{W\overline{Gg}}{\Delta + W} \qquad \text{Equation (ii)}$$

Thus, the new weight $(\Delta + W)$ acts now through the new centre of gravity G', whose position has just been found. Note the similarity of the expressions.

Equation (i) involves a knowledge of the position of b, the centre of buoyancy of the added layer of buoyancy. If the layer is thick, it must be determined from the ship geometry—in fact, it is probably as quick to determine the position of B' directly from the shape of the whole ship. Frequently, however, additions are small in comparison with the total displacement and b can be taken half way up a slice assumed to have parallel sides. It is convenient to find the approximate thickness of this slice by using a device called the *tonf per inch immersion* (TPI) or *tonnef per metre immersion* (TPM). The general abbreviation is TPI.*

The tonf per inch immersion of a waterplane is the weight required to effect a parallel sinkage of the ship at that waterline of one inch. If the waterplane area is A_w ft^2,

$$\text{weight required} = \frac{A_w \times \tfrac{1}{12} \text{ft}^2}{u} \times \text{ft} \times \frac{\text{tonf}}{\text{ft}^3}$$

i.e. $$\text{TPI} = \frac{A_w}{12u} \text{ tonf}$$

$$\text{TPI} = \frac{A_w}{420} \quad \text{for salt water}$$

* Tonf (or tonnef) parallel immersion

For an additional weight W, therefore, the parallel sinkage in inches is given approximately by W/TPI; for wallsided vessels this expression is, of course, precise. This is an extremely useful expression and figures for TPI are calculated for all waterplanes for a ship, forming an important part of the hydrostatic data. Values vary from 6·0 for an ocean tug to 300 for a supertanker.

In old metric units, the weight required to effect a parallel sinkage of one metre is

$$A_\text{w}\,\text{m}^2\,\rho\frac{\text{kg}}{\text{m}^3}\frac{\text{Mg}}{1000\,\text{kg}}\frac{\text{g}}{\text{g}}$$

i.e. TPM $= \rho A_\text{w} 10^{-3}$ tonnef per metre with A_w in m² and ρ in kg/m³. For salt water, $\rho = 1025$ kg/m³, whence TPM $= 1\cdot025\,A_\text{w}$.

In SI units, meganewtons per metre immersion

$$= A_\text{w}\,\text{m}^2\,\rho\frac{\text{kg}}{\text{m}^3}\frac{9\cdot807\,\text{m}}{\text{s}^2}\frac{\text{newton s}^2}{\text{kg m}}\frac{\text{MN}}{10^6\,\text{N}}$$

$$= 9\cdot807\rho A_\text{w} 10^{-6}$$

which for salt water becomes $0\cdot01005\,A_\text{w}$ MN/m

tonnef per metre $= 40 \times$ tonf per inch

MN per m immersion $= 0\cdot392 \times$ tonf per inch

Of course, arguments are completely reversed if weights are removed and there is a parallel rise. What happens if the weight of the ship remains the same and the density of the water in which it is floating is changed? Let us examine, at first, a body of displacement Δ floating in water of weight density w_1 which passes into water of lower weight density w_2. It will sink deeper because the water is less buoyant. The weight and buoyancy have not changed because nothing has been added to the body or taken away

$$\therefore\quad \Delta = \nabla_1 w_1 = \nabla_2 w_2$$

$$\frac{\nabla_1}{\nabla_2} = \frac{w_2}{w_1}$$

Fig. 3.9

The volume of the layer $= \nabla_2 - \nabla_1$

$$= \nabla_2\left(1 - \frac{w_2}{w_1}\right)$$

Now, this layer is made up of water of weight density w_2

$$\therefore \quad \text{weight of layer} = \nabla_2 w_2\left(1 - \frac{w_2}{w_1}\right)$$

$$= \Delta\left(1 - \frac{w_2}{w_1}\right)$$

The approximate thickness of this layer in inches is given by this expression divided by the TPI in w_2 water; if the TPI is known in w_1 water,

$$\text{TPI}_2 = \text{TPI}_1 \frac{w_2}{w_1} = \text{TPI}_1 \frac{u_1}{u_2}$$

The approximate thickness of the layer is also, of course, given by its volume above, divided by the waterplane area

$$A_W = 12\,\text{TPI}_1 u_1 = \frac{12\,\text{TPI}_1}{w_1}$$

Taking first moments of the volume about B the rise of the centre of buoyancy,

$$\overline{BB^1} = \frac{(\nabla_2 - \nabla_1)\overline{Bb}}{\nabla_2}$$

$$= \left(1 - \frac{w_2}{w_1}\right)\overline{Bb}$$

It has been assumed that the increases in draught are small and that TPI is sensibly constant over the change. There are occasions when a greater accuracy is needed. What is the relationship between the change in displacement and TPI? It will be remembered from Chapter 2 (Fig. 2.19) that the change in volume of displacement,

$$\text{change in } \nabla = \int_{WL_1}^{WL_2} A_W\, dT$$

$$\therefore \quad \text{change in } \Delta = \int_{WL_1}^{WL_2} \frac{A_W}{u}\, dT = 12\int_{WL_1}^{WL_2} (\text{TPI})\, dT \quad \text{if } A_W \text{ is in ft}^2 \text{ and } T \text{ in ft}$$

Writing this another way,

$$\frac{1}{12}\frac{d\Delta}{dT} = \text{TPI}$$

or for one metre trim, $\dfrac{\Delta \overline{GM_L}}{L}$

64 Basic ship theory

With an adjustment for units, the slope of the displacement curve with respect to draught, gives the TPI; displacement is the integral curve of TPI, i.e. displacement is represented by the area under the curve of TPI plotted against draught.

Displacement of a ship is calculated with some accuracy during its early design to a series of equally spaced waterlines. Although the curve of displacement is plotted, it cannot be read to the required accuracy at intermediate waterlines. To find the displacement at an intermediate waterline, therefore, to the nearest tabulated displacement is added (or subtracted) the integral of the TPI curve between the tabulated waterline and the required waterline. For example, suppose Fig. 3.10 shows an extract of the curves of displacement and TPI at the 19 ft and 21 ft waterlines. The displacement at say 19 ft $10\frac{1}{2}$ in. cannot accurately be read from the displacement curve; TPI can be read with sufficient accuracy at say, 19 ft, 19 ft $5\frac{1}{4}$ in. and 19 ft $10\frac{1}{2}$ in., integrated by Simpson's first rule and the displacement of the slice added to 4921 to give 5471, to an accuracy of 1 tonf, if such accuracy is needed. Worked example 4, illustrates this.

Fig. 3.10

Trim

TRIM

Trim is the difference in draughts forward and aft. An excess draught aft is called trim *by the stern*, while an excess forward is called trim *by the bow*. It is important to know the places at which the draughts are measured and trim, unless it is obvious, is usually referred to *between perpendiculars* or *between marks*. Used as a verb, trim refers to the act of angular rotation about the O*y*-axis, from one angular position to another. There is also another important use of the word trim which must be excluded for the time being; in relation to submarines, trim is also the relationship between weight and buoyancy. So far as surface ships are concerned,

$$\text{trim} = T_A - T_F$$

and the angle of trim $\theta = \dfrac{T_A - T_F}{L}$

Flotation and trim 65

Fig. 3.11 Trim

where L is the horizontal distance between the points at which T_A and T_F are measured.

If a ship is trimmed without change of displacement, it must rotate about the centre of flotation. This can be shown by writing down the condition that there shall be no change in displacement, i.e. that the volumes of emerged and immersed wedges are equal (Fig. 3.12)

$$2 \int y_F(x_F \theta) \, dx = 2 \int y_A(x_A \theta) \, dx$$

i.e. $\int xy \, dx$ forward $= \int xy \, dx$ aft, which is the condition for the centre of area of the waterplane.

Fig. 3.12

A ship trims, therefore, about the centre of flotation of the waterplane. If a small weight is added to the ship, to avoid trim it must be added at the centre of

Fig. 3.13 *Addition of weight at the centre of flotation*

flotation; the centre of buoyancy of the additional layer will also be at the centre of flotation and there is no out-of-balance moment (Fig. 3.13).

CHANGES OF DRAUGHT WITH TRIM

Because a ship trims about the centre of flotation, the draught at that position does not alter with trim. It does alter everywhere else, including amidships where the mean draught between perpendiculars occurs. Now, the displacement of a ship is recorded for different mean draughts but at a specified design trim. Should the ship be floating at a different trim, it is necessary to imagine the ship being trimmed about the centre of flotation (which does not alter the displacement) until it is brought to the designed trim; the revised mean draught is calculated and so the displacement pertinent to that draught can be found. Suppose that a ship is floating t out of designed trim at waterline WL and needs to be brought to the designed trim W_1L_1 (Fig. 3.14). The change of trim $t = W_1W + LL_1 = NL_1$. By the principle of similar triangles, the correction to the mean draught,

$$d = \frac{a}{L}t$$

where a is the distance of the CF from amidships. From this revised mean draught, the displacement can be found from the ship's hydrostatic data. Had the displacement been found first from the hydrostatic data for the ship floating at the actual mean draught, it would have been necessary to correct the displacement for the amount out of designed trim; this is clearly the displacement of a layer of thickness at/L which is

$$\text{trim correction} = \frac{at}{L} \cdot \text{TPI}$$

Whether this is positive or negative depends upon the position of the CF and whether the excess trim is by bow or stern. Instead of attempting to remember rules to govern all cases, the student is advised to make a sketch similar to Fig. 3.14 on every occasion. For the case drawn, when the CF is abaft amidships and there is an excess trim by the bow, the trim correction is negative, i.e. the displacement given by the hydrostatic data for the actual mean draught to waterline WL is too great.

Fig. 3.14

The principle of similar triangles is especially useful in calculating draughts at various positions along the ship, e.g. at the draught marks which are rarely at the perpendiculars. To calculate the effect of changes of trim on draughts at the marks, a simple sketch should be made to illustrate what the change at the marks must be; in Fig. 3.15, a change of trim t between perpendiculars causes a change of draught at the forward marks of bt/L and at the after marks of ct/L. Remember, all distances are measured from the CF!

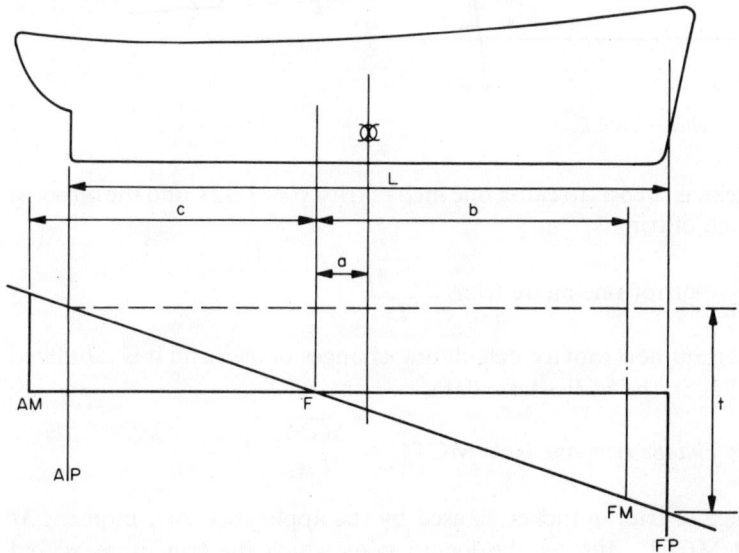

Fig. 3.15

68 Basic ship theory

MOMENT CAUSING TRIM

The trim rotation θ is caused by a moment M. What is the relationship between M and θ? In Chapter 2, we examined the rotation of any floating body, and discovered that it appeared to rotate about a point called the metacentre which was at a height I/V above the centre of buoyancy. Examine now the particular case of rotation in the longitudinal vertical plane. Let us apply a moment M at the CF causing a rotation θ, immersing a wedge of water aft and causing a wedge to emerge forward. The change in underwater shape due to the movement of the wedges, causes B to move aft to, say, B_1. The buoyancy Δ acts vertically upwards, at right angles to the new waterline; the weight continues to act vertically downwards through the centre of gravity G which has not moved. The application of a moment M therefore has caused a couple $\Delta\overline{GZ}$, $\overline{GZ}$ being the perpendicular distance between the lines of buoyancy and weight, i.e.

$$M = \Delta\overline{GZ}$$

For small angles, $\sin\theta$ is approximately equal to θ

$$\therefore \quad M = \Delta\overline{GM_L}\theta$$

Fig. 3.16 *Moment applied at the CF*

If the angle of trim is such as to cause one inch of trim, $\theta = 1/12L$ and the moment to cause one inch of trim is

$$\Delta\overline{GM_L}\frac{1}{12L} \quad \text{or for one metre trim,} \quad \frac{\Delta\overline{GM_L}}{L}$$

This is an important new tool for calculating changes of trim and it is tabulated for each waterline in the hydrostatic data,

$$\text{Moment to change trim one inch, MCT1}'' = \frac{\Delta\overline{GM_L}}{12L}$$

Thus, the change of trim in inches, caused by the application of a moment M is given by $M/\text{MCT1}''$. Just as the length over which the trim is measured

Flotation and trim 69

requires specifying, so does the MCT1″ require the length to be stated and, frequently, this standard is MCT1″ BP (between perpendiculars).

In practice, $\overline{GM_L}$ and $\overline{BM_L}$ are both large numbers and close together. ($\overline{BG}$ may be one per cent of $\overline{BM_L}$.) An approximation to MCT1″ is given by

$$\text{MCT1″ approx.} = \frac{\Delta \overline{BM_L}}{12L}$$

$$= \frac{\Delta}{12L} \frac{I_L}{\nabla} = \frac{I_L}{420L} \text{ for salt water} \qquad \text{Equation (iii)}$$

In metric units, the moment to change trim one metre or the *one metre trim moment* is $\Delta \overline{GM_L}/L$ tonnef m with Δ in tonnef or MN m with Δ in MN. For salt water, approximately,

$$\text{One metre trim moment} = \frac{\Delta \overline{BM_L}}{L} = 1{\cdot}025\frac{I}{L} \text{ tonnef m}$$

$$= 0{\cdot}01005\frac{I}{L} \text{ MN m} \qquad \text{Equation (iii)}$$

with I and L in metre units.

$$\text{One metre trim moment} = 12{\cdot}19 \times \text{MCT1″ tonnef m}$$

$$= 0{\cdot}120 \times \text{MCT1″ MN m}$$

MCT can be used for the general case, typical values being:

	tonf ft	tonnef m	MN m
60 ft (18 m) fishing vessel	2·5	30	0·3
300 ft (90 m) submarine, surfaced	150	1800	18
350 ft (110 m) frigate	450	5500	54
500 ft (150 m) dry cargo vessel	1750	20000	210
800 ft (240 m) aircraft carrier	5500	70000	650
1000 ft (300 m) supertanker	16000	200000	1900

ADDITION OF WEIGHT

It is a principle of applied mechanics that, for statical considerations, the effects of a force P acting on a body are exactly reproduced by a parallel force P at a distance h from the original line plus a moment Ph. In other words, the body shown in Fig. 3.17 behaves in precisely the same way under the action of the force and moment shown dotted as it does under the action of the force shown full. This is a useful principle to apply to the addition of a weight to a ship which causes it to sink by a shape awkward to assess. If the weight be assumed replaced by a force W and a moment Wh at the centre of flotation, the separate effects of each can be readily calculated and added:

(a) the force W at the centre of flotation causes a parallel sinkage W/TPI,
(b) the moment Wh causes a change of trim Wh/MCT

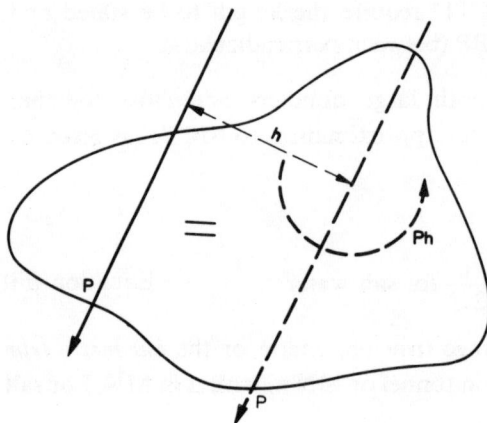

Fig. 3.17

The changes of draught at any position of the ship's length can be calculated for each movement and added, algebraically, taking care to note the sign of each change. See worked example 5.

Fig. 3.18

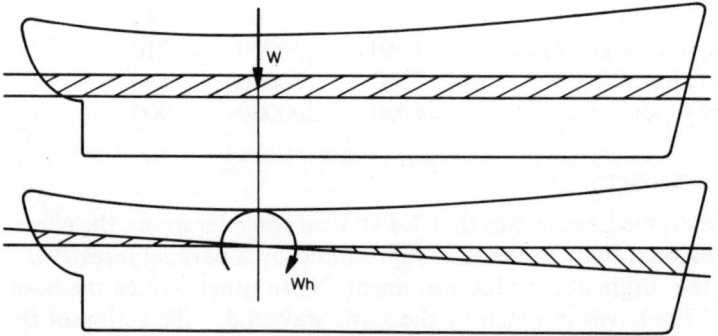

Fig. 3.19

One particular case of added weight (a negative addition, in fact) is worthy of special mention. When a ship grounds or docks, there is an upwards force at the point of contact. This is assumed replaced by a vertical force at the CF plus a moment which cause, respectively, a parallel rise and a trim. What causes the force is of little interest in this context. A fall of water level, equal to the change of draught at the point of contact is calculated from the combined effects of a parallel rise and a trim. Any attempt to treat the problem in one step is likely to meet with failure and the approach of Fig. 3.20 is essential. Worked example 6 illustrates the method.

Fig. 3.20

While we are now in a position to assess the effects of a small added weight, let us return for a moment to the exact behaviour of the ship so that we have a real understanding of what is happening. Referring to Fig. 3.21, before the addition of weight W, B, G and M were in a vertical line. The addition of the weight alters the position of all three but they must, of course, finally be in a straight line, a line perpendicular to the new waterline. What are the movements of B, G and M? G must move along a straight line joining G and g and the distance it moves could be calculated by an expression similar to Equation (ii) on p. 61. B moves upwards along the straight line Bb_1 due to the parallel sinkage to B_1 and then moves to B_2 such that B_1B_2 is parallel to bb. $\overline{BB'_1}$ can be calculated from Equation (i) on p. 60. M moves up by virtue of B moving up to B_1 and, assuming I constant, down because ∇ has increased; $\overline{BM} = I/\nabla = wI/\Delta$ and $\overline{B_1M_1} = wI/(\Delta + W)$ so that

$$\overline{BM} - \overline{B_1M_1} = wI\left(\frac{1}{\Delta} - \frac{1}{\Delta + W}\right)$$

$$= \frac{wIW}{\Delta(\Delta + W)}$$

Fig. 3.21

We have assumed that I has not appreciably changed and that the vertical component of $\overline{B_1B_2}$ is negligible. Thus, from the three movements calculated, a drawing could be made and the angle of trim measured. Clearly, the use of MCT is quicker.

LARGE WEIGHT ADDITIONS

While the use of MCT and TP1 is permissible for moderate additions of weight, the assumptions implicit in their use break down if the addition becomes large or the resulting trim is large. No longer is it possible to assume that I does not change, that TPI is constant or the longitudinal position of the CF unchanged. An approach similar to Fig. 3.21 is essential, viz.:

(a) calculate new position of G as already described or by considering the two components,

$$\overline{GG'} = \frac{Wc}{\Delta + W} \quad \text{and} \quad \overline{G'G_1} = \frac{Wd}{\Delta + W}$$

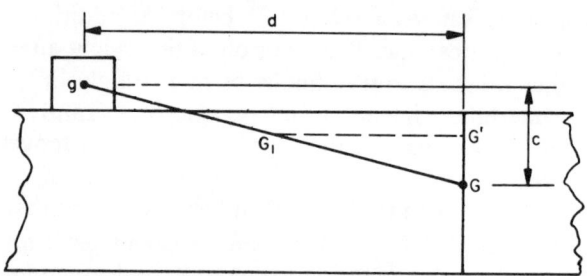

Fig. 3.22 *Movement of* G

(b) calculate new position of B in two steps
  (i) the change in B due to the addition of a parallel slab; the displacement of the slab must, of course, be equal to the additional weight and its centre of buoyancy b_1 may be assumed on a line joining the centres of flotation of the two waterplanes at a height determined by the areas of the two waterplanes. Then

$$\overline{BB'_1} = \frac{We}{\Delta + W} \quad \text{and} \quad \overline{B'_1 B_1} = \frac{Wf}{\Delta + W}$$

Fig. 3.23 *Movement of* B

  (ii) the change in position of B_1 due to the trimming of the waterplane (Fig. 3.24). The geometry of the wedges must be examined and the positions of b found by integrator or rule. At this stage however, we encounter a

Fig. 3.24 Trim effects on B_1

difficulty—we do not know what θ is. The calculation is therefore made for two or more trial values of θ, giving positions of B_2 applicable to each. As before

$$\overline{B_1 B_2'} = \frac{Wh}{\Delta + W} \quad \text{and} \quad \overline{B_2' B_2} = \frac{Wj}{\Delta + W}$$

(c) examine the trigonometry of B and G, knowing that they must be in vertical lines (Fig. 3.25). Having plotted the trial values of B_2, the choice of correct position of B_2 to correspond to the correct θ is best carried out graphically by trial and error. Having made such a judgment, the position is re-checked.

Fig. 3.25

This is a laborious process. A preferable approach is to regard the ship as an entirely new one with a revised position of G and a trim found from the Bonjean curves to give B vertically beneath G and the correct displacement. This, in fact, is how the design trim of the ship is initially determined.

DETERMINATION OF DESIGN TRIM

As described later, the early stages of ship design involve a trial and error process of matching the longitudinal positions of B and G. For a given displacement and position of G, it will at some stage be necessary to find the position of the LCB

74 Basic ship theory

and the trim resulting. Similar requirements occur in bilging and launching calculations, which are discussed in later chapters.

To find the draught and trim corresponding to a specified displacement and LCG position, it is necessary first to estimate the approximate likely waterline. Accuracy in the estimate is not important. The trial waterline is placed on a profile on which the Bonjean curve has been drawn for each ordinate so that the areas up to the waterline can be read off (Fig. 3.26). These areas and their longitudinal moments are then integrated in the usual fashion to find the displacement and LCB position. The waterplane offsets are then found, by projecting the waterline on to an offset body plan and the properties of the waterplane, in particular LCF, TPI and MCT (using the approximation of Equation (iii) on p. 69) are calculated. The ship may then be subjected to the calculations for parallel sinkage to alter the trial waterline to a new one giving the required displacement; it may then be trimmed to give the required position of LCB. If the parallel sinkage or trim are large to achieve this, a second trial waterline will be necessary and a similar adjustment made.

Fig. 3.26

CHANGE OF WATER DENSITY

A ship moving from sea water to river will be subjected to a parallel sinkage and a trim. Let us examine why.

It is necessary, to study the problem clearly, again to separate parallel sinkage and trim. Because the river water has a smaller weight density and is therefore less buoyant, the ship will sink deeper. We have already found on p. 63 that

$$\text{the volume of layer} = \nabla_2 \left(1 - \frac{w_2}{w_1}\right)$$

and

$$\text{weight of layer} = \nabla_2 w_2 \left(1 - \frac{w_2}{w_1}\right)$$
$$= \Delta \left(1 - \frac{w_2}{w_1}\right)$$

w being weight density, not the reciprocal.

Now the volume that previously provided sufficient buoyancy had its centre of buoyancy at B, in line with G. The addition of a layer, which has its centre of buoyancy at F, the centre of flotation, causes an imbalance. As drawn (Fig. 3.27), a trim by the bow is caused and the wedges of added and lost buoyancy introduced by the trim restore equilibrium (Fig. 3.28).

Fig. 3.27

Fig. 3.28

If e is the horizontal distance between LCF and LCB, the moment causing trim is

$$\Delta e \left(1 - \frac{w_2}{w_1}\right)$$

The trim is then

$$\frac{\Delta e}{\text{MCT}} = \Delta e \left(1 - \frac{w_2}{w_1}\right) \times \frac{L}{\Delta \text{GM}_L} = \text{approx } \Delta e \left(1 - \frac{w_2}{w_1}\right) \times \frac{L}{Iw_2}$$

It must be remembered that the trim occurs in w_2 water and MCT must be related to that; if the value of MCT is given for w water, approximately, since MCT is proportional to wI/L,

$$\text{MCT}_2 = \text{MCT} \times \frac{w_2}{w}$$

It is not difficult to produce formulae for changes in draught for particular changes of condition and to invent rules which give the direction of trim. The student is advised to commit none to memory. Each problem should be tackled with a small diagram and an understanding of what actually happens. Summarizing, the process is

(a) using Archimedes' principle, calculate the volume and thence the weight of the layer,

(b) calculate the parallel sinkage using TPI pertinent to the new water,
(c) calculate the trim due to the movement of the layer buoyancy from B to F, using MCT pertinent to the new water. Worked example 7 is an illustration.

Hydrostatic data

Throughout its life, a ship changes its weight and disposition of cargo, its draught and trim, and freeboard; the density of the water in which it floats varies. Its stability, discussed later, also changes. If its condition in any stated set of circumstances is to be estimated, its condition in a precise state must be known so that the effect of the changes from that state can be calculated. This precise state is known as the design condition. For ocean going ships, it is calculated for sea water of reciprocal weight density 35 ft^3/tonf; (occasionally, for ships confined to fresh water, 36 ft^3/tonf is used). In metric units, a specific volume of 99·5 m^3/MN or 0·975 m^3/tonnef is employed for salt water. For this water the tools necessary to calculate changes from the design or load waterline are calculated for a complete range of waterlines. Also calculated are the geometrical properties of the underwater form for the range of waterlines.

Collectively, this information is known as the hydrostatic data. It is presented either in tabular form when intermediate values are interpolated or as a set of curves, which are called the *hydrostatic curves*.

HYDROSTATIC CURVES

The following properties are plotted against draught to form the hydrostatic curves

(i) Centre of bouyancy above keel, $\overline{KB}$
(ii) Transverse metacentre above keel, $\overline{KM}$
(iii) CB aft of amidships
(iv) CF aft of amidships
(v) Displacement
(vi) Tonf per inch immersion (tonnef per centimetre immersion)
(vii) Change of displacement for one inch (one metre) change of trim
(viii) Moment to change trim one inch (one metre trim moment).

Occasionally, certain other properties are also plotted, such as longitudinal $\overline{KM}$, area of wetted surface and some of the geometric coefficients.

The first four items are all items of ship geometry and are affected neither by the density of the water nor by the ship's weight. Items (v), (vi) and (vii) are all related to the weight density of the water. Item (viii) is also related to the weight density of the water and alone is affected by the vertical position of the ship's centre of gravity, albeit only slightly. Accepting the approximation of Equation (iii) on p. 69, all of these last four properties are corrected in the same way when their values are required in water of different densities; if the property is known in water of reciprocal weight density u_1 and it is required in water of reciprocal density u_2, property in u_2 water = property in u_1 water $\times \dfrac{u_1}{u_2}$

u_1 will often be equal to 35 ft³/tonf or 0·975 m³/tonnef.

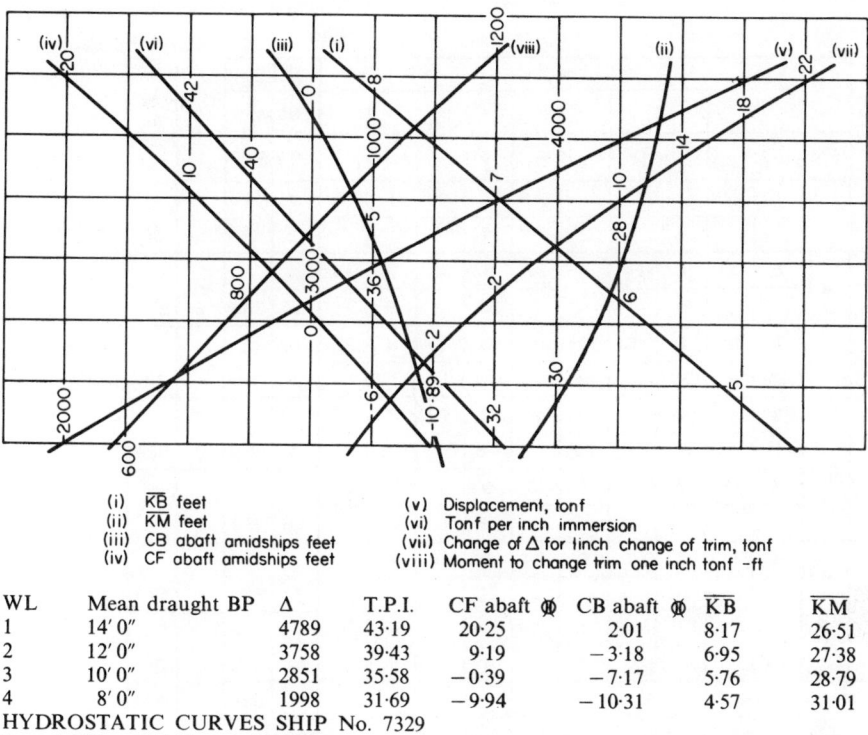

(i) $\overline{KB}$ feet
(ii) $\overline{KM}$ feet
(iii) CB abaft amidships feet
(iv) CF abaft amidships feet
(v)   Displacement, tonf
(vi) Tonf per inch immersion
(vii) Change of Δ for 1inch change of trim, tonf
(viii) Moment to change trim one inch tonf -ft

WL	Mean draught BP	Δ	T.P.I.	CF abaft ⌀	CB abaft ⌀	$\overline{KB}$	$\overline{KM}$
1	14′ 0″	4789	43·19	20·25	2·01	8·17	26·51
2	12′ 0″	3758	39·43	9·19	−3·18	6·95	27·38
3	10′ 0″	2851	35·58	−0·39	−7·17	5·76	28·79
4	8′ 0″	1998	31·69	−9·94	−10·31	4·57	31·01

HYDROSTATIC CURVES SHIP No. 7329
Length BP = 507′ 2″, Breadth extreme = 53′ 1″, Draught to 1WL = 14′ 0″, Trim BP = zero.

Fig. 3.29 Typical hydrostatic curves

CALCULATION OF HYDROSTATIC DATA

The traditional manner of calculating the hydrostatic data is so methodical that it lends itself very readily to programming for a computer. Each of the properties listed above is calculated for each of the waterlines of the ship by the methods already described in this and the previous chapters. The offsets are set down in tabular form as shown in Fig. 3.30 which has been compiled for illustration purposes for a simple ship shape—in practice 21 ordinates and several more waterlines are usual. Offsets are set down in tabular fashion to correspond to the orthogonal sections explained by Fig. 2.3. The table is known as the *displacement table* and the complete sheet of calculations as a *displacement sheet*.

The waterline offsets are set down in vertical columns and each is operated upon by the vertical column of Simpson's multipliers. The sums of these columns are functions (i.e. values proportional to) of waterplane areas which, operated upon by the horizontal multipliers and summed give a function of the displacement. Levers applied to these functions result in a function of VCB. This whole

78 Basic ship theory

process applied, first, to the ordinates by the horizontal multipliers and, secondly, to the functions of ordinate areas by the vertical multipliers and levers results in a function of displacement and a function of LCB. Clearly, the two functions of displacement should be the same and this comprises the traditional corner check.

Ordinate number	S.M.	WATERLINES									Vertical sections		Lever	FNS for momts
		5		4		3		2		1	FNS of area	Mults of area		
		1		4		2		4		1				
1	1	1	1	1	1	1	1	1	1	1	1			
		1		4		2		4		1	12	12	3	36
2	4	5	20	6	24	7	28	8	32	9	36				
		5		24		14		32		9	84	336	2	672
3	2	7	14	8	16	9	18	10	20	11	22				
		7		32		18		40		11	108	216	1	216
4	4	9	36	10	40	11	44	12	48	13	52				
		9		40		22		48		13	132	528	0	924
5	2	6	12	7	14	8	16	9	18	10	20				
		6		28		16		36		10	96	192	1	192
6	4	4	16	5	20	6	24	7	28	8	32				
		4		20		12		28		8	72	288	2	576
7	1	1	1	1	1	1	1	1	1	1	1				
		1		4		2		4		1	12	12	3	36
FNS of area		100		116		132		148		164		1584		804
Mults. area		100		464		264		592		164	1584			120
Levers		4		3		2		1		0				
FNS for mts.		400		1392		528		592		0	2912			

Fig. 3.30 *A simplified displacement sheet*

There will frequently be an appendage below the lowest convenient waterline which must be added to the main body calculations. Areas of this appendage at each ordinate are measured by planimeter and positions of centres of areas either spotted or, if the appendage is considerable, measured by integrator. The effects of the appendage are then included, as described in Chapter 2.

With the offsets for each waterplane so conveniently presented by the displacement table, it is a simple matter to calculate by the methods described in Chapter 2, area, position of CF and the second moments of area for each waterplane. Displacements and CB positions are calculated by adding or subtracting slices from the nearest waterplane calculations.

If Tchebycheff spacings of ordinates are adopted, the Simpson multipliers are, of course, dispensed with in one direction. A form of displacement table in which this is done is not unusual.

Flotation and trim 79

The lengthy process of direct calculation has been replaced by computer processing. The process clearly comprises a large number of simple arithmetical steps performed in a logical sequence and repeated for different input data. Offsets may be orthogonal as in Fig. 3.30 or radial. This type of calculation is very readily adaptable to digital computing and programs are available for most common computers often combined with the calculations of later chapters.

THE METACENTRIC DIAGRAM

As has already been discussed, the positions of B and M are dependent only on the geometry of the ship and the waterplane at which it is floating. They can, therefore, be determined without any knowledge of the actual condition of ship loading which causes it to float at that waterline.

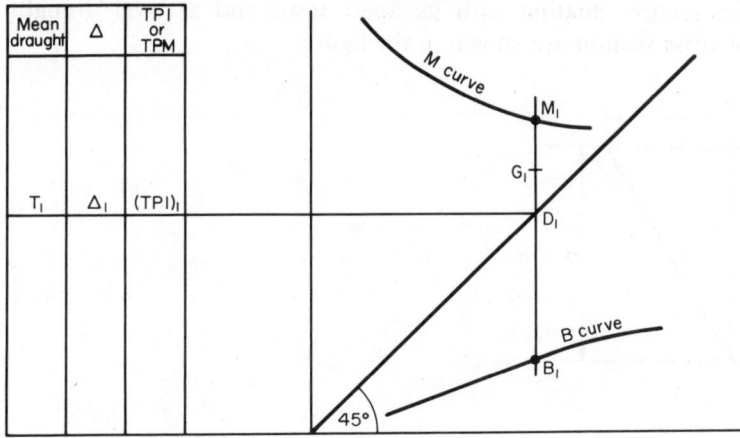

Fig. 3.31 Metacentric diagram

The metacentric diagram is a convenient way of defining variations in relative heights of B and M for a series of waterlines parallel to the design or load waterplane. Such a diagram is shown in Fig. 3.31 and it is constructed as follows. The vertical scale is used to represent draught and a line is drawn at 45 degrees to this scale. For a given draught T_1 a horizontal line is drawn intersecting the 45 degree line in D_1 and a vertical line is drawn through D_1. On this vertical line, a distance $\overline{D_1 M_1}$ is set out to represent the height of the metacentre above the waterplane and $\overline{D_1 B_1}$ to represent the depth of the centre of buoyancy below the waterplane. This process is repeated a sufficient number of times to define adequately the loci of the metacentre and centre of buoyancy. These two loci are termed the M and B curves. As drawn, M_1 lies above the waterplane but this is not necessarily always the case and the M curve may cross the 45 degree line. A table is constructed to the left of the diagram, in which are listed the displacements and TPI values for each of a number of draughts corresponding to typical ship conditions. These conditions must, strictly, be reduced to a common trim so that the loci of M and B will be continuous. In practice, however, not much error is involved in using the diagram for conditions other than the standard condition provided that the difference in trim is not excessive and provided that the draught is that at the centre of flotation.

In addition to the M and B curves, it is usual to show the positions of G for the conditions chosen. These positions can be obtained by methods discussed in Chapter 4.

Since $\overline{KB}$ is approximately proportional to draught over the normal operating range, the B curve is usually nearly straight for conventional ship shapes. The M curve, on the other hand, usually falls steeply with increasing draught at shallow draught then levels out and may even begin to rise at very deep draught.

Worked examples

EXAMPLE 1. Construct a metacentric diagram for a body with constant triangular cross-section floating with its apex down and at level draught. Dimensions of cross-section are shown in the figure.

Fig. 3.32

Solution:

Fig. 3.33

For a given draught T_1, $\overline{KB} = \frac{2}{3}T_1$. Hence, the B curve is a straight line passing through 0, at an angle β to the vertical such that

$$\tan \beta = \frac{T_1}{\frac{2}{3}T_1}$$

i.e.

$$\beta = \tan^{-1} 1.5$$

Breadth of waterplane at draught $T_1 = c\dfrac{T_1}{H}$

$$\therefore \quad \overline{B_1 M_1} = \dfrac{I}{\nabla} = \dfrac{\frac{1}{12}(cT_1/H)^3 L}{\frac{1}{2}(cT_1/H)T_1 L}$$

$$= \dfrac{1}{6}\dfrac{c^2 T_1}{H^2}$$

$$\therefore \quad \overline{KM_1} = \overline{KB_1} + \overline{B_1 M_1} = \dfrac{2}{3}T_1 + \dfrac{1}{6}\left(\dfrac{c^2}{H^2}\right)T_1$$

$$= \dfrac{T_1}{6}\left(4 + \dfrac{c^2}{H^2}\right)$$

Hence, in this case, since c and H are constants, the M curve is also a straight line through 0 but at an angle γ to the vertical such that

$$\tan \gamma = \dfrac{T_1}{T_1(4+c^2/H^2)/6} = \dfrac{6H^2}{4H^2 + c^2}$$

EXAMPLE 2. Construct a metacentric diagram for a vessel of constant circular cross-section floating at uniform draught.

Solution:

Fig. 3.34

For any inclination at any draught the buoyancy force must, from geometric considerations, pass through the centre of the circular cross-section. Hence, the M curve is a horizontal straight line.

The expression for $\overline{KB}$ is more complicated, but general considerations show that the curve must become tangential to the M curve when $T_1 = 2R$ and that its general form will be as indicated. If it is assumed that for small draughts the circle can be approximated to by a parabola, it can be shown that the tangent to the B curve at 0 is given by

$$\beta = \tan^{-1} \tfrac{5}{3}$$

82 Basic ship theory

EXAMPLE 3. When the tide falls, a moored barge grounds in soft homogeneous mud of specific gravity 1·35. With the keel just touching the mud, the barge was drawing a level 1·65 m of salt water of reciprocal weight density 0·975 m³/tonnef. The tide falls a further 18 cm.

Assuming that the barge is box shaped 25 m long and 5 m in breadth, calculate the draught after the tide has fallen. What weight must be removed to free the barge from the mud?

Solution: When floating free

$$\Delta = \frac{1\cdot 65 \times 25 \times 5}{0\cdot 975} \, m^3 \, \frac{tonnef}{m^3} = 211\cdot 5 \text{ tonnef.}$$

Fig. 3.35

When in mud,

$$\text{buoyancy supplied by salt water} = \frac{1\cdot 47}{1\cdot 65} \times 211\cdot 5 = 188\cdot 4 \text{ tonnef}$$

$$\text{buoyancy needed from mud} = 211\cdot 5 - 188\cdot 4 = 23\cdot 1 \text{ tonnef}$$

$$\text{buoyancy provided by mud} = x \times 25 \times 5 \times 1\cdot 35 = 23\cdot 1$$

$$\therefore \quad x = \frac{23\cdot 1}{25 \times 5 \times 1\cdot 35} = 0\cdot 14 \text{ m}$$

$\therefore$ draught when tide has fallen = 1·61 m

weight to be removed to clear mud = 23·1 tonnef

(the draught x could also have been obtained by taking a proportion of the 18 cm fall in tide in the ratio of the S.Gs of mud and salt water, $(1\cdot 35 \times 0\cdot 975) x = 0\cdot 18$.

EXAMPLE 4. Hydrostatic data for a ship show the following

Draught	19 ft 6 in.	21 ft 9 in.	24 ft 0 in.
Displacement (tonf)	8421	9927	11447
TPI	50·56	52·08	52·82

Calculate the displacement at a draught of 22 ft 8 in.

Solution: The TPI curve gives values of TPI at 22 ft 2½ in. and 22 ft 8 in. of 52·27 and 52·44 by plotting

WL	TPI	SM	f(V)
22 ft 8 in.	52·44	1	52·44
22 ft 2½ in.	52·27	4	209·08
21 ft 9 in.	52·08	1	52·08
			313·60

$$\text{displacement of addition} = \frac{5 \cdot 5}{3} \times 313 \cdot 6 \text{ in.} \frac{\text{tonf}}{\text{in.}}$$

$$= 574 \cdot 9 \text{ tonf}$$

∴ Δ to 22 ft 8 in. waterline = 10,502 tonf

(the best obtainable from interpolation of the displacement curve would have been a straight line relationship giving $\Delta = 9927 + \frac{11}{27} \times (11{,}447 - 9927) = 10{,}546$ tonf). We would have obtained a sufficiently accurate answer in this case by assuming the TPI to be constant at its 22 ft 2½ in. value, linearly interpolated between the two top waterplanes, i.e.

$$52 \cdot 08 + \frac{5 \cdot 5}{27} \times 0 \cdot 74 = 52 \cdot 23$$

then

$$\Delta = 9927 + 11 \times 52 \cdot 23 = 10{,}502 \text{ tonf}$$

EXAMPLE 5. During a voyage, a cargo ship uses up 320 tonnef of consumable stores and fuel from the fore peak, 85 m forward of midships.

Before the voyage, the forward draught marks 7 m aft of the forward perpendicular, recorded 5·46 m and the after marks, 2 m aft of the after perpendicular, recorded 5·85 m. At this mean draught, the hydrostatic data show the ship to have tonnef per metre = 4400, one metre trim moment BP = 33,200 tonnef m BP, CF aft of midships = 3 m. Length BP = 195 m. Calculate the draught mark readings at the end of the voyage, assuming that there is no change in water density.

Solution:

$$\text{Parallel rise} = \frac{320}{4400} = 0 \cdot 073 \text{ m}$$

Moment trimming = 320(85 + 3) tonnef m.

$$\text{Trim BP (195 m)} = \frac{320 \times 88}{33{,}200} = 0 \cdot 848 \text{ m.}$$

$$\text{Draught change at FM due to trim} = \frac{93 \cdot 5}{195} \times 0 \cdot 848 = 0 \cdot 406 \text{ m.}$$

84 *Basic ship theory*

$$\text{Draught change at AM due to trim} = \frac{96 \cdot 5}{195} \times 0{\cdot}848 = 0{\cdot}420 \text{ m}.$$

New draught at FM $= 5{\cdot}46 - 0{\cdot}07 - 0{\cdot}41 = 4{\cdot}98$ m.

New draught at AM $= 5{\cdot}85 - 0{\cdot}07 + 0{\cdot}42 = 6{\cdot}20$ m.

A clear sketch is essential for a reliable solution to problems of this sort.

Fig. 3.36

EXAMPLE 6. A fishing vessel grounds on a rock at a point 13·4 m from the FP when the depth of water is 0·3 m above low tide. Before grounding, the vessel was drawing 1·60 m at the FP and 2·48 m at the AP. At this mean draught, TPI in MN per metre immersion = 3·5, one metre trim moment = 13 MN m and CF is 1 m forward of midships. The ship is 49 m BP. Calculate the force at the keel and the new draughts at low tide.

Solution: Let the force at the rock be P MN and replace it by a force P MN and a moment $10{\cdot}1P$ MN m at the CF.

$$\text{Parallel rise due to } P = \frac{P}{3 \cdot 5} \text{ m}$$

$$\text{Change of trim due to } 10{\cdot}1P = \frac{10{\cdot}1P}{13} \text{ m BP}$$

$$\text{Change of draught at rock due to trim} = \frac{10{\cdot}1}{49} \times \frac{10{\cdot}1P}{13} \text{ m}$$

Flotation and trim 85

Fig. 3.37

$$\text{Total change of draught at rock} = \frac{P}{3\cdot 5} + \frac{10\cdot 1}{49} \times \frac{10\cdot 1 P}{13} \text{ m}$$

$$= \text{fall of tide} = 0\cdot 3 \text{ m}$$

$$\therefore \quad P(0\cdot 286 + 0\cdot 160) = 0\cdot 3$$

$$\therefore \quad P = 0\cdot 673 \text{ MN}$$

Then parallel rise due to $P = 0\cdot 192$ m.

Change of trim due to $10\cdot 1 P = 0\cdot 523$ m.

$$\text{Change of draught at FP due to trim} = \frac{23\cdot 5}{49} \times 0\cdot 523 = 0\cdot 251 \text{ m}$$

$$\text{Change of draught at AP due to trim} = \frac{25\cdot 5}{49} \times 0\cdot 523 = 0\cdot 272 \text{ m}.$$

New draught at FP $= 1\cdot 600 - 0\cdot 192 - 0\cdot 251 = 1\cdot 157$ m.

New draught at AP $= 2\cdot 480 - 0\cdot 192 + 0\cdot 272 = 2\cdot 560$ m.

(Because the final trim is large, it is unlikely that the answer can be relied upon to within 10 cm.)

EXAMPLE 7. The hydrostatic curves (prepared for water of reciprocal weight density 35 ft³/tonf) for a guided missile destroyer show it to have the following particulars at a mean draught of 17 ft 2 in. at which it is floating with a 12 in. stern trim in water of reciprocal weight density 35·9 ft³/tonf:

Length BP	560 ft
Designed trim	2 ft 6 in. by stern
Displacement	7940 tonf
CB abaft amidships	2·4 ft
CF abaft amidships	20·4 ft
TPI	69·4
MCT1"	1720 tonf ft

86 Basic ship theory

Calculate (a) the true displacement, (b) the new draught and trim when the ship puts to sea in water of reciprocal weight density 35·2 ft³/tonf.

Fig. 3.38

Solution: As shown in Fig. 3.38, because the hydrostatic curves assume a 2 ft 6 in. trim, they overestimate the displacement by the shaded layer of thickness

$$\frac{20\cdot 4}{560} \times 18 \text{ in.} = 0\cdot 66 \text{ in.}$$

This layer is composed of 35·9 ft³/tonf water, so that the relevant TPI is

$$69\cdot 4 \times \frac{35}{35\cdot 9}$$

and the displacement of the layer

$$= 0\cdot 66 \times 69\cdot 4 \times \frac{35}{35\cdot 9} = 44\cdot 5 \text{ tonf}$$

Now the displacement to WL $= 7940 \times \dfrac{35}{35\cdot 9}$

$$= 7940 - 7940\left(\frac{35\cdot 9 - 35}{35\cdot 9}\right)^*$$

$$= 7741 \text{ tonf}$$

∴   displacement to W_1L_1 (and W_2L_2) $= 7741 - 44\cdot 5 = 7696$ tonf.   (a)

In moving from 35·9 to 35·2 water, which is more buoyant, there is a parallel rise:

Volume of layer $= 7696(35\cdot 9 - 35\cdot 2) = 5387$ ft³

This is a layer of 35·9 water, weight

$$\frac{5387}{35\cdot 9} \text{ tonf} = 149\cdot 6 \text{ tonf}$$

* (Note the important artifice used to obtain the displacement to WL by calculating the difference by slide rule.)

$$\text{TPI in } 35 \cdot 9 \text{ water} = 69 \cdot 4 \times \frac{35}{35 \cdot 9}$$

$$\therefore \quad \text{layer thickness} = \frac{5387}{69 \cdot 4 \times 35} = 2 \cdot 2 \text{ in.}$$

Moment causing trim = $149 \cdot 6 (20 \cdot 4 - 2 \cdot 4) = 2695$ tonf ft.

Trim occurs in $35 \cdot 2$ water for which $MCT1'' = 1720 \times \dfrac{35}{35 \cdot 2}$

$$\therefore \quad \text{trim by stern} = \frac{2695}{1720} \times \frac{35 \cdot 2}{35} = 1 \cdot 58 \text{ in.}$$

Fig. 3.39

Change in mean draught due to $1 \cdot 58$ in. trim by stern

$$= -\frac{20 \cdot 4}{560} \times 1 \cdot 58 \text{ in.} = -0 \cdot 06 \text{ in.}$$

total reduction in mean draught = $2 \cdot 26$ in.

$\therefore \quad$ in water of RWD $35 \cdot 2$ ft^3/tonf

$\qquad$ mean draught = 16 ft $11\frac{3}{4}$ in. $\hfill$ (b)

$\qquad$ stern trim = $13\frac{1}{2}$ in.

Problems

1. (*a*) Calculate the reciprocal weight density of petrol in m^3/MN, given that its specific gravity is 0·70.

   (*b*) A pressure of $3 \cdot 75$ MN/m^2 is experienced by a submarine. If 1 lb = 0·4536 kg and 1 in. = 2·54 cm, convert this pressure to lbf/in^2. Put $g = 9 \cdot 81$ m/s^2.

2. A floating body has a constant triangular section, vertex downwards and has a constant draught of 12 m in fresh water, the breadth at the waterline being 24 m. The keel just touches a quantity of mud of specific gravity 2. The water level now falls 6 m. How far will the body sink into the mud? $\hfill$ (AP & S)

3. A wallsided ship goes aground on a mudbank so that its draught marks record a mean draught of 7 ft. Before going aground, the draught of the ship in salt water was 8 ft 10 in. The area of the waterplane is 4180 ft^2. What volume of oil of specific gravity 0·92 should be pumped out to free the ship?

Supposing, before pumping can begin, the tide falls a further foot and the ship sinks a further 6 in. into the mud, displacing a total of 1900 ft^3 of mud. What would be the reciprocal weight density of the mud? (HMDTC)

4. A homogeneous wooden pontoon of square section, having a specific gravity of 0·5 is made to float in fresh water with its sides vertical by covering one of its faces completely with a strip of metal having a specific gravity of 8·0.

Show that G coincides with M if the thickness of the strip is approximately one nineteenth ($\frac{1}{90}$) of its width. (HMDTC)

5. A model of a ship is built to float in water of 62·5 lbf/ft^3 weight density. It has the following geometric properties:

Length BP, 6·0 ft;   Area of waterplane, 691 in^2
Draught, 5·5 in.;   Trans. MI of waterplane, 12,450 in^4
$\overline{\text{KB}}$, 3·0 in.;   Volume of displacement, 4150 in^3

The centre of gravity as built is 7·2 in. above the keel. Where must a 25 lbf weight be placed to bring G below M, presuming the model to be wallsided at the waterline? (HMDTC)

6. The TPMs (tonnef per metre immersion) of a wallsided ship floating at a draught of 2·75 m is 940. Its displacement at this draught is 3335 tonnef and the VCB is 1·13 m below the waterline. The centre of gravity of the ship is 3·42 m above the keel. The transverse second moment of area of the waterplane is 7820 m^4.

Calculate the shifts of B and G and the new position of M when a load of 81·2 tonnef is placed 3·05 m off the centreline on a deck 8·54 m above the keel and by constructing the movements on squared paper, estimate, to the nearest degree, the heel of the ship.

7. The half ordinates of the waterplane of a barge, 50 m long, are 0·0, 3·0, 4·5, 5·0, 4·2 and 1·0 m. Its volume of displacement is 735 m^3 and the CG is 2·81 m above the keel. The draught is 3·0 m.

A block of SG 7·0, having a volume of 10 m^3 has to be raised from the deck in a cage. Using an approximate formula for the position of B, estimate the height to which the weight can be raised before G is higher than M.

8. The tonf per inch immersion of a ship at the waterlines, which are 5 ft apart, are given below. In addition, there is an appendage having a displacement of 1480 tonf with its centre of buoyancy 3 ft 3 in. below 7 WL.

Waterline	1	2	3	4	5	6	7
TPI	195	184	169	153	135	108	46

Calculate the displacement of the ship and the vertical position of the centre of buoyancy of the ship. (HMDTC)

9. The TPIs of the waterlines of a vessel, which are 7 ft apart, are:

WL	6	5½	5	4	3	2	1
TPI	20	44	64	88	108	124	132

If there is a 110 tonf appendage whose c.b. is 3 ft below 6WL, find the displacement and the position of the CB of the whole vessel. (RNATE)

10. A yacht of mass displacement 9·5 tonnes to 1 WL in fresh water has a CB 0·25 m below 1 WL. If the distance between WLs is 0·15 m, plot a curve of VCB against draught. The areas of A, 1, 2 and 3 WLs are respectively 28·4, 28·0, 26·8 and 25·2 m². Quote VCB at $2\frac{1}{2}$ WL.

11. A guided missile destroyer is 510 ft long BP and displaces 6130 tonf in salt water when the draught mark readings are 14 ft $10\frac{1}{4}$ in. forward and 15 ft $3\frac{1}{2}$ in. aft. The distances of the draught marks from amidships are 230 ft forward and 275 ft aft. The second moment of area of the waterplane is $82·3 \times 10^6$ ft⁴ about the centre of flotation which is 5 ft abaft amidships. The waterplane area is 17,500 ft².

Calculate the new draughts when 140 tonf of missiles are embarked at a mean distance of 190 ft abaft amidships. Illustrate on a bold diagram, the forces and movements involved and state any assumptions made. (HMDTC)

12. The longitudinal moment of inertia about the CF of the waterplane of a depot ship floating in fresh water is 190×10^6 ft⁴. The length BP is 684 ft and the draught marks are 32 ft abaft the FP and 8 ft abaft the AP. The area of the waterplane is 48,000 ft². Draught marks read 17 ft $3\frac{1}{4}$ in. forward and 22 ft $2\frac{1}{2}$ in. aft.

When 444 tonf of oil with its c.g. 200 ft abaft amidships are pumped out, the reading of the after marks is observed to change to 16 ft $10\frac{1}{2}$ in.

Deduce the position of the CF of the waterplane and the reading of the forward marks. (HMDTC)

13. For a mean draught of 4·0 m with a 0·5 m trim by the stern, the ship's book shows a destroyer to have the following particulars:

$$\text{displacement, mass} = 2300 \text{ tonne}$$
$$\text{TPM} = 910$$
$$\text{MCT BP} = 3010 \text{ tonnef m}$$
$$\text{CF abaft amidships} = 6·85 \text{ m}$$
$$\text{CB abaft amidships} = 2·35 \text{ m}$$

The ship is 102 m BP and is floating where the water has an SG = 1·02 at draughts of 3·50 m forward and 4·50 m aft.

Find, to the nearest half centimetre the draught at the propellers, which are 13 m forward of the AP, when the ship has moved up river to water of SG = 1·01.

14. A ship, displacement 7620 tonnef, floats at draughts of 4·10 m forward and 4·70 m aft. The forward marks are 2·1 m aft of the FP and the after marks are 19·8 m forward of the AP. The ship is 170 m between perpendiculars, has a tonnef per centimetre of 22·4 and the CF is 5·8 m aft of amidships. Determine the new draughts at the marks if a weight of 100 tonnef is placed 18·3 m forward of amidships.

One metre trim moment BP = 20,700 tonnef m.

15. The following are the particulars of an aircraft carrier: Displacement = 44,000 tonf, mean draught BP = 38·4 ft, trim by stern between marks = 7·3 ft, TPI = 84·2, MCT1″ BP = 2550 tonf ft. CF abaft amidships = 40 ft, LBP = 720 ft, forward marks abaft FP = 33 ft, after marks before AP = 52 ft.

Calculate the new draughts at the marks when 530 tonf of aircraft are embarked with their c.g. 260 ft before amidships.

(RNATE)

16. A box-shaped barge of length 20 m beam 5 m and mean draught 1·45 m floats with a trim of 30 cm by the stern in water of specific gravity 1·03. If it moves into water of SG = 1·00, what will be its new draughts forward and aft?

17. The buoy mooring cable on a badly moored vessel is vertical and just taut when it has an even draught of 3 m. The vessel is 50 m long and has a TPM = 250 and CF 4 m abaft amidships. MCT is 1300 tonnef m. The mooring cable passes over the bow bullring 5 m before the FP.

Calculate the new draughts at the perpendiculars when the tide has risen 0·8 m.

(RNATE)

18. A cargo ship, displacing 5500 tonf, floats at draughts of 15 ft 0 in. forward and 16 ft 6 in. aft, measured at marks 230 ft forward of and 170 ft abaft amidships.

The vessel grounds on a rock 75 ft forward of amidships. What is the force on the bottom when the tide has fallen 1 ft and what are then the draughts at the marks? TPI = 52; CF is 15 ft abaft amidships; MCT1″ BP is 1300 tonf ft; LBP is 480 ft.

19. The draught marks of a ship, 61 m long BP, are 6·1 m aft of the FP and 12·2 m before the AP. The MN per m immersion is 3·570 and the one metre trim moment BP is 7·66 MN m. The CF is 2·45 m abaft amidships and the draught mark readings forward and aft are respectively 2·67 and 3·0 m.

The vessel goes aground on a ridge of rock 9·15 m from the FP. If the tide is falling at an average rate of 81 cm/hr, how long will it be before the freeboard at the AP is reduced by 1·22 m?

What will then be the draught mark readings?

20. A ship 360 ft long, has a design trim of 2 ft by the stern, an after cut-up 75 ft from the after perpendicular and a $\overline{KG}$ of 16 ft. When the after cut-up just touches level blocks, the trim out of normal is measured as 3 ft by the stern and the water level in the dock is 13·28 ft above the blocks.

Calculate (i) the initial displacement and LCG; (ii) the force on the after cut-up and the water level above the blocks when the ship just sues all along.

Hydrostatic data for design trim:

Mean draught (ft)	Displacement (tonf)	LCB (ft aft)	VCB (ft)	LCF (ft aft)	$\overline{BM_L}$ (ft)
12·0	2220	7·62	7·4	21·88	943
11·5	2079	6·66	7·1	21·43	983
11·0	1939	5·64	6·8	20·76	1026
10·5	1800	5·58	6·5	19·61	1070

(HMDTC)

21. A new class of frigates has the following hydrostatic particulars at a mean draught of 4 m as calculated for water of 1025 kg/m³ : TPM = 720, MCT = 3000 tonnef m, CF abaft amidships = 4 m, CB abaft amidships = 1 m, displacement = 2643 tonnef.

When one of the class was launched at Portsmouth, where the mass density of water is 1025 kg/m³, it took the water with a mean draught of 3·98 m and a stern trim of 0·6 m.

Supposing it to be in an exactly similar condition, how would you expect a sister ship to float after launch on the Clyde, where the water has a speciffic gravity of 1·006?

All draughts are at the perpendiculars 120 m apart. (RNATE)

22. A ship of 5000 tonf and 500 ft between perpendiculars, has its centre of gravity 5 ft abaft amidships, floats in salt water of 35 ft³/tonf and has draughts of 10 ft 3 in. at the forward perpendicular and 14 ft 6 in. at the after cut-up, which is 30 ft before the after perpendicular.

Estimate the draughts before docking in water of reciprocal weight density 35·7 ft³/tonf.

The TPI is originally 50, MCT1″ is 625 tonf ft increasing at the rate of 50 tonf ft per foot increase of draught. The centre of flotation is 25 ft abaft amidships. (HMDTC)

23. A Great Lakes bulk carrier has hydrostatic curves drawn for water of reciprocal weight density 36 ft³/tonf, which show the following information:

Mean draught BP	28 ft	32 ft
Displacement	24,259 tonf	28,032 tonf
Trim by stern	12 in.	12 in.
TPI	78·4	78·8
MCT1″ BP	775 tonf ft	779 tonf ft
CF forward of midships	3·8 ft	2·2 ft
CB aft of midships	12 ft	8·0 ft

The draughts forward and aft in river water of reciprocal weight density 35·8 ft³/tonf are respectively 30 ft 6 in. and 31 ft 6 in. The length between perpendiculars is 580 ft.

Calculate the draughts when the ship reaches the open sea. (HMDTC)

24. The following are the half ordinates in m of a vessel for which the waterlines are 1·75 m apart and ordinates 25 m apart. Determine its volume and the position of the centre of volume below 1WL.

		WLs			
Ords.	5	4	3	2	1
1	0	0	0	0	0
2	1	2	3	4	6
3	2	3	5	7	8
4	3	5	7	8	9
5	2	4	6	8	9
6	1	2	4	6	6
7	0	0	0	0	0

25. Given the half breadths of the waterlines of a ship as shown below, work out the displacement of the main body up to the 1 WL. The WLs are 4 ft 6 in. apart and the ordinates 72 ft.

	Half breadths in feet at ordinates				
	FP	2	3	4	AP
1 WL	1·1	21·3	30·2	27·6	4·4
2 WL	0·8	20·7	29·9	26·7	1·1
3 WL	0·5	18·9	29·0	24·9	1·8
4 WL	0·0	16·2	26·6	21·0	2·9

26. It is desired to fit a gun mounting weighing 20 tonf to a ship without altering the draught at the propellers which are 30 ft forward of the after perpendicular. The draughts are 8 ft forward and 9 ft aft and other particulars of the ship before the gun is added are: LBP = 140 ft, displacement = 260 tonf, MCT1″ = 65 tonf ft, CF abaft amidships = 7 ft, TPI = 5·6.

Where should the gun be mounted? What are the resulting draughts forward and aft?

27. Construct a metacentric diagram for a vessel of rectangular cross-section.

28. Construct metacentric diagrams for prisms, apex downwards,

(*a*) having a parabolic cross-section 6 m deep by 3 m wide at the top;
(*b*) having a section of an isosceles triangle, half apex angle 15 degrees and height 8 m.

4 Stability

Most readers will have been annoyed as children to find that the boats they made of blocks of wood and cotton reels so often turned turtle when they put them in the bath. Soon, they will have discovered that a large wood screw in the bottom of the boat put matters to right. This was an excellent practical introduction to an important aspect of ship design known as ship stability.

Stability and equilibrium are not, of course, considerations confined to ships and before studying such an application it is necessary to define the subject with some precision.

EQUILIBRIUM

A rigid body is said to be in a state of equilibrium when the resultant of all the forces acting on it is zero and the resultant moment of the forces is also zero.

STABILITY

If a rigid body, when subject to a small disturbance from a position of equilibrium, tends to return to that state it is said to possess positive stability or, to be in a state of stable equilibrium. If, following the disturbance, the body remains in its new position, then it is said to be in a state of neutral equilibrium or to possess neutral stability. If, following the disturbance, the excursion from the equilibrium position tends to increase, then the body is said to be in a state of unstable equilibrium or to possess negative stability.

The ship is a complex structure and is not in the mathematical sense a rigid body. However, for the purpose of studying stability it is permissible so to regard it. Throughout this chapter the ship will be regarded as a rigid body in calm water and not underway. If the ship is in waves or is underway there are hydrodynamic forces acting on the ship which may affect the buoyancy forces. This problem is discussed briefly in later sections. In Ref. 1 it is stated:

'It is reported that certain destroyers, when underway, show an apparent loss in transverse metacentric stability. These vessels are said to take a more pronounced heel when making turns than would be expected from their transverse stability characteristics. Further, they often hold this inclination after straightening out on a new course.'

Nevertheless, for stability purposes, it is usual to ignore hydrodynamic forces except for high speed craft. In the case of fast motor boats, the hydrodynamic forces are, in fact, the predominant factor in assessing stability. (See Ref. 2.)

For *equilibrium*, the buoyancy force and weight must be equal and the two forces must act along the same straight line. For a floating body this line must be vertical.

DISTURBANCE FROM STATE OF EQUILIBRIUM

Any small disturbance can be resolved into three components of translation and three of rotation with reference to the ship's body axes. The conventional axes are defined as in Fig. 4.1, the positive directions being indicated by the arrows.

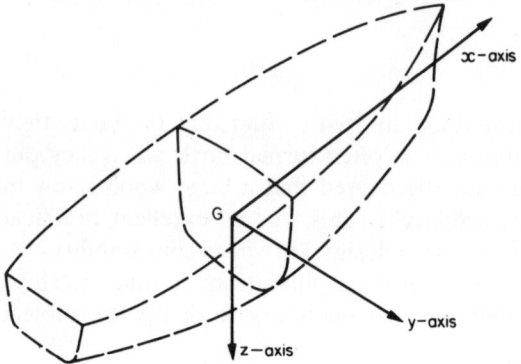

Fig. 4.1 Body axes

Consider each component of a disturbance in turn.

Translation along the x-axis, which is horizontal, leads to no resultant force so that the ship is in neutral equilibrium for this type of disturbance.

Translation along the y-axis also leads to no resultant force so that the ship is in neutral equilibrium for this type of disturbance.

For a floating body, translation along the z-axis in the positive direction results in an augmented buoyancy force which will tend to move the ship in the negative sense of z, i.e. it tends to return the ship to its state of equilibrium and the ship is thus stable for this type of disturbance. The special case of a totally submerged body is considered later.

Rotation about the x-axis, heel, results in a moment acting on the ship about which no generalization is possible and the ship may display stable, neutral or unstable equilibrium.

Rotation about the y-axis, trim, leads to a condition similar to that for heel.

Rotation about the z-axis, yaw, results in no resultant force or moment so that the ship is in neutral equilibrium for this type of disturbance.

The above results are summarized in Table 4.1.

Table 4.1
Summary of equilibrium conditions

Axis	Equilibrium condition for	
	Translation along:	Rotation about:
x	Neutral	Stable, neutral or unstable
y	Neutral	Stable, neutral or unstable
z	Stable	Neutral

It is clear from Table 4.1 that the only disturbances which herein demand study are the rotations about the x- and y-axes. In principle, there is no distinction between these two but, for the ship application, the waterplane characteristics are such that it is convenient to study the two separately. Also, for small rotational disturbances at constant displacement any skew disturbance can be regarded as compounded of

(a) the stability exhibited by the ship for rotations about the x-axis—referred to as its *transverse stability*;
(b) the stability exhibited by the ship for rotations about the y-axis—referred to as its *longitudinal stability*.

Fig. 4.2 Action of buoyancy force and weight for small rotational disturbance

Initial stability

Consider the irregular shaped body shown in Fig. 4.2 floating in a state of equilibrium. In the equilibrium state, the centre of buoyancy, B_0, and the centre of gravity, G, must lie on the same vertical line. If the body is now subjected to a rotational disturbance, by turning it through a small angle β at constant displacement, the centre of buoyancy will move to some new position, B. For convenience, in Fig. 4.2 the angular disturbance is shown as being caused by a pure moment about G, but it will be realized that the condition of constant displacement will, in general, require translational movements of G by forces as well.

The weight and buoyancy forces continue to act vertically after rotation but, in general, are separated so that the body is subject to a moment Δ $\overline{GZ}$ where Z is the foot of the normal from G on to the line of action of the buoyancy force. As drawn, this moment tends to restore the body to the original position. The couple is termed the *righting moment* and $\overline{GZ}$ is termed the *righting lever*.

Another way of defining the line of action of the buoyancy force is to use its point of intersection, M, with the z-axis. As the angle β is indefinitely diminished

M tends to a limiting position termed the *metacentre*. For small values of β it follows that

$$\overline{GZ} = \overline{GM} \sin \beta$$
$$\simeq \overline{GM} \beta$$

The distance $\overline{GM}$ is termed the *metacentric height* and is said to be positive when M lies above G. This is the condition of stable equilibrium, for should M lie below G the moment acting on the body tends to increase β and the body is unstable. If M and G coincide the equilibrium is neutral. (See Fig. 4.3.)

Fig. 4.3 *The three stability conditions*

ADJUSTMENT OF TRANSVERSE METACENTRIC HEIGHT BY SMALL CHANGES OF DIMENSIONS

The ship's form can be altered by increasing ordinates in the x, y and z directions such that all dimensions in any one direction are altered in the same ratio. This ratio need not be the same for all directions. This method of form changing has the advantage of maintaining the coefficients of fineness unaltered and is often used in the early stages of ship design. For instance, it may be necessary to decrease draught at the expense of the beam to ensure that the ship will be able to negotiate canals or harbour entrances. In this case,

$$\Delta = (\text{constant}) \times L \times B \times T$$

Hence

$$\log \Delta = \log(\text{constant}) + \log L + \log B + \log T$$

and differentiating

$$\frac{d\Delta}{\Delta} = \frac{dL}{L} + \frac{dB}{B} + \frac{dT}{T}$$

Thus, if the percentage changes in the main dimensions are small, their sum will provide the percentage change in the displacement.

Similarly as shown in Chapter 3,

$$\overline{BM} = \frac{I_T}{V} = (\text{constant}) \times \frac{B^2}{T}$$

and by the same process

$$\frac{d\overline{BM}}{\overline{BM}} = 2\frac{dB}{B} - \frac{dT}{T}$$

Also

$$\frac{d\,\overline{BM}}{\overline{BM}} = \frac{d\,\overline{BG} + d\,\overline{GM}}{\overline{BM}}$$

$$= \frac{d\,\overline{BG} + d\,\overline{GM}}{\overline{BG} + \overline{GM}}$$

Some special cases are worth considering.

(a) Where it is desired to change beam only, the increase in displacement is given by

$$d\Delta = \Delta \frac{dB}{B}$$

and the effect on $\overline{GM}$ is deduced as follows:

$$\frac{d\,\overline{BG} + d\,\overline{GM}}{\overline{BM}} = 2\frac{dB}{B}$$

If it is assumed that $\overline{KG}$ remains unaltered then $d\,\overline{BG} = 0$ and

$$d\,\overline{GM} = 2\overline{BM} \cdot \frac{dB}{B}$$

Since, in general, $\overline{BM}$ is greater than $\overline{GM}$ the percentage increase in metacentric height is more than twice that in beam.

(b) If it is desired to keep the displacement and draught unaltered, the length must be decreased in the same ratio as the beam is increased, that is

$$-\frac{dL}{L} = \frac{dB}{B}$$

Provided the assumption that $\overline{KG}$ is unchanged remains true the change in metacentric height is as above.

(c) To maintain constant displacement and length the draught must be changed in accord with

$$\frac{dT}{T} = -\frac{dB}{B}$$

This change in draught may, or may not, cause a change in $\overline{KG}$. There is a number of possibilities two of which are dealt with below.

(i) $\overline{KG}$ = (constant) × T. But $\overline{KB}$ = (constant) × T also, i.e. $\overline{BG} = \overline{KG} - \overline{KB}$ = (constant) × T.

It should be noted that these constants of proportionality are not necessarily the same, hence

$$\frac{d\overline{BG}}{\overline{BG}} = \frac{dT}{T} = -\frac{dB}{B}$$

It has been shown that

$$\frac{d\overline{BG} + d\overline{GM}}{\overline{BG} + \overline{GM}} = 2\frac{dB}{B} - \frac{dT}{T} = \frac{3\,dB}{B}$$

Hence

$$-\overline{BG}\frac{dB}{B} + d\overline{GM} = 3(\overline{BG} + \overline{GM})\frac{dB}{B}$$

and

$$d\overline{GM} = (4\overline{BG} + 3\overline{GM})\frac{dB}{B}$$

(ii) $\overline{KG}$ = constant. Since

$$\overline{BG} = \overline{KG} - \overline{KB}$$

in this case, the change in $\overline{BG} = d\overline{BG}$

$$= -(\text{change in } \overline{KB})$$
$$= -\overline{KB}\frac{dT}{T} = \overline{KB}\frac{dB}{B}$$

As before

$$d\overline{BG} + d\overline{GM} = 3(\overline{BG} + \overline{GM})\frac{dB}{B}$$

$$d\overline{GM} = (3\overline{BG} + 3\overline{GM} - \overline{KB})\frac{dB}{B}$$

$$d\overline{GM} = (4\overline{BG} + 3\overline{GM} - \overline{KG})\frac{dB}{B}$$

EXAMPLE 1. A ship has the following principal dimensions: $L = 360$ m, $B = 42$ m, $T = 12$ m, $\Delta = 1200$ MN, $\overline{KB} = 7$ m, $\overline{KM} = 21$ m, $\overline{KG} = 18$ m.

It is desired to reduce draught to 11 m, keeping length and displacement constant and coefficients of fineness constant. Assuming $\overline{KG}$ remains unaltered, calculate the new $\overline{GM}$ and the new beam.

Solution:

$$\frac{d\Delta}{\Delta} = 0 = \frac{dL}{L} + \frac{dB}{B} + \frac{dT}{T}$$

Hence

$$\frac{dB}{B} = \frac{1}{12} \quad \therefore \quad dB = \frac{42}{12} = 3\cdot5 \text{ m}.$$

i.e.

new beam $= 45\cdot5$ m.

$$\frac{d\,\overline{BM}}{\overline{BM}} = 2\frac{dB}{B} - \frac{dT}{T} = 2\times\frac{1}{12} + \frac{1}{12} = \frac{1}{4}$$

$$d\,\overline{BM} = 14\times\frac{1}{4} = 3\cdot5 \text{ m}.$$

Because $\overline{KB}$ is proportional to T

$$\frac{d\,\overline{KB}}{\overline{KB}} = \frac{dT}{T} = -\frac{1}{12}$$

and

$$d\,\overline{KB} = -\frac{7}{12}$$

Now

$$\overline{GM} = \overline{KB} + \overline{BM} - \overline{KG}$$

$$\therefore \quad \text{new } \overline{GM} = 3 + (-\tfrac{7}{12}) + 3\cdot5$$

$$= 5\cdot92 \text{ m}.$$

EFFECT OF MASS DENSITY

It is clear that a critical feature in the study of initial stability is the vertical position of the centre of gravity. It is instructive to consider a homogeneous rectangular block of material floating freely as shown in Fig. 4.4.

Fig. 4.4 Homogeneous block floating freely

The density of the block must be less than that of the water in which it floats, or else it would sink. If the density is C times that of the water, equating weight and buoyancy shows that

$$C \times LBH = LBT$$

i.e.

$$C = \frac{T}{H}$$

Now for a rectangular block

$$\overline{KB} = \frac{T}{2}$$

$$\overline{BM} = \frac{I}{V} = \frac{1}{12} \frac{B^3 L}{BLT} = \frac{B^2}{12T}$$

$$\overline{KG} = \frac{H}{2}$$

and

$$\overline{GM} = \overline{KB} + \overline{BM} - \overline{KG} = \frac{T}{2} + \frac{B^2}{12T} - \frac{H}{2}$$

$$= \frac{CH}{2} + \frac{B^2}{12CH} - \frac{H}{2}$$

$$= \frac{H}{2}(C-1) + \frac{B^2}{12CH}$$

The condition for positive stability is that

$$\overline{GM} > 0$$

i.e.

$$\frac{H}{2}(C-1) + \frac{B^2}{12CH} > 0$$

Similar expressions can be derived for homogeneous blocks of other cross-sectional shapes.

EXAMPLE 2. A rectangular block of homogeneous material is 20 m long, 5 m wide and 5 m deep. It is floating freely in fresh water with its longest dimension horizontal. Calculate the range of specific gravity over which the block will be unstable transversely.

Solution: As derived above, the block will be unstable if

$$\frac{H}{2}(C-1) + \frac{B^2}{12CH} < 0$$

i.e.

$$\frac{5}{2}(C-1)+\frac{25}{12C\times 5} < 0$$

$$C-1+\frac{1}{6C} < 0$$

$$6C^2 - 6C + 1 < 0$$

When $C = 0$, the block has zero draught and the inequality is not satisfied, i.e. the block is stable.

When $C = \frac{1}{2}$, the left-hand side $= \frac{6}{4} - 3 + 1$. This is less than zero so that the inequality is satisfied.

When $C = 1$, the other possible extreme value, the inequality is not satisfied.

The block is therefore stable at extreme values of C but unstable over some intermediate range. This range will be defined by the roots of the equation

$$6C^2 - 6C + 1 = 0$$

$$C = \frac{6 \pm \sqrt{(36-24)}}{12} = \frac{6 \pm \sqrt{12}}{12}$$

i.e.

$$C = 0{\cdot}211 \quad \text{or} \quad 0{\cdot}789$$

Hence the block is unstable if the specific gravity lies within the range 0·211 to 0·789.

EFFECT OF FREE SURFACES OF LIQUIDS

It is quite a common experience to find it difficult to balance a shallow tray or tin containing water. Stability is essentially a problem of balance, and it is therefore necessary to investigate whether a tank of liquid in a ship affects the ship's initial stability. The problem is considered below in relation to transverse stability, but similar considerations would apply to the case of longitudinal stability.

In practice, a ship has tanks with several different liquids—fresh water for drinking or for boilers, salt water for ballast, fuels of various types and lubricating oils—so the problem must be examined with allowance made for the fact that the density of the liquid may not be the same as that of the sea water in which the ship is floating.

In the following, the subscript s is used to denote quantities associated with the ship or the sea water in which she floats and the subscript ℓ to denote the liquid or the tank in which it is contained.

Let the ship be floating initially at a waterline WL and let it be heeled through a small angle ϕ to a new waterline $W_1 L_1$. Since by definition the surface of the liquid in the tank is free, it will also change its surface inclination, relative to the tank, by the same angle ϕ. (See Fig. 4.5.)

Fig. 4.5 Liquid free surface

In Chapter 3, it was shown that for small angles of inclination the transfer of buoyancy is given approximately by the expression

$$\Delta_s \frac{I_s}{\nabla_s} \phi = \rho_s I_s \phi g$$

It follows that, by similar arguments, the transfer of weight due to the movement of the liquid in the tank is approximately

$$\Delta_\ell \frac{I_\ell}{\nabla_\ell} \phi = \rho_\ell I_\ell \phi g$$

This being a transfer of weight opposes the righting moment due to the transfer of buoyancy and results in the effective righting moment acting on the ship being reduced to

$$\Delta_s \overline{GM}_s \phi - \rho_\ell I_\ell \phi g$$

Thus, if $\overline{GM}_F$ is the effective metacentric height allowing for the action of the liquid free surface

$$\Delta_s \overline{GM}_F \phi = \Delta_s \overline{GM}_s \phi - \rho_\ell I_\ell \phi g$$

and therefore

$$\overline{GM}_F = \overline{GM}_s - \frac{\rho_\ell I_\ell}{\Delta_s} g$$

$$= \overline{GM}_s - \left(\frac{\rho_\ell}{\rho_s}\right) \frac{I_\ell}{\nabla_s}$$

It should be noted that the effect of the free surface is independent of the position of the tank in the ship; the tank can be at any height in the ship, at any position along its length and need not be on the middle-line. The effect is also independent of the amount of liquid in the tank provided the second moment of area of the free surface is substantially unchanged when inclined. A tank which is almost empty or almost full can suffer such a change in second moment of area and it is for this reason that if, during an inclining experiment (see later), tanks cannot be completely full or empty they are specified to be half full.

It is usual to regard the free surface effect as being a virtual rise of the centre of gravity of the ship, although it will be appreciated that this is merely a matter of convention.

A similar effect can arise from the movements of granular cargoes stowed in bulk such as grain. Here, however, there is no simple relation between the angle of inclination of the ship and the slope of the surface of the cargo. At small angles of heel the cargo is not likely to shift so there is no influence on initial stability.

The effect of a free liquid surface on stability at larger angles of heel is discussed later.

EFFECT OF FREELY SUSPENDED WEIGHTS

It is more difficult to balance a pole with a weight freely suspended from its top than it is to balance the same pole with the same weight lashed securely to the pole. It is of interest to the naval architect to know what effect weights suspended freely in a ship have on the stability of the ship. Such a practical situation arises when a ship unloads her cargo using her own derricks. Consider the moment the cargo load is lifted from the hold before any translation of the load has taken place. The effect on transverse stability will normally be more critical than that on longitudinal stability, although the principles involved are the same.

Fig. 4.6 Freely suspended weight

Referring to Fig. 4.6, let the weight W be suspended freely from a point S a distance h above the centroid of mass of the weight. Let the ship be floating at a waterline WL and consider it being heeled through a small angle ϕ to a new waterline $W_1 L_1$. The weight, being freely suspended, will move until it is again vertically below S, i.e. its suspending wire will move through an angle ϕ. Thus, as far as the ship is aware the line of action of the weight of the cargo being lifted always passes through S. Hence, the effect on the ship is as though the weight W were placed at S.

104 Basic ship theory

It will be noted that this result is independent of the magnitude of the angle of heel provided the movement of the suspended weight is not restricted in any way.

THE WALL-SIDED FORMULA

Fig. 4.7 *Wall-sided formula*

A ship is said to be wall-sided if, for the angles of inclination to be considered, those portions of the outer bottom covered or uncovered by the moving waterplane are vertical with the ship upright. No practical ships are truly wall-sided, but many may be regarded as such for small angles of inclination—perhaps up to about 10 degrees.

Referring to Fig. 4.7, let the ship be inclined from its initial waterline WL to a new waterline $W_1 L_1$ by being heeled through a small angle ϕ. Since the vessel is wall-sided, WL and $W_1 L_1$ must intersect on the centre line.

The volume transferred in an elemental wedge of length δL where the beam is b is

$$\delta L \left(\frac{1}{2} \times \frac{b}{2} \times \frac{b}{2} \tan \phi \right) = \left(\frac{b^2}{8} \tan \phi \right) \delta L$$

Moment of transfer of volume for this wedge in a direction parallel to WL

$$= \frac{b^2}{8} \tan \phi \, \frac{2b}{3} \delta L$$

Hence, for the whole ship, moment of transfer of volume is

$$\int_0^L \frac{b^3}{12} \tan \phi \, dL$$

Hence, horizontal component of shift of B, $\overline{BB'}$ is given by

$$\overline{BB'} = \frac{1}{\nabla} \int_0^L \frac{b^3}{12} \tan \phi \, dL$$

$$= \frac{I}{\nabla} \tan \phi = \overline{BM} \tan \phi$$

Similarly, vertical shift $\overline{B'B''}$ is given by

$$\overline{B'B''} = \frac{1}{\nabla} \int_0^L \frac{b^2}{8} \tan\phi \tfrac{1}{3} b \tan\phi \, dL$$

$$= \frac{I}{2\nabla} \tan^2\phi = \frac{\overline{BM}}{2} \tan^2\phi$$

By projection on to a plane parallel to $W_1 L_1$

$$\overline{GZ} = \overline{BB'} \cos\phi + \overline{B'B''} \sin\phi - \overline{BG} \sin\phi$$

$$= \overline{BM}\left[\sin\phi + \frac{\tan^2\phi}{2} \sin\phi\right] - \overline{BG} \sin\phi$$

$$= \sin\phi\left[\overline{BM} - \overline{BG} + \frac{\overline{BM}}{2} \tan^2\phi\right]$$

i.e.

$$\overline{GZ} = \sin\phi\left[\overline{GM} + \frac{\overline{BM}}{2} \tan^2\phi\right]$$

For a given ship if $\overline{GM}$ and $\overline{BM}$ are known, or can be calculated, $\overline{GZ}$ can readily be calculated using this formula.

Wall-sided vessel containing a tank with vertical sides containing liquid

Fig. 4.8 *Wall-sided ship with liquid contained in a wall-sided tank*

Let the density of the liquid in the tank be ρ times that of the water in which the ship is floating.

Referring to Fig. 4.8, horizontal and vertical shifts of B will be as calculated for the ship without a tank. In addition, however, the centroid of mass of the liquid in the tank will suffer movements

$$\overline{gg'} = \frac{I_\ell}{\nabla_\ell} \tan\phi$$

and

$$\overline{g'g''} = \frac{I_\ell}{2\nabla_\ell} \tan^2\phi$$

Hence the centre of gravity of the ship, G, will suffer movements of

$$\overline{GG'} = \frac{I_\ell}{V_\ell} \tan \phi \times \rho \frac{V_\ell}{V_s} = \rho \frac{I_\ell}{V_s} \tan \phi$$

and

$$\overline{G'G''} = \rho \frac{I_\ell}{2V_s} \tan^2 \phi$$

Thus, the presence of the free surface will effectively reduce $\overline{GZ}$ to $\overline{GZ}_F$ where

$$\overline{GZ}_F = \sin \phi \left[\left(\overline{GM} - \rho \frac{I_\ell}{V_s} \right) + \left(\overline{BM} - \rho \frac{I_\ell}{V_s} \right) \frac{\tan^2 \phi}{2} \right]$$

EXAMPLE 3. Calculate the ordinates of the curve of $\overline{GZ}$ for a wall-sided ship up to 15 degrees of heel given that $\overline{GM} = 3$ ft and $\overline{BM} = 18$ ft.

Solution:

$$\overline{GZ} = \left[\overline{GM} + \frac{\overline{BM}}{2} \tan^2 \phi \right] \sin \phi$$

$$\overline{GZ} = [3 + 9 \tan^2 \phi] \sin \phi$$

Values of $\overline{GZ}$ for varying values of ϕ can be computed as in the table below.

ϕ (deg)	$\tan \phi$	$\tan^2 \phi$	$9 \tan^2 \phi$	$3+9 \tan^2 \phi$	$\sin \phi$	$\overline{GZ}$ (ft)
0	0	0	0	3	0	0
3	0·052	0·0027	0·0243	3·024	0·052	0·157
6	0·105	0·0110	0·0990	3·099	0·105	0·325
9	0·158	0·0250	0·2250	3·225	0·156	0·503
12	0·213	0·0454	0·4086	3·409	0·208	0·709
15	0·268	0·0718	0·6462	3·646	0·259	0·944

Complete stability

CROSS CURVES OF STABILITY

So far, only stability at small angles of inclination has been discussed. In practice, it is necessary to have a knowledge of stability at large angles of inclination, particularly in the transverse plane. In the following sections, transverse stability at large angles is considered. In principle, the concepts are equally applicable to longitudinal stability but, in practice, they are not normally required because of the relatively small angles of trim a ship can accept for reasons other than stability.

Referring to Fig. 4.9, let the ship be floating initially at a waterline WL. Now let it be heeled through some angle ϕ to a new waterline $W_1 L_1$ such that the displacement remains constant. The buoyancy force Δ will act through B_1 the new position of the centre of buoyancy, its line of action being perpendicular to $W_1 L_1$. If Z_1 is the foot of the perpendicular dropped from G on to the line of action of the buoyancy force then the righting moment acting on the ship is given by $\Delta \overline{GZ}_1$.

Fig. 4.9 Stability at large angles

This is similar to the concept applied to stability at small angles of heel but, in this case, it is not possible to make use of the concept of a metacentre as the buoyancy force does not intersect the ship's middle line plane in a fixed point.

It should be noted that, in general, a ship when heeled will also trim to maintain its longitudinal equilibrium. This can usually be ignored but where it is significant, the points shown in Fig. 4.9 must be regarded as projections of the true points on to a transverse plane of the ship.

Since the displacement to $W_1 L_1$ is the same as that to WL, it follows that the volumes of the immersed and emerged wedges are equal.

Let

δ = buoyancy force associated with immersed wedge

b_1, b_2 = centroids of volume of the emerged and immersed wedges respectively

h_1, h_2 = feet of perpendiculars from b_1, b_2 on to $W_1 L_1$

R = Foot of the perpendicular from B on to the line of action of the buoyancy force through B_1.

Then

$$\Delta \overline{BR} = \delta \overline{h_1 h_2}$$

and righting moment acting on the ship is given by

$$\Delta \overline{GZ} = \Delta \overline{BR} - \Delta \overline{BG} \sin \phi$$
$$= \Delta \left[\frac{\delta}{\Delta} \overline{h_1 h_2} - \overline{BG} \sin \phi \right]$$

This formula is sometimes known as *Atwood's Formula*, although it was known and used before Atwood's time.

Unfortunately, G depends upon the loading of the ship and is not a fixed position. It is therefore more convenient to think in terms of an arbitrary, but fixed, pole S and its perpendicular distance $\overline{SZ}$ from the line of action of the buoyancy force. $\overline{SZ}$ then depends only on the geometry of the ship and can be calculated for various angles of heel and for various values of displacement without reference to a particular loading condition. Since the position of S is known, when G has been calculated for a particular condition of loading, $\overline{GZ}_1$ can always be calculated from the equation

$$\overline{GZ}_1 = \overline{SZ} + \overline{SG} \sin \phi \quad \text{(S above G)}$$

Where a whole range of ship conditions is required, it is usual to plot values of $\overline{SZ}$ against displacement for each of a number of angles of inclination as shown in Fig. 4.10. These curves are known as *Cross Curves of Stability*.

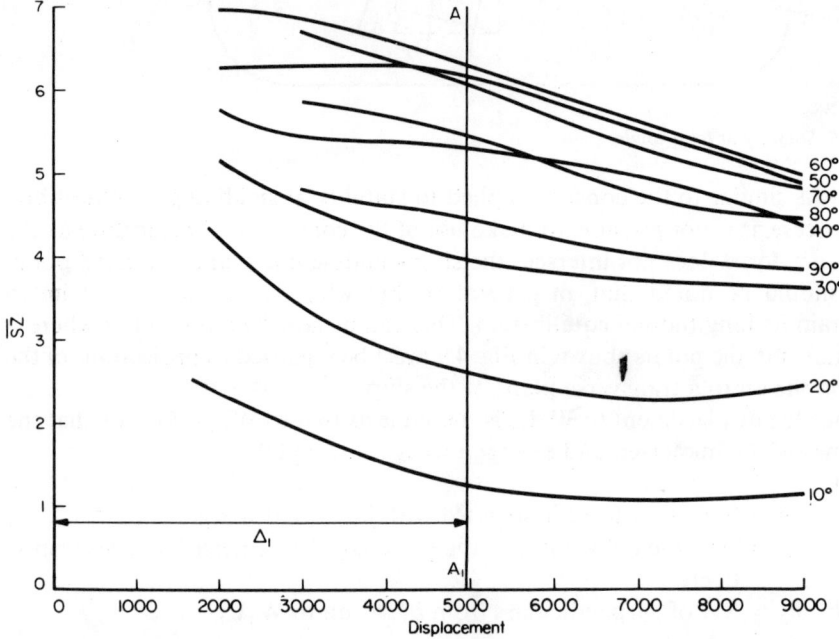

Fig. 4.10 Cross curves of stability

This form of plotting avoids the need to determine inclined waterplanes for precise displacements. It is convenient usually to adopt a set of waterlines which intersect at the same point on the ship's middle line. Then, if a plot of $\overline{SZ}$ against angle of inclination is required at a constant displacement Δ_1, this can be obtained by reading off the $\overline{SZ}$ values along a vertical line AA_1 in Fig. 4.10.

If a whole range of ship conditions is not required, the $\overline{SZ}$ curve for constant displacement can be obtained directly as follows:

Referring to Fig. 4.11, let WL be the upright waterline, W_1L_1 the inclined waterline at the same displacement and W_2L_2 the waterline at the inclination of W_1L_1 passing through the intersection of WL with the centre line of the ship. Let

δ = bouyancy of immersed or emerged wedge between WL and W_1L_1

δ_1 = emerged buoyancy between WL and W_2L_2

δ_2 = immersed buoyancy between WL and W_2L_2

Fig. 4.11 Derivation of $\overline{SZ}$ values for constant displacement

Then, buoyancy of layer between W_1L_1 and W_2L_2 is $\delta_2 - \delta_1$ and let this force act through point F_2 in W_2L_2. If the layer is thin, then F_2 may be regarded as the centroid of the waterplane W_2L_2.

Let

b_1, b_2 be the centroids of the wedges between WL and W_1L_1
b'_1, b'_2 be the centroids of the wedges δ_1 and δ_2
h_1, h_2 projections of b_1, b_2 on to W_2L_2
h'_1, h'_2 projections of b'_1, b'_2 on to W_2L_2

Then

$$\delta \overline{h_1 h_2} = \delta_1 \overline{Oh'_1} + \delta_2 \overline{Oh'_2} - (\delta_2 - \delta_1) \cdot \overline{OF_2}$$

DERIVATION OF CROSS CURVES OF STABILITY

It is now usual to derive data for the plotting of cross curves from a digital computer. If a computer is not available one of the manual methods must be used and since these illustrate more clearly the principles involved they will be described here.

Integrator methods

The integrator was described in Chapter 2. It is essentially a machine which measures the area lying within a closed curve and the first and second moments of that area about a datum line—the axis of the integrator. The integrator can be used in two ways.

The 'all-round' method

A body plan for the ship is prepared to as large a scale as is convenient for the integrator to work with. On this body plan is marked the position of the selected pole S, and radiating from S a series of lines representing the angles of heel for which $\overline{SZ}$ is to be measured. Then, on a separate sheet of tracing paper is marked off a series of parallel lines to represent waterlines, spaced so as to cover adequately the range of displacement over which it is desired to study the ship's stability. A line normal to the waterlines is drawn to represent the centre line of the ship when upright.

For each angle to be studied, the tracing paper is set up over the body plan with the 'centre line' passing through S and the 'waterlines' at the correct angle and covering the required range of draught. The integrator is then set up so that its axis lies along the 'centre line' drawn on the tracing paper—see Fig. 4.12.

Fig. 4.12 *Use of integrator in 'all-round' method*

Then, provided the scaling factors to be applied to the dial readings have been accurately assessed, the integrator can be used to determine the area shown cross-hatched in Fig. 4.12 and the moment of that area about the axis of the integrator. This can be repeated for each section of the ship. If a Simpson body plan is used, the areas and moments must be set out in tabular form, multiplied by the appropriate factor and summated to give the total volume of the ship up to the chosen waterline and the moment about the line through S. Displacement and $\overline{SZ}$ follow and the process can be repeated for each waterline and then for other angles of heel having adjusted the position of the body plan below the tracing paper. All the data required for plotting the cross curves of stability are now available except insofar as it may be necessary to allow for appendages.

If a Tchebycheff body plan is used then, since the multiplying factor is the same for all sections of the ship, it is possible to move the integrator round all sections in turn and note only the difference between the first and final readings on the dials. In the same way, the number of readings involved with a Simpson body plan can be reduced by dealing with all sections having the same multiplier without stopping.

The 'figure of eight' method

This method makes use of the fact that the only differences between the upright and an inclined condition are the immersed and emerged wedges. By passing the integrator point round these two wedges in opposite senses—i.e. in a figure of eight motion as in Fig. 4.13—the moment of transfer of buoyancy and the change in displacement are obtained.

Fig. 4.13 'Figure of eight' method

Barnes's method

This method makes use of the general formula derived above for the transfer of buoyancy, viz.

$$\delta \overline{h_1 h_2} = \delta_1 \overline{Oh'_1} + \delta_2 \overline{Oh'_2} - (\delta_2 - \delta_1)\overline{OF_2}$$

and the various terms are evaluated using radial integration

Fig. 4.14 Radial integration for Barnes's method of deriving statical stability data

By considering the element of angle $\delta\alpha$ in Fig. 4.14 and applying the principles of radial integration

$$\delta_1 \overline{Oh'_1} + \delta_2 \overline{Oh'_2} = \int_0^L \int_0^\phi \left[\tfrac{1}{2} r_1^2 \, d\alpha \frac{2r_1}{3} + \tfrac{1}{2} r_2^2 \, d\alpha \frac{2r_2}{3} \right] \cos(\phi - \alpha) \, dx$$

$$= \int_0^L \int_0^\phi \left(\frac{r_1^3 + r_2^3}{3} \right) \cos(\phi - \alpha) \, dx \, d\alpha$$

This double integral can be evaluated by drawing intermediate radial waterlines at equal increments of heel and measuring the offsets r_ϕ at the appropriate stations. The same process can be followed to evaluate

$$\delta_2 = \int_0^L \int_0^\phi \tfrac{1}{2} r_2^2 \, d\alpha \, dx$$

$$\delta_1 = \int_0^L \int_0^\phi \tfrac{1}{2} r_1^2 \, d\alpha \, dx$$

The area and first moment of area of waterplane W_2L_2 are given by the expressions

$$\text{Area} = \int_0^L r_\phi \, dx$$

First moment of area about fore and aft axis through 0

$$= \int_0^L \frac{r_\phi^2}{2} \, dx$$

By dividing the moment by the area the value of $\overline{OF}_2$ is found.
Substituting in Atwood's formula

$$\overline{SZ} = \left(\frac{\delta_1 \overline{Oh'_1} + \delta_2 \overline{Oh'_2} - (\delta_2 - \delta_1)\overline{OF}_2}{\Delta} \right) - \overline{BS} \sin \phi$$

Evaluating this expression for various values of ϕ gives the values of $\overline{SZ}$ at constant displacement.

An adaptation of Barnes's method, if a whole range of ship displacements are to be covered, would be to find the displacement Δ_ϕ corresponding to waterline W_2L_2 through O and the corresponding $\overline{SZ}$, viz:

$$\Delta_\phi = \Delta + \delta_2 - \delta_1$$

$$\overline{SZ}_\phi = \left(\frac{\delta_1 \overline{Oh'_1} + \delta_2 \overline{Oh'_2}}{\Delta_\phi} \right) - \overline{BS} \sin \phi$$

These values correspond to those obtained by the integrator method.

Reech's method

Fig. 4.15 Reech's method

Let B_α and M_α be the positions of the centre of buoyancy and metacentre corresponding to inclined waterplane $W_\alpha L_\alpha$. From the definition of pro-metacentre (see p. 20), if B_α moves to $B_{\alpha+\delta\alpha}$ for a very small additional inclination $\overline{B_\alpha B_{\alpha+\delta\alpha}} = \overline{B_\alpha M_\alpha}\delta_\alpha$, and $\overline{B_\alpha B_{\alpha+\delta\alpha}}$ is parallel to $W_\alpha L_\alpha$

$$\delta y = \overline{B_\alpha M_\alpha} \cos \alpha \, \delta\alpha$$
$$\delta z = -\overline{B_\alpha M_\alpha} \sin \alpha \, \delta\alpha$$

It follows by radial integration that from waterplane $W_1 L_1$ the position of B_1 relative to B can be expressed as (y, z) where

$$y = \int_0^\phi \overline{B_\alpha M_\alpha} \cos \alpha \, d\alpha$$

$$z = -\int_0^\phi \overline{B_\alpha M_\alpha} \sin \alpha \, d\alpha$$

The negative sign for z signifies only that B_1 is 'higher' than B. Hence

$$\overline{SZ} = y \cos \phi - z \sin \phi - \overline{BS} \sin \phi$$
$$= \cos \phi \int_0^\phi \overline{B_\alpha M_\alpha} \cos \alpha \, d\alpha + \sin \phi \int_0^\phi \overline{B_\alpha M_\alpha} \sin \alpha \, d\alpha - \overline{BS} \sin \phi$$

To evaluate this expression, it is necessary to determine a series of inclined waterlines at constant displacement and for each waterplane obtain the value of $\overline{BM}$ by finding the values of the second moment of area and dividing by the volume of displacement.

Use of model to obtain curve of statical stability

It has been noted that one limitation of the methods described above to determine the statical stability of a ship is the neglect of trim induced by the heeling of the ship. This can be overcome by finding the true equilibrium waterplane at each inclined waterplane, but this leads to considerable complication. One method of automatically allowing for the effects of trim is to use a scale model of the ship, applying to it known heeling moments and noting the resulting angles of heel.

Normally, the expense of making an accurately scaled model is not justified, but the method can be used where a model already exists for other purposes such as the conduct of ship tank tests. The method is particularly useful where there are large changes in waterplane shape for small changes in heel. Such changes can occur with forms which have large rise of floor, very rounded bilges, and/or long well-rounded cut-ups.

Prohaska's method

Reference 3 considers the stability lever $\overline{GZ}$ as composed of two parts, viz:

$$\overline{GZ} = \overline{GM} \sin \phi + \overline{MS}$$

The quantity $\overline{MS}$, which, in a projection on a transverse plane, is the distance from the upright metacentre to the line of action of the buoyancy force, is termed the residuary stability lever (see Fig. 4.16). For convenience in non-dimensional plotting, a coefficient C_{RS} is employed for which

$$C_{RS} = \frac{\overline{MS}}{\overline{BM}_{upright}}$$

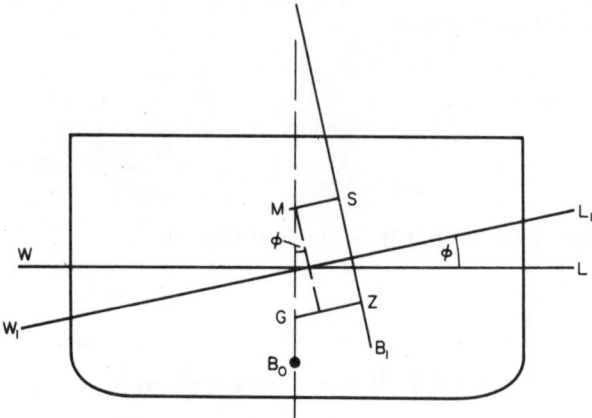

Fig. 4.16

By the use of displacement sheets, the co-ordinates of the centres of buoyancy for 90 and 180 degrees inclination can be calculated relative to those for the upright ship. Also, the metacentric radii for 0, 90 and 180 degrees can be calculated. Using this data and other geometric form data, Prohaska reduces the derivation of the residual stability curve to a calculation in tabular form. The tables used are based on calculations performed on forty-two forms having form characteristics covering the usual merchant ship field, backed up by mathematical treatments assuming that the stability curve can be approximated by a trigonometric series. By its nature the method is approximate, but for general ship forms lying within the range of parameters considered, accuracy comparable with that achieved by the so-called 'exact' methods is obtained.

ACCURACY OF STABILITY CALCULATIONS

Before embarking upon lengthy and tedious calculations, it is as well to decide the standards of accuracy required. Each proposed method of calculation should then ideally be critically examined to ensure that it neither falls short of that standard nor wastes undue effort in striving for greater accuracy.

There are no accepted standards of accuracy and it would be inappropriate to attempt to lay them down rigidly in this present book. However, the following considerations are of significance:

(a) It is not possible to define precisely the conditions the ship will have to survive in service, but it is known that particular ships on certain trade routes have proved successful with certain stability standards. Unfortunately, it is also known that others failed to survive and this is of greater importance. Such failures can usually be traced to either a misjudgement of the stability margins necessary to cope with damage, shifting cargo, etc, or the fact that the ship encountered some freak weather condition which it would have been unreasonable to design against.

(b) Some inaccuracy is bound to arise from the use of scale drawings to define the form of the ship and the use of displacement sections coupled with approximate integration rules. The latter point is discussed in Chapter 2 and the former objection can be checked in due course from the lines on the scrieve board or mould loft floor. There will be certain discrepancies between the form of the ship as built and as drawn.

(c) In the early design stages, it is very difficult to assess closely the displacement or $\overline{KG}$ although both are checked in due course by means of the inclining experiment.

(d) There will be variations in loading, and perhaps of form, during the life of the ship.

It can be argued that (a) and (d) are taken account of in specifying the basic standards of stability aimed at, as discussed later. However, they do serve to emphasize the absurdity of trying to specify a ship's stability curves to a high degree of accuracy.

Item (c) must also be taken into account as a margin applied to the final desired stability to determine the design standard. It is suggested that, unless a closely similar ship is available, it is difficult to assess displacement by calculation to closer than about 3–4 per cent and $\overline{KG}$ within ± 6 in. (0·15 m). Typically, this might represent less than 5 per cent of the actual $\overline{KG}$ value but, proportionately, its effect on stability is much greater. It is suggested that, for most practical purposes, $\overline{GZ}$ values within, say, ± 5 per cent should suffice.

CURVES OF STATICAL STABILITY

It was explained earlier, that it is usually convenient to derive cross curves of stability from purely geometric considerations by making use of an arbitrary pole about which to measure righting moments. It was also seen, that it simplifies the work in deriving stability curves if displacement is allowed to vary as the ship is inclined and if both displacement and righting lever are calculated for each waterline.

For practical applications, however, it is necessary to present stability in the form of righting moments or levers about the centre of gravity, as the ship is heeled at constant displacement. Such a plot will in general appear as in Fig. 4.17 and is known as a *statical stability curve*.

The curve of statical stability, or $\overline{GZ}$ curve as it is commonly called, is derived from the cross curves of stability by setting up a vertical line such as AA_1 for displacement Δ_1 shown on Fig. 4.10. The $\overline{SZ}$ value corresponding to each angle of inclination plotted can be read off and then, using Fig. 4.9 and the $\overline{SG}$ known for the particular loading of the ship,

$$\overline{GZ} = \overline{SZ} - \overline{SG} \sin \phi$$

Fig. 4.17 *Curve of statical stability*

MAIN FEATURES OF THE $\overline{GZ}$ CURVE

Certain features of the $\overline{GZ}$ curve are of particular significance and are useful parameters with which to define the stability possessed by a given design. They include:

(a) **Slope at the origin.** For small angles of heel, the righting lever is proportional to the angle of inclination, the metacentre being effectively a fixed point. It follows, that the tangent to the $\overline{GZ}$ curve at the origin represents the metacentric height.

(b) **Maximum $\overline{GZ}$.** This is proportional to the largest steady heeling moment that the ship can sustain without capsizing, and its value and the angle at which it occurs are both important.

(c) **Range of stability.** At some angle, often greater than 90 degrees, the $\overline{GZ}$ value reduces to zero and becomes negative for larger inclinations. This angle is known as the *angle of vanishing stability* and the range of angle (OC in Fig. 4.17) for which $\overline{GZ}$ is positive is known as the *range of stability*. For angles less than this, a ship will return to the upright state when the heeling moment is removed.

(d) **Angle of deck edge immersion.** For most ship forms, there is a point of inflexion in the curve (shown in Fig. 4.17 as occurring at angle OA) corresponding roughly to the angle at which the deck edge becomes immersed.

Fig. 4.18

In general, of course, the angle at which the deck edge is immersed varies along the length, but is within a fairly narrow band for the larger sections amidships which exert most influence upon the stability. This point is not so much of interest in its own right as in the fact that it provides guidance to the designer upon the possible effect on stability of certain design changes.

(e) Area under the curve. The area under the curve represents the ability of the ship to absorb energy imparted to it by winds, waves or any other external agency. This concept is developed more fully later.

ANGLE OF LOLL

A special case arises when $\overline{GM}$ is negative but $\overline{GZ}$ becomes positive at some reasonable angle of heel. This is illustrated in Fig. 4.19 as ϕ_1. If the ship is

118 Basic ship theory

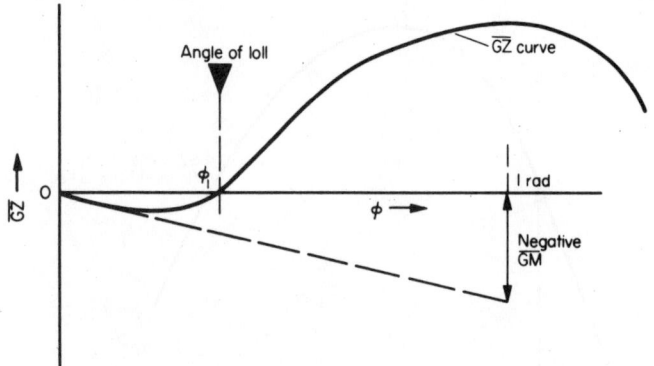

Fig. 4.19 Angle of loll ϕ_1

momentarily at some angle of heel less than ϕ_1, the moment acting due to $\overline{GZ}$ tends to increase the heel. If the angle is greater than ϕ_1, the moment tends to reduce the heel. Thus the angle ϕ_1 is a position of stable equilibrium. Unfortunately, since the $\overline{GZ}$ curve is symmetrical about the origin, as ϕ_1 is decreased, the ship eventually passes through the upright condition and will then suddenly lurch over towards the angle ϕ_1 on the opposite side and overshoot this value before reaching a steady state. This causes an unpleasant rolling motion which is often the only direct indication that the heel to one side is due to a negative $\overline{GM}$ rather than to a positive heeling moment acting on the ship.

As a special case, consider a wall-sided vessel with negative $\overline{GM}$. In this case,

$$\overline{GZ} = \sin\phi(\overline{GM} + \tfrac{1}{2}\overline{BM}\tan^2\phi)$$

$\overline{GZ}$ is zero when $\sin\phi = 0$. This merely demonstrates that the upright condition is one of equilibrium. $\overline{GZ}$ is also zero when $\overline{GM} + \tfrac{1}{2}\overline{BM}\tan^2\phi = 0$. i.e. when

$$\tan\phi = \pm\sqrt{\left(-\frac{2\overline{GM}}{\overline{BM}}\right)}$$

Also, in this case, the slope of the $\overline{GZ}$ curve at ϕ_1 will be given by

$$\frac{d\,\overline{GZ}}{d\phi} = \cos\phi(\overline{GM} + \tfrac{1}{2}\overline{BM}\tan^2\phi) + \sin\phi\,\overline{BM}\tan\phi\sec^2\phi$$

$$= 0 + \overline{BM}\tan^2\phi_1/\cos\phi_1 \quad (\text{putting }\phi = \phi_1)$$

$$= -2\overline{GM}/\cos\phi_1$$

EFFECT OF FREE LIQUID SURFACES ON STABILITY AT LARGE ANGLES OF INCLINATION

It was shown earlier, that the effect of a free liquid surface on initial stability is equivalent to a reduction in the metacentric height of

$$\left(\frac{\rho_\ell}{\rho_s}\right)\frac{I_\ell}{\nabla_s}$$

This was derived by considering the transfer of weight of liquid which occurred in opposition to the righting moment induced by the transfer of buoyancy at the waterplane. The same principle can be applied to any form of tank at any angle of heel.

Fig. 4.20 *Effect on stability of free surface at large angles of heel*

Referring to Fig. 4.20, let a ship initially floating at waterline WL be inclined, at constant displacement, through angle ϕ. Then if wl is the upright free surface of liquid in the tank shown, the surface when inclined becomes $w_1 l_1$ also at angle ϕ to wl.

Knowing the shape of the tank, the transfer of weight can be computed and translated into an effective reduction in the righting moment due to transfer of buoyancy in the wedges between WL and $W_1 L_1$. It follows, by analogy with the upright case, that the reduction in *slope* of the $\overline{GZ}$ curve at angle ϕ will be given by

$$\left(\frac{\rho_\ell}{\rho_s}\right) \frac{(I_\ell)_\phi}{\nabla_s}$$

where $(I_\ell)_\phi$ is the moment of inertia of the liquid surface at angle ϕ.

If the tank is not a simple geometric shape, the transfer of weight can be computed using an integrator or any of the other methods discussed on p. 109 *et seq.* for the derivation of cross curves of stability. Even so, it is fairly tedious to evaluate for sufficient angles of inclination in order to define the effective $\overline{GZ}$ curve precisely, and it is common for some simplifying assumption to be made.

In the Ship Department of the Ministry of Defence, it is the usual practice to compute the metacentric height and the $\overline{GZ}$ value for 45 degrees heel allowing for the free surface. The effective $\overline{GZ}$ curve up to 45 degrees inclination is then constructed by drawing the curve through the 45 degree spot, following the general character of the uncorrected curve and fairing into the modified tangent at the origin. For angles greater than 45 degrees, the reduction of $\overline{GZ}$ at 45 degrees is applied as a constant correction. This method is illustrated in Fig. 4.21.

120 *Basic ship theory*

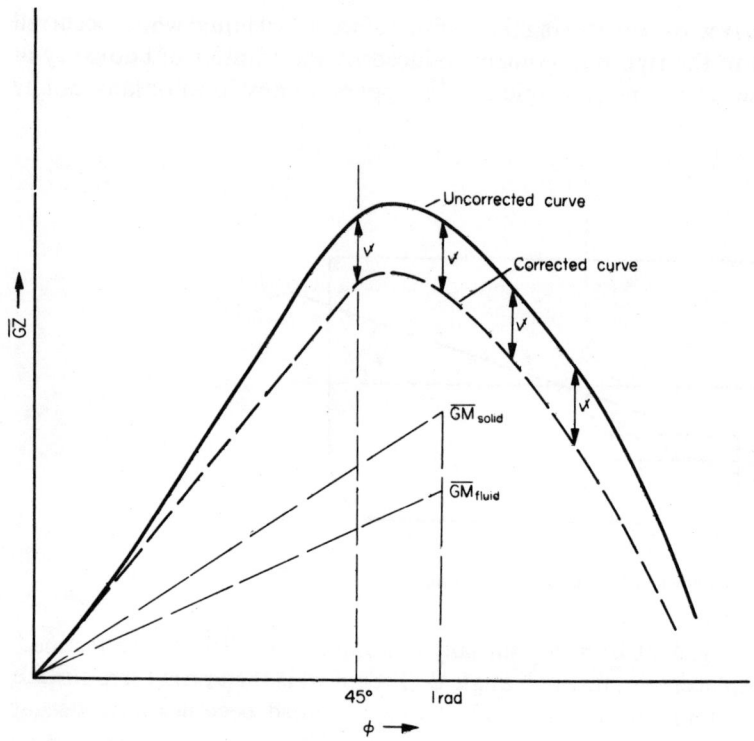

Fig. 4.21 $\overline{GZ}$ *curve corrected for free surface*

SURFACES OF B, M, F AND Z

When a body floats in water, there are unique positions of the centre of buoyancy, metacentre, centre of flotation of the waterplane and Z, the foot of the perpendicular from the c.g. on to the line of the buoyancy force. If the body is rotated at constant displacement, these points will, in general, move to new positions. Considering all possible inclinations B, M, F and Z trace out surfaces which are fixed relative to the body. The simplest case to consider is that of a sphere as in Fig. 4.22.

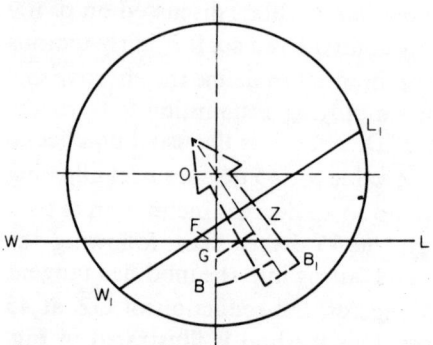

Fig. 4.22 *Sphere floating in fluid at* WL

Let the sphere float at a waterline WL as shown (the argument is unaffected if WL is above the centre of the sphere, O). Then, by arguments of symmetry it follows that for any inclination, OB will be constant, OF will be constant, F being the foot of the perpendicular from O on to WL, and M will always be at O. Thus, in this case, M is a single point and the surfaces traced out by B and F are spheres of radius OB and OF, respectively. As the sphere rotates, the angle OZG is always a right angle. Hence, the locus of Z is a sphere with $\overline{OG}$ as diameter.

Interest, as far as a ship is concerned, is usually centred on transverse stability, i.e. on rotation at constant displacement about a fore and aft axis. In this case, B, M, F and Z trace out lines across the surfaces discussed above. The projections of these traces on to a plane normal to the axis of rotation are termed the *curves of B, M, F and Z* and it is of interest to study certain of their characteristics. For a symmetrical ship form, of course, all curves will be symmetrical about the middle line of the ship.

B *curve or curve of buoyancy*

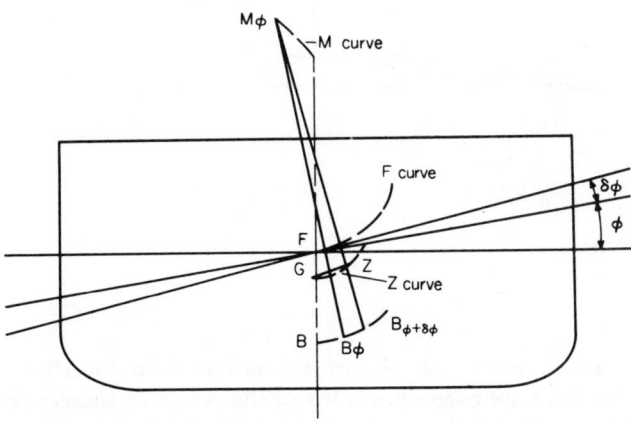

Fig. 4.23 Curves of B, M, F *and* Z

Let B_ϕ and $B_{\phi+\delta\phi}$ be the positions of the centre of buoyancy corresponding to inclinations ϕ and $\phi+\delta\phi$. Then $\overline{B_\phi B_{\phi+\delta\phi}}$ is parallel to the line joining the centroids of volume of the two wedges between the waterplanes at ϕ and $\phi+\delta\phi$. In the limit, $\overline{B_\phi B_{\phi+\delta\phi}}$ becomes the tangent to the curve of buoyancy and this tangent must be parallel to the corresponding waterplane.

The projections of the lines of action of buoyancy through B_ϕ and $B_{\phi+\delta\phi}$ intersect in a point which, in the limit, becomes M_ϕ, called the *prometacentre* and

$$\overline{B_\phi M_\phi} = \frac{I_\phi}{\nabla}$$

The co-ordinates of the point on the curve of buoyancy corresponding to any given inclination ϕ have already been shown to be

$$y = \int_0^\phi \overline{B_\alpha M_\alpha} \cos \alpha \, d\alpha$$

$$z = -\int_0^\phi \overline{B_\alpha M_\alpha} \sin \alpha \, d\alpha$$

The M curve or metacentric curve

The metacentric curve is the projection of the locus of pro-metacentres, for inclinations about a given axis, on to a plane normal to that axis.

Fig. 4.24 *Metacentric curve*

Let $W_1 L_1$ and $W_2 L_2$ be two waterlines at relative inclination of $\delta\phi$ and let B_1 and B_2, M_1 and M_2 be the corresponding positions of the centre of buoyancy and pro-metacentre. Let C_M be the centre of curvature of the metacentric curve at M_1. Then $\overline{C_M M_1}$ is normal to $\overline{B_1 M_1}$ and therefore parallel to $W_1 L_1$.

Referring to Fig. 4.24

$$\overline{M_1 M_2} = \delta(\overline{B_\phi M_\phi}) = \overline{C_M M_1}\, \delta\phi$$

and in the general case

$$\overline{C_M M_\phi} = \frac{d\overline{B_\phi M_\phi}}{d\phi} = \frac{1}{\nabla} \frac{dI_\phi}{d\phi}$$

The F curve or curve of flotation

For very small changes in inclination successive waterplanes intersect in a line through their centres of flotation. In the limit, therefore, the waterplane at any angle is tangential to the curve of flotation at the point corresponding to that inclination.

Fig. 4.25 Curve of flotation

Let W_1L_1 and W_2L_2 be waterplanes at a relative inclination $\delta\phi$ and B_1 and B_2, F_1 and F_2 and M_1 and M_2 their respective centres of buoyancy and flotation and pro-metacentres. Let the lines through F_1 and F_2 normal to W_1L_1 and W_2L_2 intersect in C_F which, in the limit, as $\delta\phi$ diminishes, will become the centre of curvature of the F curve.

Now, consider a small layer added to each waterline, the added volume of buoyancy in each case being δV. Then let B_1B_2 take up new positions $B_1'B_2'$ and so on. Effectively, δV is added at F_1 and F_2 for the two inclinations and B_1, B_1' and F_1 will lie on a straight line as will B_2, B_2' and F_2.

By taking moments

$$\frac{\overline{B_1B_1'}}{\overline{B_1F_1}} = \frac{\delta V}{V + \delta V} = \frac{\overline{B_2B_2'}}{\overline{B_2F_2}}$$

Also $\overline{B_1B_2}$, $\overline{B_1'B_2'}$ and $\overline{F_1F_2}$ are parallel, and

$$\overline{B_1B_2} = \overline{B_1M_1}\,\delta\phi = \frac{I_1}{V}\delta\phi, \text{ if } \delta\phi \text{ is small.}$$

Hence

$$\frac{\overline{B_1F_1}}{\overline{B_1B_1'}} = \frac{\overline{B_1B_2} - \overline{F_1F_2}}{\overline{B_1B_2} - \overline{B_1'B_2'}}$$

By substitution, this becomes

$$\frac{V + \delta V}{\delta V} = \frac{\dfrac{I_1}{V}\delta\phi - \overline{C_FF_1}\,\delta\phi}{\dfrac{I_1}{V}\delta\phi - \dfrac{I_1 + \delta I}{V + \delta V}\delta\phi}$$

From which it follows that, in the limit,

$$C_F F_1 = \frac{dI}{d\nabla}$$

This is known as Leclert's theorem.

The Z curve

Fig. 4.26 *Z curve*

The Z curve is the projection on to a transverse plane of the foot of the perpendicular from G on to successive lines of action of the buoyancy force.

Curves of **B, M, F** *and* **Z** *for a typical ship*

The form of the B, M, F and Z curves is illustrated in Fig. 4.27 for a 20,000 tonf depot ship. The principal features of this design are:

	20,000 tonf depot ship	
Deep displacement, tonf (MN)	19,300	(192)
L.B.P., ft (m)	675	(206)
Beam, ft (m)	75·8	(23·1)
Mean draught, ft (m)	22·2	(6·8)
Block coefficient	0·595	
Prismatic coefficient	0·617	
Waterplane coefficient	0·755	

INFLUENCE OF SHIP FORM ON STABILITY

It has been shown how a designer, faced with a given form and loading condition, can assess the stability characteristics of his ship. It is unlikely that his first choice of form will satisfy his requirements completely. Initial stability, maximum $\overline{GZ}$ and range may all be too great or too small. Perhaps one feature alone may need modification. How then is the designer to modify his form to produce the required result? The effect of small changes in principal dimensions

Fig. 4.27

on initial stability has already been discussed, and if only such a change is required this method might be adopted provided that the consequential changes in stability at large angles are acceptable.

In general, however, there must be a certain amount of 'trial and error' in the process. That is to say, the designer must make certain changes, recalculate the stability and assess what additional changes may be necessary. The electronic computer is a great help in this type of investigation as, by its use, extensive stability data can be obtained in a very short time. Indeed, if the range of forms the designer has to deal with is limited, the computer can produce a 'methodical series' of forms from which the designer can select a suitable design.

Although the designer cannot predict precisely the steps necessary to effect a desired change in stability characteristics, it is essential that he know the general effect of changing the ship form in a specified manner. The following comments are intended as a general qualitative guide to the changes that can be expected. It will be appreciated that, in general, it is impossible to vary one parameter alone without some consequential change being required in some other factor.

Length

If length is increased in proportion to displacement, keeping beam and draught constant, the transverse $\overline{KB}$ and $\overline{BM}$ are unchanged. In general, increasing length increases $\overline{KG}$ so reducing initial stability although this will not be the case for a truly geometrically similar ship.

If length is increased at the expense of beam, there will be a reduction in stability over the full range. If length is increased at the expense of draught, there will, in general, be an increase in initial stability but a reduction at larger angles.

Beam

Of the form parameters which can be varied by the designer, the beam has the greatest influence on transverse stability. It has been shown that

$$\overline{BM} \propto \frac{B^2}{T}$$

Thus $\overline{BM}$ will increase most rapidly if beam is increased at the expense of the draught. If freeboard remains constant, the angle of deck edge immersion will decrease and stability at larger angles will be reduced. If the total depth of ship remains constant, then stability will be reduced by the increase in $\overline{BG}$ and, although this is offset by the increased beam at small angles, the stability at larger angles will suffer.

Draught

Reduction in draught in proportion to a reduction in displacement increases initial stability, leads to greater angle of deck immersion but reduces stability at large angles.

Displacement

Changes in length, beam and draught associated with displacement are discussed above. If these parameters are kept constant then displacement increases lead to a fatter ship. In general, it can be expected that the consequential filling out of the waterline will more than compensate for the increased volume of displacement and $\overline{BM}$ will increase. Fattening of the ship in this way is also likely to lead to a fall in G. These changes will also, in general, enhance stability at all angles.

Centre of gravity

The best way, but often the most difficult, of achieving improved stability at all angles is to reduce the height of the centre of gravity above the keel. This is clear from a consideration of the formulae used to derive $\overline{GZ}$ in earlier sections of this chapter. What is perhaps not so immediately obvious, but which cannot be too highly emphasized, is that too high a value of $\overline{KG}$ results in poor stability at larger angles no matter what practical form changes are made.

The effect of change in $\overline{KG}$, if not associated with any change of form, is given directly by the relationship

$$\overline{GZ} = \overline{SZ} - \overline{SG} \sin \phi$$

For a more thorough review of the influence of form changes, the student is advised to consult papers published in the various transactions of learned bodies such as Refs. 3 and 4. The broad conclusion from Prohaska's work, is that the ratios of beam to draught and depth of ship have a comparatively greater influence on stability than that caused by the variation of the fullness parameters of the forms.

STABILITY OF A COMPLETELY SUBMERGED BODY

Fig. 4.28 Stability of completely submerged body

As in the case of surface ships there will be a position of rotational equilibrium when B and G are in the same vertical line. Let us determine the condition for stable equilibrium for rotation about a horizontal axis.

Since the body is completely submerged, the buoyancy force always acts through B. Viewing this another way, in the absence of any waterplane $\overline{BM}$ must be zero so that B and M become coincident. If the body is inclined through an angle ϕ, the moment acting on it is given by

$$\Delta \overline{BG} \sin \phi$$

It is clear from Fig. 4.28, that this will tend to bring the body upright if B lies above G. This then is the condition for stable equilibrium. If B and G coincide, the body has neutral stability and if B lies below G it is unstable.

Both the transverse and longitudinal stability of a submerged body are the same and the $\overline{GZ}$ curve becomes a sine curve as in Fig. 4.29. A submarine is typical although the relative positions of B and G, and therefore the stability in the two directions, may be changed by flooding or emptying tanks.

128 Basic ship theory

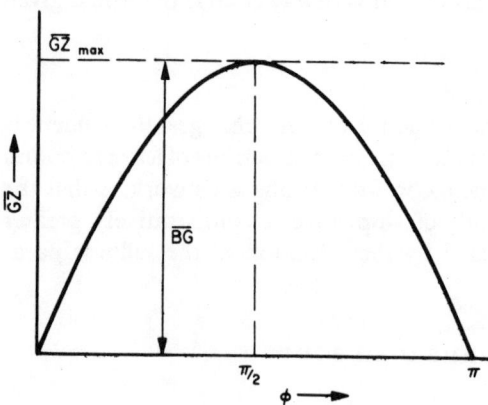

Fig. 4.29 *Statical stability curve for submarine*

Another mode of stability of a completely submerged body which is of interest is that associated with depth of submersion. If the body in Fig. 4.28 is initially in equilibrium, and is disturbed so as to increase its depth of submersion it is subject to greater hydrostatic pressure. This causes certain compression of the body which, if the body is more readily compressed than water, leads to a reduction in the buoyancy force. The weight of the body remains constant so a resultant downward force is created. This will tend to increase the depth of submersion still further. In these circumstances—applicable to a submarine—the body is unstable in depth maintenance.

Generally, in the case of a submarine the degree of instability is no great embarrassment and, in practice, the effect is usually masked by changes in water density associated with temperature or salinity as depth changes. It becomes important, however, with deep submergence research vehicles.

Dynamical stability

The *dynamical stability* of a ship at a given angle of heel is defined as the work done in heeling the ship to that angle very slowly and at constant displacement, i.e., ignoring any work done against air or water resistance.

Consider a ship with a righting moment curve as shown in Fig. 4.30.

Let the righting moment at an angle of heel ϕ be M_ϕ. Then, the work done in heeling the ship through an additional small angle $\delta\phi$ is given approximately by

$$M_\phi \, \delta\phi$$

Hence, the total work in heeling to an angle Φ is

$$\int_0^\Phi M_\phi \, d\phi$$

$$= \int_0^\Phi \Delta \overline{GZ}_\phi \, d\phi$$

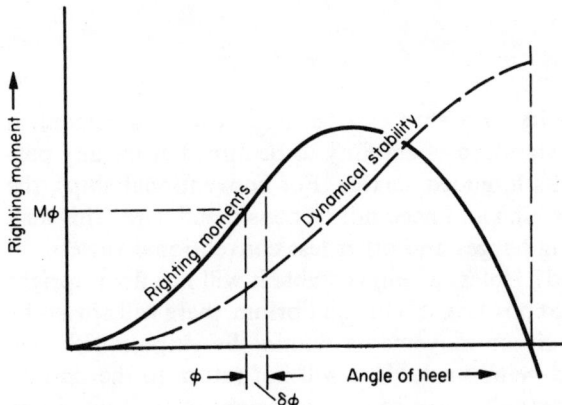

Fig. 4.30

The dynamical stability at any angle, therefore, is proportional to the area under the statical stability curve up to that angle.

There is an alternative way of determining the work done in heeling a ship. Weight and displacement forces remain constant during the process but they are separated vertically, thereby raising the potential energy of the ship.

Referring to Fig. 4.9, let B move to B_1 when ship is heeled from waterline WL to waterline W_1L_1. Increased vertical separation $= \overline{B_1Z_1} - \overline{BG}$. Hence, dynamical stability at angle ϕ is given by

$$\Delta(\overline{B_1Z_1} - \overline{BG})$$

Let v be the volume of the immersed or emerged wedge, let their centroids of volume be at b_1 and b_2 and let h_1 and h_2 be the feet of perpendiculars dropped from b_1 and b_2 on to W_1L_1.
Then

$$\overline{B_1R} = \frac{v(b_1h_1 + b_2h_2)}{\nabla}$$

Now

$$\overline{B_1Z_1} = \overline{B_1R} + \overline{BG}\cos\Phi$$

Therefore

$$\overline{B_1Z_1} = \frac{v(b_1h_1 + b_2h_2)}{\nabla} + \overline{BG}\cos\Phi$$

and the dynamical stability is given by

$$\Delta\left[\frac{v(b_1h_1 + b_2h_2)}{\nabla} - \overline{BG}(1 - \cos\Phi)\right]$$

This formula is known as *Moseley's Formula*. Although this expression can be evaluated for a series of angles of heel, and the curve of dynamical stability drawn, its application is laborious and not often used.

Stability assessment

STABILITY STANDARDS

Having shown how the stability of a ship can be defined and calculated, it remains to discuss the actual standard of stability to be aimed at for any particular ship bearing in mind its intended service. For conventional ships, the longitudinal stability is always high and need not be considered here. This may not be true for offshore drilling barges and other less conventional vessels.

Why then is stability needed? Unless a ship is stable it will not float upright because, although in the upright position it is in equilibrium, there will always be disturbances—from the sea, air or movements within the ship—which will force it out of the upright and being unstable it will not return to the upright position. Even if it does not actually capsize, i.e. turn right over, it would be unpleasant to be in a ship which lolled to one side or the other of the upright. Thus one need for stability arises from the desire to have the ship float upright. Although, in theory, a very small metacentric height would be sufficient for this purpose, it must be adequate to cover all conditions of loading of the ship and growth in the ship during its life. If the ship is to operate in very cold climates, allowance will have to be made for the topweight due to ice forming on the hull and superstructure.

Next, it is necessary to consider circumstances during the life of the ship which will cause it to heel over. These include

(a) The action of the wind which will be most pronounced in ships with high freeboard or large superstructure;
(b) the action of waves in rolling the ship. This will be most important for those ships which have to operate in large ocean areas, particularly the North Atlantic;
(c) the action of the rudder and hull forces when the ship is manoeuvring;
(d) loading and unloading cargoes.

The ship may be subject to several of the above at the same time. In addition, the ship may, on occasion, suffer damage leading to flooding or she may suffer from shifting cargo in very rough weather. These aspects of the design are dealt with in more detail in the next chapter.

The standards of stability aimed at by various navies are not generally available but Ref. 5 discusses the standards specified for US naval surface ships. The authors point out that if a ship experiences a heeling moment in perfectly calm water it would be sufficient if the curve of statical stability had a lever in excess of that represented by the heeling moment. In practice, it is also necessary to allow a certain reserve of dynamical stability to enable the ship to absorb the energy imparted to it by waves or by a gusting wind.

Certain relaxations are made for ships operating in coastal waters and for ships in service, but for new design intact ships to operate in ocean areas the following criteria are specified.

(a) *Beam winds and rolling*

A wind heeling arm curve is calculated and is superimposed on the statical stability curve for the intact ship as in Fig. 4.31. A simple formula for calculating the heeling arm due to wind is

$$\text{Heeling arm} = \frac{0.0035 V^2 A l \cos^2 \phi}{2240 \Delta} \text{ ft}$$

Fig. 4.31 Stability criteria for beam wind and rolling

where V = nominal wind velocity, knots (taken as 100 knots). A = projected area (ft^2) of ship above waterline and l = lever arm from half draught to the centroid of the projected area. Δ = displacement in tonf.

More accurately, the formula

$$\text{Heeling arm} = \frac{0.004 V^2 A l \cos^2 \phi}{2240 \Delta} \text{ ft}$$

can be used when the wind speed V at each height above the sea surface is taken from Fig. 9.22 for a nominal wind velocity of 100 knots. In this case, it is necessary to divide A into a number of convenient horizontal strips and carry out a vertical integration.

If A and l are measured in metres and Δ in MN, the two equations become

$$\text{Heeling arm} = 0.17 \times 10^{-6} \frac{AV^2 l}{\Delta} \cos^2 \phi \text{ m}$$

$$\text{Heeling arm} = 0.19 \times 10^{-6} \frac{AV^2 l}{\Delta} \cos^2 \phi \text{ m}$$

The angle ϕ_s at which the two curves cross, is the steady heel angle the ship would take up if the wind were perfectly steady and there were no waves and the corresponding righting arm is $\overline{GZ}_s$. To allow for the rolling of the ship the curves are extended back to a point 25 degrees to windward of ϕ_s and the areas

132 Basic ship theory

A_1 and A_2 shown shaded in Fig. 4.31 are computed. For stability to be regarded as adequate the following conditions must be met by USN ships:

$\overline{GZ}_s$ not more than $0.6 \times \overline{GZ}_{max}$
Area A_1 not less than $1.4 \times$ Area A_2.

(b) *Lifting of heavy weights over the side*

Fig. 4.32

Again, the heeling arm curve is superimposed on the statical stability curve (Fig. 4.32) the heeling arm being taken as

$$\frac{Wa}{\Delta} \cos \phi$$

where W = weight of lift, a = transverse distance from centre line to end of boom and Δ = displacement, including weight of lift.

The stability criteria applied by the USN are

$\overline{GZ}_s$ not more than $0.6 \times \overline{GZ}_{max}$
ϕ_s not greater than 15 degrees

Shaded area not less than 40 per cent of the total area under the statical stability curve.

(c) *Crowding of passengers to one side*

The same formula and criteria are used as for case (b), except that, in this case,

W = weight of passengers
a = distance from centre line of ship to c.g. of passengers.

(d) *Heeling during a high speed turn*

When a ship is turning steadily, it must be acted upon by a force directed towards the centre of the circle and of value

$$\frac{\Delta \text{(steady speed)}^2}{g \text{(radius of turn)}} = \frac{\Delta V^2}{gR}$$

Stability

This problem is discussed in more detail in Chapter 13, but, approximately, the heeling moment acting on the ship is given by

$$\frac{\Delta V^2}{gR}\left(\overline{KG} - \frac{T}{2}\right)\cos\phi$$

The heeling arm curve is then

$$\frac{V^2}{gR}\left(\overline{KG} - \frac{T}{2}\right)\cos\phi$$

and can be plotted as in Fig. 4.32. The stability criteria adopted are as for case (b) above.

In Ref. 6, the standards of stability adopted by Japan are presented and discussed. As with the USN standards, they are essentially standards for metacentric height, maximum $\overline{GZ}$ and dynamical stability.

So far, only minimum standards have been mentioned. Why not then make sure and design the ship to have a very large metacentric height? In general, this could only be achieved by considerably increasing the beam partially at the expense of draught. This will increase the resistance of the ship at a given speed, and may have adverse effects on stability at large angles of heel and following damage. It will also lead to more violent motion in a seaway which may be unpleasant to passengers and indeed dangerous to all personnel. In addition, the larger beam may make it impossible to negotiate certain canals or dock entrances. Hence the designer is faced with providing adequate but not excessive stability.

THE INCLINING EXPERIMENT

It has been shown that, although much of the data used in stability calculations depends only on the geometry of the ship, the position of the centre of gravity must be known before the stability can be assessed finally for a given ship condition. Since $\overline{KG}$ may be perhaps ten times as great as the metacentric height, it must be known very accurately if the metacentric height is to be assessed with reasonable accuracy.

$\overline{KG}$ can be calculated for a variety of conditions provided it is accurately known for one precisely specified ship condition. It is to provide this basic knowledge that the *inclining experiment* is carried out. The term 'experiment' is a misnomer in the scientific sense but it is universally used. It would be better called a stability survey. The purposes of the inclining experiment are to determine the displacement and the position of the centre of gravity of the ship in an accurately known condition. It is usually carried out when the ship is as nearly complete as possible during initial building and, in the case of warships, may be repeated at intervals during her life as a check upon the changing armaments, etc. For instance, an additional inclining may be carried out following an extensive modernization or major refit.

The experiment is usually carried out by moving weights across the deck under controlled conditions and noting the resulting angle of heel. The angles are normally kept small so that they are proportional to the heeling moment, and the proportionality factor provides a measure of the metacentric height. The angle of heel is usually recorded using long pendulums rigged one forward and one aft in the ship, perhaps through a line of hatches. The pendulum bobs may be immersed in water or oil to damp their motion.

Conduct of an inclining experiment

Fig. 4.33 *Movement of weights during an inclining experiment*

The principal steps in the carrying out of an inclining experiment are:

(a) The ship is surveyed to determine weights to be removed, to come on board or be moved for final completion.
(b) The state of all tanks is noted accurately.
(c) The draughts are accurately read at each set of draught marks, including amidships, on both sides of the ship.
(d) The density of the water in which the vessel is floating is measured at a number of positions and depths around the ship.
(e) Weights, arranged on the deck in four groups, shown in Fig. 4.33, are moved in the following sequence:
weights A to a position in line with weights C
weights B to a position in line with weights D
weights A and B returned to original positions
weights C to a position in line with weights A
weights D to a position in line with weights B
weights C and D returned to original positions
The weight groups are often made equal.
(f) The angle of heel is recorded by noting the pendulum positions before the first movement of weight and after each step given above.

Analysis of results

Due to the shift of a weight w through a distance d, G will move parallel to the movement of the weight to G′ where

$$\overline{GG'} = \frac{wd}{\Delta}$$

Fig. 4.34 Analysis of results

Since $\overline{GG'}$ is normal to the centre-line plane of the ship

$$\overline{GM} = \overline{GG'}/\tan \phi$$

$$= \frac{wd}{\Delta \tan \phi}$$

If the movement of each pendulum, length l, is measured as y on a horizontal batten

$$\tan \phi = \frac{y}{l}$$

The displacement can be determined from the measurements of draught and water density. The latter are averaged and the former are used to determine the trim of the vessel. The amount of hog or sag present can be determined if the ship is provided with amidship draught marks. When hog or sag is detected it is usual to assume, in calculating the displacement, that the ship takes up a parabolic curve. The mean draught is calculated from the draughts at the ends of the ship and is increased or reduced by 70 per cent of the sag or hog respectively. Similarly, it may be possible to find the extent of any stern drop.

Hence, $\overline{GM}$ can be calculated for each transfer of weight provided the metacentre remains fixed up to the maximum angle of heel used. Typically, this should be of the order of 3 or 4 degrees and presents no problem for most ships. If equal weight transfers are made, this is readily confirmed if the angle changes are equal. If unequal weight transfers are used, an approximate check can be made by dividing the angles by the respective weights and comparing the results. If it is suspected that the relationship between angle and heeling moment is not linear, the results obtained must be plotted as a statical stability curve and the tangent at the origin determined.

The data can be analysed in various ways. One possible method is to produce a table of the asymmetric moment applied at each stage (m_1, m_2, etc.) and the corresponding pendulum deflections (d_1, d_2, etc.). The moment values are squared and the moments and deflections multiplied together as illustrated below:

136 Basic ship theory

Weight movement (Fig. 4.33)	Applied moment m	m^2	Measured deflection d	$m \times d$
A to C	m_1	m_1^2	d_1	$m_1 d_1$
B to D	m_2	m_2^2	d_2	$m_2 d_2$
A and B returned	0	0	d_3	0
C to A	$-m_4$	m_4^2	d_4	$-m_4 d_4$
D to B	$-m_5$	m_5^2	d_5	$-m_5 d_5$
C and D returned	0	0	d_6	0
		$\sum m^2$		$\sum md$

The average deflection per unit applied moment is given by $\sum md / \sum m^2$.

It will be noted that, in this method of analysis, the deflections measured when all weights are returned to their original positions play no part in the analysis. They are used at the time of the experiment to indicate whether any loose weights, or liquids in tanks have moved from one side to another.

The datum readings are used in a second method of analysis in which the deflection of the pendulum per unit applied moment is calculated for each shift of weights. This is illustrated below:

Weight moment (Fig. 4.33)	Applied moment, m	Measured deflection, d	Change in deflection per unit change of moment
A to C	m_1	d_1	d_1/m_1
B to D	m_2	d_2	$(d_2-d_1)/(m_2-m_1)$
A and B returned	0	d_3	$(d_3-d_2)/(0-m_2)$
C to A	$-m_4$	d_4	$(d_4-d_3)/(-m_4)$
D to B	$-m_5$	d_5	$(d_5-d_4)/(-m_5+m_4)$
C and D returned	0	d_6	$(d_6-d_5)/m_5$

The average deflection per unit change of moment is taken as the mean of the figures in the last column.

EXAMPLE 4. A ship of 6000 tonnef displacement is inclined. The ballast weights are arranged in four equal units of 10 tonnef and each is moved transversely through a distance of 10 m. The pendulum deflections recorded are 31, 63, 1, −30, −62 and 0 cm with a pendulum length of 7 m. Calculate the metacentric height at the time of the experiment.

Solution: Since the moment is applied in equal increments of 100 tonnef m, each such increment can be represented by unity in the table as below, using the first method of analysis:

Applied moment Units of 100 tonnef m m	m^2	Deflection d cm	$m \times d$
1	1	31	31
2	4	63	126
0	0	1	0
−1	1	−30	30
−2	4	−62	124
0	0	0	0
	$\sum m^2 = 10$		$\sum md = 311$

∴ Mean deflection per unit moment = 31·1 cm, i.e. the pendulum is deflected through 31·1 cm for each 100 tonnef m of applied moment

$$\text{Angle of heel} = \frac{\text{Pendulum deflection}}{\text{Pendulum length}}$$

$$= \frac{31 \cdot 1}{700} = 0 \cdot 0444 \text{ radians.}$$

For small angles

Applied moment = $\Delta \overline{\text{GM}} \phi$

∴ 100 = 6000 $\overline{\text{GM}}$ 0·0444

∴ $\overline{\text{GM}}$ = 0·375 m

Applying the second method of analysis would have given:

Change of moment Units of 100 tonnef m	Change in pendulum deflection (cm)	Pendulum deflection per unit change of moment
1	31	31
1	32	32
−2	−62	31
−1	−31	31
−1	−32	32
2	62	31

Hence mean pendulum deflection = $\dfrac{188}{6}$

= 31·3 cm

This represents less than one per cent difference compared with the answer obtained by the first analysis. This is within the general limits of accuracy of the experiment.

Precautions to be taken

The importance of obtaining an accurate result has already been emphasized and certain precautions must be taken to ensure that accuracy is obtained.

These are really a matter of common sense and include

(a) The ship must be floating upright and freely without restraint from ropes.
(b) There should be no wind on the beam.
(c) All loose weights should be secured.
(d) All cross-connections between tanks should be closed.
(e) Tanks should be empty or pressed full. If neither of these conditions is possible, the level of liquid in the tank should be such that the free surface effect is readily calculable and will remain sensibly constant throughout the experiment.
(f) The number of men on board should be kept to a minimum and they should go to specified positions for each reading of the pendulums.
(g) Any mobile equipment used to move the weights across the deck must return to a known position for each set of readings.

It should be noted that (c), (d), (f) and (g) will, to some extent, be checked by the accuracy with which the pendulums return to their zero readings following the return of weights to their original positions half way through the experiment and again at the end. If the pendulum reading fails to take up a steady value but slowly increases or diminishes, it is likely that liquid is passing between tanks through an open cross-connection.

Heeling trials

These trials are mentioned only because they are commonly confused with the inclining experiment. In fact, the two are quite unrelated. Heeling trials are carried out to prove that the ship, and the equipment within her, continue to function when the vessel is held at a steady angle of heel. For instance, pumps may fail to maintain suction, bearings of electric motors may become overloaded, boats may not be able to be lowered by the davits clear of the ship, etc.

For warships, the trials are usually carried out for angles of heel of 5, 10 and 15 degrees although not all equipment is required to operate up to the 15 degree angle.

Tilt test

This is another test carried out in warships which is quite unrelated to the inclining experiment but is sometimes confused with it. The tilt test is carried out to check the alignment of items of armament—gun turrets, missile launchers, directors—with respect to each other and to a reference datum in the ship.

Problems

1. A small weight is added to a wall-sided ship on the centre line and at such a position as to leave trim unchanged. Show that the metacentric height is reduced if the weight is added at a height above keel greater than $T - \overline{\text{GM}}$, where T is the draught.

Stability 139

2. Prove that for a wall-sided ship, the vertical separation of B and G at angle of heel ϕ is given by

$$\cos\phi[\overline{BG}+\tfrac{1}{2}\overline{BM}\tan^2\phi]$$

where $\overline{BG}$ and $\overline{BM}$ relate to the upright condition. Show that when the ship has a free surface in a wall-sided tank the corresponding expression is

$$\overline{BG}_V = \cos\phi[\overline{BG}_S+\tfrac{1}{2}(\overline{BM}-\overline{G_S G_F})\tan^2\phi]$$

where subscripts S and F relate to the solid and fluid centres of gravity.

3. Show that the dynamical stability of a wall-sided vessel up to angle ϕ is given by the expression

$$\Delta[\overline{BG}(\cos\phi-1)+\tfrac{1}{2}\overline{BM}\tan\phi\sin\phi]$$

4. Prove the wall-sided formula.

A rectangular homogeneous block 30 m long × 7 m wide × 3 m deep is half as dense as the water in which it is floating. Calculate the metacentric height and the $\overline{GZ}$ at 15 degrees and 30 degrees of heel.

5. The statical stability curve for a cargo ship of 10,000 tonnef displacement is defined by

ϕ (degrees)	0	15	30	45	60	75	90
$\overline{GZ}$ (m)	0	0·275	0·515	0·495	0·330	0·120	−0·100

Determine the ordinate of the dynamical stability curve at 60 degrees and the change in this figure and loss in range of stability if the c.g. of the ship is raised by 0·25 m.

6. A hollow triangular prism whose ratio of base to height is 1:2 floats vertex downwards. Mercury of density 13·6 is poured in to a depth of 1 m and water is then poured on top till the draught of the prism is 4 m. Calculate $\overline{GM}$ solid and fluid assuming the prism weightless.

7. A ship has the following principal dimensions: length 120 m, beam 14 m, draught 4 m, displacement 30 MN. The centres of buoyancy and gravity are 2·5 m and 6 m above keel and the metacentre is 7 m above keel.

Calculate the new metacentric height and beam if draught is reduced to 3·6 m, keeping length, displacement, $\overline{KG}$ and coefficients of fineness unaltered.

8. The model of a ship, 5 ft long, is found to be unstable. Its waterplane has an area of 550 in^2 and a transverse MI of 5500 in^4. The draught is 4·6 in. and the volume of displacement is 2200 in^3 in fresh water.

If G is originally 6 in. above the keel, how far above the keel must a weight of 20 lb be put to just restore stability? $\overline{KB} = 2\cdot5$ in.   (RNATE)

9. A hollow prism has a cross section in the form of an isosceles triangle. It floats apex down in fresh water with mercury, of specific gravity 13·5, dropped into it to make it float upright.

If the prism may be assumed weightless by comparison and has an included angle of 90 degrees, express the fluid metacentric height in terms of the draught T.

140 Basic ship theory

10. A ship is floating in fresh water at a draught of 14 ft when a weight of 420 tonf is placed 42 ft above the keel and 14 ft to port. Estimate the angle of heel.

In sea water, the hydrostatic curves show that at a draught of 14 ft, TPI = 72; displacement = 36,000 tonf; $\overline{KM}$ = 26 ft; $\overline{KB}$ = 8 ft. Before the weight is added $\overline{KG}$ = 19 ft. (RNATE)

11. The raft shown has to support a weight which would produce a combined height of the centre of gravity above the keel of 3·5 m. The draught is then uniformly 1 m.

What is the minimum value of d—the distance apart of the centre lines of the baulks—if the $\overline{GM}$ must not be less than 2 m?

Fig. 4.35

12. A homogeneous solid is formed of a right circular cylinder and a right circular cone of the same altitude h on opposite sides of a circular base radius r. It floats with the axis vertical, the whole of the cone and half of the cylinder being immersed. Prove that the metacentric height is $3r^2/10h - 21h/80$, so that for equilibrium r must be greater than $0·935h$. (AP & S)

13. A ship of 50 MN (5100 tonnef) displacement has a metacentric height of 1 m. Suppose 1·0 MN of fuel to be shifted so that its centre of gravity moves 6 m transversely and 2 m vertically up, what would be the angle of heel of the vessel, if it were upright before the movement? No free surface effects are produced.

14. A prismatic log of wood, of specific gravity 0·75, whose uniform transverse section is that of an isosceles triangle, floats in fresh water with the base of the section horizontal and vertex upwards. Find the least vertical angle of the section for these conditions to hold. (AP & S)

15. A pontoon raft 10 m long is formed by two cylindrical pontoons 0·75 m diameter spaced 2 m apart between centres and is planked over with wood forming a platform 10 m × 3 m.

When laden, the raft floats with the cylindrical pontoons half immersed in river water and its centre of gravity when laden is 1 m above the water-line. Calculate the transverse and longitudinal metacentric heights.

16. Describe the procedure required to carry out an inclining experiment. The displacement of a vessel as inclined in sea water is 75 MN, 0·3 MN of ballast with a spread of 15 m causes a deviation of 0·2 m on a 4 m pendulum. The net weight to go on includes 7 MN of fuel (s.g. = 0·85) with a KG of 6 m. The transverse M.I. of the fuel surface is 1000 m⁴ units. If the value of $\overline{KM}$ is 9 m and is kept at this value for the increased draught, find the final $\overline{GM}$.

17. Determine the transverse metacentric height from the following data obtained from an inclining experiment:

Length of pendulum = 20 ft
Mean deflection = 8·25 in.
Shift of weight = 20 tonf through 56 ft
Draughts at perpendiculars fwd. = 17 ft 9½ in.
                          aft. = 19 ft 1¼ in.
Density of water = 35·2 ft³/tonf
Length BP = 565 ft

The hydrostatic particulars for normal trim of 2 ft by the stern and water 35·0 ft³/tonf are:

Draught (mean BP) (ft)	Displacement (tonf)	TPI	CF. aft of ⌽ (ft)
18·0	10,524	49·8	30·0
18·5	10,823	50·0	31·1

(AP & S)

18. During an inclining experiment on a 60 MN guided missile destroyer weights in units of 0·05 MN are moved 10 m transversely. Deflections at the bottom of a pendulum 4 m long are defined by the following table:

Weight movement	Pendulum reading (m)
0	0
(a) 0·05 MN to port	0·023
(b) 0·05 MN to port	0·049
(a) & (b) returned	0·003
(c) 0·05 MN to starboard	−0·021
(d) 0·05 MN to starboard	−0·045
(c) & (d) returned	−0·001

Calculate the metacentric height as inclined.

19. A crane in a cargo liner, of 50 MN displacement and $\overline{GM}$ 1 m, lifts a weight of 0·2 MN from a cargo hold through a vertical height of 10 m. If the height of the crane's jib is 20 m above the hold and the radius of the jib is 10 m, calculate the reduction in $\overline{GM}$ caused by lifting the weight.

What is the approximate angle of heel caused by turning the crane through 30 degrees assuming it is initially aligned fore and aft?

20. A fire in the hangar of an aircraft carrier, floating in water of 35 ft³/tonf, is fought by dockside fire tenders using fresh water. When the fire is under control the hangar, which is 360 ft long and 80 ft broad, is found to be flooded to a depth of 3 ft. If the hangar deck is 23 ft above the original c.g. of the ship, what is the resultant $\overline{GM}$? The following particulars apply to the ship before the fire:

Displacement = 43,000 tonf $\overline{KB}$ = 19 ft
Mean draught = 39 ft 2 in. $\overline{BM}$ = 23 ft
TPI = 120 $\overline{GM}$ = 11·5 ft

21. The following particulars apply to a new cruiser design:

Deep displacement	12,500 tonnef
Length on WL	200 m
$\overline{KG}$	8 m
$\overline{GM}_T$	1·5 m
Area of waterplane	3000 m²
Draught	6 m
Depth of hull amidships	14 m
Beam	21 m

A proposal is made to increase the armament by the addition of a weight of 200 tonnef, the c.g. 2 m above the upper deck. Find the amount by which the beam must be increased to avoid loss of transverse stability assuming other dimensions unchanged. Assume water of 0·975 m³/tonne.

22. A pontoon has a constant cross-section in the form of a trapezium, width 6 m at the keel, 10 m at the deck and depth 5 m. At what draught will the centre of curvature of the curve of flotation be at the deck level?

23. Show that a wall-sided vessel with negative $\overline{GM}$ lolls to an angle given by

$$\tan \phi = \pm \left(\frac{2\overline{GM}}{\overline{BM}}\right)^{\frac{1}{2}}$$

A body of square cross-section of side 6 m has a metacentric height of -0.5 m when floating at a uniform draught of 3 m. Calculate the angle of loll.

24. Derive an expression for the radius of curvature of the metacentric locus.

Prove that in a wall-sided vessel, the radius of curvature of the metacentric locus is given by $3\,\overline{BM}\,\sec^3 \phi \tan \phi$ where $\overline{BM}$ relates to the upright condition.

25. The half-ordinates in metres of a waterplane for a ship of 5 MN, 56 m long are 0·05, 0·39, 0·75, 1·16, 1·63, 2·12, 2·66, 3·07, 3·38, 3·55, 3·60, 3·57, 3·46, 3·29, 3·08, 2·85, 2·57, 2·26, 1·89, 1·48, and 1·03. If $\overline{KB}$ is 1·04 m and $\overline{KG}$ is 2·2 m calculate the value of $\overline{GM}$ assuming the ship is in water of 0·975 m³/Mg.

26. A computer output gives the following data for plotting cross curves of stability ($\overline{KS} = 15$ ft).

ϕ (deg)	Dispt. (tonf)	$\overline{SZ}$ (ft)	Dispt. (tonf)	$\overline{SZ}$ (ft)	Dispt. (tonf)	$\overline{SZ}$ (ft)
10	1300	3·12	2350	2·08	3580	1·60
	4890	1·29	6200	1·10	7660	1·08
20	1410	4·89	2430	3·78	3660	3·05
	4950	2·62	6330	2·35	7830	2·30
30	1580	5·56	2600	4·76	3820	4·31
	5130	3·94	6550	3·79	8100	3·69
40	1810	5·84	2870	5·45	4120	5·38
	5500	5·23	6870	4·98	8350	4·60
50	2100	6·24	3270	6·29	4570	6·23
	5850	5·87	7150	5·48	8450	5·08
60	2530	6·90	3680	6·69	4950	6·30
	6200	5·89	7400	5·49	8600	5·11

(continued on p. 143)

(continued from p. 142)

φ (deg)	Dispt. (tonf)	$\overline{SZ}$ (ft)	Dispt. (tonf)	$\overline{SZ}$ (ft)	Dispt. (tonf)	$\overline{SZ}$ (ft)
70	2950	6·70	4030	6·37	5300	5·93
	6500	5·47	7620	5·13	8770	4·87
80	3250	5·81	4370	5·63	5530	5·26
	6680	4·82	7830	4·58	8970	4·42
90	3670	4·67	4630	4·51	5740	4·32
	6900	4·08	8050	3·91	9170	3·85

Plot the cross curves of stability and deduce the $\overline{GZ}$ curves for the following conditions:

(a) $\Delta = 3710$ tonf; $\overline{GM} = 1·92$ ft, $\overline{KG} = 21·84$ ft
(b) $\Delta = 4275$ tonf; $\overline{GM} = 2·80$ ft, $\overline{KG} = 20·20$ ft
(c) $\Delta = 4465$ tonf; $\overline{GM} = 2·88$ ft, $\overline{KG} = 19·90$ ft
(d) $\Delta = 4975$ tonf; $\overline{GM} = 3·56$ ft, $\overline{KG} = 18·70$ ft

Plot the $\overline{GZ}$ curves and find the angles of vanishing stability.

27. A ship of displacement 50 MN has a $\overline{KG}$ of 6·85 m. The $\overline{SZ}$ values read from a set of cross curves of stability are as below:

φ	10	20	30	40	50	60	70	80	90
$\overline{SZ}$ (m)	0·635	1·300	1·985	2·650	3·065	3·145	3·025	2·725	2·230

Assuming that $\overline{KS}$ for the curves is 5 m, calculate the ordinates of the $\overline{GZ}$ curve and calculate the dynamical stability up to 80 degrees.

28. A passenger liner has a length of 200 m, a beam of 25 m, a draught of 10 m and a metacentric height of 1 m. The metacentric height of a similar vessel having a length of 205 m, beam 24 m, draught of 10·5 m is also 1 m. Assuming that $\overline{KG}$ is the same for the two vessels, calculate the ratio of $\overline{KB}$ to $\overline{BM}$ in the original vessel. What is the ratio of the displacements of the two vessels?

29. A vessel 72 ft long floats at 6 ft draught and has 4·5 ft freeboard, with sides above water vertical. Determine the $\overline{GZ}$ at 90°, assuming $\overline{KB} = 3·5$ ft and $\overline{KG} = 5$ ft with the vessel upright. The half-ordinates of the waterplane are 0·8, 3·3, 5·4, 6·5, 6·8, 6·3, 5·1, 2·8 and 0·6 ft. The displacement is 100 tonf and the middle-line plane is rectangular in shape. (AP & S)

30. For a given height of the centre of gravity and a required standard of stability (i.e. $\overline{GM}$), what is the relationship between a ship's length, beam, draught and volume of displacement?

State your assumptions clearly.

A ship is designed to the following particulars:

Displacement 10,000 tonf; draught 24 ft; beam 56 ft, $\overline{GM}$ 3·5 ft; G above WL 4·0 ft; TPI 48.

Alterations involve 100 tonf extra displacement and 1 ft rise of c.g.

What increase in beam will be necessary to maintain $\overline{GM}$, assuming that the depth of the ship remains unaltered and the small alterations in dimensions will not further alter the position of the c.g. or weight?

Assume the ship to be wall-sided and that length, waterplane coefficients and block coefficients are unchanged. (HMDTC)

31. A ship of 1500 tonf displacement carries 150 tonf of oil fuel in a rectangular tank 30 ft long, 20 ft wide and 20 ft deep. If the oil is assumed solid the ship has a $\overline{GM}$ of 4·90 ft and the following values of $\overline{GZ}$:

angle (deg)	15	30	45	60	75	90
$\overline{GZ}$ (ft)	1·35	2·72	3·17	2·18	0·60	−1·13

Taking the density of the oil as 40 ft³/tonf, find the values of $\overline{GZ}$ at 30, 45 and 75 degrees allowing for the mobility of the fuel, and state the initial $\overline{GM}$ (fluid) and the angle of vanishing stability. (HMDTC)

32. Prove Atwood's formula for calculating $\overline{GZ}$ for a ship at an angle of heel ϕ.

A simple barge has a constant cross-section throughout its length, a beam B at the waterplane and straight sides which slope outwards at an angle α to the vertical (beam increasing with draught).

If the barge is heeled to an angle ϕ, prove that the heeled waterplane will cut the upright waterplane at a horizontal distance x from the centre line where:

$$x = \frac{B}{2\tan\phi\tan\alpha}[1-\{1-(\tan\phi\tan\alpha)^2\}^{\frac{1}{2}}]$$

If $B = 20$ ft, $\alpha = 10°$ and $\phi = 30°$, calculate the value of x, and then, by calculation or drawing, obtain the $\overline{GZ}$ at 30° of heel if $\overline{B_0G} = 4·6$ ft and the underwater section area = 140 ft². (HMDTC)

33. State the purposes of an inclining experiment. Explain the preparations at the ship before the experiment is performed.

Calculate the change in $\overline{GM}$ due to the addition of 150 tonf, 36 ft above the keel of a frigate whose particulars before the addition are given below:

Displacement = 2700 tonf $\overline{KG}$ = 21·3 ft
TPI   = 18 $\overline{KB}$ = 8·2 ft
Draught   = 14·0 ft $\overline{BM}$ = 18·5 ft

(RNATE)

34. Derive an expression for the radius of curvature of the curve of flotation in terms of the waterplane characteristics and the volume of displacement (Leclert's theorem).

A homogeneous prism with cross-section as an isosceles triangle, base width B and height H, floats with its apex downwards in a condition of neutral equilibrium. Show that the radius of curvature of the curve of flotation in this condition is

$B^2H/(4H^2+B^2)$

(RNC)

References

1. Saunders, H. E. Hydrodynamics in ship design, *SNAME*, 1965.
2. Du Cane, P. *High speed small craft*, David & Charles, 1974.
3. Prohaska, C. W. Residuary stability, *TINA*, 1947.
4. Prohaska, C. W. Influence of ship form on transverse stability, *TINA*, 1951.
5. Sarchin, T. H. and Goldberg, L. L. Stability and buoyancy criteria for US naval surface ships, *TSNAME*, 1962.
6. Yamagata, M. Standard of stability adopted in Japan, *TRINA*, 1959.
7. Thomson, G. and Tope, J. E. International considerations of intact stability standards, *TRINA*, 1970.
8. Welford, S. The development of the self-righting lifeboat, *The Naval Architect*, July, 1974.
9. Nadeinski, V. P. and Jens, J. E. L. The stability of fishing vessels, *TRINA*, 1968.
10. Odabaşi, A. Y. Ultimate stability of ships, *TRINA*, 1977.

5 Hazards and protection

The naval architect needs to be more precise than the old and loved hymn, because he must ask himself why those on the sea are in peril and what he can do to help them. Hazard to those sailing in well designed ships arises through mishandling, misfortune or an enemy and these can cause flooding, fire, explosion, structural damage or a combination of these. It is the job of the naval architect to ensure that the effects do not result in immediate catastrophe and that they can be counteracted by equipment provided in the ship, at least up to a substantial level of damage. He must further ensure that when the damage is such that the ship will be lost, workable equipment is provided to save all life possible. To this end, the naval architect must anticipate the sort of mishandling and misfortune possible and the probable intent of any enemy, so that he may design his ship to mitigate the effects and render counter action readily available.

This chapter is concerned with this anticipation. It seeks to define the hazards in sufficiently precise terms and to describe the forms of protection and life saving possible. Some of these forms are demanded by international and national regulations; such regulations do not, however, remove the need to understand the problems.

Despite all that anticipation and regulation can achieve, losses at sea continue. Excluding yachts and special ships, 160 vessels of all sizes are still lost every peace-time year. Nearly half of these are wrecked, sixteen are lost by fire, eighteen by collision and forty founder, are abandoned, or are missing. While these figures represent only a tiny percentage of ships in use, they remain an anxiety to naval architects as well as to masters, owners and safety authorities. Reference 1 gives an informative summary of losses of merchant ships over a forty year period.

Flooding and collision

WATERTIGHT SUBDIVISION

Excluding loading in excess of the reserve of buoyancy, a ship can be sunk only by letting water in. Water may be let in by collision, grounding, by enemy action or by operation of a system open to the sea. A compartment which has been opened to the sea is said to have been *bilged*. However the water is let in, there is a need to isolate the flooded volume for the following reasons:

(a) to minimize the loss of transverse stability,
(b) to minimize damage to cargo,
(c) to prevent *plunge*, i.e. loss of longitudinal stability,
(d) to minimize the loss of reserve of buoyancy.

Ideally, a ship should sustain more and more flooding without loss of stability until it sinks bodily by loss of its reserve of buoyancy. This is *foundering*. The dangerous effect of asymmetric moment on the $\overline{GZ}$ curve was discussed in the last chapter; the ideal way to avoid such a possibility, is to subdivide the entire ship transversely and this is a major aim of the designer. It is not often wholly possible, but it is nowadays a major feature of most ships even at the expense of increasing the volume of water admitted. Free surface can also cause appreciable loss of transverse stability as discussed in Chapter 4. The effects of free surface can be minimized by longitudinal bulkheads which are undesirable and, better, by sills; because the loss of stability is proportional to the cube of the width of free surface, the effect of this type of subdivision is considerable (see Fig. 5.1). The sill reduces the effect of shallow flooding but cannot cure the effect of excessive transverse flooding.

Fig. 5.1 Effect of a sill

Extensive watertight subdivision is an inconvenience to everyone. The ship is larger, more expensive to build, access around the ship is inconvenient and cargo becomes more difficult to stow and more expensive to handle. A compromise between degree of safety and economics must be found. Generally, this results in watertight volumes larger in merchant ships than in warships, and a greater tendency in the former to plunge when damaged. Regulations to minimize this possibility in the behaviour of merchant ships are dealt with later in the chapter under 'Damage Safety Margins'.

Certain watertight subdivision is incorporated into a ship with the direct intention of isolating common and likely forms of damage. Collision, for example, is most likely to let water in at the bow. For this reason, all ships must have a collision bulkhead, which is a main transverse watertight bulkhead continuous to the uppermost watertight deck; SOLAS 1960 (Ref. 3) recommended a second collision bulkhead for ships over 100 metres in length. In merchant ships, it may not be pierced by access holes and be not less than five per cent of the ship's length from the bow. Flooding caused by grounding is isolated by the provision of a second watertight skin, formed in merchant ships by a watertight tank top and margin strake and, in warships, by the inner bottom. Merchant ships over 249 ft in length are required to have a double bottom which is continuous from collision to afterpeak bulkheads. This provides useful tank capacity. The double bottom also provides some protection against non-contact underbottom explosions, although to be most effective it should be only partially filled with liquid (usually oil fuel), which causes large free surface losses. The effects of contact explosion by torpedo or mine are minimized in large warships by the provision at the sides of sandwich protection comprising watertight compartments containing air or fluid (see Fig. 5.2). The basic principle is to absorb the energy of the explosion without allowing water to penetrate to the ship's vitals.

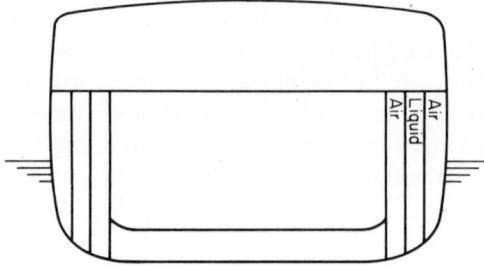

Fig. 5.2 Sandwich protection

Special subdivision is required in ships having a nuclear reactor. The reactor, primary circuit and associated equipment must be in a containment pressure vessel which should be so supported in the ship that it accepts no strain from the ship. It must be protected from damage by longitudinal bulkheads between it and the ship's side, by an extra deep double bottom and by cofferdam spaces longitudinally (Fig. 5.3).

Fig. 5.3 Reactor protection

FLOTATION CALCULATIONS

In order to assess a ship's ability to withstand damage, it is first necessary in the design stages to define the degrees of flooding to be examined. A range of examples will be chosen normally based, for a warship, on an expert assessment of likely weapon damage or, for a merchant ship, on statutory figures given in the United Kingdom by the Dept. of Trade in the Merchant Shipping (Construction) Rules. For each of these examples, it is necessary to discover.

(a) the damaged waterline, heel and trim,
(b) the damaged stability for which minimum standards are laid down in the same Rules.

Consider, first, a central compartment of a rectangular vessel open to the sea (Fig. 5.4).

Fig. 5.4 A central compartment open to the sea

As a result of this flooding, the ship sinks from WL to W_1L_1. The amount of weight added to the ship by the admission of water is represented by ABFE and the additional buoyancy required exactly to support it is represented by W_1L_1LW. To calculate the added weight to the depth AE, it is necessary to guess the new waterline and then verify that the guess is correct; trial and error will yield an answer. There is a better way to approach the problem. Instead of thinking of an increase in ship weight, the flooded portion CDFE must be thought of as a loss of buoyancy which must be made up by the buoyancies of W_1ACW and BL_1LD. The lost buoyancy CDFE can be calculated exactly because it is up to the original waterline only, and the additional buoyancy up to W_1L_1 can be calculated from the tonf parallel immersion of the waterplane excluding the portion AB. Weight and buoyancy of the portion ABDC cancel each other out. The ship's weight is unchanged. These two approaches are known generally as the '*added weight method*' and the '*lost buoyancy method*' respectively.

Compartments of ships open to the sea do not fill totally with water because some space is already occupied by structure, machinery or cargo. The ratio of the volume which can be occupied by water to the total gross volume is called the *permeability*. Typical values are

Space	Permeability (per cent)
Watertight compartment	97 (warship) / 95 (merchant ship)
Accommodation spaces	95
Machinery compartments	85
Coal bunkers, stores, cargo holds	60

Permeabilities should be calculated or assessed with some accuracy. Gross floodable volume should therefore be multiplied by the permeability to give the lost buoyancy or added weight. Formulae for the calculation of permeability for merchant ships are given in the Merchant Shipping (Construction) Rules.

Often, a watertight deck will limit flooding of a compartment below the level of the new waterline. But for a possible free surface effect due to entrapped air, the compartment may be considered pressed full and its volume calculated. In this case, the new waterline, heel and trim are best calculated by regarding the flooding as a known added weight whose effects are computed by the methods described in Chapters 3 and 4.

Where there is no such limitation and the space is free flooding, heel, trim and parallel sinkage are calculated by regarding the flooding as lost buoyancy in a manner similar to that already described for a central compartment. Now, because the ineffective area of waterplane is not conveniently central, the centre of flotation will move and the ship will not heel about the middle line. The procedure is therefore as follows:

(i) calculate permeable volume of compartment up to original waterline;
(ii) calculate TPI, longitudinal and lateral positions of CF for the waterplane with the damaged area removed;
(iii) calculate revised second moments of areas of the waterplane about the CF in the two directions and hence new $\overline{BM}$s;
(iv) calculate parallel sinkage and rise of CB due to the vertical transfer of buoyancy from the flooded compartment to the layer;
(v) calculate new $\overline{GM}$s
(vi) calculate angles of rotation due to the eccentricity of the loss of buoyancy from the new CFs.

This is best illustrated by an example.

Fig. 5.5

EXAMPLE. A compartment having a plan area at the waterline of 100 m² and centroid 70 m before midships, 13 m to starboard is bilged. Up to the waterline obtaining before bilging, the compartment volume was 1000 m³ with centres of volume 68·5 m before midships, 12 m to starboard and 5 m above keel. The permeability was 0·70.

Before the incident the ship was floating on an even draught of 10 m at which the following particulars obtained

Displacement mass, 30,000 tonnes $\overline{KM}$ long, 170 m
$\overline{KG}$, 9·40 m WP area, 4540 m²
$\overline{KM}$ transverse, 11·40 m CF, 1 m before midships
$\overline{KB}$, 5·25 m LBP, 220 m

Calculate the heel and trim when the compartment is bilged.

Solution: Refer to Fig. 5.5. Use the lost buoyancy method.

(i) Permeable volume = $0·70 \times 1000 = 700$ m³

(ii) Damaged WP area = 4440 m²

$$\text{Movement of CF aft} = \frac{110 \times (70-1)}{4440} = 1·55 \text{ m}$$

$$\text{Movement to of CF port} = \frac{100 \times 13}{4440} = 0·29 \text{ m}$$

(iii) Original transverse I

$I = (11·40 - 5·25) \times 1·025 \times 30{,}000 = 189{,}110$ m⁴

Damaged transverse I

$I = 189·11 \times 10^3 - 100 \times 13^2 - 4440 \times (0·29)^2 = 171{,}850$ m⁴

(ignoring I of the damage about its own axis)

$$\text{Damaged transverse } \overline{BM} = \frac{171{,}850}{1·025 \times 30{,}000} = 5·59 \text{ m}$$

Original long. I

$I = (170·0 - 5·25) \times 1·025 \times 30{,}000 = 5·066 \times 10^6$ m⁴

Damaged long. I

$I = 5·066 \times 10^6 - 100 (69)^2 - 4440 (1·55)^2 = 4·579 \times 10^6$ m⁴

Damaged long. $\overline{BM}$

$$\overline{BM} = \frac{4·579 \times 10^6}{1·025 \times 30{,}000} = 148·9 \text{ m}$$

(iv) Parallel sinkage $= \dfrac{700}{4440} = 0\cdot 16$ m

Rise of B $= \dfrac{700\,(10 + 0\cdot 08 - 5)}{1\cdot 025 \times 30{,}000} = 0\cdot 12$ m

(v) Damaged transverse $\overline{GM} = 5\cdot 25 + 0\cdot 12 + 5\cdot 59 - 9\cdot 40 = 1\cdot 56$ m

Damaged long. $\overline{GM} = 5\cdot 25 + 0\cdot 12 + 148\cdot 9 - 9\cdot 40 = 144\cdot 9$ m

(vi) Angle of heel $= \dfrac{700 \times 12\cdot 29}{1\cdot 025 \times 30{,}000 \times 1\cdot 56} \times \dfrac{180}{\pi} = 10\cdot 3°$

Angle of trim $= \dfrac{700 \times (68\cdot 5 - 1 + 1\cdot 55)}{1\cdot 025 \times 30{,}000 \times 144\cdot 9} = 0\cdot 01085$ rads

Change of trim $= 0\cdot 01085 \times 220 = 2\cdot 39$ m between perps.

Note that displacement and $\overline{KG}$ are unchanged.

The principal axes of the waterplane, as well as moving parallel to their original positions, also rotate. The effects of this rotation are not great until a substantial portion of the waterplane has been destroyed.

This approach to the flotation calculations is satisfactory for trim which does not intersect keel or deck and for heel up to about 10 degrees. Thereafter, it is necessary to adopt a trial and error approach and to calculate the vertical, athwartships and longitudinal shifts of the centre of buoyancy for several trial angles of waterplanes. That angle of waterplane which results in the new centre of buoyancy being perpendicularly under the centre of gravity is the correct one. This is illustrated for the transverse plane in Fig. 5.6, in which the transfer of buoyancy from b to the two wedges (one negative) results in a move of the centre of buoyancy of the whole from B to B_1. $\overline{B_1 G}$ must be perpendicular to $W_1 L_1$. To ensure that the displacement is unaltered, several waterlines parallel to $W_1 L_1$ will be necessary at each angle as described presently under 'Damaged Stability Calculations', Fig. 5.8. These calculations are often performed with the aid of a planimeter or integrator. The calculations can also be performed by a digital computer.

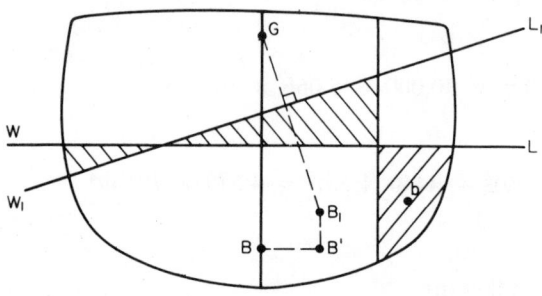

Fig. 5.6

DAMAGED STABILITY CALCULATIONS

Consider, first, the effect of a flooded compartment on initial stability. Let us show that, whether the flooding be considered an added weight or a lost buoyancy, the result will be the same.

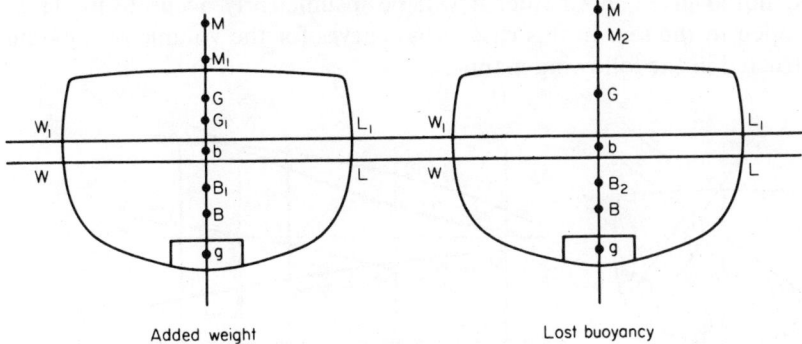

Fig. 5.7

Consider a ship of displacement Δ admitting a weight w having a free surface i as shown in Fig. 5.7. Regarding as an added weight,

$$\text{Rise of B} = \overline{BB_1} = \frac{w\overline{Bb}}{\Delta + w}$$

$$\text{Fall of G} = \overline{GG_1} = \frac{w\overline{Gg}}{\Delta + w}$$

New $\overline{GM} = \overline{B_1M_1} - \overline{B_1G_1} = \overline{B_1M_1} - \overline{BG} + \overline{BB_1} + \overline{GG_1}$

i.e.

$$\overline{G_1M_1} = \rho\frac{(I_1 - i)}{\Delta + w} - \overline{BG} + \frac{w}{\Delta + w}(\overline{Bb} + \overline{Gg})$$

$$\text{Righting moment} = (\Delta + w)\overline{G_1M_1}\phi = \{\rho(I_1 - i) - \Delta\overline{BG} - w\overline{BG} + w(\overline{Bb} + \overline{BG} + \overline{Bg})\}\phi$$

$$= \{\rho(I_1 - i) - \Delta\overline{BG} + w\overline{bg}\}\phi$$

Regarding as a loss of buoyancy,

$$\text{Rise of B} = \overline{BB_2} = \frac{w\overline{bg}}{\Delta}$$

New $\overline{GM} = \overline{B_2M_2} - \overline{B_2G} = \overline{B_2M_2} - \overline{BG} + \overline{BB_2}$

$$\overline{GM_2} = \rho\frac{(I_1 - i)}{\Delta} - \overline{BG} + \frac{w\overline{bg}}{\Delta}$$

Righting moment $= \Delta\overline{GM_2}\phi = \{\rho(I_1 - i) - \Delta\overline{BG} + w\overline{bg}\}\phi$ as before.

154 Basic ship theory

Thus, so far as righting moment is concerned (and this is what the ship actually experiences), it does not matter whether the flooding is regarded as added weight or lost buoyancy although $\overline{GM}$ and $\overline{GZ}$ values will not be the same. The lost buoyancy method is also called the *constant displacement method*.

It is probable that the approximate method of correcting the $\overline{GZ}$ curve for contained liquid given in Chapter 4 will be insufficiently accurate for large volumes open to the sea. In this case, cross curves for the volume of flooding are constructed in the following manner:

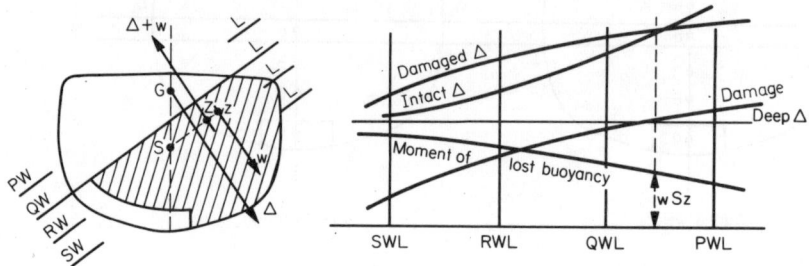

Fig. 5.8

For each angle of heel, a series of parallel waterlines P, Q, R, S, is drawn. For each of these waterlines, the weight of flooding and its lever $\overline{Sz}$ from the pole of the ship's cross curves are calculated by integrator, computer or direct mensuration, i.e. by one of the methods used for the ship itself and described in Chapter 4. The weight of flooding up to each waterline is added to the deep displacement to give a damaged displacement which is plotted on a base of WL together with $w\overline{Sz}$. Intact displacement to the same base will be available from the calculations which led to the cross curves for the ship (if not, they must be calculated). Where these two lines cross is the point of vertical equilibrium for that angle and $w\overline{Sz}$ can be read off. Now the restoring lever $\overline{SZ}$ for the intact ship at displacement $\Delta + w$ can be read directly from the cross curves. Then the damaged righting moment is given by

$$(\Delta + w)\overline{SZ} - \Delta\overline{SG} \sin \phi - w\overline{Sz}$$

A righting lever corresponding to the original displacement Δ is given by dividing this expression by Δ. This procedure is repeated for all angles. The damaged GZ curve will, in general, appear as in Fig. 5.9. The point at which the curve crosses the ϕ-axis, at angle ϕ_1, represents the position of rotational equilibrium; this will be zero when the flooding is symmetrical about the middle line.

With symmetrical flooding, the upright equilibrium position may not be one of stable equilibrium. In this case, the $\overline{GZ}$ curve will be as in Fig. 5.10 where ϕ_2 is the angle of loll. The significance of the angle of loll is discussed in Chapter 4. If the $\overline{GZ}$ curve does not rise above the ϕ-axis the ship will capsize; if little area is left above, capsizing will occur dynamically.

Hazards and protection 155

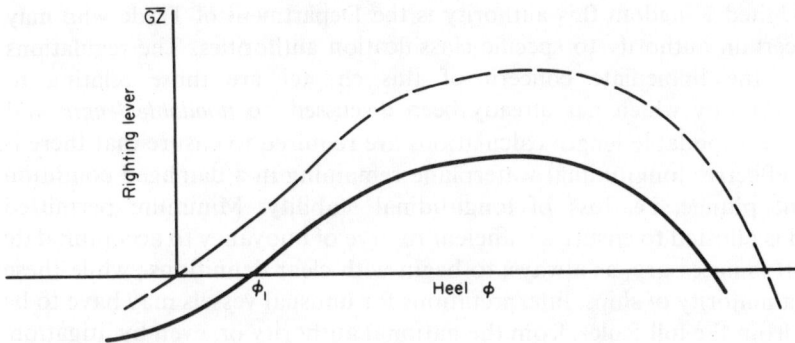

Fig. 5.9 Damaged $\overline{GZ}$ curve

Standards of damaged stability are not easy to define precisely. The 1960 SOLAS conference (Ref. 3) demanded a minimum of 0·05 m (2 in.) of $\overline{GM}$ by the constant displacement method in the standard damaged condition for merchant ships. It is important, also, to decide the adequacy of range, maximum $\overline{GZ}$ and angle of maximum stability, particularly for warships which do not conform to the margin line standards discussed presently. Trim in a warship can cause rapid loss of waterplane inertia and deterioration of damaged stability and this is one reason why the low quarter deck destroyers common in the second world war have been replaced by modern flush deck, high freeboard frigates.

The fact that ships may take up large angles of heel following damage is recognized in the regulations governing ship construction, e.g. watertight doors must be able to be opened up to angles of heel of 15 degrees.

The Merchant Shipping (Passenger Ship Construction) Rules incorporate the UK requirements for a minimum 0·05 m $\overline{GM}$ and various heel minima.

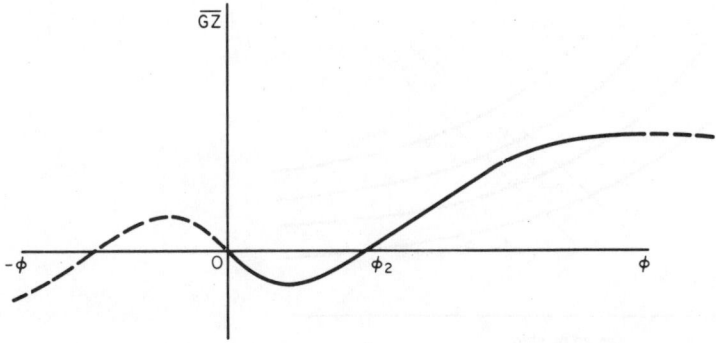

Fig. 5.10

DAMAGE SAFETY MARGINS

Minimum standards of behaviour of merchant ships under damaged conditions are agreed by international convention and enforced by national authority.

For the United Kingdom this authority is the Department of Trade who may delegate certain authority to specific classification authorities. The regulations which are the immediate concern of this chapter are those relating to damaged stability which has already been discussed, to *floodable length* and to *freeboard*. Floodable length calculations are required to ensure that there is sufficient effective longitudinal waterplane remaining in a damaged condition to prevent plunge, i.e. loss of longitudinal stability. Minimum permitted freeboard is allotted to ensure a sufficient reserve of buoyancy to accommodate damage. It is necessary, as always, to begin with clear definitions; while these embrace a majority of ships, interpretations for unusual vessels may have to be obtained from the full Rules, from the national authority or, even by litigation.

The *bulkhead deck* is the uppermost continuous weathertight deck to which transverse watertight bulkheads are carried.

The *margin line* is 3 in (75 mm) below the upper surface of bulkhead deck at side.

The *floodable length* at any point in the length of a ship is the length, with that point as centre, which can be flooded without immersing any part of the margin line when the ship has no list.

Formulae are provided in the Rules for the calculation of a *factor of subdivision* which must be applied to the floodable length calculations. This factor depends on the length of the ship and a *criterion numeral* which is intended to represent the criterion of service of the ship and is calculated from the volumes of the whole ship, the machinery spaces and the accommodation spaces and the number of passengers. Broadly, the factor of subdivision ensures that one, two or three compartments must be flooded before the margin line is immersed and ships which achieve these standards are called one-, two- or three-compartment ships. Compartment standard is an inverse of the factor of subdivision. As indicated in Fig. 5.11, very small ships would be expected to have a one-compartment and large passenger ships a three-compartment standard.

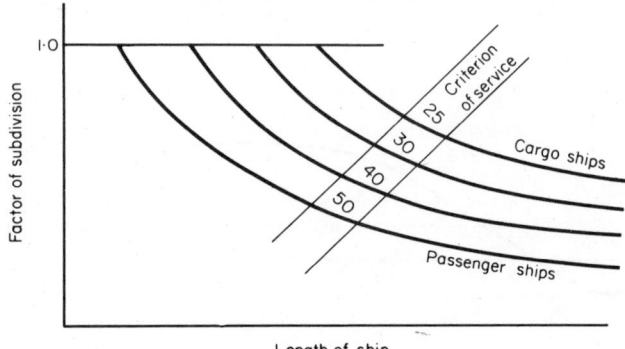

Fig. 5.11 *Factor of subdivision*

The product of the floodable length and the factor of subdivision gives the *permissible length*. With certain provisos concerning adjacent compartments, a compartment may not be longer than its permissible length. Flooding calculations, either direct or aided by standard comparative parametric diagrams available in the United Kingdom from the Department of Trade can produce curves similar to those shown in Fig. 5.12 for floodable and permissible lengths and in general, a triangle erected from the corners of a compartment with height equal to base must have an apex below the permissible length curve. The base angle of this triangle is $\tan^{-1} 2$ if vertical and horizontal scales are the same. Lines at this angle, called the forward and after terminals, terminate the curves at the two ends of the ship. The steps in the curve are due to different permeabilities of compartments; in the initial determination of bulkhead spacing for the ship on this basis, it is necessary to complete sets of permissible length curves for a range of permeabilities.

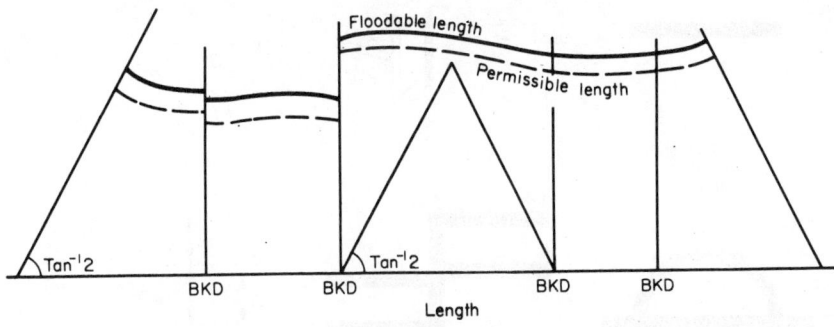

Fig. 5.12 Floodable and permissible length curves

Summarizing, the steps to be taken to carry out the floodable length calculations are as follows:

(a) Define bulkhead deck and margin line;
(b) calculate factor of subdivision;
(c) calculate permeabilities;
(d) assess floodable lengths;
(e) plot permissible lengths.

Calculations are conveniently carried out in methodical manner in a standard tabulated form recommended by the Department of Trade.

The second important insurance against damage in merchant ships is the allocation of a statutory freeboard. The rules governing the allocation of freeboard are laid down by an international Load Line Convention, of which one was held in 1966, and ratified nationally by each of the countries taking part—by the United Kingdom in the Merchant Shipping (Loadline) Rules, 1968. Because the amount of cargo which can be carried is directly related to the minimum permissible freeboard, the authorities are anxious to be fair and exact and this tends to produce somewhat complicated rules. The intention, however, is clear enough. The intention is to provide a simple visual check that a laden ship has sufficient reserve of buoyancy and to relate, therefore, the watertight volume above the laden waterline to a height which can be readily measured. This clearly involves the geometry of the ship, and the statutory calculation of freeboard involves water density, ship's length, breadth, depth, sheer, size of watertight superstructures and other relevant geometrical features of the ship. The Rules require minimum standards of closure in watertight boundaries before allowing them to be counted in the freeboard calculation. Standards for hatch covers, crew protection, freeing port areas, ventilators and scuttles are enforced by these Rules.

The freeboard thus calculated results in a *load line* which is painted boldly on the ship's side in the form shown in Fig. 5.13. Because the density of water affects the reserve of buoyancy and weather expectation varies with season and location, different markings are required for Winter North Atlantic (WNA), Winter (W), Summer (S), Tropical (T), Fresh (F) and Tropical Fresh (TF).

Fig. 5.13 Load line markings

LOSS OF STABILITY ON GROUNDING

The upward force at the keel due to docking or grounding, whose magnitude was found in Chapter 3, causes a loss of stability. Let the force at the keel be w. Consider a slightly inclined vessel before and after the application of this force (Fig. 5.14).

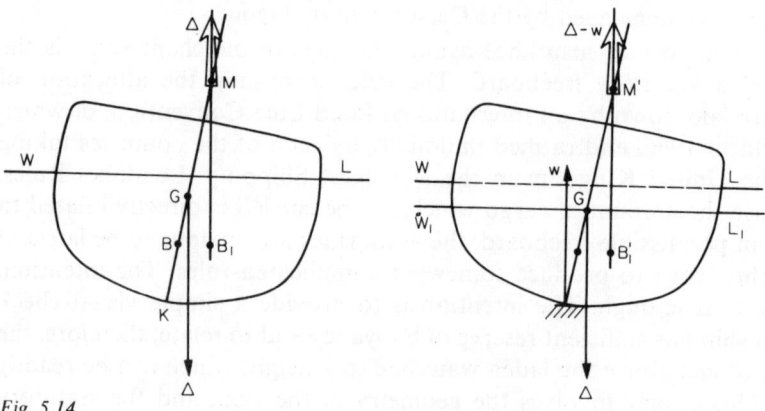

Fig. 5.14

The righting moment at inclination ϕ before the application of w is, of course, $\Delta\overline{GM} \sin \phi$. After application, the righting moment is

$$(\Delta - w)\overline{GM}' \sin \phi - w\overline{KG} \sin \phi = \Delta\left(\overline{GM}' - \frac{w}{\Delta}\overline{KM}'\right) \sin \phi$$

The movement of M to M' is due, as described in Chapter 3 to (a), the fall of B due to the removal of the layer of buoyancy at the waterline, (b), the change in $\overline{BM}$ due to the differences in I and volume of displacement ∇.

BERTHING AND ICE NAVIGATION

A ship has no brakes and is slow to respond to the propulsive machinery; unexpected currents and gusts of wind can make a ship awkward to handle. Despite dexterous handling by the Master, there will be occasions when a ship comes alongside heavily and may be indented by fenders or catamarans or tugs. Local internal structural stiffening is often fitted in the vicinity of the waterline to afford some protection, and the waterline strake may be increased in thickness.

Similar stiffening is fitted in ships intended for navigation in ice and Lloyd's Register lays down three degrees of stiffening dependent on the type of ice to be negotiated, making a note against the ship to this effect in the Register Book. This is not to be confused with the stiffening required in an ice breaker which is much more formidable, since to perform its task, the ice breaker is driven to ride up on the ice, allowing its weight to break the ice.

Safety of life at sea

Representatives of nearly 100 seafaring nations contribute to the Inter-governmental Maritime Consultative Organization (IMCO) which is an organization formed in 1959 under the auspices of the United Nations, intended to promote co-operation amongst all countries on the questions relating to ships. This organization promotes discussion on such topics as tonnage measurement, safety of life and standards of construction. It convened the Load Line Convention of 1966, the one previous having been held in 1930 and it has taken over the functions of the International Conferences on the Safety of Life at Sea (SOLAS) four of which have been held, in 1914 (following the *Titanic* disaster), in 1929, 1948 and 1960. The topics with which the SOLAS Conferences concerned themselves were standards of construction, watertight subdivision, damage behaviour, damage control, fire protection, life-saving appliances, dangerous cargoes, nuclear machinery protection, safety of navigation and many other aspects of safety. Following the 1960 SOLAS Conference, IMCO set up a dozen or so sub committees dealing actively with stability and subdivision, fire protection, bulk cargoes, oil pollution, tonnage, signals and other aspects of safety.

FIRE

In the design and construction of a ship, it is necessary to provide means to contain fire, the most feared, perhaps, of all the hazards which face the mariner. During 1963, two major ship fires led to the deaths of 158 people. A third disaster in which the liner *Lakonia* caught fire in the Atlantic, caused the deaths of 128. When it is appreciated that these disasters occurred in peacetime, with so many modern aids available, the seriousness of fire as a hazard can be seen. The causes of fires are manifold—electrical short circuits, chemical reactions, failure of insulation, ingress of hot particles. Whatever the cause, however, there are two factors about fire which give the clue to its containment,

(a) fire cannot be sustained below a certain temperature which depends upon the particular material;
(b) fire cannot be sustained without oxygen.

Thus, to put a fire out, it must be cooled sufficiently or it must be deprived of oxygen. A ship must be designed readily to permit both.

The principal method of cooling a fire is to apply water to it and this is most efficiently done by fine spray. Automatic sprinkler systems are often fitted, actuated by bulbs which burst at a temperature of about 80°C, permitting water to pass. Passenger vessels must embody arrangements whereby any point in the ship can be reached by two hoses delivering a specified quantity of water.

Deprivation of oxygen is effected in a variety of ways. The watertight subdivision of the ship is conveniently adapted to provide vertical zone fire boundaries built to particular standards of fire resistance that can be closed off in the event of a fire. The fire itself can be smothered by gas or foam provided by portable or fixed apparatus.

Regulations for merchant ships registered in the United Kingdom are contained in the Merchant Shipping (Fire Appliances) Rules and allied publications issued by Government bodies. These specify the constructional materials, method of closing the fire boundaries, the capacities of pumps and the provision of fire-fighting appliances. While the quantities depend upon the particular classes of ship, the principles of fire protection in merchant ships and warships are similar:

(a) the ship is subdivided so that areas may be closed off by fire boundaries; this also prevents the spread of smoke, which hampers firefighters and makes it difficult to find the seat of the fire;
(b) a firemain of sufficient extent and capacity is provided, with sufficient cross connections to ensure supply under severe damage;
(c) fixed foam, or inert gas smothering units are provided in machinery spaces and in most cargo holds;
(d) sufficient small portable extinguishers are provided to put out a small fire before it spreads;
(e) fire control plans are supplied to the Master and a fire fighting headquarters provided.

Hazards and protection

Some cargoes contain or generate their own oxygen and are not therefore susceptible to smothering. Cooling by spraying or flooding is the only means of extinguishing such fires and any extensive flooding thus caused brings with it the added hazard of loss of stability.

LIFE-SAVING EQUIPMENT

Ships must conform to the safety regulations of the country with whom they are registered. For the United Kingdom, the Merchant Shipping (Life-Saving Appliances) Rules govern the number and types of lifeboats, liferafts, lifebuoys and buoyant apparatus to be carried by each ship. These depend upon the class of ship and the service for which it is intended. In general, sufficient lifeboats and liferafts for one half of the number of persons designed to be carried, are to be provided on each side of the ship. They must be capable of launch with up to 15 degrees of heel on the ship in either direction. Each lifeboat is to be constructed to minimum standards of reserve of buoyancy, block coefficient and cubic capacity and the importance of gravity davits under damaged conditions (up to 15 degrees heel and 10 degrees trim), is emphasized in the Rules.

ANCHORING

Lives of the crew and the value of ship and cargo are often entrusted totally to the anchor—an item of safety equipment much taken for granted. Bower anchors carried by ships need to hold the ship against the pull of wind and tide. Refs. 11 and 19 show how to calculate the forces due to wind and tide to enable the naval architect to select the size of cable and an anchor of sufficient holding pull. Classification societies define an equipment number to represent the windage and tide forces and relate this to the cable and to approved anchor designs.

The qualities required of a good anchor are:

(a) it must bite quickly into the sea bed;
(b) it must hold well in all types of sea bed;
(c) it must be stable, i.e. not rotate out of the sea bed;
(d) it must not foul the cable and must be easy to weigh;
(e) it must be sufficiently strong and easy to make.

Efficiency of the anchor itself is measured by the ratio of holding pull to anchor weight which may nowadays exceed 10 in most sea beds. However, the efficiency of the mooring depends also upon the length of cable veered and the depth of water, the ratio of these being the scope. The scope must be sufficient to ensure a horizontal pull on the anchor shank. Figure 5.15 shows some typical relationships for bower anchors.

Ideally, the holding pull of the anchor should be slightly less than its own proof load and slightly more than the total wind and tide drag on the ship, while the proof load of the cable should be slightly greater than both.

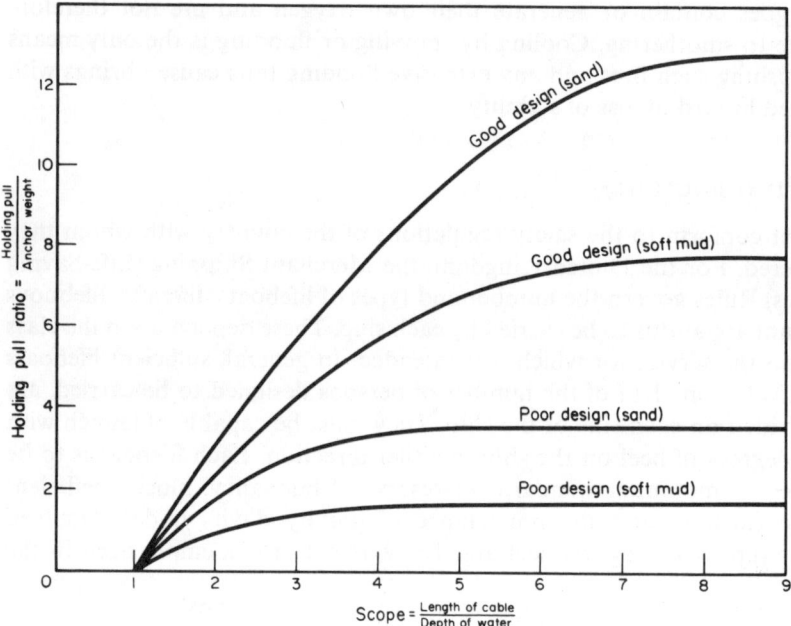

Fig. 5.15 *Characteristics of anchoring*

DAMAGE CONTROL

The importance of a damage control organization is recognized in both merchant shipping and warship circles. Because of its greater complexity and its need to defend itself from nuclear, chemical and bacteriological attack as well as explosion and flooding, the organization in a warship is more complex. However, the Master of a merchant ship is required to be familiar with the damage control characteristics of his ship, to institute and drill an effective organization and to ensure that damage control plans are kept displayed.

The aim is to organize the ship in order rapidly to ascertain the damage, to isolate the incident and to take corrective action. The ship is constructed to make this as easy as possible; watertight subdivision is arranged as already discussed; watertight doors and hatches must be operable at 15 degrees of heel and are marked in levels of importance; minimum standards of damaged stability are met; pumping, flooding and fire-fighting systems are arranged to facilitate action under conditions of damage; electrical supplies are arranged with a view to providing sufficient breakdown capacity and duplication. All important systems are cross connected to ensure continuity of supplies following damage.

In a warship, information and control is concentrated in a central compartment with several subsidiary control posts each controlling one of the sections of the ship into which it is divided for purposes of damage control. Displayed in the headquarters is the flooding board which shows the watertight subdivision of the ship and the approximate heel and trim which would result from the flooding of any watertight compartment. Also displayed is information on the pumping, electrical, ventilation and other systems. A comprehensive communication network is available in the headquarters. With this organization, the damage control officer is able to appreciate the position and order corrective action.

Because a ship is most easily sunk by loss of transverse stability, the most urgent corrective action, once flooding has been contained by the closure of boundaries, is to reduce the angle of heel. This is most effectively done by counterflooding, i.e. flooding a compartment on the side opposite the damage and the extent necessary is indicated by the flooding board. In merchant ships, various regulations govern the limiting angle of heel, the maximum allowed after corrective action being 7 degrees (Ref. 2). Open cross connection of wing tanks is desirable. SOLAS Conference 1960 recommended a maximum time of 15 min for the correction of asymmetric flooding. Having taken immediate corrective measures, the damage control officer may order reinforcement of bulkheads by shoring or the repair of leaks by wedges, boxes and concrete and the slower time repair of damage and restoration of supplies as far as is possible.

If A is the area of a hole and d is its distance below the waterline, the velocity of inflow of water, v, is given approximately by $v = 8\sqrt{d}$ ft/s, d being in feet, or $4\cdot5\sqrt{d}$ m/s, d being in metres. The volume of water admitted by the hole is KvA, where K is a coefficient of contraction at the hole. Assuming a value of 0·625 for K,

$$\text{inflow} = 5A\sqrt{d}\text{ ft}^3/\text{s, with } A \text{ in ft}^2, \quad \text{or } \tfrac{11}{4}A\sqrt{d}\text{ m}^3/\text{s, with } A \text{ in m}^2$$

Thus, a 15 cm diameter hole, 16 m below the waterline would admit

$$\frac{11}{4} \times \frac{\pi}{4} \times 0\cdot0225 \times 4 \times 1\cdot025 \times 60 = 12 \text{ tonnes of salt water per minute.}$$

UNCOMFORTABLE CARGOES

Grain, oil, explosive, hygroscopic materials, liquid gas and radioactive materials are some of the cargoes which may provide an intrinsic hazard to a ship and for which a large network of rules exists. These cannot be examined in a book of this size beyond a brief mention of their existence.

In the nineteenth century, when loading was not supervised by port surveyors, grain ships were lost because voids were left under the decks. Grain and similar cargoes may shift when the ship rolls at sea, providing an upsetting moment which, if greater than the ship's maximum righting moment, causes it to capsize; if it is less, the ship heels, which may cause a further shift of the grain, causing a larger angle of heel, which may immerse openings or capsize the ship. Protection for deep sea ships is now provided as follows:

(a) In special bulk carriers, either upper wing tanks are fitted thus making the holds 'self-trimming' and reducing the free surface in them when full, or at least two longitudinal curtain bulkheads are used to break up the free surface.
(b) In general cargo carriers (mostly two deckers), shifting boards are fitted in the upper parts of the ship, usually on the centre line in conjunction with

large feeder boxes. These feeders supply grain for settlement to those voids which fill in bad weather while limiting the slack surface produced higher up. When the ship's stability is adequate, feeders may be replaced by deep saucers of bagged cargo plugging the hatches.

(In both types of ship, when it is necessary for compartments to be partly filled, the shift of grain can be restricted by overstowing with bagged grain, or by strapping down with dunnage platforms and wires, or by carrying the shifting boards down through the grain.)

(c) In both classes of ship, it is now customary to carry grain stability information so that for bulk carriers the angle of heel after an assumed shift of grain can be found before loading and kept under 5 degrees, and in a general cargo ship, the stability required for the method of loading can be predetermined. In both cases, the loading is then planned to meet the stability requirements. To provide what is probably the most effective protection, the principal grain exporting countries appoint surveyors to check fittings and stability before loading. Later, they supervise the stowing of the grain so that voids are reduced as far as is practicable.

Oils and petrols are hazardous if they are volatile, i.e. if, at normal temperatures they emit a vapour that can accumulate until an explosive mixture with air is created. The vapour may be ignited at any mixture if it is raised to a critical and well defined temperature known as the flashpoint. For heavy and crude oils, this temperature is quite high, often above the temperature of a cigarette. Cleaning of empty crude oil tanks by steam hoses has led to several disastrous explosions due to the discharge of electrostatic build-up in the swirling fluid. Light oil vapour can be ignited by match, electrical spark, spark caused by friction or electrostatics, by overheating of bearings or loss of insulation.

Regulations, in general, provide for:

(a) total isolation of a dangerous oil cargo where possible;
(b) the removal of any possibility of creating ignition or overheating;
(c) adequate ventilation to prevent a build up of vapour to an explosive mixture;
(d) a comprehensive fire warning and fighting system.

Cofferdams to create an air boundary to oil spaces are a common requirement.

Explosives may be carried by ships which comply with the Merchant Shipping (Dangerous Goods) Rules. Because they must carry explosives where there is, in wartime, considerable risk of ignition by an enemy, the carriage of explosives in warships requires especial study. General regulations are contained in Naval Magazines and Explosive Regulations but these must be reviewed in the light of every new weapon development. The carriage of cordite in silk bags which were ignited by flash in the *Queen Mary* at Jutland and, probably, *Hood* in the second world war has been long discontinued; fixed robust ammunition is now carried alongside delicate guided weapons and torpedoes, some with exotic fuels. No ship construction can prevent the ingress of all offensive weapons, although the probability of causing catastrophic damage can be reduced. Structure can be arranged to minimize the effects of any incident and to this end the magazines are:

(a) isolated and provided with flashtight boundaries;
(b) kept cool by adequate insulation, ventilation and the prohibition of any electrical and mechanical devices which can be a source of unacceptable heat;
(c) provided with vent plates which permit an excessive pressure caused by burning to be vented to atmosphere;
(d) provided with fire detection and fighting facilities, often automatic.

Each dangerous or uncomfortable cargo must be examined on its own merits. Hygroscopic materials such as sisal may absorb much moisture and become so heavy that safe limits of deadweight or stability are broken; they may also swell and cause structural damage. Liquid gas is carried at very low temperatures and, if it leaks, may render the steel with which it comes in contact so brittle that it fractures instantly. Radioactive materials must, of course, have their radiations suitably insulated. Hydrogen peroxide combusts in contact with grease. Even some manure gives off dangerous organic gases.

NUCLEAR MACHINERY

A nuclear reactor is simply a type of boiler. Instead of producing heat by burning oil, a reactor produces heat by controlled decay of radioactive material. The heat is removed by circulation in a primary circuit, whence it is transferred at a heat exchanger to a secondary circuit to turn water into steam for driving the turbines. Whatever else can go wrong with the reactor there is no possibility whatever of a nuclear explosion, i.e. an explosion involving nuclear fission. There are, nevertheless, some unpleasant hazards associated with a reactor, viz.:

(a) under normal operation, dangerous gamma-rays are emitted from materials, activated by neutron bombardment. All personnel serving in the ship, who would be damaged by such rays must be protected by shielding of lead or other dense material. In the first nuclear merchant ship, the *Savannah*, there were nearly 2000 tons of shielding and there is similar shielding in nuclear submarines. Such heavy concentrated weight gives strength problems. Embrittlement of some materials by this irradiation is a further hazard;
(b) by mishandling or by accident, precise control of decay may be lost and radioactive fission products may be released. To contain such products, the reactor must be surrounded by a containment vessel which is made with scrupulous care to withstand the pressure build up due to the most serious credible accident. Safety devices are also built into the automatic control equipment which regulates the behaviour of the reactor. The subdivision of the ship referred to earlier is aimed at reducing the chances of loss of control by collision or grounding damage.

The 1960 SOLAS Conference made a series of recommendations for the safety of ships with nuclear reactors and these have now been incorporated into national law and classification society rules. In addition to the cofferdam protection discussed earlier, two-compartment standards are required.

Reference 16, the Merchant Shipping Acts 1965 and the classification society rules give further details.

Other hazards

MECHANICAL SHOCK

If one jumped off a chair and landed without bending knees or ankles, the body would suffer an unpleasant and perhaps damaging shock because the momentum of the body would be destroyed in a short time and distance causing high deceleration; bending the knees lengthens the time of arrest and reduces the deceleration to a value acceptable to the body. China subject to the same treatment may break while polystyrene will not. Almost all objects suffer some form of mechanical shock during their lives and must be designed to meet it. Ships suffer shock when grounding or berthing heavily.

A particular and difficult form of shock caused to ships and equipment carried in them, is that due to an underwater explosion which may be some distance from the ship. Near miss bombs, pressure mines, anti-submarine explosions, nuclear bombs and the effects of a warship's own weapons are typical. Reference 15 gives approximate values of acceleration and deceleration associated with different experiences as follows:

Experience	Approx. g	Approx. duration (s)
Metal box, 3 ft drop	400	0·002
Wooden box, 3 ft drop	100	0·004
Car crash	20–100	<0·1
Lorries on rough road	3	<0·2
Aircraft catapult	6	1·5
Small missile boost	30	0·2
Earthquakes	0·3	—
Underwater explosion		
Items on ship's hull	1000	0·002
Items on bottom plating	10,000	0·0005

The shock reaching an object in a ship from an explosion varies according to the object's weight, type of mounting and position in the ship; a typical velocity time record of an item in a ship subjected to non-contact explosion is shown in Fig. 5.16. The motion of the item is very complex, but its behaviour can be closely represented by a definition of maximum velocity, period, mean acceleration and mean deceleration expressed usually in g's. To allow for such effects, any rigidly mounted item of equipment is designed to withstand statically the force associated with these number of g's, i.e. its own mass multiplied by the shock g. The shock experienced by a flexible item depends upon the stiffness of support. There is a maximum magnification of shock when the natural period of vibration of the item approximates to the shock disturbing period. Other factors are relevant, for example, some materials, notably mild steel, exhibit an increase in yield point by a factor up to two under high rates

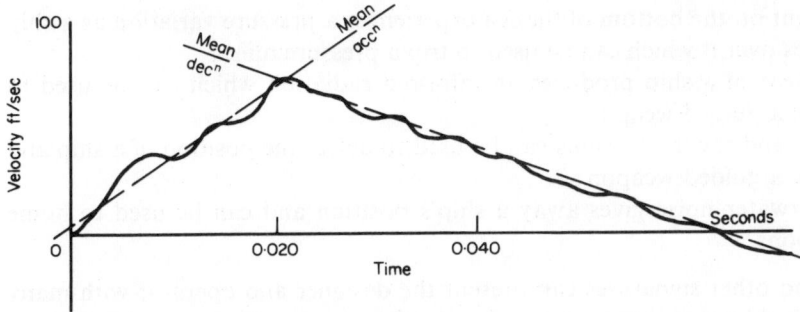

Fig. 5.16 Velocity-time record at an object

of strain; such factors enhance protection. There is, of course, no standard of enemy action and the values to be used are specified by different navies such that the essential equipment continues to work as long as the hull remains tight and this results in requirements often for several hundred g's.

As a general guide to good practice in resisting all types of shock, the designer should

(a) avoid brittle materials such as cast iron;
(b) minimize stress concentrations; corners must, of course, be well rounded;
(c) avoid overhangs, cantilevers;
(d) minimize weights;
(e) ensure that pipes and cables are secure;
(f) ensure that two parts of an item cannot move independently unless flexibly coupled;
(g) ensure adequate clearances for shock movements.

Often, it will be uneconomical to design equipment to withstand the full shock loading. It is then necessary to reduce the shock reaching the item by mounting it on a shock attenuating device, just as the body of the jumper is protected by the bending of his legs. The energy is absorbed more slowly. Such devices are basically damped springs or yielding straps. They need to be properly matched to the equipment, however, as a piece of rubber, for example, which provided an item of equipment with a natural frequency coincident with the excitation frequency of the shock pulse, would, in fact, amplify that input.

Reference 17 gives more detail of shock requirement and testing.

SHIP SIGNATURES

In order to inflict damage an enemy must first find and identify his prey. A ship has many different signatures which help an enemy to detect and classify it:

(a) it has a natural magnetism which can be used to trip the fuse of a magnetic mine; such a signature can be counteracted by passing a current around cables wound round the inside of the ship. This is known as *de-gaussing*. Such magnetism can also be caused by induced eddy currents in a ship, particularly an aluminium alloy ship, rolling and cutting the earth's magnetic lines of force;

(b) a point on the bottom of the sea experiences a pressure variation as a ship passes over it which can be used to trip a pressure mine;
(c) the heat of a ship produces an infra-red radiation which can be used to home a guided weapon;
(d) radio and radar emissions can be used to detect the position of a ship and home a guided weapon;
(e) underwater noise gives away a ship's position and can be used to home weapons.

These and other signatures can present the designer and operator with many problems. Although eradication of a signature is usually impossible, it may often be reduced to a level at which detection is difficult.

ENEMY ACTION

There are two important principles on which the protection of a ship against enemy attack is based:

(a) the offensive medium must be prevented from reaching the ship;
(b) the effect of the offensive medium, presumed to have hit, must be minimized.

(a) may be effected by a counter weapon such as an anti-missile missile, or it may be achieved by seducing the weapon from its expected path by electronic or other countermeasures. Reduced target size and signature or increased manoeuvrability help.

(b) is achieved by dispersion and duplication of important men and equipment and by fitting armour, protective plating, venting plates and automatic quenching equipment.

Gas, bacteria and radioactive particles must be excluded by the crash closing of an airtight boundary. Deposits are washed away by a pre-wetting system which drenches the whole ship in salt water spray. A large air burst explosion such as that from a nuclear weapon causes a blast effect followed by a slight suction, each of which may cause structural damage against which the ship may be designed.

The effects of a ship's weapons on the ship itself must be catered for; blast, shock, heating, scouring, chemical deposit, recoil loading, noise and physical obstruction. High intensity transmissions by modern radio and radar can be hazardous to personnel and can trigger weapons which have not been properly shielded. This type of radiation hazard is called radhaz.

A good example of protection by dispersion is afforded by the unitization of machinery in large warships. Each unit, which may comprise more than one watertight compartment, is self-contained, e.g. in a steam turbine ship it would include boiler, steam turbine, gearing and auxiliaries. The total electrical generating capacity of the ship would also be divided amongst the various units (Fig. 5.17). A ship designed for about 30 knots on two units could attain more than 25 knots on one unit. Thus, keeping one unit available after damage, affords considerable mobility to the ship. A ship unable to move would be a sitting duck for further attack. This may be demonstrated by an example.

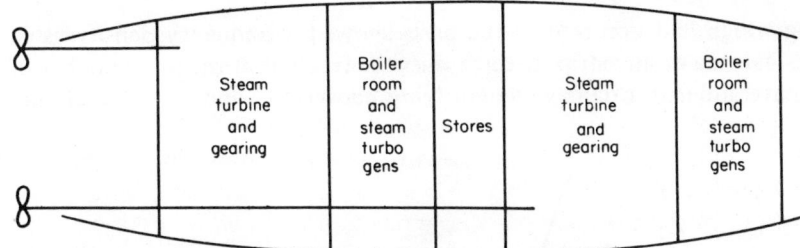

Fig. 5.17 Unitized machinery

EXAMPLE 2. A ship 200 m in length has two machinery units, each 25 m in length, separated by a length of 15 m. The distance of the propellers aft of the aftermost unit is 20 m. Calculate the probability of losing 100 and 50 per cent of the propulsive power using the following assumptions:

(a) power on a given shaft is lost if its associated machinery unit is flooded;
(b) a hit in way of a shaft damages the shaft on that side of the ship;
(c) the starboard shaft is longer;
(d) the damage front of the weapon, i.e. the distance over which the outer bottom is violated, is 20 m;
(e) the weapon is equally likely to strike anywhere along the length of the ship.

Solution: A weapon hit on either side of the ship will cause flooding of the forward unit if it strikes between points A and B in Fig. 5.18. The starboard shaft is damaged by any one hit on the starboard side between C and D.

Fig. 5.18

For a starboard side hit between Q and S, all power is out of action while a hit between P and Q or S and U destroys 50%. Thus

$$\text{Probablity of losing all power} = \frac{45}{200} = 0.225.$$

$$\text{Probablity of losing at least half power} = \frac{95}{200} = 0.475.$$

Similarly for a port side hit:

$$\text{Probablity of losing all power} = \frac{RS}{200} = 0.025$$

Vulnerability

The statistics of ship casualties over many years enables us to depict the frequency of events which has occurred in the past and to use that pattern to predict the likelihood of a particular event in the future. For example, it would not be surprising to discover that all of the lengths of damage due to collision and grounding which had occurred in the past, showed a frequency density as in Fig. 5.19. The area of any strip δx represents the fraction of the total number of ships to have suffered a damage length lying between x_1 and $x_1 + \delta x$ of ship length.

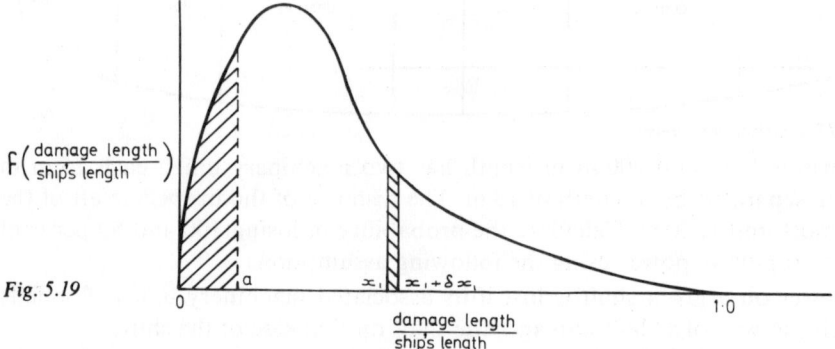

Fig. 5.19

This information could be used to predict that the probability of a damage length equal to a fraction a of ship length or less occurring to any ship in the future is given by the area shaded up to a. This is the basis for a new approach to ship vulnerability promulgated for merchant ships by IMCO in 1973. The probability of two or more independent events is found by multiplying together their separate probabilities. Thus, the probability that a ship in collision will suffer a damage length l and a penetration from the side d and at the same time be in a condition with a permeability μ is given by

$$p(l) \times p(d) \times p(\mu)$$

Moreover, this must be compounded with the probability of collision at a certain position along the length of the ship. Probability of collision or grounding occurring at all is clearly dependent upon the routeing of the ship which is affected by the weather, sea state and traffic density met; it will be high in the English Channel or St Lawrence and low in the Indian Ocean. It must also depend upon the number and competence of the crew.

The effects upon the ship of a stated set of damage can be found in terms of trim, flotation and stability for which permissible values have already been declared. Thus, the vulnerability of the ship—that is to say the likelihood of unacceptable damage occurring—can be determined from the architecture of the ship and the probability density functions for: position of damage; length of damage; penetration of damage; permeability at the time of damage; occurrence of an incident; crew competence.

'Standard' shapes for the first four of these have been proposed by IMCO who have also described how they should be applied. There are so many variables that computer programs have been written for the calculation. Similar standard functions have been in use by various navy departments for some while to determine the vulnerabilities of warships which are subjected to weapons with different homing devices and explosive content.

It is not easy, once it is acknowledged that nothing is absolutely safe or absolutely reliable, to declare a probability of catastrophe which, however tiny, is nevertheless acceptable. Actuaries have had to make such judgments for many years of course in settling the levels of premium for insurance involving human life. Such a cold declaration in monetary terms does not commend itself to the public, whose outrage at a particular catastrophe may be whipped up by the press. Nevertheless, a standard of acceptable probability must be declared and this will fall to national authorities and insurers, generally on the basis of what has been found acceptable in the past.

Environmental Pollution

Besides ensuring that the ship can meet the hazards imposed on it by the environment, it is important to ensure that the ship itself does not hazard the environment. As a result of the work of IMCO, stringent requirements are laid down to restrict or totally prevent pollution in certain areas of sea particularly those close to land and in land-locked seas such as the Mediterranean. These deal with oil, sewage, food disposal and packaging materials. Ships must either store waste products or process them on board. Sewage treatment plants can be fitted to turn raw sewage into an inoffensive effluent that can be pumped overboard; incinerators can burn many packaging materials; crushers can compact waste so that it can be stored more conveniently.

Problems

1. A water lighter is in the form of a rectangular barge, 42·7 m long by 5·5 m beam, floating at an even draught of 2·44 m in sea water. Its centre of gravity is 1·83 m above the keel. What will be the new draughts at the four corners if 20 m^3 of fresh water are pumped out from an amidships tank whose centre of volume is 0·3 m from the port side and 0·91 m above the keel? Ignore free surface effects.

2. A box-form vessel, 150 ft long, 50 ft wide and 20 ft deep floats on an even keel with a draught of 6 ft in salt water. A transverse watertight bulkhead is fitted 25 ft from the forward end. If the compartment thus formed is open to the sea, estimate the new draughts forward and aft to the nearest inch.

3. A methane carrier, displacing 6000 m^3 floats at draughts of 5·1 m forward and 5·8 m aft, measured at marks which are 80·5 m forward and 67·5 m aft amidships. The vessel grounds, on a falling tide, on a rock at a position 28 m forward of amidships. Calculate the force on the ship's bottom and the new draughts after the tide has fallen 25 cm.

The rock then ruptures the bottom and opens to the sea, a compartment between two transverse bulkheads 14·5 m and 28·5 m forward of amidships and between two longitudinal bulkheads 5·2 m each side of the centre line. Estimate the draughts of the ship when the tide has risen to float the ship free.

The hydrostatic curves show for about these draughts:
WP area = 1850 m²   Length BP = 166 m
CF abaft amidships = 6 m
$\overline{GM_L}$ = 550 m

4. A catamaran is made up of two hulls, each 80 m long and with centres 30 m apart. The constant cross-section of each hull has the form of an equilateral triangle, each side being of 10 m length. The draught of the craft is 4 m and its $\overline{KG}$ is 10 m.

172 Basic ship theory

Calculate the heeling couple and the angle of heel necessary to bring one hull just clear of the water, assuming that the broadside wind force does not effectively increase the displacement.

Each of the hulls has main bulkheads 10 m each side of amidships. If these central compartments were both open to the sea, calculate the virtual $\overline{GM}$ of the craft in the bilged condition, comparing the added weight and lost buoyancy methods.
(HMDTC)

5. A ship displacing 2200 tonf and 360 ft in length has grounded on a rock at a point 110 ft forward of amidships. At low water the draughts forward and aft are 8·92 and 13·24 ft respectively. Given the following hydrostatic particulars of the ship in level trim and taking the $\overline{KG}$ as 16·53 ft, calculate; (i) the force on the rock at low tide; (ii) the virtual $\overline{GM}$ at low tide; (iii) the rise in tide necessary to refloat the ship.

Mean draught (ft)	Displacement (tonf)	LCB (ft aft)	VCB (ft)	LCF (ft aft)	$\overline{BM}_L$ (ft)	$\overline{BM}_T$ (ft)
12·0	2220	7·62	7·42	22·88	943	12·16
11·0	1939	5·64	6·83	20·76	1026	13·57

6. A ship, for which the hydrostatic particulars of the preceding question apply at level trim, has a length of 360 ft and displaces 2035 tonf at level trim and with a $\overline{KG}$ of 16·67 ft. A collision causes uncontrollable flooding of the auxiliary machinery space. Calculate (a) the final draughts at the forward and aft perpendiculars; (b) the virtual $\overline{GM}$ in the bilged condition. Particulars of the flooded compartment are as follows: after bulkhead, 20 ft forward of amidships, length of compartment, 20 ft, beam above 10 ft waterline assumed constant at 38 ft, area of section assumed constant at 320 ft² up to 10 ft waterline, centroid of section above keel, 6·6 ft. Hydrostatic data may be linearly extrapolated when required.
(HMDTC)

7. A rectangular pontoon, 300 ft × 12 ft × 4 ft draught, is divided by a longitudinal bulkhead at the middle line and by four equally spaced transverse bulkheads. The metacentric height is 2 ft. Find the draughts at the four corners when one corner compartment is bilged. Ignore rotation of the principal axes of the waterplane.
(AP & S)

8. A box-shaped vessel 100 m long and 20 m broad, floats at a draught of 6 m forward and 10 m aft, the metacentric height being 2·25 m. Find the virtual metacentric height when the keel just touches level blocks throughout its length.
(AP & S)

9. A vessel of box form, 150 ft long and 25 ft broad, floats at an even draught of 8 ft, and has a watertight deck 8½ ft above the keel. If a central compartment, 30 ft long, bounded by two transverse bulkheads extending up to the deck, is bilged, what will be (a) the new draught of the vessel, (b) the alteration in metacentric height if the water admitted is regarded as lost buoyancy (AP & S)

10. A ship 120 m long and floating at a level draught of 4·0 m has a displacement vol = 3140 m³. Its centre of gravity is 5·1 m above the keel and, at the 4 m waterline, the TPM = 1200, MCT = 8000 tonnef m/m, $\overline{KB}$ = 2·2 m and the centre of flotation is 5·1 m abaft amidships.

After striking a rock at a point 2 m abaft the fore perpendicular, the foremost 7 m are flooded up to the waterline. The displacement lost up to the 4 m waterline is 40 m³ with its centre of buoyancy, 4·5 m abaft the FP and 2 m above the keel. Twenty square metres of waterplane are lost, with the centroid 4·5 m abaft the FP

Making reasonable assumptions, estimate: (*a*) the force on the rock immediately after the accident; (*b*) the force on the rock when the tide has fallen 30 cm; (*c*) the rise of tide necessary to lift the bow just clear of the rock. rock. (RNC)

11. The following particulars refer to a 30,000 tonf aircraft carrier:

length, 700 ft $\overline{KB}$, 16 ft
beam, 90 ft $\overline{KG}$, 30 ft
draught, 28 ft TPI, 100
$\overline{GM}_T$, 6 ft

The design is modified by increasing all athwartships dimensions by 3 per cent, and all longitudinal dimensions by 2 per cent. The weight of the flight deck armour is adjusted to limit the increase in displacement to 900 tonf. It should be assumed that the height of the flight deck above keel remains constant at 70 ft and that the weight of the ship varies directly as the length and beam.

In compiling the flooding board for the ship, a compartment 60 ft long by 20 ft wide is assumed flooded, and open to the sea. If the compartment extends the full depth of the ship, with its centre 40 ft to starboard of the middle line, estimate the resulting angle of heel. The effects of changing trim should be ignored. (RNC)

12. A vessel of length 120 m between perpendiculars floats at a uniform draught of 5·0 m with the following particulars:

Displacement, 3000 tonnef
WP area, 1300 m²
CF abaft amidships, 3 m
CB above keel, 2·70 m
CG above keel, 4·52 m
Transverse metacentre above keel, 6·62 m
MCT BP, 7300 tonnef m/m

It may be assumed to be wall-sided in the region of the waterplane.

The vessel is involved in an accident in which 60 tonnef outer bottom (with centre of gravity at keel level and 3·2 m from the middle line) are torn away and a compartment 3·1 m wide and 7·9 m long is opened to the sea.

Estimate the resulting angle of heel, assuming that the compartment extends from keel level to above the new waterplane and neglecting any change of trim. The centroids of volume and plan area of the flooded compartment are 3·0 m from the middle line.

13. A ship 120 m BP for which hydrostatic and other data are given in question 12, floats at a uniform draught of 5·0 m.

The vessel grounds on a rock at keel level, 20 m forward of amidships and 3·0 m from the middle line. Making reasonable assumptions, calculate the force on the rock and the angle of heel when the tide has fallen 15 cm. (RNC)

14. A rectangular pontoon 12 ft deep, 36 ft wide and 105 ft long is divided into

174 *Basic ship theory*

three equal sections by two transverse bulkheads. The centre compartment is further subdivided into three equal compartments by two longitudinal bulkheads. All compartments extend the full depth of the pontoon. The centre of gravity is 6 ft above the keel.

The pontoon is damaged in such a way that the three central compartments are open to the sea at keel level. Of the three compartments, the centre one is vented at deck level and the wing compartments are airtight above keel level. The draught after damage is 7·18 ft and the depth of water in the wing tanks is 1·71 ft. The position of the centre of gravity of the pontoon may be assumed unaffected.

Calculate the virtual metacentric height in the damaged condition, assuming that the height of the sea water barometer is 33 ft. (RNC)

15. A ship floating at a draught of 2 m has a hole of area 0·3 m² in the bottom at the keel, giving access to a rectangular compartment right across the ship. The compartment is 10 m long and has an even permeability of 0·80 throughout. This ship has initially WP area = 300 m². Its length is 70 m, beam 8 m and it does not trim due to the damage. Calculate how long it will be before the maximum flooded draught occurs.

16. Calculate the probability of losing half and total power of worked example 1, assuming that there was no 15 m separation of the machinery units.

References

1. Beer, W. J. Analysis of world shipping losses, *TRINA*, 1969.
2. *Merchant Shipping (Passenger Ship Construction) Rules*, HMSO, 1965.
3. SOLAS 1960, published for IMCO by HMSO.
4. Sarchin, T. H. and Goldberg, L. L. Stability and buoyancy criteria for US naval surface ships, *TSNAME*, 1962.
5. *Instructions to surveyors for the survey of passenger ships*. Vols. I and II, Dept. of Trade, HMSO.
6. *Merchant Shipping (Loadline) Rules*, HMSO, 1968.
7. *Merchant Shipping (Fire Appliances) Rules*, HMSO, 1965.
8. Symposium on fire in ships, *TINA*, 1957.
9. Nash, P. and Ashton, L. A. Research in fire-fighting and protection in ships, *TRINA*, 1965.
10. *Merchant Shipping (Life Saving Appliances) Rules*, HMSO, 1965.
11. Dove, H. L. and Ferris, G. S. Development of anchors, *TRINA*, 1960.
12. Buckle, A. K. Anchoring and mooring equipment on ships, *TRINA*, 1974.
13. Tope, J. E. Carriage of bulk grain without temporary fittings, *TRINA*, 1971.
14. *Merchant Shipping (Grain) Rules*, HMSO, 1965.
15. *Merchant Shipping (Dangerous Goods) Rules*, HMSO, 1965.
16. Murray Smith, D. R., Whiteside, H. N. E. and Manson, A. C. Safety aspects of nuclear propulsion of merchant ships, *TRINA*, 1961.
17. Wishart, P. B. *The merits of shock testing with particular reference to shock in ships*, Society of Environmental Engineers, 1966.
18. *The carriage of dangerous goods and explosives in ships* (The Blue Book), HMSO, 1968.
19. Aguirre, J. E. and Boyce, T. R. Estimation of wind forces on offshore drilling platforms, *TRINA* 1974.
20. Chemical data guide for bulk shipping by water, US Coastguards, 1969.
21. Lee, E. C. B. and Lee, K. *Safety and survival at sea*, Cassell, 1971.
22. Symposium on marine pollution, *RINA*, 1973.
23. Clarke, D. and Wellman, F. Stopping of large tankers and the feasibility of using auxiliary braking devices, *TRINA*, 1971.

6 The ship girder

Few who have been to sea in rough weather can doubt that the structure of a ship is subject to strain. Water surges and crashes against the vessel which responds with groans and shudders and creaks; the bow is one moment surging skywards, the next buried beneath green seas; the fat middle of the ship is one moment comfortably supported by a wave and the next moment abandoned to a hollow. The whole constitutes probably the most formidable and complex of all structural engineering problems in both the following aspects:

(a) the determination of the loading
(b) the response of the structure.

As with most complex problems, it is necessary to reduce it to a series of unit problems which can be dealt with individually and superimposed. The smallest units of structure which have to be considered are the panels of plating and single stiffeners which are supported at their extremities by items which are very stiff in comparison; they are subject to normal and edge loads under the action of which their dishing, bowing and buckling behaviour relative to the supports may be assessed. Many of these small units together constitute large flat or curved surfaces of plating and sets of stiffeners called grillages, supported at their edges by bulkheads or deck edges which are very stiff in comparison; they are subject to normal and edge loading and their dishing and buckling behaviour as a unit relative to their supports may be assessed. Finally, many bulkheads, grillages and decks, together constitute a complete hollow box whose behaviour as a box girder may be assessed. It is to this last unit, the whole ship girder, that this chapter is confined, leaving the smaller units for later consideration.

Excluding inertia loads due to ship motion, the loading on a ship derives from only two sources, gravity and water pressure. It is impossible to conceive a state of the sea whereby the loads due to gravity and water pressure exactly cancel out along the ship's length. Even in still water, this is exceedingly unlikely

Fig. 6.1

176 Basic ship theory

but in a seaway where the loading is changing continuously, it is inconceivable. There is therefore an uneven loading along the ship and, because it is an elastic structure, it bends. It bends as a whole unit, like a girder on an elastic foundation and is called the *ship girder*. The ship will be examined as a floating beam subject to the laws deduced in other textbooks for the behaviour of beams.

In still water, the loading due to gravity and water pressure are, of course, weight and buoyancy. The distribution of buoyancy along the length follows the curve of areas while the weight is conveniently assessed in unit lengths and might, typically, result in the block diagram of Fig. 6.2. (Clearly, the areas representing total weight and total buoyancy must be equal.) This figure

Fig. 6.2 Still water hogging

would give the resultants dotted which would make the ship bend concave downwards or *hog*. The reverse condition is known as *sagging*. Because it is not difficult to make some of the longer cargo ships break their backs when badly loaded, consideration of the still water hogging or sagging is vital in assessing a suitable cargo disposition. It is the first mate's yardstick of structural strength.

It is not difficult to imagine that the hog or sag of a ship could be much increased by waves. A long wave with a crest amidships would increase the upward force there at the expense of the ends and the hogging of the ship would be increased. If there were a hollow amidships and crests towards the ends sagging would be increased (Fig. 6.3). The loads to which the complete hull girder is subject are, in fact:

(*a*) those due to the differing longitudinal distribution of the downward forces of weight and the upward forces of buoyancy, the ship considered at rest in still water;

Fig. 6.3 Sagging on a wave

(b) the additional loads due to the passage of a train of waves, the ship remaining at rest;
(c) loads due to the superposition on the train of waves of the waves caused by the motion of the ship itself through still water;
(d) the variations of the weight distribution due to the accelerations caused by ship motion.

Consideration of the worst likely loading effected by (a) and (b) is the basis of the standard calculation, performed as a means of comparing the structural strengths of different ships. The effects of (c) and (d) are smaller and are not usually taken into account except partly by the statistical approach to the problem, outlined later.

The standard calculation

It is supposed that the ship never meets a sea which imposes more severe bending on the ship than that caused by a single wave of length equal to the ship's length with

(a) a crest amidships and a hollow at each end causing maximum hogging, and
(b) a hollow amidships and a crest at each end causing maximum sagging.

The ship is assumed to be momentarily still, balanced on the wave with zero velocity and acceleration and the response of the sea is assumed to be that appropriate to static water. In this condition, the curves of weight and buoyancy are deduced. Subtracted one from the other, the curves give a curve of net loading p'. Now, a fundamental relationship at a point in an elastic beam is

$$p' = \frac{dS}{dx} = \frac{d^2M}{dx^2}$$

where p' is the load per unit length, S is the shearing force, M is the bending moment, and x defines the position along the beam.

$$\therefore \quad S = \int p' \, dx \quad \text{and} \quad M = \int S \, dx$$

Fig. 6.4 Loading curve, p'

Thus, the curve of loading p' must be integrated along its length to give a curve of shearing force and the curve of shearing force must be integrated along its length to give the bending moment curve. From the maximum bending moment, a figure of stress can be obtained,

$$\text{stress } \sigma = \frac{M}{I} y$$

I/y being the modulus of the effective structural section.

A closer look at each of the constituents of this brief summary is now needed.

Fig. 6.5 Simplified structural section

THE WAVE

Whole books have been written about ocean waves. Nevertheless, there is no universally accepted standard ocean wave which may be assumed for the standard longitudinal strength calculation. While the shape is agreed to be trochoidal, the observed ratios of length to height are so scattered that many 'standard' lines can be drawn through them. Fortunately, this is not of primary importance; while the calculation is to be regarded as comparative, provided that the same type of wave is assumed throughout for design and type ships, the comparison is valid.

A trochoid is a curve produced by a point at radius r within a circle of radius R rolling on a flat base. The equation to a trochoid with respect to the axes shown in Fig. 6.6, is

$$x = R\theta - r \sin \theta$$
$$z = r(1 - \cos \theta)$$

Fig. 6.6 *Construction of a trochoid*

One accepted standard wave is that having a height from trough to crest of one twentieth of its length from crest to crest. In this case, $L = 2\pi R$ and $r = h/2 = L/40$ and the equation to the wave is

$$x = \frac{L}{2\pi}\theta - \frac{L}{40}\sin \theta$$

$$z = \frac{L}{40}(1 - \cos \theta)$$

The co-ordinates of this wave at equal intervals of x are:

$\dfrac{x}{L/20}$	0	1	2	3	4	5	6	7	8	9	10
$\dfrac{z}{L/20}$	0	0·034	0·128	0·266	0·421	0·577	0·720	0·839	0·927	0·982	1·0

Research has shown that the $L/20$ wave is somewhat optimistic for wavelengths from 300 ft up to about 500 ft in length. Above 500 ft, the $L/20$ wave becomes progressively more unsatisfactory and at 1000 ft is probably so exaggerated in height that it is no longer a satisfactory criterion of comparison. This has resulted in the adoption of a trochoidal wave of height $1.1\sqrt{L}$ as a standard wave in the comparative longitudinal strength calculation. This wave has the equation

$$x = \frac{L}{2\pi}\theta - \frac{1.1\sqrt{L}}{2}\sin \theta \qquad x, z \text{ and } L \text{ in feet}$$

$$z = \frac{1.1\sqrt{L}}{2}(1 - \cos \theta)$$

180 Basic ship theory

The $1{\cdot}1\sqrt{L}$ wave has the slight disadvantage that it is not non-dimensional, and units must be checked with care when using this wave and the formulae derived from it. Co-ordinates for plotting are conveniently calculated from the equations above for equal intervals of θ. In metric units $1{\cdot}1\sqrt{L} = 0{\cdot}607\sqrt{L}$.

The length of the wave is, strictly, taken to be the length of the ship on the load waterline; in practice, because data is more readily available for the displacement stations, the length is often taken between perpendiculars (if this is different) without making an appreciable difference to the bending moment. Waves of length slightly greater than the ship's length can, in fact, produce theoretical bending moments slightly in excess of those for waves equal to the ship's length, but this is not an important factor while the calculation continues to be comparative.

WEIGHT DISTRIBUTION

Consumable weights are assumed removed from those parts of the ship where this aggravates the particular condition under investigation; in the sagging condition, they are removed from positions near the ends and, in the hogging condition, they are removed amidships. The *influence lines* of a similar design should be consulted before deciding where weights should be removed, and the decision should be verified when the influence lines for the design have been calculated (see p. 192), provided that the weights are small enough.

The longitudinal distribution of the weight is assessed by dividing the ship into a large number of intervals. Twenty displacement intervals are usually adequate. The weight falling within each interval is assessed for each item or group in the schedule of weights and tabulated. Totals for each interval divided by the length give mean weights per unit length. It is important that the centre of gravity of the ship divided up in this way should be in the correct position. To ensure this, the centre of gravity of each individual item should be checked after it has been distributed.

One of the major items of weight requiring distribution is the hull itself, and this will sometimes be required before detailed structural design of the hull has been completed. A useful first approximation to the hull weight distribution is obtained by assuming that two-thirds of its weight follows the still water buoyancy curve and the remaining one-third is distributed in the form of a trapezium, so arranged, that the centre of gravity of the whole hull is in its correct position (Fig. 6.7).

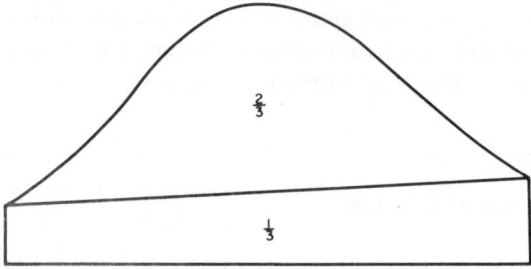

Fig. 6.7 *Approximate hull weight distribution*

Having obtained the mean weight per foot for each interval, this is plotted as the mid-ordinate of the interval and a straight line is drawn through it, parallel to the chord of the buoyancy curve. This is a device for simplifying later stages of the calculation which introduces usually insignificant inaccuracies. A sawtooth distribution of weight per unit length, as shown in Fig. 6.3, results.

BUOYANCY AND BALANCE

The wave is drawn on tracing paper and placed over the contracted profile of the ship on which the Bonjean curve has been drawn at each ordinate. Figure 6.8 shows one such ordinate. It is necessary for equilibrium to place the wave at a draught and trim such that

(a) the displacement equals the weight and
(b) the centre of buoyancy lies in the same vertical plane as the centre of gravity.

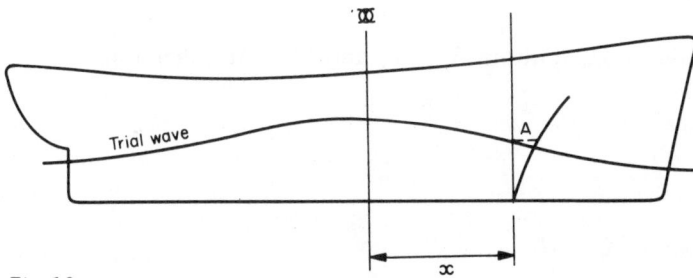

Fig. 6.8

Simple hydrostatic pressure is assumed; the areas immersed at each ordinate can be read from the Bonjean curves where the wave profile cuts the ordinate, and these areas are subjected to normal approximate integration to give displacement and LCB position. The position of the wave to meet the two conditions can be found by trial and error. It is usual to begin at a draught to the midships point of the trochoid about 85 per cent of still water draught for the hogging condition and 120 per cent for the sagging wave. A more positive way of achieving balance involves calculating certain new tools (Ref. 1). Consider a typical transverse section of the ship, x m forward of amidships, at which the Bonjean curve shows the area immersed by the first trial wave surface to be A m².

If ∇ m³ and M m⁴ are the volume of displacement and the moment of this volume before amidships for the trial wave surface, then, over the immersed length,

$$\nabla = \int A \, dx \quad \text{and} \quad M = \int Ax \, dx$$

Suppose that ∇_0 m³ and M_0 m⁴ are the volume of displacement and moment figures for equilibrium in still water and that ∇ is less than ∇_0 and M is less than M_0. The adjustment to be made to the trial wave waterline is therefore a parallel sinkage and a trim by the bow in order to make $\nabla = \nabla_0$ and $M = M_0$.

Let this parallel sinkage at amidships be z_0 and the change of trim be m radians, then the increased immersion at the typical section is

$$z = (z_0 + mx) \text{ m}$$

Let the slope of the Bonjean curve be $s = dA/dz$ m. Assuming that the Bonjean curve is straight over this distance, then

$$A + zs = A + (z_0 + mx)s \text{ m}^2$$

Fig. 6.9

In order to satisfy the two conditions, $\nabla = \nabla_0$ and $M = M_0$, therefore,

$$\int [A + (z_0 + mx)s] \, dx = \nabla_0$$

and

$$\int [A + (z_0 + mx)s]x \, dx = M_0$$

Now put

$$\int s \, dx = \delta\nabla \text{ m}^2$$

$$\int sx \, dx = \delta M \text{ m}^3$$

$$\int sx^2 \, dx = \delta I \text{ m}^4$$

Then

$$z_0 \cdot \delta\nabla + m\delta M = \nabla_0 - \nabla$$

and

$$z_0 \cdot \delta M + m\delta I = M_0 - M$$

$\delta\nabla$, δM and δI can all be calculated by approximate integration from measurement of the Bonjean curves. From the pair of simultaneous equations above the required sinkage z_0 and trim m can be calculated. A check that this wave position in fact gives the required equilibrium should now be made. If the trial waterplane was a poor choice, the process may have to be repeated. Negative values of z_0 and m, mean that a parallel rise and a trim by the stern are required.

The ship girder

Having achieved a balance, the curve of buoyancy per metre can be drawn as a smooth curve. It will have the form shown in Fig. 6.2 for the hogging calculation and that of Fig. 6.3 for the sagging condition.

LOADING, SHEARING FORCE AND BENDING MOMENT

Because the weight curve has been drawn parallel to the buoyancy curve, the difference between the two, which represents the net loading p' for each interval, will comprise a series of rectangular blocks. Using now the relationship $S = \int p' \, dx$, the loading curve is integrated to obtain the distribution of shearing force along the length of the ship. The integration is a simple cumulative addition starting from one end and the shearing force at the finishing end should, of course, be zero; in practice, due to the small inaccuracies of the preceding steps, it will probably have a small value. This is usually corrected by canting the base line, i.e. applying a correction at each section in proportion to its distance from the starting point.

The curve of shearing force obtained is a series of straight lines. This curve is now integrated in accordance with the relationship $M = \int S \, dx$ to obtain the distribution of bending moment M. Integration is again a cumulative addition of the areas of each trapezium and the inevitable final error, which should be small, is distributed in the same way as is the shearing force error. If the error is large, the calculations must be repeated using smaller intervals for the weight distribution.

The integrations are performed in a methodical, tabular fashion as shown in the example below. In plotting the curves, there are several important features which arise from the expression

$$p' = \frac{dS}{dx} = \frac{d^2 M}{dx^2}$$

which will assist and act as checks. These are

(a) when p' is zero, S is a maximum or a minimum and a point of inflexion occurs in the M curve,
(b) when p' is a maximum, a point of inflexion occurs in the S curve,
(c) when S is zero, M is a maximum or minimum.

A typical set of curves is shown in Fig. 6.10.

EXAMPLE 1. The mean immersed cross-sectional areas between ordinates of a ship, 300 m in length, balanced on a hogging wave, as read from the Bonjean curves are given below, together with the mass distribution. The second moment of area of the midship section is 752 m^4 and the neutral axis is 9·30 m from the keel and 9·70 m from the deck.

Calculate the maximum direct stresses given by the comparative calculation and the maximum shearing force.

Making the assumption that the second moment of area is constant along the length, estimate the difference in slope between ordinates number 4 and 10 and the deflection of the middle relative to the ends.

184 *Basic ship theory*

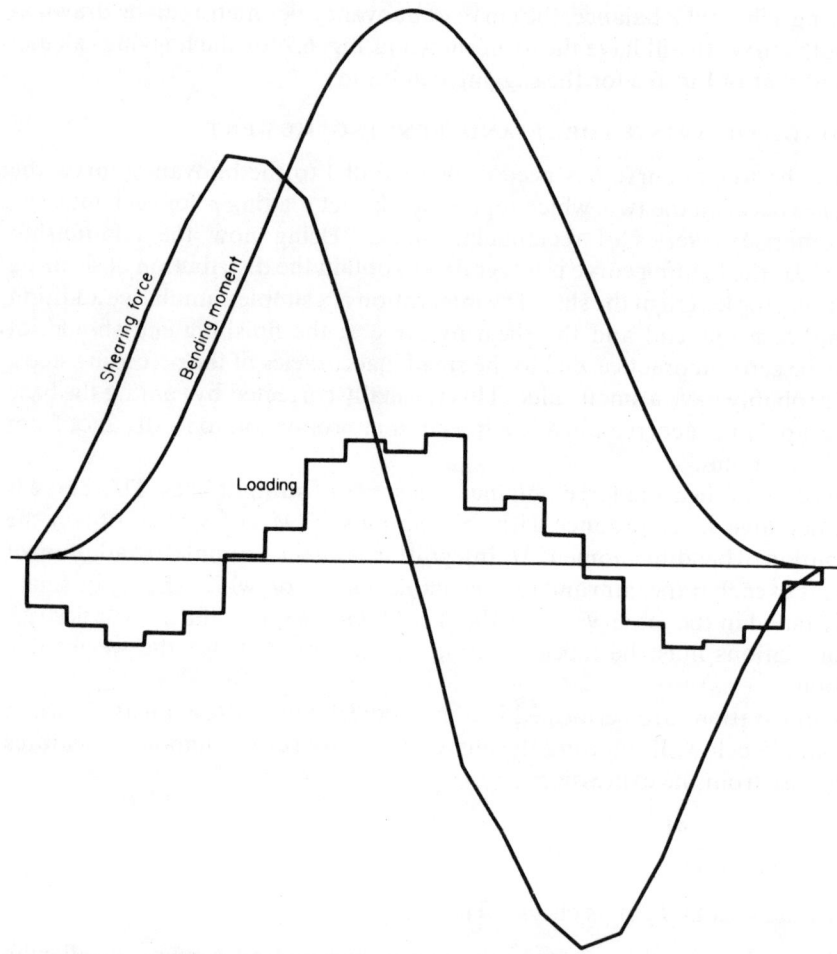

Fig. 6.10 *Typical loading, shearing force and bending moment curves*

Ordinate	11	10	9	8	7	6	5	4	3	2	1
Area A, m²		10·5	49·5	243	490	633	565	302	71	2·5	0·5
Mass M, Mg	5030	6790	10,670	9900	9370	7830	9260	6400	4920	2690	

Solution: Integrate in tabular form using trapezoidal rule

Ordinate spacing = 30 m

$$\text{Weight per metre} = \frac{M}{30}\frac{\text{Mg}}{\text{m}} \cdot \frac{9\cdot81\,\text{m}}{\text{s}^2} \cdot \frac{1000\,\text{kg}}{\text{Mg}} = 327M, \text{N/m}$$

$$\text{Buoyancy per metre} = A\,\text{m}^3 \cdot \frac{1\cdot026\,\text{Mg}}{\text{m}^3} \cdot \frac{9\cdot81\,\text{m}}{\text{s}^2} \cdot \frac{1000\,\text{kg}}{\text{Mg}} = 10{,}060A, \text{N/m}$$

The ship girder 185

a Ord.	b wt./m 327M $\frac{10^6}{(MN)}$	c buoy./m 10,060A $\frac{10^6}{(MN)}$	d load/m b−c (MN)	e δSF 30d (MN)	f SF Σe (MN)	g mid SF (MN)	h δBM 30g (MN m)	i BM Σh (MN m)	j corrn.	k BM (MN m)
1					0			0		0
	0·880	0·005	0·875	26·25		13·13	394			
2					26·25			394	−4	390
	1·609	0·025	1·584	47·52		50·01	1500			
3					73·77			1894	−8	1886
	2·093	0·714	1·379	41·37		94·46	2834			
4					115·14			4728	−12	4716
	3·028	3·038	−0·010	−0·30		114·99	3450			
5					114·84			8178	−16	8162
	2·560	5·684	−3·124	−93·72		67·98	2039			
6					21·12			10,217	−20	10,197
	3·064	6·368	−3·304	−99·12		−28·44	−853			
7					−78·00			9364	−24	9340
	3·237	4·929	−1·692	−50·76		−103·38	−3101			
8					−128·76			6263	−28	6235
	3·489	2·445	1·044	31·32		−113·10	−3393			
9					−97·44			2870	−32	2838
	2·220	0·498	1·722	51·66		−71·61	−2148			
10					−45·78			722	−36	686
	1·645	0·106	1·539	46·17		−22·70	−681			
11					0·39			41	−40	1

Maximum shearing force = 128·76 MN
Maximum bending moment = 10,220 MN m (by plotting column k)

$$\text{Keel stress} = \frac{10{,}220 \text{ MN m}}{752 \text{ m}^4} \times 9.3 \text{ m} = 126.5 \text{ MN/m}^2 \ (8.2 \text{ tonf/in}^2)$$

$$\text{Deck stress} = \frac{10{,}220}{752} \times 9.7 = 132 \text{ MN/m}^2 \ (8.6 \text{ tonf/in}^2)$$

$$\text{Slope} = \frac{1}{EI}\int M \, dx = \frac{dy}{dx} = \frac{10^{-6}}{0.208 \times 752} \int M \, dx \quad \text{and} \quad y = \int \frac{dy}{dx} \cdot dx$$

Columns e and h are not strictly necessary to this table since the multiplier 30 could have been applied at the end; they have been included merely to give the student an idea of the values expressed in meganewtons.

a Ord	b BM (MN m)	c mid BM	d Σc (MN m²)	e mid d	f Σe	g y = 5·75f (×10⁻⁶)	h chord	i h−g
1	0		0		0	0	0	
		195		98				
2	390		195		98			
		1138		764				
3	1886		1333		862			
		3301		2984				
4	4716		4634		3846			
		6439		7854				
5	8162		11,073		11,700	0·066	0·484	0·418
		9180		15,663				
6	10,197		20,253		27,363	0·154	0·605	0·451
		9769		25,138				

(continued on p. 186)

(continued from p. 185)

a Ord	b BM (MN m)	c mid BM	d Σc (MN m^2)	e mid d	f Σe	g $y = 5{\cdot}75f$ ($\times 10^{-6}$)	h chord	i h−g
7	9340		30,022		52,501	0·296	0·726	0·430
		7788		33,916				
8	6235		37,810		86,417			
		4537		40,079				
9	2838		42,347		126,496			
		1762		43,228				
10	686		44,109		169,724			
		343		44,280				
11	1		44,452		214,004	1·209	1·209	

$$\text{Difference in slope 4–10 Ords.} = \frac{10^{-6}}{0{\cdot}208 \times 752}(44{,}109 - 4634) \times 30 = 0{\cdot}0076 \text{ radians}$$

$$= 0{\cdot}0076 \times \frac{180}{\pi} \times 60 = 26 \text{ minutes of arc}$$

$$\text{Deflection } y = \frac{30 \times 30 \times 10^{-6}}{0{\cdot}208 \times 752}f = 5{\cdot}75f \times 10^{-6}$$

Central deflection = 0·451 m

Column h is necessary because, as shown in Fig. 6.11 by integrating from no. 1 ord., zero slope has been assumed there; to obtain deflection relative to the ends, the chord deflection must be subtracted.

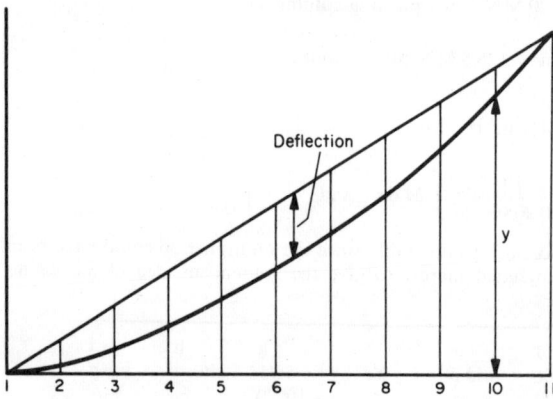

Fig. 6.11

SECOND MOMENT OF AREA

It is now necessary to calculate the second moment of area, I, of the section of the ship girder. For a simple girder this is a straightforward matter. For a ship girder composed of plates and sections which may not extend far longitudinally or which might buckle under compressive load or which may be composed of differing materials, a certain amount of adjustment may be judged necessary. Unless there is some good reason to the contrary (such as inadequate jointing in a wood sheathed or armoured deck), it is assumed here that local structural design has been sufficient to prevent buckling or tripping or other forms of load shirking. In fact, load shirking by panels having a width/thickness ratio in excess of seventy is likely and plating contribution should be limited to seventy times the thickness (see Chapter 7). No material is assumed to contribute to the section modulus unless it is structurally continuous for at least half the length of the ship amidships. Differing materials are allowed for in the manner described later. It is of interest that the Minoans, perhaps in 2500 B.C. the first designers of ships that ventured out of sight of land, also had doubts about what material contributed to longitudinal strength. They assisted the section modulus by ropes wound longitudinally over the deck and under the keel.

Having decided which material to include, the section modulus is calculated in a methodical, tabular form. An *assumed neutral axis* (ANA) is first taken near the mid-depth. Positions and dimensions of each item forming the structural mid-section are then measured and inserted into a table of the following type:

Table 6.1
Modulus calculation

1	2	3	4	5	6	7
Item	A (in^2 or cm^2)	h (ft or m)	Ah (in^2 ft or cm^2 m)	Ah^2 (in^2 ft^2 or cm^2 m^2)	k^2 (ft^2 or m^2)	Ak^2 (in^2 ft^2 or cm^2 m^2)
Each item above ANA						
Totals above ANA ΣA_1			$\Sigma A_1 h_1$	$\Sigma A_1 h_1^2$		$\Sigma A_1 k_1^2$
Each item below ANA						
Totals below ANA ΣA_2			$\Sigma A_2 h_2$	$\Sigma A_2 h_2^2$		$\Sigma A_2 k_2^2$

where A = cross-sectional area of item, h = distance from ANA, k = radius of gyration of the structural element about its own NA.

Fig. 6.12

Subscript 1 is used to denote material above the ANA and subscript 2 for material below.

$$\text{Distance of true NA above ANA} = \frac{\Sigma A_1 h_1 - \Sigma A_2 h_2}{\Sigma A_1 + \Sigma A_2} = d$$

Second moment of area about true NA
$= \Sigma A_1 h_1^2 + \Sigma A_2 h_2^2 + \Sigma A_1 k_1^2 + \Sigma A_2 k_2^2 - (\Sigma A_1 + \Sigma A_2)d^2 = I$

Lever above true neutral axis from NA to deck at centre $= y_D$

Lever below true neutral axis from NA to keel $= y_K$

The strength section of some ships is composed of different materials, steel, light alloy, wood or plastic. How is the second moment of area calculated for these composite sections? Consider a simple beam composed of two materials, suffixes a and b. From the theory of beams, it is known that the stress is directly proportional to the distance from the neutral axis and that, if R is the radius of curvature of the neutral axis and E is the elastic modulus,

$$\text{stress } \sigma = \frac{E}{R} h$$

Fig. 6.13 Composite section

Consider the typical element of area A of Fig. 6.13. For equilibrium of the cross-section, the net force must be zero, therefore

$$\Sigma(\sigma_a A_a + \sigma_b A_b) = 0$$

$$\Sigma\left(\frac{E_a}{R} A_a h_a + \frac{E_b}{R} A_b h_b\right) = 0$$

i.e.

$$\Sigma\left(A_a h_a + \frac{E_b}{E_a} A_b h_b\right) = 0$$

Now the contribution to the bending moment by the element A is the force σA multiplied by the distance from the neutral axis, h. For the whole section,

$$M = \Sigma(\sigma_a A_a h_a + \sigma_b A_b h_b)$$

$$= \frac{E_a}{R} \Sigma\left(A_a h_a^2 + \frac{E_b}{E_a} A_b h_b^2\right)$$

$$= \frac{E_a}{R} \cdot I_{\text{eff}}.$$

where I_{eff} is the effective second moment of area.

It follows from the equations above that the composite section may be assumed composed wholly of material a, provided that an effective area of material b, $(E_b/E_a)A_b$, be used instead of its actual area. The areas of material b used in columns 2, 4, 5 and 7 of Table 6.1 must then be the actual areas multiplied by the ratio of the elastic moduli. The ratio E_b/E_a for different steels is approximately unity; for wood/steel it is about $\frac{1}{16}$ in compression and $\frac{1}{25}$ in tension. For aluminium alloy/steel it is about $\frac{1}{3}$ and for glass reinforced plastic/steel it is between $\frac{1}{15}$ and $\frac{1}{30}$. The figures vary with the precise alloys or mixtures and should be checked.

BENDING STRESSES

Each of the constituents of the equation, $\sigma = (M/I)y$, has now been calculated, maximum bending moment M, second moment of area, I, and the levers y for two separate conditions, hogging and sagging. Values of the maximum direct stress at deck and keel arising from the standard comparative longitudinal strength calculation can thus be found.

Direct stresses occurring in composite sections are, following the work of the previous section

in material a, $\quad \sigma_a = \dfrac{E_a y}{R} = \dfrac{M}{I_{\text{eff}}} y$

in material b, $\quad \sigma_b = \dfrac{E_b y}{R} = \dfrac{M y}{I_{\text{eff}}} \dfrac{E_b}{E_a}$

It is at this stage that the comparative nature of the calculation is apparent, since it is now necessary to decide whether the stresses obtained are acceptable or whether the strength section needs to be modified. It would, in fact, be rare good fortune if this was unnecessary, although it is not often that the balance has to be repeated in consequence. The judgment on the acceptable level of stress is based on a comparison with similar ships in similar service for which a similar calculation has previously been performed. This last point needs careful checking to ensure that the same wave has been used and that the same assumptions regarding inclusion of material in weight and modulus calculations are made. For example, a device was adopted many years ago to allow for the presence of rivet holes, either by decreasing the effective area of section on the tension side by $\frac{2}{11}$ or by increasing the tensile stress in the ratio $\frac{11}{9}$. Although this has long been known to be an erroneous procedure, some authorities continue to use it in order to maintain the basis for comparison.

Stresses different from those found acceptable for the type ships may be considered on the following bases:

(a) Length of ship. An increase of acceptable stress with length is customary on the grounds that standard waves at greater lengths are less likely to be met. This is more necessary with the $L/20$ wave than the $1 \cdot 1 \sqrt{L}$ wave for which the probability varies less with length. If a standard thickness is allowed for corrosion, it will constitute a smaller proportion of the modulus for larger ships.

(b) Life of ship. Corrosion allowance is an important and hidden factor. Classification societies demand extensive renewals when survey shows the plating thicknesses and modulus of section to be appreciably reduced. It could well be economical to accept low initial stresses to postpone the likely time of renewal. Comparison with type ship ought to be made before corrosion allowance is added and the latter assessed by examining modern corrosion protection.

(c) Conditions of service. Classification societies permit a reduced modulus of section for service in the Great Lakes or in coastal waters. Warship authorities must consider the likelihood of action damage by future weapons and the allowance to be made in consequence. Warships are not, of course, restricted to an owner's route.

(d) Local structural design. An improvement in the buckling behaviour or design at discontinuities may enable higher overall stress to be accepted.

(e) Material. Modern high grade steels permit higher working stresses and the classification societies encourage their use, subject to certain provisos.

(f) Progress. A designer is never satisfied; a structural design which is entirely successful suggests that it was not entirely efficient in the use of materials and he is tempted to permit higher stresses next time. Such progress must necessarily be cautiously slow.

A fuller discussion of the nature of failure and the aim of the designer of the future occurs later in the chapter. Approximate values of total stress which have been found satisfactory in the past are given below:

Ships	Wave	Design stresses Deck		Keel	
		tonf/in^2	MN/m^2	tonf/in^2	MN/m^2
100 m frigate	$L/20$	7	110	6	90
150 m destroyer	$L/20$	8	125	7	110
200 m general cargo vessel	$1\cdot1\sqrt{L}$	7	110	6	90
250 m aircraft carrier	$L/20$	9	140	8	125
300 m oil tanker	$1\cdot1\sqrt{L}$	9	140	8	125

SHEAR STRESSES

The shearing force at any position of the ship's length is that force which tends to move one part of the ship vertically relative to the adjacent portion. It tends to distort square areas of the sides into rhomboids. The force is distributed over the section, each piece of material contributing to the total. It is convenient to consider shear stress, the force divided by the area and this is divided over the cross-section of a simple beam according to the expression

$$\tau = \frac{SA\bar{y}}{Ib}$$

$A\bar{y}$ is the moment about the NA of that part of the cross-section above section PP where the shear stress τ is required. I is the second moment of area of the

Fig. 6.14 Shear loading on a ship girder

whole cross-section and b is the total width of material at section P (Fig. 6.15). The distribution of shear stress over a typical cross-section of a ship is shown in Fig. 6.14. The maximum shear stress occurs at the neutral axis at those points along the length where the shearing force is a maximum. A more accurate distribution would be given by shear flow theory applied to a hollow box girder, discussed presently.

Fig. 6.15

Acceptable values of shear stress depend on the particular type of side construction. Failure under the action of shear stress would normally comprise wrinkling of panels of plating diagonally. The stress at which this occurs depends on the panel dimensions, so while the shear stress arising from the standard longitudinal strength calculation clearly affects side plating thickness and stiffener spacings, it does not have a profound effect on the structural cross-section of the ship.

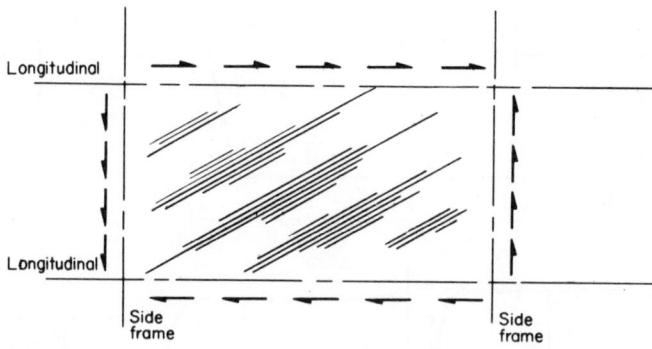

Fig. 6.16

Already, there is a tendency to assume that the stresses obtained from the standard comparative calculation actually occur in practice, so that the design of local structure may be effected using these stresses. Because local structure affected by the ship girder stresses cannot otherwise be designed, there is no choice. Strictly, this makes the local structure comparative. In fact, the stresses obtained by the comparative calculation for a given wave profile have been shown by full scale measurements to err on the safe side so that their use involves a small safety factor. Often, other local loading is more critical. This is discussed more fully under 'Criterion of failure.'

Extensions to the standard calculation

The standard calculation has been in use for many years as the yardstick of ship girder strength. Investigators continue to strive to make it entirely representative of the ship's behaviour and future trends are discussed later in the chapter under 'The nature of failure'. Before examining the philosophy, it is necessary to consider several extensions to and variations of the standard comparative approach.

INFLUENCE LINES

The ship will not often, even approximately, be in the condition assumed for the standard calculation. It is important for designers and operators to know at a glance, the effect of the addition or removal of weight on the longitudinal strength. Having completed the standard calculation, the effects of small additions of weight are plotted as influence lines in much the same way as for bridges and buildings. (See Fig. 6.17.)

An influence line shows the effect on the *maximum* bending moment of the addition of a unit weight at any position along the length. The height of the line at P represents the effect on the maximum bending moment at X of the addition of a unit weight at P. Two influence lines are normally drawn, one for the hogging and one for the sagging condition. Influence lines could, of course, be drawn to show the effect of additions on sections other than that of the maximum BM but are not generally of much interest.

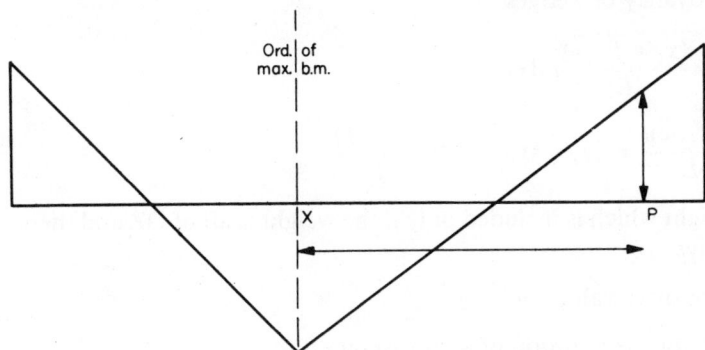

Fig. 6.17

Consider the addition of a weight P, x aft of amidships, to a ship for which the hogging calculation has been performed as shown in Fig. 6.18. It will cause a parallel sinkage s and a change of trim t over the total length L. If A and I are the area and least longitudinal second moment of area of the curved waterplane and the ship is in salt water of reciprocal weight density u, then, approximately,

$$\text{sinkage } s = \frac{uP}{A} \quad \text{and} \quad \text{trim } t = \frac{P(x-f)uL}{I}$$

Fig. 6.18

The increase in bending moment at OZ is due to the moment of added weight less the moment of buoyancy of the wedges aft of OZ less the moment of buoyancy of the parallel sinkage aft of OZ.

$$\text{Moment of buoyancy of parallel sinkage about OZ} = \frac{sM_a}{u} = \frac{PM_a}{A}$$

Moment of buoyancy of wedges

$$= \frac{1}{u}\int 2yx_1 \times \frac{(x_1 - \overline{f-e})}{L} t\, dx_1$$

$$= \frac{I_a t}{uL} - \frac{M_a(f-e)t}{uL} = \{I_a - M_a(f-e)\}\frac{P(x-f)}{I}$$

Moment of weight which is included only if the weight is aft of OZ and therefore only if positive

$$= P[x-e], \text{ positive values only.}$$

Increase in·BM for the addition of a unit weight,

$$\frac{\delta M}{P} = -\{I_a - M_a(f-e)\}\frac{(x-f)}{I} - \frac{M_a}{A} + [x-e]$$

Note that this expression is suitable for negative values of x (i.e. for P forward of amidships), provided that the expression in square brackets, [ ], is discarded if negative. A discontinuity occurs at OZ, the ordinate of maximum bending moment. The influence lines are straight lines which cut the axis at points about 0·2–0·25 of the length from amidships. It is within this length, therefore, that weights should be removed to aggravate the hogging condition and outside this length that they should be removed to aggravate the sagging condition.

Certain simplifying assumptions are sometimes made to produce a simpler form of this equation. There is little point in doing this because no less work results. However, if $(f-e)$ is assumed negligible, n put equal to I_a/I and F put equal to M_a/A

$$\frac{\delta M}{P} = -n(x-f) - F + [x-e]$$

This gives the results shown in Fig. 6.19.

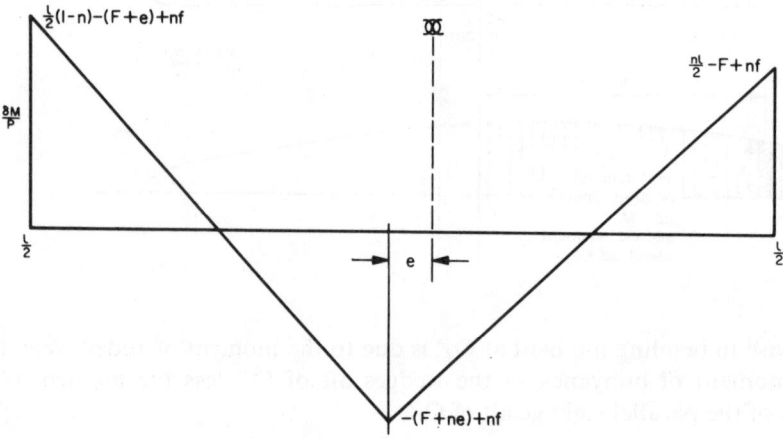

Fig. 6.19

A note of caution is necessary in the use of influence lines. They are intended for small weight changes and are quite unsuitable for large changes such as might occur with cargo, for example. In general, weight changes large enough to make a substantial change in stress are too large for the accuracy of influence lines.

CHANGES TO SECTION MODULUS

Being a trial and error process, the standard calculation will rarely yield a suitable solution first time. It will almost always be necessary to return to the structural section of the ship to add or subtract material in order to adjust the resulting stress. The effect of such an addition, on the modulus I/y, is by no means obvious. Moreover, it is not obvious in the early stages, whether the superstructure should be included in the strength section or whether the construction should be such as to discourage a contribution from the superstructure. Some measure of the effect of adding material to the strength section is needed if we are to avoid calculating a new modulus for each trial addition.

In order to provide such a measure, consider (Fig. 6.20) the addition of an area a at a height z above the neutral axis of a structural section whose second moment of area has been calculated to be Ak^2, area A, radius of gyration k and levers y_1 to the keel and y_2 to the deck. Now

$$\text{stress } \sigma = \frac{M}{I/y}$$

Fig. 6.20

For a given bending moment, stress will *not* be increased if the section modulus I/y is not reduced
i.e. if

$$\frac{I+\delta I}{y+\delta y} - \frac{I}{y} > 0$$

$$Iy + y\,\delta I - Iy - I\,\delta y > 0$$

i.e. if

$$\frac{\delta I}{I} > \frac{\delta y}{y}$$

With the addition of the area a, the rise of the neutral axis

$$= \frac{az}{A+a} = \delta y$$

The new second moment of area

$$I + \delta I = I + az^2 - (A+a)\left(\frac{az}{A+a}\right)^2$$

$$\therefore \quad az^2 - \frac{a^2 z^2}{A+a} = \delta I = \frac{A a z^2}{A+a}$$

Now δI is positive and $\delta y/y_2$ is negative so that $\delta I/I$ will certainly be greater than $\delta y/y$ at the deck, provided that the material is added within the section ($z < y_2$). There must therefore be a reduction of stress at the deck.

At the keel, the condition $\delta I/I > \delta y/y$ becomes

$$\frac{A a z^2}{A k^2 (A+a)} > \frac{az}{y_1(A+a)}$$

i.e.

$$z > \frac{k^2}{y_1}$$

To achieve a reduction in stress at the keel as well, therefore, the material must be added at a height greater than k^2/y_1 from the neutral axis. For a thin walled cylinder, k^2/y is one-half the radius and for ships the value is 0·6–0·8 of the half depth.

If the material is added above the deck, as a superstructure might be, the maximum stress above the neutral axis occurs not at the deck, y_2, but in the new material at z.

$$\therefore \quad \delta y = z - \frac{az}{A+a} - y_2 = \frac{Az}{A+a} - y_2$$

The condition $\delta I/I > \delta y/y$ becomes

$$\frac{A a z^2}{A k^2 (A+a)} > \frac{Az}{y_2(A+a)} - 1$$

i.e.

$$\frac{az^2}{k^2} + a > \frac{Az}{y_2} - A$$

$$a > \frac{A(z/y_2 - 1)}{(z^2/k^2 + 1)}$$

If, therefore, the material is added above the deck, there is a minimum area at any height z, for which there will be a reduction in deck stress. The stress in the material having less area than this minimum will be greater than it was in the original deck. This minimum required area to ensure the same deck stress can be plotted against z as shown in Fig. 6.21. When material is added above the section, there will be reduced keel stress.

The position is not quite so simple if the added material is a superstructure and attention is drawn to p. 216.

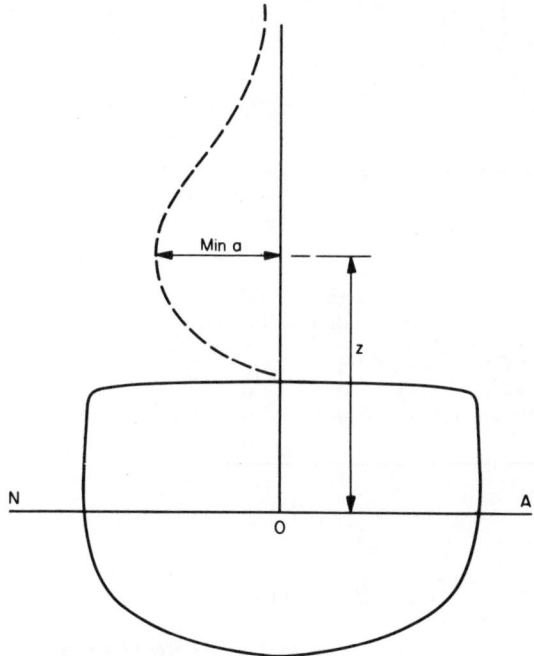

Fig. 6.21

EXAMPLE 2. In converting a steel survey ship, it is proposed to extend the short forecastle for the whole length of the ship and to arrange the structure so that it contributes 100 per cent to the hull girder. The new structure is wholly of light alloy. Estimate the new nominal stresses due to the change in section modulus, assuming that the bending moment remains unchanged.

Before conversion: BM = 25,000 tonf ft, I = 40,000 in² ft², A = 700 in², y, deck = 9·5 ft; y, keel = 10·0 ft.

Added structure: side plating 7·5 ft × ⅜ in., stiffened by one 4·0 in² girder at mid-height; deck plating 36 ft × ⅜ in. stiffened by five 4·0 in² girders with centre of area 3 in. below the deck.

E, light alloy: 10×10^6 lbf/in²
E, steel: 30×10^6 lbf/in²

Solution:

Fig. 6.22

Above upper deck

Item	A (in^2)	h (ft)	Ah (in^2 ft)	Ah^2 (in^2 ft^2)	k^2 (ft^2)	Ak^2 (in^2 ft^2)
two sides	67·5	3·75	253	949	4·7	318
two side girders	8·0	3·75	30	113	0	0
deck	162·0	7·5	1215	9113	0	0
five deck girders	20·0	7·25	145	1051	0	0
	257·5	6·38	1643	11,226		318

New effective area $= 700 + \frac{1}{3} \times 257·5 = 785·8$ in^2

Movement of neutral axis $= \dfrac{\frac{1}{3} \times 257·5(9·5 + 6·38)}{785·8} = 1·73$ ft

I about old NA $= 40,000 + \frac{1}{3}\{11,226 + 318 - 257·5(6·38)^2 + 257·5(6·38 + 9·5)^2\}$
$= 62,009$ in^2 ft^2

I about new NA $= 62,009 - 785·8(1·73)^2 = 59,652$ in^2 ft^2

y, new deck $= 15·27$ ft

y, keel $= 11·73$ ft

Old stresses were, σ, keel $= \dfrac{25,000}{40,000} \times 10·0 = 6·25$ tonf/in^2 (steel)

σ, deck $= \dfrac{25,000}{40,000} \times 9·5 = 5·94$ tonf/in^2 (steel)

New stresses are, σ, keel $= \dfrac{25,000}{59,650} \times 11·73 = 4·92$ tonf/in^2 (steel)

σ, deck $= \dfrac{1}{3} \times \dfrac{25,000}{59,650} \times 15·27 = 2·13$ tonf/in^2 (alloy)

σ, deck $= \dfrac{25,000}{59,650} \times 7·77 = 3·26$ tonf/in^2 (steel)

SLOPES AND DEFLECTIONS

The bending moment on the ship girder has been found by integrating first the loading p' with respect to length to give shearing force S, and then by integrating the shearing force S with respect to length to give M. There is a further relationship with which students will already be familiar.

$$M = EI\frac{d^2y}{dx^2}$$

or

$$\frac{dy}{dx} = \frac{1}{E}\int\frac{M}{I}dx \quad \text{and} \quad y = \int\frac{dy}{dx}dx$$

Thus, the slope at all points along the hull can be found by integrating the M/EI curve and the bent shape of the hull profile can be found by integrating the slope curve. It is not surprising that the errors involved in integrating approximate data four times can be quite large. Moreover, the calculation of the second moment of area of all sections throughout the length is laborious and the standard calculation is extended this far only rarely—it might be thus extended, for example, to give a first estimate of the distortion of the hull between a master datum level and a radar aerial some distance away. It may also be done to obtain a deflected profile in vibration studies.

HORIZONTAL FLEXURE

Flexure perpendicular to the plane with which we are normally concerned may be caused by vibration, flutter, uneven lateral forces or bending while rolling. Vibrational modes are discussed in Chapter 9. Unsymmetrical bending can be resolved into bending about the two principal axes of the cross-section. The only point in the ship at which the maxima of the two effects combine is the deck edge and if the ship were to be balanced on a standard wave which gave a bending moment M, the stress at the deck edge would be

$$\sigma = \frac{Mz}{I_{yy}}\cos\theta + \frac{My}{I_{zz}}\sin\theta$$

Fig. 6.23

However, it is not quite so easy as this; if the ship were heading directly into a wave train, it would not be rolling. Only in quartering or bow seas will bending and rolling be combined and, in such a case, the maximum bending moments in the two planes would not be in phase, so that the deck edge effect will be less than that obtained by superposition of the two maxima. Some limited research into this problem indicates that horizontal bending moment maxima are likely to be of the order of 40 per cent of the vertical bending moment maxima and the ratio of the stresses is likely to be about 35 per cent in common ship shapes. The increase in deck edge stress over that obtained with head seas is thought to be of the order of 20–25 per cent. This is an excellent reason to avoid stress concentrations in this area.

BEHAVIOUR OF A HOLLOW BOX GIRDER

The simple theory of bending of beams assumes that plane sections of the beam remain plane and that the direct stress is directly proportional to the distance from the neutral axis. A deck parallel to the neutral axis would therefore be expected to exhibit constant stress across its width. In fact, the upper flange of a hollow box girder like a ship's hull can receive its load only by shear at the deck edge. The diffusion of this shear into a plane deck to create the direct stresses is a difficult problem mathematically; the diffusion from the edge elements across the deck is such that the plane sections do not remain plane, and the mathematics shows that the direct stresses reduce towards the middle of the deck. This has been borne out by observations in practice. The effect is known as *shear lag* and its magnitude depends on the type of loading and dimensions of the ship; it is more pronounced, for example, under concentrated loads. In common ship shapes, it accounts for a difference in stress level at mid-deck of only a few per cent. It is more important in the consideration of the effects of superstructures and of the effective breadth of plating in local strength problems which will be discussed later.

Fig. 6.24 Direct stresses in practice

WAVE PRESSURE CORRECTION

This is usually known as the *Smith Correction* (Ref. 2). In calculating the buoyancy per unit length at a section of the ship, the area of the section given by the Bonjean curve cut by the wave surface was taken. This assumes that the pressure at a point P on the section is proportional to the depth h of the point below the wave surface and the buoyancy = $w \int h \, dB = w \times$ area immersed (Fig. 6.25).

Fig. 6.25

It is shown in Chapter 9, that this simple hydrostatic law is not true in a wave because the wave is caused by the orbital motion of water particles. It can be shown that the pressure at a point P in a wave at a depth h below the wave surface is the same as the hydrostatic pressure at a depth h', where h' is the distance between the mean (or still water) axis of the surface trochoid and the subsurface trochoid through P (Fig. 6.26). Thus, the buoyancy at a section of a ship is

$$w \int h' \mathrm{d}B = w \times (\text{effective area immersed}).$$

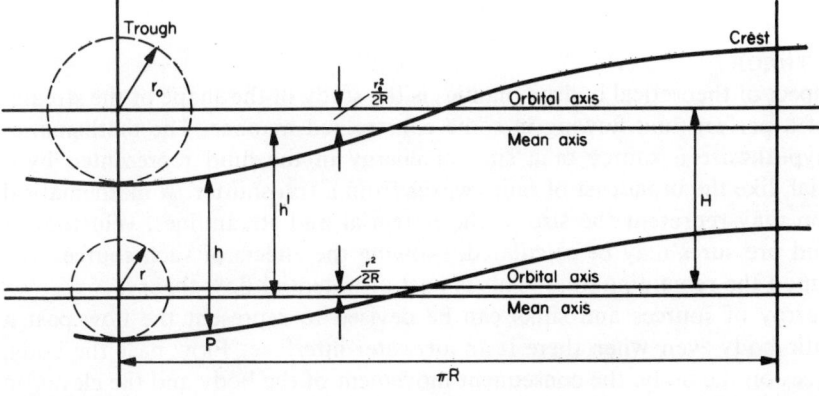

Fig. 6.26

Setting up h' from the sub-surface trochoid through P and similar heights from a series of sub-surface trochoids drawn on the wave profile, the effective immersed area up to W'L is obtained. New Bonjean curves can thus be plotted (Fig. 6.27). The formula for h' is

$$h' = H - \frac{r_0^2}{2R}\left\{1 - \exp\left(-\frac{2H}{R}\right)\right\}$$

Fig. 6.27

An approximation to the Smith correction is:

$$\text{corrected wave BM} = \text{wave BM} \times \exp\left(-\frac{nT}{L}\right)$$

where T is the draught, L the length and n a constant given by:

Block coeff. C_B	n, sagging	n, hogging
0·80	5·5	6·0
0·60	5·0	5·3

STRIP THEORY

One aspect of theoretical hydrodynamics is the study of the shape of the streamlines of a perfect fluid flowing in some constrained manner. The mathematics may hypothesize a source or a sink of energy in the fluid represented by a potential, like the broadcast of radio waves from a transmitter. A mathematical function may represent the size of the potential and streamlines, velocities of flow and pressures may be calculated, showing the effects of such sources and sinks upon the remaining fluid. This is part of potential flow theory.

An array of sources and sinks can be devised to represent the flow past a prismatic body even when there is an air/water interface. Flow past the body, the forces on the body, the consequent movement of the body and the elevation or depression of the interface can all be calculated. A ship can be represented by a series of short prismatic bodies or strips, all joined together and the total forces and bending moments upon such a hull calculated, the different elevations representing the self-generated waves. Waves imposed upon the ship may also be represented in the same way. The potential functions needed for this representation are pulsating ones and interference occurs between waves created and imposed. These are affected by the beam of the ship relative to the wave length of the self-generated waves and this has resulted in several different approaches to strip theory using slightly different but important assumptions. There are other important assumptions concerned with the boundaries. The general term strip theory embraces all such studies, including slender body theory and systematic perturbation analysis.

This mathematics is beyond the scope of this book. However, it is of such importance that the student must be aware of its existence and the way in which it is used because it is largely supplanting the work described in this chapter. This is because the digital computer is now available to effect the vast amount of computation to which the mathematics leads and which renders hand manipulation of strip theory virtually impossible. Neither, while it would be readily possible, is it any longer necessary to confine our attention to the simplistic concept of a single trochoidal wave. Strip theory provides the means of tackling the more realistic problem of random seas which is discussed presently. It is sufficient, for the time being to understand that by means of strip theory, the shear forces and bending moments upon a hull of specified form, proceeding in a specified sea may be calculated to a fair degree of accuracy and that computer programs are available which effect such computation.

STRUCTURAL DYNAMICS

The true problem of overall ship girder behaviour is that of an elastic shell moving through a wave system of infinite variability, each affecting the other. Loading upon the ship is affected by the ship's own response so that the whole system is dynamic and ought to be treated as such. Different modes of vibration will be stimulated when there is matching between a component of the wave loading and a particular response of the ship, as in the case known as springing (Ref. 3). Of course, many of these responses are of no interest. The low modes—including the two node mode of the standard static calculation—are of predominant interest and are very strongly affected by damping. It would thus be preferable to treat the longitudinal strength problem as one in structural dynamics. The mathematics necessary for this (Ref. 4) is available and incidentally, provides the rigid body movements of roll, pitch and heave into the bargain.

Unfortunately, a lack of knowledge of the damping characteristics and virtual masses in various modes and imprecise knowledge of the structural behaviour of a non-uniform open box girder, prevents an immediate application of this approach. Such problems may in time yield to research and make such a modal attack profitable, possibly in conjunction with other changes.

LONGITUDINAL STRENGTH STANDARDS BY RULE

The standard longitudinal strength calculation is often performed by ship owners and builders on merchant ship designs and such calculations are found acceptable by the classification societies as a measure of the longitudinal strength. Responsible as they are for many thousands of ships, however, the societies would find it difficult to carry out the calculations themselves for each vessel as a step in the classification, and such relative accuracy may not be strictly necessary in ships with characteristics very similar to successful type ships. For example, ships with large amounts of parallel middle body and traditional disposition of cargo and machinery are conducive to design by rule. There is a fundamental difference in design philosophy between warships and merchant ships which has already been touched on in Chapter 1.

Over the years, the classification societies built up massive experience of the craft of ship construction and as a result they compiled rules and tables specifying the scantlings of each individual plate and stiffener. The only requirement for ship section modulus was a discredited formula specified by international conference in 1930. During the 1950s there was a fundamental change of approach, and the societies devised ingenious formulae to represent the standard calculation and to specify minimum section moduli, in order to continue the rule approach to structural design on a rational basis. The rules were eminently successful in that they safely permitted the rapid expansion in size of tankers and development of other ship types with the minimum of structural calculation.

The rules are all based on the logical division of the total bending moment into two parts,

(a) the still water bending moment,
(b) the wave bending moment.

The wave bending moment is that due to the superposition of a wave on the still water condition. It is determined by the geometry of the ship and the wave and is in no appreciable way influenced by the disposition of cargo. In fact, with the principal dimensions of the ship settled, there is nothing that the designer can do to reduce wave bending moment. For an $L/20$ wave, the wave bending moment is represented closely by a formula of the type, const $\times$ BL^3

and for a $1\cdot 1\sqrt{L}$ wave by a const $\times$ $BL^{2\cdot 5}$

Fig. 6.28 *Wave bending forces*

The constant depends on the type of ship and the prismatic or block coefficient and is best determined by reference to previous similar ships, compared on this basis. The $L/20$ constant for a frigate is about $7N/m^3$ (20×10^{-6} tonf/ft^3). The formula for the minimum midship section modulus I/y given by Lloyd's Register for the loaded condition is the greater of

$I/y = fKB\,(C_B + 0.70) \times 10^5$ cm^3
or $I/y = 1/3\,fKB\,(C_B + 0.70) \times 10^5 + 92$ SWBM $(C_B + 0.20)$ cm^3
where $f = 0.85$ or 0.90 if there are empty holds

$\quad C_B =$ block coefficient at load draught or at $T = 0.45L$ if this is greater but C_B is not to be taken as less than 0.60.
$K = 0.985 \quad 2.382 \quad 4.594 \quad 7.722 \quad 11.437$
at L(m) $= 100 \quad\quad 150 \quad\quad 200 \quad\quad 250 \quad\quad 300$

The first part of this formula implies a wave bending moment of the form constant x $(C_B + 0.70) \times BL^{2.25}$ approximately. For reasons which are given presently, classification societies are adopting indices for L between 2.25 and 2.5. Requirements vary slightly between classification societies and between ship types and conditions.

The still water bending moment can be simply calculated in a manner similar to that described for the standard calculation although, of course, the difficulties of balance on the wave do not occur. The still water bending moment arises from the relative distribution of weight and buoyancy along the length. Weight distribution is affected by the construction of hull and disposition of machinery and cargo. Buoyancy distribution in still water is affected by the geometry of the hull, primarily by length and block coefficient. If it is assumed that the maximum bending moment occurs amidships, it can be represented by couples caused by the weight and buoyancy forces forward and aft,

$\quad$ max. SWBM $=$ (moment buoyancy $-$ moment weight)$_{\text{forward}}$

$\quad\quad\quad\quad\quad\quad = $ (moment buoyancy $-$ moment weight)$_{\text{aft}}$

While these values can be calculated fairly readily from lines plan and weight distribution, formulae have been deduced for first estimates for ships with traditional forms. Regarding the maximum still water bending moment as the difference between the 'mean' of the buoyancy and weight moments forward and aft, Lloyd's Register gives the mean position of the LCB half body (i.e. the mean of the distances from amidships for both halves) as aL, a being given by the following table

Draught	a
$0.06L$	$0.179C_B + 0.063$
$0.05L$	$0.189C_B + 0.052$
$0.04L$	$0.199C_B + 0.041$
$0.03L$	$0.209C_B + 0.030$

C_B is that at draught $= 0.06L$

Fig. 6.29

The mean weight moment is calculated by meaning the forward and after moments of weights of hull, machinery and cargo, the hull constituent of which is taken as $0.24L$ for tankers, $0.23L$ for shelter deck cargo ships and $0.215L$ for passenger ships with large amidships superstructures. If cL is the mean LCG of forward and after bodies, obtained this way,

$$\text{max. still water bending moment} = \frac{\Delta}{2}(a-c)L$$

Since the values of c and a are close, they must be calculated with some accuracy. The shearing force appropriate to this still water bending moment is given approximately by

$$\text{max. still water shearing force} = \frac{6 \times \text{SWBM}}{L}$$

Acceptable stresses vary with the different classification societies and the formulae in use. Those appropriate to the formulae above are about 120 MN/m^2 for the wave BM and 70 MN/m^2 for the still water BM for oil tankers fitted with an approved method of cathodic protection against corrosion destined for world wide service. Somewhat lower stresses are usual in cargo and passenger ships. The required modulus to meet these figures is determined by a combination of the separate demands of wave and still water, designed to encourage small still water bending moments. Clearly, since this critical feature is under the control of the ship's master, the company must issue to him precise instructions as to the acceptable loading in his ship. Indeed, not infrequently, loading of particular tanks must, in the terms of the classification be expressly forbidden in some conditions, if still water stress is to be kept below the figures permitted by the classification society.

Criterion of failure

A longitudinal structural failure of a ship is imagined by children as a jagged fracture amidships, with the extremities of the ship disappearing beneath the waves in the manner pictured by caricaturists. This is not a sufficiently exact or accurate conception of failure. How can the acceptable level of behaviour of the ship be defined?

Fig. 6.30

FULL-SCALE TRIALS

There have been several attempts to measure the behaviour of the ship girder by loading ships and recording their behaviour at various positions by strain gauges and measurements of deflection. *Neverita* and *Newcombia, Clan Alpine* and *Ocean Vulcan* were subject to variations in loading by filling different tanks while they were afloat. *Wolf, Preston, Bruce* and *Albuera* were supported at the middle or the ends in dry dock and weight added until major structural failure occurred. Many ships have been to sea with strain gauges fitted so that changes in strain level can be recorded in waves. Fortunately, only a few ships have failed while at sea, providing further evidence of ultimate behaviour.

Probably, the most important deduction from all of these measurements is that, if the loading is known, stresses can be deduced with sufficient accuracy by the simple theory of bending. Stress, however, does not cause failure, although it might be a measure of the phenomena that do. Failure, in the case of the three destroyers loaded to destruction in dry dock, was by buckling of the bottom at a stress less than three-quarters of the yield. This stress was, in fact, two or three times that assumed acceptable by the standard calculation. The most striking conclusion from the examination of major fractures in ships at sea, is that the cracks almost invariably begin at obvious stress concentrations and may or may not be propagated according to the quality of the steel. (Stress concentrations and brittle fracture are discussed later.)

While full scale trials have been successful in connecting a known loading with stress level, the information connecting loading with the sea is still sparse. This is the principal difficulty in improving the approach to longitudinal strength, and this difficulty is being slowly removed by a big programme of statistical strain measurements on ships at sea. Assessment of residual strain due to the processes of manufacture is a further difficulty.

THE NATURE OF FAILURE

Stress has never caused any material to fail. Stress is simply a convenient measure of the material behaviour which may 'fail' in many different ways. 'Failure' of a structure might mean permanent strain, cracking, unacceptable deflection, instability, a short life or even a resonant vibration. Some of these criteria are conveniently measured in terms of stress. In defining an acceptable level of stress for a ship, what 'failure' do we have in mind?

Structural failure of the ship girder may be due to one or a combination of (a) Cracking, (b) Fatigue failure, (c) Instability.

It is a fact that acceptable stress levels are at present determined entirely by experience of previous ships in which there have been a large number of cracks in service. The fact that these might have been due to poor local design is at present largely disregarded, suggesting that some poor local design or workmanship somewhere in the important parts of the hull girder is inevitable.

So far as instability is concerned, this is essentially a local problem in surface ships, unless considering ultimate longitudinal strength (Ref. 9). Buckling of longitudinal structure between frames or transverse bulkheads must be prevented to permit the hull girder to develop its strength up to a point where fatigue or extensive cracking cannot be prevented. Since this is possible up to the full plastic moment of the ship section, instability is not a suitable criterion for design of the hull girder, although it is very important, of course, in the consideration of local stiffener and panel behaviour.

However good the design of local structure and details might be, there is one important influence on the determination of acceptable levels of stress. The material built into the ship will have been rolled and, finally, welded. These processes necessarily distort the material so that high stresses are already built in to the structure before the cargo or sea impose any loads at all. Very little is known about these built-in stresses. Some may yield out, i.e. local, perhaps molecular, straining may take place which relieves the area at the expense of other areas. The built-in stress clearly affects fatigue life to an unknown degree. It may also cause premature buckling. Thus, with many unknowns still remaining, changes to the present practice of a stress level determined by a proliferation of cracks in previous ships, must be slow and cautious.

STRUCTURAL RELIABILITY

Variability in strength due to material and manufacturing tolerances can be represented by a probability density function, the area up to a particular value of the abscissa being the probability that that value will not be exceeded. So also can the variability in the loading as discussed next. Each can be expressed in terms of longitudinal bending moment. The likelihood of applied bending moment exceeding M is given by the area to the right of M shown shaded in Fig. 6.31 under the overlap of the tails of the distributions. Similarly, the common area to the left of the overlap represents the probability that the strength will be less than M. The probability that the strength will be less than M and the load more than M is the product of these two areas. This is the probability of failure and it lies somewhere between 10^{-8} and 10^{-4} for different ships. Such an approach is an important development in determining a rational failure criterion. References 7, 8 discuss the concept but some work remains to be done before it becomes the standard by which longitudinal strength is judged.

Fig. 6.31

STATISTICAL DETERMINATION OF LOADING

An important change has occurred in the approach to longitudinal bending of ships in recent years. Instead of using a standard wave bending moment calculation as a basis of comparison, an estimate is made of the probability of a ship exceeding a particular wave bending moment by relating the response of the ship to the seas that it encounters during its life.

A detailed account of how the motion response of the ship to the sea is determined is given in Chapter 12. The problem in determining the probabilities of causing particular levels of bending moment is basically the same. Briefly, it is as follows:

(*a*) Select the energy spectra pertaining to the seas for which the ship is intended.
(*b*) Create encounter spectra for the ship speeds of interest by correcting the stationary wave spectrum.
(*c*) Measure the bending moment response operators for each component wave in a model tank or in a full size similar ship, or calculate by strip theory.
(*d*) Apply the response operators to the encounter spectra to give bending moment spectra.
(*e*) Fit the bending moment spectrum to a known probability distribution and calculate the probability of exceeding particular values of bending moment.
(*f*) Compound this probability with the probabilities of meeting each sea state.

While this gives an outline of the process there are yet certain difficulties in applying it. Oceanographers are not in complete agreement about the type of energy spectra applicable to different seas. Correction for encounter speed is straightforward. Some disparity between the bending moment response operators calculated by strip theory and those measured in towing tank experiments occurs. Strip theory includes numerous simplifying assumptions. Furthermore, correlation of model and ship response operators has yet to be firmly established. Some extrapolation of measurements on ships needs to be made to predict likely extreme values of bending moment which occur with great rarity.

Fig. 6.32 *Energy spectra*

Despite these present difficulties, the statistical determination of bending moments is already in use by the classification societies. Converting the bending moments to an effective wave of height h/L applied in the standard calculation, the probability of meeting a wave exceeding h/L is as shown in Fig. 6.34. It is observed that a wave height of $1 \cdot 1\sqrt{L}$ results in a differing probability for different lengths of ship while the $L/20$ wave gives a bigger variation. A wave height proportional to $L^{0 \cdot 3}$ to $L^{0 \cdot 4}$ is thought to give an approximately constant probability and is responsible for the index of 2·3–2·4 for L in the formulae used by different classification societies for wave bending moment.

Fig. 6.33 *Response operators*

A ship at sea for 20 years may experience 10^8 reversals of strain, so that the probability of meeting an extreme value once in a lifetime is of the order of 10^{-8}. The extreme bending moment associated with this probability happens to be about the same as had been found acceptable for many thousands of ships in the past. Comparison with previous ships and the arguments already put forward in this chapter must continue to determine acceptable stresses (Refs. 12, 13).

Fig. 6.34

Discontinuities

Every schoolboy knows that a steel nail is most easily broken by notching it at the desired point of fracture and bending it. What he may not know is that he has introduced a stress concentration at the notch so that bending causes a local stress higher than the material can withstand.

A stress concentration is a localized area in a structure at which the stress is significantly higher than in the surrounding material. It can conveniently be conceived as a disturbance or a discontinuity in the smooth flow of the lines of stress such as a stick placed in a fast flowing stream would cause in the water flow. There are two types of discontinuity causing stress concentrations in ships:

(a) discontinuities built into the ship unintentionally by the methods of construction, e.g. rolling, welding, casting, etc.;
(b) discontinuities deliberately introduced into the structural design for reasons of architecture, use, access, e.g. hatch openings, superstructures, door openings, etc.

Stress concentrations cannot be totally avoided either by good design or high standards of workmanship. Their effects, however, can be minimized by attention to both and it is important to recognize the effects of stress concentrations on the ship girder. Many ships and men were lost because these effects were not recognized in the early Liberty ships of the 1940s.

In general, stress concentrations may cause yield, brittle fracture or buckling. There is a certain amount of theory which can guide the designer, but a general understanding of how they arise is more important in their recognition and treatment because it is at the detail design stage that many can be avoided or minimized.

THEORY

The classical mathematical theory of elasticity has produced certain results for holes and notches in laminae. The stress concentration factors at A and B of

Fig. 6.35 of an elliptical hole in an infinite plate under uniform tension in the direction of the b-axis are given by

$$j_A = \frac{\text{stress}_A}{\sigma} = -1$$

$$j_B = \frac{\text{stress}_B}{\sigma} = 1 + \frac{2a}{b}$$

Fig. 6.35

For the particular case of a circular hole, $a = b$ and $j_B = 3$, i.e. the stress at the sides of a circular hole is three times the general tensile stress level in the plate, while at top and bottom there is a compressive stress equal to the general stress level. If a crack is thought of, ideally, as a long thin ellipse, the equation above gives some idea of the level of stress concentration at the ends; a crack twenty times as long as its width, for example, lying across the direction of loading would cause a stress, at the ends, forty-one times the general stress level and yielding or propagation of the crack is likely for very modest values of σ.

A square hole with radiused corners might be represented for this examination by two ellipses at right angles to each other and at 45 degrees to the direction of load. For the dimensions given in Fig. 6.36, the maximum stress concentration factor at the corners is given approximately by

$$j = \frac{1}{2}\sqrt{\frac{b}{r}}\left\{1 + \frac{\sqrt{(2b + 2r)}}{\sqrt{b} - \sqrt{r}}\right\}$$

Figure 6.37 shows the effect of the variation of corner radius r on length of side b for a square hole with a side parallel to the direction of stress and for a square hole at 45 degrees. The figure shows

(a) that there may be a penalty of up to 25 per cent in stress in failing to align a square hole with rounded corners with the direction of stress;

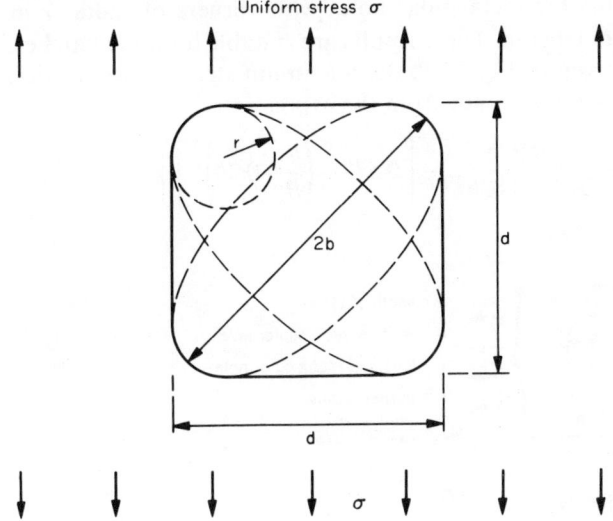

Fig. 6.36

(b) that there is not much advantage in giving a corner radius greater than about one-sixth of the side;
(c) that the penalty of corner radii of less than about one-twentieth of the side, is severe. Rim reinforcement to the hole can alleviate the situation.

Fig. 6.37

214 Basic ship theory

Reference 14 gives results for rectangular holes with corners of radius r in a finite plate under uniform tension. These results are suitable for large hatches. With the dimensions as given in Fig. 6.38, the maximum stress concentration factor can be found with good accuracy from the expression,

$$j_{max} = \frac{2-0.4^{B/b}}{2-0.4^{l/B}}\left\{1+\frac{0.926}{1.348-0.826^{2 0r/B}}\left[0.577-\left(\frac{b}{B}-0.24\right)^2\right]\right\}$$

Fig. 6.38 Rectangular hole in finite plate

It is of importance that the maximum stress occurs always about 5–10 degrees around the corner and the zero stress 50–70 degrees round. Butts in plating should be made at this latter point. Figure 6.39 shows the results for a hole with $l = B$. Note that the concentration factor is referred not to the stress in the clear plate but to the stress at the reduced section.

Fig. 6.39 Stress concentration factor for a hole with $l = B$

BUILT-IN STRESS CONCENTRATIONS

The violent treatment afforded a plate of mild steel during its manufacture, prevents the formation of a totally unstrained plate. Uneven rolling or contraction, especially if cooling is rapid, may cause areas of strain, even before the plate is selected for working into a ship. These are often called 'built in' or 'locked up' stresses (more accurately, strains). Furthermore, during the processes of moulding and welding, more strains are built in by uneven cooling. However careful the welders, there will be some, perhaps minute, holes, cracks and slag inclusions, lack of penetration and undercutting in a weld deposit. Inspection of important parts of the structure will minimize the number of visual defects occurring, and radiography can show up those below the surface, but lack of homogeneity cannot be observed by normal inspection procedures, even though the 'built-in' stress may exceed yield. What then happens to them when the ship is subjected to strain?

In ductile materials, most of the concentrations 'yield out', i.e. the concentration reaches the yield point, shirks further load and causes a re-distribution of stress in the surrounding material. If the concentration is a crack, it may propagate to an area of reduced stress level and stop. If it becomes visible, a temporary repair is often made at sea by drilling a circular hole at its end, reducing the concentration factor. This is a common first aid treatment. There is considerably more anxiety if the material is not so ductile as mild steel, since it does not have so much capacity for 'yielding out'; furthermore, a high yield steel is often employed in places where a general high stress level is expected so that cracks are less able to propagate to areas of reduced stress level and stop. A further anxiety in all materials is the possibility of fatigue, since concentrations at which there is, locally, a high stress level will be able to withstand few reversals.

Fig. 6.40 Yielding out

BRITTLE FRACTURE

Cracks then, cannot be prevented, although they can be minimized. It is important to ensure that they do not cause sudden catastrophic failure before they are observed and rectified. The rapid propagation of fractures, usually at low temperatures, has been experienced in structures and has resulted in the loss of ships. The phenomenon is known as brittle fracture and it has occurred in mild steels which were expected to be ductile. Much has been written about the subject and intensive research in the 1950s resulted in a satisfactory means of preventing brittle fracture. Briefly, the behaviour of steels under impact was found to change quite suddenly over a short range of *transition temperatures*; structures which were satisfactory at one temperature failed suddenly as the temperature was reduced. The likelihood of brittle fracture is now reduced, by specifying a type of steel which is 'notch tough' down to sufficiently low temperatures, the notch toughness being measured by an Izod or similar impact test. Steelmakers have met this requirement by a study of the metallurgical factors, important amongst them being the ratio of manganese to carbon in the steel.

There are other causes of brittle fracture. Normal yielding may be inhibited at 'bunched' structural junctions or in very thick plating causing a state of tri-axial tension which may cause a fracture to be brittle in a ductile material. Very high rates of loading, as in explosions, will also cause a brittle fracture.

DISCONTINUITIES IN STRUCTURAL DESIGN

In the second category of stress concentrations, are those deliberately introduced by the designer. Theory may assist where practical cases approximate to the assumptions made, as, for example, in the case of a side light or port hole. Here, in a large plate, stress concentration factors of about three may be expected. At hatches too, the effects of corner radii may be judged from Figs. 6.37 and 6.39. Finite element techniques outlined in Chapter 7 have extended the degree to which theory may be relied upon to predict the effect of large openings and other major stress concentrations.

Often, the concentrations will be judged unacceptably high and reinforcement must be fitted to reduce the values. One of the most effective ways to do this is by fitting a rim to the hole or curved edge. A thicker insert plate may also help, but the fitting of a doubling plate is unlikely to be effective unless means of creating a good connection are devised.

Designers and practitioners at all levels must be constantly on the watch for the discontinuity, the rapid change of structural pattern and other forms of stress raiser. It is so often bad local design which starts the major failure. Above all, the superposition of one concentration on another must be avoided —butt the reinforcement rim where the concentration is lowest, avoid stud welds and fittings at structural discontinuities, give adequate room between holes, grind the profile smooth at the concentration!

SUPERSTRUCTURES AND DECKHOUSES

These form important discontinuities in the ship girder. In calculating the section modulus of the ship earlier in the chapter, the effect of the addition of material was assessed on the assumption that it was entirely effective and obeyed the relationship of $\sigma = (M/I)y$. It is not, however, always fully effective and its contribution to the section modulus requires closer examination.

The only contact between the upper deck and the superstructure is along the bottom of the superstructure sides through which the strains and forces must be transmitted. Because the upper deck stretches, so also must the lower edge of the superstructure sides thus causing shear forces which tend to distort the superstructure into a shape opposite to that of the hull (Fig. 6.41). The two

Fig. 6.41

are held together, however, and there must be normal forces on the superstructure having the opposite effect. The degree of these normal forces must depend upon the flexibility of the deck beams and main transverse bulkheads if the superstructure is set in from the ship's sides. The effect of the shear forces will depend on the manner in which the shear is diffused into the superstructure, and the shear lag effects are likely to be more appreciable there than in the main hull girder.

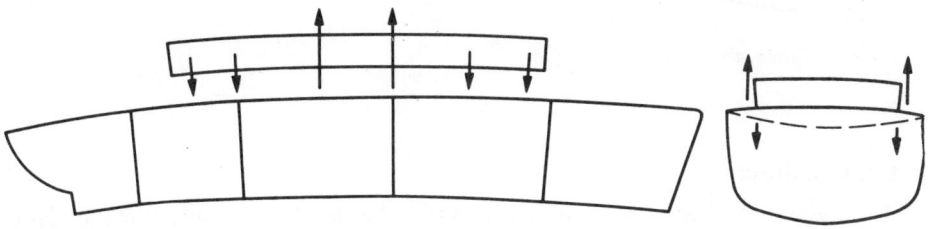

Fig. 6.42

This difficult problem has been satisfactorily solved in Refs. 15 and 16. In the former reference, the effects of shear lag are ignored and the results are suitable for the middle portions of long superstructures. Reference 16 embraces the effects of shear diffusion but ignores the concentrated forces from main transverse bulkheads, and it is suitable for short superstructures or for those which extend out to the ship's side. An efficiency of superstructure is defined as

$$\eta = \frac{\sigma_0 - \sigma}{\sigma_0 - \sigma_1}$$

where σ_0 is the upper deck stress which would occur if there were no superstructure present, σ is the upper deck stress calculated and σ_1 is the upper deck stress with a fully effective superstructure. Curves are supplied from which the factors leading to the efficiency may be calculated. As might be expected, the efficiency depends much on the ratio of superstructure length to its transverse dimensions.

218 *Basic ship theory*

The square ends of the superstructure constitute major discontinuities, and may be expected to cause large stress concentrations. They must not be superimposed on other stress concentrations and should be avoided amidships or, if unavoidable, carefully reinforced. For this reason, expansion joints are to be used with caution; while they relieve the superstructure of some of its stress by reducing its efficiency, they introduce stress concentrations which may more than restore the stress level locally. To assist the normal forces, superstructure ends should coincide with main transverse bulkheads.

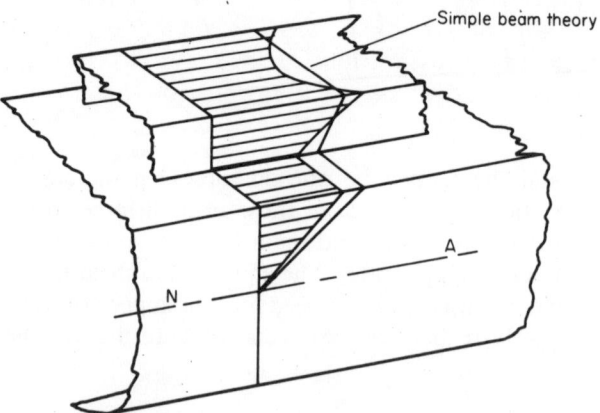

Fig. 6.43 *Direct stress in a superstructure*

Conclusions

The student may be forgiven if he began this chapter safely assured by the static calculation (sometimes called Reed's method) and ended it aware of some considerable uncertainty. As the proceedings of the International Ship Structures Congress bear witness, this is precisely the current situation. Naval architects are rapidly adopting the statistical approach to ship girder loading and are preparing to marry it to structural reliability when sufficient information about strength variability is to hand. They await the results of the long process of data collection at sea to refine their standards of acceptability.

Large computer programs are already providing assessment on this new basis and are usually integrated into suites which perform finite element analysis of the whole hull and its components. Reed's method plays no part in this process. However, it remains a quick, cheap and safe process either for initial estimates or for those designers without immediate access to expensive computing facilities. Reed's method can itself be effected by simple programs, often in conjunction with hydrostatic curves and it continues to provide a useful starting point in structural design. Subsequently designers will usually wish to embark upon consultancy with a classification society in the full structural design and analysis process using more elegant programs.

Problems

1. A landing craft of length 200 ft may be assumed to have a rectangular cross-section of beam of 28 ft. When empty, draughts are 1·5 ft forward and 3·5 ft aft and its weight is made up of general structure weight assumed evenly distributed throughout the length, and machinery and superstructure weight spread evenly over the last 40 ft. A load of 100 tonf can be carried evenly distributed over the first 160 ft, but to keep the forward draught at a maximum of 2 ft, ballast water must be added evenly to the after 40 ft.

Draw the load, shearing force and bending moment diagrams for the loaded craft when in still water of specific volume of 35 ft^3/tonf. Determine the position and value of the maximum bending moment acting on the craft. (HMDTC)

2. State the maximum bending moment and shearing force in terms of the weight and length of a vessel having the weight uniformly distributed and the curve of buoyancy parabolic and quote deck and keel moduli. Where do the maximum shearing force and bending moment occur? (AP & S)

3. The barge shown in the figure floats at a uniform draught of 1 m in sea water when empty.

A heavy weight, uniformly distributed over the middle 5 m of the barge, increases the draught to 2 m. It may be assumed that the buoyancy curves for the barge (loaded and unloaded) and the weight distribution of the unloaded barge are constant over the parallel length of the barge, decreasing linearly to zero at the two ends.

Draw curves of buoyancy, weight, loading, shear force and bending moment for the barge loaded and at rest in salt water.

Fig. 6.44

(HMDTC)

4. A rectangular barge is 80 ft long and has a beam of 14 ft. The weight distribution of the partially loaded barge is shown in the figure below. The barge is floating at rest in still water. Draw curves of loading, shearing force and bending moment, stating the maximum shearing force and bending moment and the positions where they act.

Fig. 6.45

(HMDTC)

5. A barge, 70 m long, has the cross-section shown. The empty weight is 420 tonnef evenly distributed over the whole length, whereas the load is spread evenly over the middle 42 m of length. Draw the curves of load, shearing force and bending moment for the barge, when it is loaded and balanced on a sea wave whose profile gives draughts, symmetrical about amidships, as follows:

Section	FE	2	3	4	5	Amidships
Draught (m)	5·00	4·55	3·61	2·60	2·10	2·00

Fig. 6.46

(HMDTC)

6. A steel barge of constant rectangular section, length 72 ft, floats at a draught of 5 ft when loaded. The weight curve of the loaded barge may be regarded as linear, from zero at the two ends to a maximum at the mid-length. The structural section is shown below. If the stress in the deck in still fresh water is not to exceed 1·5 tonf/in^2, estimate the thickness of the plating if this is assumed to be constant throughout.

Fig. 6.47

(HMDTC)

7. In a calculation of the longitudinal strength for the sagging condition, the following mean ordinates in tonnef/m were found for sectional lengths of a ship each 12 m long, starting from forward:

Section	1	2	3	4	5	6	7	8	9	10	11
Weight		8·3	12·6	24·2	48·2	66·2	70·0	65·1	40·7	23·3	13·0	6·0
Buoyancy	24·8	40·6	39·2	33·6	28·2	30·0	39·6	48·7	47·4	36·0	9·5

Draw the shearing force and bending moment diagrams and state the positions and values of the maxima. (AP & S)

8. A dumb lighter is completely wall-sided, 100 m long, 20 m maximum beam and it floats at a draught of 6 m in still water. The waterline is parabolic and symmetrical about amidships with zero ordinates at the ends. The weight is evenly distributed along its length.

If the vessel is 15 m deep, has a sectional second mt. = 30 m⁴ and has a neutral axis 6 m from the keel, find the maximum hogging stress when balanced on an $L/20$ wave.

The coordinates of a trochoid are:

$\dfrac{x}{L/20}$	0	1	2	3	4	5	6	7	8	9	10
$\dfrac{z}{L/20}$	0	0·018	0·073	0·161	0·280	0·423	0·579	0·734	0·872	0·964	1·0

9. The following data apply to the half-section modulus of a ship girder 45 ft deep with an assumed neutral axis 20 ft above the keel:

	Area (in²)	1st moment about ANA (in² ft)	2nd moment about ANA (in² ft²)
Above ANA	930	16,020	331,740
Below ANA	1072	14,820	243,460

Find the stresses in the keel and upper deck if the bending moment is 200,000 tonf ft. (AP & S)

10. The data given below applies to a new frigate design. Draw the curves of loading, shearing force and bending moment for the frigate and calculate the maximum stresses in the keel and deck given that:

2nd moment of area of section about NA = 92,500 in² ft²
total depth = 34·5 ft
NA above keel = 13 ft
length = 360 ft

Ordinate	1	2	3	4	5	6	7	8	9	10	11
Buoyancy (tonf/ft)	0·90	8·05	10·16	9·26	6·80	5·80	6·15	7·46	8·91	8·89	6·32
Weight (tonf/ft)		3·8	5·6	5·8	11·9	10·2	9·9	10·4	9·9	5·3	3·6

(HMDTC)

11. The particulars of a structural strength section 13 m deep, taken about mid-depth, are as follows:

	Area (m²)	1st moment (m³)	2nd moment (m⁴)
Above mid-depth	0·33	1·82	12·75
Below mid-depth	0·41	2·16	14·35

On calculation, the maximum stress in the upper deck, for the hogging condition, is found to be 122 MN/m². Determine how many longitudinal girders must be welded to the upper deck to reduce the stress to 100 MN/m² under the same loading conditions, given that

(a) area of cross-section of each girder = 0·002 m²
(b) c.g. of each girder can be considered to be at the height of the upper deck,
(c) second moment of each girder about its own c.g. is negligible.

(HMDTC)

12. Calculate the deck and keel moduli of the structural section given below. Calculate the maximum stresses due to a sagging bending moment of 37,380 tonf ft.

Fig. 6.48

The centre of area of each girder and longitudinal may be assumed to lie in the plating to which it is attached. Second moments of girders about their own c.gs are negligible.

13. The forecastle of a destroyer is to be extended in aluminium alloy, over the midships area by the structure shown below. Details of the existing steel structural midship section are as follows:

Depth, keel to upper deck	20 ft
Neutral axis below upper deck	12·6 ft
Total area of section	750 in^2
Second moment of area about NA	81,000 in^2 ft^2
Calculated upper deck hogging stress	6·85 tonf/in^2

Calculate the stress in the deck of the alloy extension and the new keel stress for the same bending moment.

The value of E for alloy should be taken as $\frac{1}{3}$ that for steel

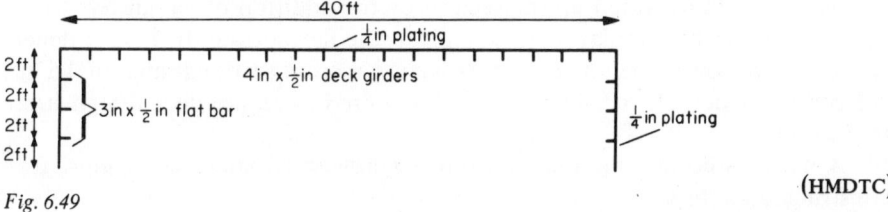

Fig. 6.49

(HMDTC)

14. An aluminium superstructure made up of a deck 10 m wide supported on two sides 3 m deep, is to be included for strength purposes with the steel structural section whose particulars are as follows:

total area of section	0·545 m^2
second moment of area	10·29 m^4
depth of section	14 m
height of NA above keel	7·20 m

Since the design stresses are already large, it is proposed to replace the steel upper deck by one of aluminium of the same cross-sectional area of 0·09 m^2.

Making reasonable first assumptions and assuming that stiffeners can be taken with the plating, determine the area/metre run of the aluminium superstructure deck and sides (assumed constant for deck and sides), to maintain the same keel stress as before.

Take E for aluminium to be $\frac{1}{3}$ that for steel.

15. A rectangular vessel is 15 m broad and 10 m deep and has deck plating 5 mm thick and sides and bottom 9 mm thick. At a certain section, it is subjected to a hogging bending moment of 65 MN m and a shearing force of 3·15 MN. Calculate, in accordance with classical beam theory,

(a) Maximum tensile and compressive stresses,

(b) Maximum shearing stress. (AP & S)

16. If, in the previous example, the deck and bottom were 9 mm thick and the sides 5 mm thick, what would then be the stresses? (AP & S)

17. A barge has a rectangular waterline 61 m long with a beam of 5·34 m.

224 Basic ship theory

When it is floating in calm sea water, the position of the maximum longitudinal bending moment is 6·1 m abaft amidships.

Deduce, from first principles, the influence lines, showing the effect on the maximum still water BM of the addition of a unit concentrated weight at any position along the length of the barge. What is the effect of an addition (a) at the extreme after end, (b) at the point of maximum BM?

Check that the effect of a load uniformly distributed along the length is zero.

18. The particulars of a structural midship section, 40 ft deep, taken about mid-depth, are as follows:

	Area (in^2)	Moment (in^2 ft)	2nd moment (in^2 ft^2)
above mid-depth	550	9000	175,000
below mid-depth	650	11,400	221,000

Displacement increases would cause deck stresses of 8 tonf/in^2 to arise in the standard sagging condition.

It is proposed to stiffen up the section by the addition of ten girders to the upper deck and five similar longitudinals to the flat bottom. If these stiffeners are to be cut down versions of T bars having a cross-sectional area of 4·5 in^2, determine the actual cross-sectional area required to reduce deck design stress to 7·5 tonf/in^2.

19. A barge is 60 m long and completely symmetrical about amidships. It is constructed of steel.

The following table gives the mean net loading between ordinates and the second moments of area of sections at regular intervals between the forward perpendicular and amidships:

	Amidships					FP
Ordinate	6	5	4	3	2	1
Load (tonnef/m)		−19	−8	7	15	5
Second moment of area (m^4)	1·77	1·77	1·77	1·60	1·28	0·42

Estimate the breakage due to this loading, which is symmetrical about amidships. $E = 209$ GN/m². (RNC)

20. The following table gives the loading diagram which was obtained after balancing a ship of length 700 ft in the standard longitudinal strength calculation:

	AE	10	9	8	7	⊕	5	4	3	2	FP
Load (tonf/ft)		9	17	18	−18	−21	−27	−18	4	24	12
$I/(10^5$ in^2 ft$^2)$	6	7·5	9	13·5	15	15	13·5	9	7·5	6	4·5

The neutral axis is 24 ft below the strength deck. Find the stress in this deck amidships.

The table also gives the MI of section at the ordinates. Estimate the relative angular movement between a missile launcher at 3 ordinate and a guidance radar amidships ($E = 3 \times 10^7$ lbf/in^2). (RNC)

21. The steel weight of a large oil tanker is 24,800 tonf. Other weights, with

their centres of gravity forward and aft of amidships are:

	Forward	Aft
Cargo	62,300 tonf at 132 ft	49,800 tonf at 121 ft
Outfit	300 tonf at 400 ft	900 tonf at 400 ft
Machinery and fuel	300 tonf at 380 ft	3400 tonf at 410 ft

The tanker has a length of 880 ft, a beam of 120 ft and a block coefficient at a draught of $0.06L$ of 0.80.

Using Murray's method, compare the section moduli required to maintain the still water stress below 3.6 tonf/in^2 and the $1.1\sqrt{L}$ sagging wave stress below 6.4 tonf/in^2.

22. The still water stress calculated for a bulk carrier by Murray's method is 75 MN/m^2. The ship is 250 m long, 35 m in beam and has a block coefficient at 15 m draught of 0.75. The actual draught is 12.5 m at which the block coefficient is 0.74. The section modulus is 28.0 m^3.

Assuming that the block coefficient remains about 0.74, estimate how much cargo should be removed from a 15 m amidships tank to reduce the stress to 60 MN/m^2.

23. A ship of length 105 m is 9 m deep. It is moored in the effluent from a power station on a cold night, which results in the keel increasing in temperature by 15°C and the upper deck falling 15°C.

Estimate the breakage resulting. The coefficient of linear expansion of steel is 0.000012 in Celsius units.

References

1. Muckle, W. The buoyancy curve in longitudinal strength calculations, *Shipbuilder and Marine Engine Builder*, Feb., 1954.
2. Smith, W. E. Hogging and sagging strains in a seaway as influenced by wave structure, *TINA*, 1883.
3. Vallentine, H. R. *Applied hydrodynamics*, Butterworths, 1969.
4. Goodman, R. A. Wave excited main hull vibration in large tankers and bulk carriers, *TRINA*, 1971.
5. Bishop, R. E. D. Eatock Taylor, R. and Jackson, K. L. On the structural dynamics of ship hulls in waves, *TRINA*, 1973.
6. Murray, J. M. Notes on the longitudinal strength of tankers, *TNEC*, 1965.
7. Murray, J. M. Further notes on the strength of tankers, *TNEC*, 1965.
8. Admiralty Ship Welding Committee. Report on hogging and sagging tests on all welded tanker MV Neverita, *Report R1* HMSO, 1946.
9. Caldwell, J. B. Ultimate longitudinal strength, *TRINA*, 1965.
10. Mansour, A. Probabilistic design concepts in ship structural safety and reliability, *TSNAME*,1972.
11. Mansour, A. and Faulkner, D. On applying the statistical approach to extreme sea loads and ship hull strength, *TRINA*, 1965.
12. Meek, M. *et al.* The structural design of the OCL container ships, *TRINA*, 1972.
13. Little, R. S. and Lewis, E. V. A statistical study of wave induced bending moments on large ocean going tankers and bulk carriers, *TSNAME*, 1971.
14. Gibsztein, M. Stress concentration at rectangular openings with rounded corners in plates of finite dimensions, *European Shipbuilding*, 1965.
15. Chapman, J. C. The interaction between a ship's hull and a longitudinal superstructure, *TINA*, 1957.
16. Caldwell, J. B. The effect of superstructures on the longitudinal strength of ships, *TINA*, 1957.
17. McCallum, J. The strength of fast cargo ships, *TRINA*, 1974.
18. Proceedings of the International Congress on Ship's Structures.

7 Structural design and analysis

It is not possible within the confines of one chapter—or even a book of this size—to present the naval architect with all that he should know about the design and analysis of the ship's structure. The object of this chapter is to provide an understanding of the structural behaviour of the ship and a recognition of the unit problems. Applied mechanics and mathematics will have provided the tools; now they must be applied to specific problems. The scope and the limitations of different theories must be known if they are to be used with success and the student needs to be aware of the various works of reference. Recognition of the problem and knowledge of the existence of a theory suitable for its solution are exceedingly valuable to the practising engineer. He rarely has the time to indulge an advanced and elegant theory when a simple approach provides an answer giving an accuracy compatible with the loading or the need. On the other hand, if he recognizes that a simple approach is inadequate, he must discard it. It is therefore understanding and recognition which this chapter seeks to provide.

Optimum design is often assumed to mean the minimum weight structure capable of performing the required service. While weight is always significant, cost, ease of fabrication and ease of maintenance are also important. Cost can increase rapidly if non-standard sections or special quality materials are used; fabrication is more difficult with some materials and, again, machining is expensive. This chapter discusses methods for assessing the minimum requirements to provide against failure. The actual structure decided upon must reflect all aspects of the problem.

The whole ship girder provides the background and the boundaries for local structural design. The needs of the hull girder for areas at deck, keel and sides must be met. Its breakdown into plating and stiffener must be determined; there is also much structure required which is not associated with longitudinal strength; finally, there are many particular fittings which require individual design. An essential preliminary to the analysis of any structure or fitting, however, is the assessment of the loading and criterion of failure.

LOADING AND FAILURE

Because it is partly the sea which causes the loading, some of the difficulties arising in Chapter 6 in defining the loading apply here also. The sea imposes on areas of the ship impact loads which have not yet been extensively measured, although the compilation of a statistical distribution of such loading continues. Until this information is available, a comparative approach is necessary; a loading which is likely to provide a suitable basis for comparison must be decided upon and used to compare the behaviour of previous successful and unsuccessful ships. For example, in designing a panel of plating in the outer bottom, hydrostatic pressure due to draught might provide a suitable basis of comparison, and examination of previous ships might indicate that when the ratio of permanent set to thickness exceeded a certain percentage of the breadth to thickness ratio, extensive cracking occurred.

Some loads to which parts of the structure are subject are known with some accuracy. Test water pressure applied during building (to tanks for example), often provides maximum loads to which the structure is subject during its life; bulkheads cannot be subjected to a head greater than that to the uppermost watertight deck, unless surging of liquid or shift of cargo is allowed for; forces applied by machinery are generally known with some accuracy; acceleration loads due to ship motion may be known statistically. More precise analytical methods are warranted in these cases.

Having decided on the loading, the next step is to decide on the ultimate behaviour, which, for brevity, will be called failure. From the point of view of structural analysis, there are four possible ways of failing, by (*a*) direct fracture, (*b*) fatigue fracture, (*c*) instability, and (*d*) unacceptable deformation.

(*a*) *Direct fracture* may be caused by a part of the structure reaching the ultimate tensile, compressive, shear or crushing strengths. If metallurgical or geometrical factors inhibit an otherwise ductile material, it may fail in a brittle manner before the normally expected ultimate strength. It should be noted, that yield does not by itself cause fracture and cannot therefore be classed as failure in this context;

(*b*) *Fatigue fracture*. The elastic fatigue lives of test specimens of materials are fairly well documented. The elastic fatigue lives of complex structures are not divinable except by test, although published works of tests on similar structural items may give a lead. The history of reversals in practical structures at sea also requires definition. Corrosion fatigue is a special case of accelerated failure under fatigue when the material is in a corrosive element such as sea water. The 'bent nail' fatigue is another special case, in which yield is exceeded with each reversal and the material withstands very few reversals;

(*c*) *Instability*. In a strut, buckling causes an excessive lateral deflection; in a plating panel, it may cause load shirking by the panel or wrinkling; in a cylinder under radial pressure, instability may cause the circumference to corrugate; in a plating stiffener it may cause torsional tripping. Most of these types of instability failure are characterized by a relatively rapid increase in deflection for a small increase in load and would generally be regarded as failure if related to the whole structure; where only part of the structure shirks its load, as sometimes happens, for example, with panels of plating in the hull girder section, overall 'failure' does not necessarily occur.

(*d*) *Deformation*. A particular deflection may cause a physical foul with machinery or may merely cause alarm to passengers, even though there is no danger. Alignment of machinery may be upset by excessive deflection.

228 *Basic ship theory*

Such deformations may be in the elastic or the elasto-plastic range. The stiffness of a structure may cause an excessive amplitude of vibration at a well used frequency. Any of these could also constitute failure.

For each unit of structure in a ship, first the loading must be decided and then the various ways in which it would be judged to have failed must be listed and examined. What are these units of structure?

STRUCTURAL UNITS OF A SHIP

There are four basic types of structure with which the ship designer must deal: (a) plating-stiffener combinations, (b) panels of plating, (c) frameworks, (d) fittings.

(a) *Plating-stiffener combinations.* The simplest form of this is a single simple beam attached to a plate. Many parallel beams supporting plating constitute a grillage with unidirectional stiffening. Beams intersecting at right angles constitute an orthogonally stiffened grillage. These various units may be initially flat or curved, loaded in any plane and possess a variety of shapes and boundaries.

(b) *Panels of plating.* These are normally rectangular and supported at the four edges, subject to normal or in-plane loads. Initially, they may be nominally flat or dished;

(c) *Frameworks.* These may be portals of one or more storeys. Frameworks may be constituted by the transverse rings of side frames and deck beams or the longitudinal ring of deck girder, bulkhead stiffeners and longitudinal. They may be circular as in a submarine. Loading may be distributed or concentrated in their planes or normal to their planes.

(d) *Fittings.* There is a great variety of fittings in ships the adequacy of whose strength must be checked. Particular ones include control surfaces such as rudders and hydroplanes, shaft brackets and spectacle plates, masts, derricks, davits and machinery seatings.

Let us examine the methods of analysis available for each of these four basic structural units.

Stiffened plating

SIMPLE BEAMS

Very many of the local strength problems in a ship can be solved adequately by the application of simple beam theory to a single stiffener-plating combination. This is permissible if the boundaries of the unit so isolated are truly represented by forces and moments that adjacent units apply to it. Frequently, when there is a series of similarly loaded units, the influence of adjacent units on the edges will be zero; similarity longitudinally might also indicate that the end slopes are zero. These edge constraints have a large influence and in many cases will not be so easily determined. It is important that the deflection of the supporting structure is negligible compared with the deflection of the isolated

Structural design and analysis 229

Fig. 7.1

beam, if the unit is to be correctly isolated; this is likely to be true if the supports are bulkheads but not if they are orthogonal beams. A summary of results for common problems in simple beams is given in Fig. 7.2. (See pp. 230 and 231.)

According to the Bernoulli–Euler hypothesis from which the simple theory of bending is deduced, sections plane before bending remain plane afterwards and

$$\sigma = \frac{M}{I} y$$

For many joists and girders this is very closely accurate. Wide flanged beams and box girders, however, do not obey this law precisely because of the manner in which shear is diffused from the webs into the flanges and across the flanges. The direct stresses resulting from this diffusion do not quite follow this law but vary from these values because sections do not remain plane. Distribution of stress across stiffened plating under bending load is as shown by the wavy lines in Fig. 7.3, and this effect is known as the shear lag effect. While the wavy

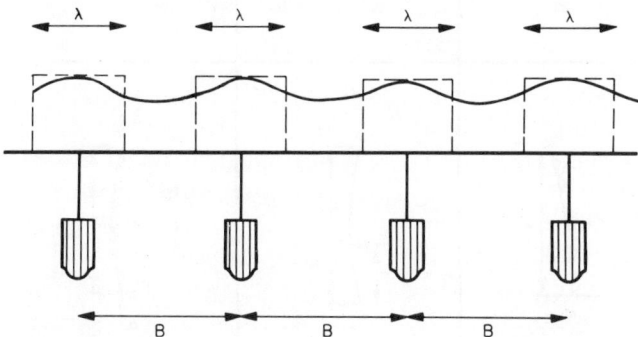

Fig. 7.3 Shear lag effects

230 Basic ship theory

Problem	Bending moments	Deflections
Cantilever with point load W at B, length l, fixed at A	$BM_A = Wl$	$\delta_B = \dfrac{Wl^3}{3EI}$
Cantilever with distributed load p', fixed at A	$BM_A = \dfrac{p'l^2}{2}$	$\delta_B = \dfrac{p'l^4}{8EI}$
Simply supported beam with point load W at distance a from A	$BM_B = Wa\left(\dfrac{l-a}{l}\right)$	$\delta = \dfrac{Wx}{6EI}\left(\dfrac{l-a}{l}\right)(2al - a^2 - x^2) + \dfrac{W}{6EI}[x-a]^{3*}$ if $a = \dfrac{l}{2}$, $\delta_B = \dfrac{Wl^3}{48EI}$ * Disregard last term if $x < a$.
Simply supported beam with distributed load p' and end axial loads P; $u = \dfrac{l}{2}\sqrt{\dfrac{P}{EI}}$	$BM_B = \dfrac{p'l^2}{8} \cdot \dfrac{2(1 - \cos u)}{u^2 \cos u}$	$\delta = \dfrac{p'l^2}{4Pu^2}\left\{\dfrac{\cos u(1 - 2x/l)}{\cos u} - 1\right\} - \dfrac{p'x(l-x)}{2P}$ if $P = 0$, $\delta_B = \dfrac{5p'l^4}{384EI}$

$BM_C = Wa\left(\dfrac{l-a}{l}\right)^2$ $BM_A = W(l-a)\left(\dfrac{a}{l}\right)^2$ if $a = \dfrac{l}{2}$, $BM_A = BM_C = \dfrac{Wl}{8}$	$\delta_{max} = \dfrac{2Wa^3}{3EI}\left(\dfrac{l-a}{l+2a}\right)^2$ if $a = \dfrac{l}{2}$, $\delta_B = \dfrac{Wl^3}{192EI}$	
$BM_A = BM_C = \dfrac{pl^2}{12}$	$\delta = \dfrac{p'x^2(l-x)^2}{24EI}$ $\delta_B = \dfrac{p'l^4}{384EI}$	
For AB $BM = \dfrac{Wl}{2u} \cdot \dfrac{\sin\dfrac{2ux}{l}\sin 2u\left(1-\dfrac{a}{l}\right)}{\sin 2u}$ max at $x = \dfrac{\pi l}{4u}$ or a For BC $BM = \dfrac{Wl}{2u} \cdot \dfrac{\sin\dfrac{2au}{l}\sin 2u\left(1-\dfrac{x}{l}\right)}{\sin 2u}$ max at $x = l\left(1-\dfrac{\pi}{4u}\right)$ or a	For AB $\delta = \dfrac{Wl}{2uP}\left\{\dfrac{\sin 2u\left(1-\dfrac{a}{l}\right)\sin\dfrac{2ux}{l}}{\sin 2u} - \dfrac{2xu}{l}\left(1-\dfrac{a}{l}\right)\right\}$ For BC $\delta = \dfrac{Wl}{2uP}\left\{\dfrac{\sin\dfrac{2au}{l}\sin 2u\left(1-\dfrac{x}{l}\right)}{\sin 2u} - \dfrac{2au}{l}\left(1-\dfrac{x}{l}\right)\right\}$	

Fig. 7.2 Beam formulae

distribution of stress cannot be found without some advanced mathematics, the maximum stress can still be found by simple beam theory if, instead of assuming that all of the plating is partially effective, it is assumed that part of the plating is wholly effective. This effective breadth of flange, λ, (Fig. 7.3), is used to calculate the effective second moment of area of cross-section. It is dependent on the type of loading and the geometry of the structure. Figure 7.4 shows the effective breadths given by Ref. 1. These values do not hold when there is appreciable panel dishing due to welding; in that common case an assumption of $\lambda = B/2$ is usually made.

There remains, in the investigation of the single stiffener-plating combination, the problem of behaviour under end load. Classical Euler theories assume perfect struts and axial loads which never occur in practice. Many designers use these or the Rankine–Gordon formula which embraces the overriding case of yield, together with a factor of safety often as high as twenty or thirty. This is not a satisfactory approach, since it disguises the actual behaviour of the member. Very often, in ship structures there will be a lateral load, which transforms the problem from one of elastic instability into one of bending with end load. Typical solutions appear in Fig. 7.2. The lateral load might be sea pressure, wind, concentrated weights, personnel load, cargo or flooding pressure. However, there will, occasionally, arise problems where there is no lateral load in the worst design case. How should the designer proceed then?

Practical structures are always, unintentionally, manufactured with an initial bow, due to welding distortion, their own weight, rough handling or processes of manufacture. It can be shown that the deflection of a strut with an initial simple bow y_0 is given by:

$$y = \frac{P_E}{P_E - P} y_0 \quad (y \text{ is the total deflection, including } y_0).$$

$P_E/(P_E - P)$ is called the *exaggeration factor*. P_E is the classical Euler collapse load, $P_E = \pi^2 EI/l^2$, l being the effective length (Fig. 7.5).

The designer must therefore decide first what initial bow is likely; while some measurements have been taken of these in practical ship structures, the designer will frequently have to make a common-sense estimate. Having decided the value, and calculated the Euler load, the designer can find the maximum deflection from the equation above.

The maximum bending moment for a member in which end rotation is not constrained is, of course,

$$\text{Max BM} = P y_{max}$$

In general, so far as end loading is concerned, the assumption of simple support is safe.

GRILLAGES

Consider the effect of a concentrated weight W on two simply-supported beams at right angles to each other as shown in Fig. 7.6. This is the simplest form of grillage. Assume that the beams, defined by suffixes 1 and 2, intersect

Structural design and analysis

Single girder, effective breadth = λ / B

L/B	Uniform load	Concentrated load		
		$\beta = 0.01$	$\beta = 0.10$	$\beta = 1.00$
0.5	0.191	0.092	0.133	0.150
1.0	0.362	0.152	0.242	0.288
2.0	0.665	0.312	0.414	0.518
4.0	0.885	0.467	0.592	0.720
6.0	0.943	0.554	0.687	0.802
8.0	0.969	0.611	0.748	0.850
10.0	0.982	0.653	0.792	0.878

Stiffened plating, effective breadth = λ / B

L/B	Uniform load	Concentrated load		
		$\beta = 0.01$	$\beta = 0.10$	$\beta = 1.00$
0.5	0.196	0.092	0.136	0.154
1.0	0.399	0.156	0.256	0.313
2.0	0.737	0.328	0.438	0.580
4.0	0.989	0.501	0.638	0.795
6.0	1.045	0.596	0.744	0.881
8.0	1.069	0.661	0.814	0.934
10.0	1.080	0.701	0.855	0.960

L = Span of simply supported beam or distance between points of zero bending moment for fixed ends (which for a uniformly distributed load is 0.58 of the span).

$\beta = \dfrac{1}{6} \dfrac{h t_w}{bt}$ for double identical flanges

$\beta = \dfrac{1}{4} \dfrac{h t_w}{bt}$ for single flanges or stiffened plating.

Fig. 7.4 Effective breadth of plating

234 Basic ship theory

Fig. 7.5

each other in the middle and that each is simply supported. What is not immediately obvious is how much the flexure of beam 1 contributes to supporting W and how much is contributed by the flexure of beam 2. Let the division of W at the middles be R_1 and R_2, then

$$R_1 + R_2 = W$$

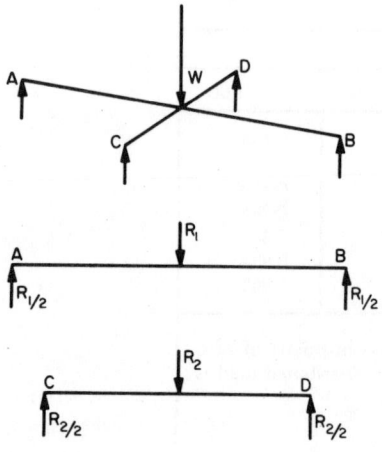

Fig. 7.6

Examining each beam separately, the central deflections are given by

$$\delta_1 = \frac{R_1 l_1^3}{48 E I_1}$$

and

$$\delta_2 = \frac{R_2 l_2^3}{48EI_2}$$

But, if the beams do not part company, $\delta_1 = \delta_2$

$$\therefore \quad \frac{R_1 l_1^3}{I_1} = \frac{R_2 l_2^3}{I_2}$$

Since $R_1 + R_2 = W$,

$$\delta = \frac{W l_1^3}{48EI_1} \times \frac{1}{\left(1 + \frac{I_2 l_1^3}{I_1 l_2^3}\right)}$$

and the maximum bending moments in the two beams are

$$\text{Max BM}_1 = \frac{R_1 l_1}{4} = \frac{W l_1}{4\left(1 + \frac{I_2 l_1^3}{I_1 l_2^3}\right)}$$

$$\text{Max BM}_2 = \frac{R_2 l_2}{4} = \frac{W l_2}{4\left(1 + \frac{I_1 l_2^3}{I_2 l_1^3}\right)}$$

This has been an exceedingly simple problem to solve. It is not difficult to see, however, that hand computation of this sort could very quickly become laborious. Three beams in each direction, unaided by symmetry could give rise to nine unknowns solved by nine simultaneous equations. Moreover, a degree of fixity at the edges introduces twelve unknown moments while moments at the intersections cause twist in the orthogonal beams. Edge restraint, uneven spacing of stiffeners, differing stiffeners, contribution from plating, shear deflection and other factors all further contribute to making the problem very difficult indeed.

Fig. 7.7

Advanced mathematical theories have been evolved to solve these problems in a variety of ways with various assumptions, and computers have been programmed to turn the theories into data sheets of use to the practising designer. The first of these data for general use were those published in Ref. 2 but quite little has been published since Refs. 3, 4 and 5. More will surely follow, particularly for the cases of the curved grillages which form much of the ship structure and for the grillages with edge loading in the plane of the grillage, combined with lateral loading.

SWEDGED PLATING

Fabrication costs can be reduced in the construction of surfaces which need not be plane, by omitting stiffeners altogether and creating the necessary flexural rigidity by corrugated or swedged plating. Main transverse bulkheads in a large oil tanker, for example, may have a depth of swedge of 25 cm. Such plating is incorporated into the ship to accept end load in the direction of the swedges as well as lateral loading. It tends to create difficulties of structural discontinuity where the swedge meets conventional stiffeners, for example where the main transverse bulkhead swedges meet longitudinal deck girders.

Buckling of some faces of the plating is possible if the swedges are not properly proportioned and it is this difficulty, together with the shear diffusion in the plating, which makes the application of simple beam theory inadequate. Development of design techniques continues and Ref. 6 gives suitable design data. Properly designed, corrugated plating is highly efficient.

Panels of plating

Knowledge of the behaviour of panels of plating under lateral pressure (sometimes called plate elements) has advanced rapidly since 1956. It is important for the designer to understand the actual behaviour of plates under this loading, so that he can select the theory or results most suitable for his application. To do this, consider how a panel behaves as the pressure is increased.

BEHAVIOUR OF PANELS UNDER LATERAL LOADING

Consider, at first, the behaviour of a rectangular panel with its four edges clamped, and unable to move towards each other. As soon as pressure is applied to one side, elements in the plate develop a flexural resistance much like the elements of a simple beam but in orthogonal directions. Theories relating the pressure to the elastic flexural resistance of the plate alone are called *small deflection theories*. As the pressure is increased and deflection of the same order as the plate thickness results, the resistance of the plate to the pressure stiffens because of the influence of membrane tension. This influence

Fig. 7.8 *Flexural resistance of a plate*

is dependent upon the deflection, since the resistance is due to the resolute of the tension against the direction of the pressure. Clearly, it has but a small influence when the deflection is small. Figure 7.9 shows a typical section through the plate; the orthogonal section would be similar. Elastic theories which take into account both flexural rigidity and membrane tension are called *large deflection theories*.

Fig. 7.9 *Membrane tension effects in a plate*

With a further increase in pressure, yield sets in, deflection increases more rapidly and the effect of membrane tension becomes predominant. The plate is partly elastic and partly plastic and theories relating to the behaviour following the onset of yield are called *elasto-plastic theories*. Yield is first reached at the middles of the two longer sides on the pressure side of the plate; soon afterwards, yield is reached on the other side of the plate and this area of plasticity spreads towards the corners. Plasticity spreads with increase in pressure in the stages illustrated in Fig. 7.10. The plastic areas, once they have developed through the thickness, are called hinges since they offer constant resistance to rotation. Finally, once the hinges have joined to form a figure of eight, distortion is rapid and the plate distends like a football bladder until the ultimate tensile strength is reached.

The precise pattern of behaviour depends on the dimensions of the panel but this description is typical. There can be no doubt that after the first onset of yield, a great deal of strength remains. Unless he has good reasons not to do so, the designer would be foolish not to take advantage of this strength to effect an economical design. Once again, this brings us to an examination of 'failure'. As far as a panel under lateral pressure is concerned, failure is likely to be either fatigue fracture or unacceptable deflection. Deflection considered unacceptable for reasons of appearance, to avoid the 'starved horse' look, might nowadays be thought an uneconomical criterion. In considering fatigue fracture, it must be remembered that any yield will cause some permanent set; removal of the load and reapplication of any lesser load will not increase the permanent set and the plate will behave elastically. A plate designed to yield under a load met very rarely, will behave elastically for all of its life save for the one loading which causes the maximum permanent set. Indeed, initial permanent set caused by welding distortion will permit the plate to behave elastically, thereafter, if this is taken as the maximum acceptable permanent set.

Fig. 7.10 *Onset of plasticity in a plate*

In ship's structures, small deflection elastic theories would be used for plates with high fluctuating loading such as those opposite the propeller blades in the outer bottom and where no permanent set can be tolerated in the flat keel, or around sonar domes, for example, in the outer bottom. Large deflection elastic theory is applicable where deflection exceeds about a half the thickness, as is likely in thinner panels. Elastoplastic theories are appropriate for large areas of the shell, for decks, bulkheads and tanks.

AVAILABLE RESULTS FOR FLAT PLATES UNDER LATERAL PRESSURE

The three ranges covered by the different theories are illustrated in Fig. 7.11. It is clear that unless the correct theory is chosen, large errors can result.

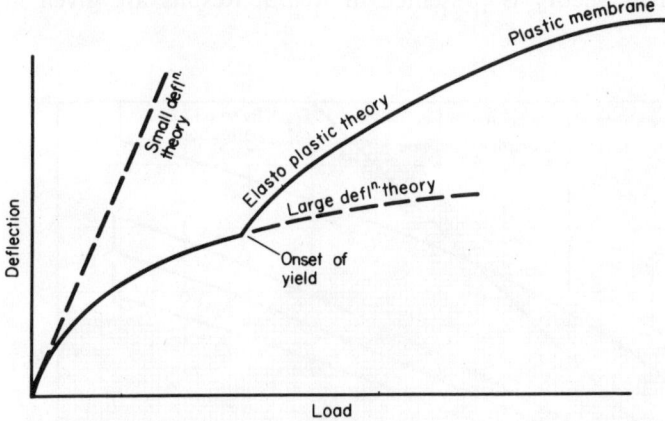

Fig. 7.11 Comparison of plate theories

Small deflection elastic theory for plates with clamped edges has been presented in Ref. 8 and in several empirical forms.

$$\text{Central deflection} = k_1 \cdot \frac{pb^4}{384D}$$

$$\text{Maximum stress} = k_2 \cdot \frac{p}{2}\left(\frac{b}{t}\right)^2$$

where

$$D = \frac{Et^3}{12(1-\nu^2)}$$

k_1 and k_2 are non-dimensional and the units should be consistent.

Fig. 7.12

n	1	1·25	1·50	1·75	2	∞
k_1	0·486	0·701	0·845	0·928	0·976	1·0
k_2	0·616	0·796	0·906	0·968	0·994	1·0

Large deflection elastic theory is presented in Ref. 9. Results are given in Fig. 7.13.

Fig. 7.13 Large deflection results

Elasto-plastic results have been presented in Ref. 10. The maximum allowable pressure is there defined, arbitrarily, as the lesser pressure which will cause either

(a) a central plastic hinge in a long plate or 1·25 times the pressure which causes yield at the centre of a square plate; or
(b) the membrane tension to be two-thirds the yield stress.

The first criterion applies to thick plates and the latter to thin plates. Design curves giving maximum permissible pressure, deflection and permanent set based on these criteria are shown in Fig. 7.14.

An important extension to plate theory is given in Ref. 11, in which pressures have been calculated which will not permit any increase in an initial permanent set, i.e. the plate, after an initial permanent set (caused perhaps by welding) behaves elastically. These results are presented in Fig. 7.15 for long plates.

References 12 and 13 make further important steps in examining the real behaviour of panels forming part of a grillage. These show that pull-in at the edges has an appreciable effect on panel behaviour, and that a panel in a grillage has not the edge constraint necessary to ensure behaviour in the manner of Fig. 7.14. The edge constraint which can give rise to membrane tension arises from the hoop effects in the plane of the boundary. Figure 7.16 gives design curves assuming that the edges of the panel are free to move inwards.

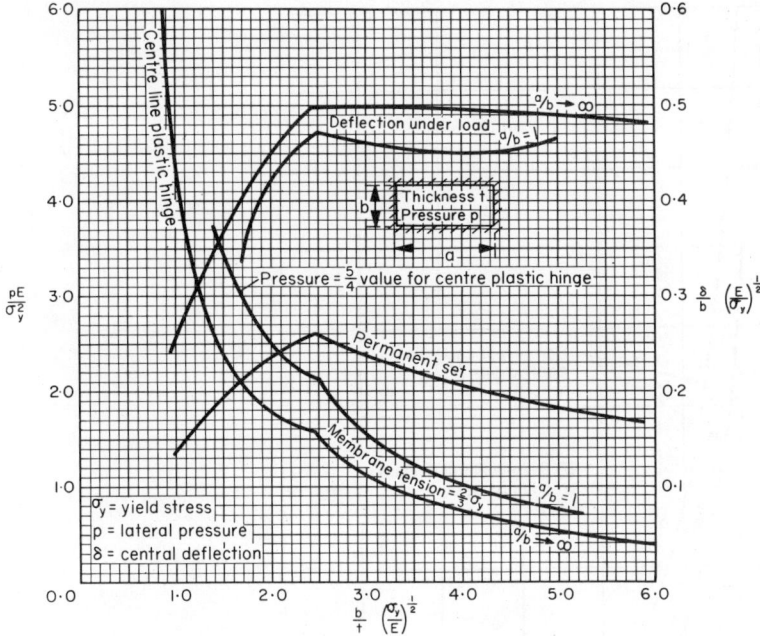

Fig. 7.14 Elasto-plastic results

EXAMPLE. Compare the design pressures suitable for a steel plate 0·56 m × 1·26 m = 6 mm yielding at 278 MN/m² assuming, (a) the edges fixed and (b) the edges free to move inwards. Calculate also the pressure which will not cause additional permanent set above an initial bow of 2·8 mm due to welding. Had the plate been initially flat, what pressure would have first caused yield?

Solution:

$$\frac{a}{b} = \frac{1\cdot26}{0\cdot56} = 2\cdot25 \quad \frac{b}{t}\left(\frac{\sigma_y}{E}\right)^{\frac{1}{2}} = \frac{0\cdot56}{0\cdot006}\left(\frac{278}{209{,}000}\right)^{\frac{1}{2}} = 3\cdot41 \text{ for which Fig. 7.14}$$

gives

$$\frac{pE}{\sigma_y^2} = 1\cdot00 \text{ approx.} \quad \text{and} \quad \frac{\delta}{b}\left(\frac{E}{\sigma_y}\right)^{\frac{1}{2}} = 0\cdot224$$

Hence,

$$\text{design pressure} = \frac{1\cdot00 \times 278^2}{209{,}000} = 0\cdot37 \text{ MN/m}^2$$

Using the same criterion of failure, viz. a permanent set coefficient of 0·224 and interpolating between the two diagrams of Fig. 7.16,

$$\frac{pE}{\sigma_y^2} = 0\cdot57 \text{ approx.}$$

242 Basic ship theory

Fig. 7.15

Hence,

$$\text{design pressure} = \frac{0.57}{1.00} \times 0.37 = 0.21 \text{ MN/m}^2$$

From Fig. 7.15, with a permanent deflection coefficient of

$$\frac{0.0028}{0.56}\left(\frac{209{,}000}{278}\right)^{\frac{1}{2}} = 0.137, \quad \text{and} \quad \frac{b}{t}\left(\frac{\sigma_y}{E}\right)^{\frac{1}{2}} = 3.41,$$

the pressure which will not cause additional permanent set is obtained from $pE/\sigma_y^2 = 0.50$, whence

$$p = \frac{0.50}{1.00} \times 0.37 = 0.185 \text{ MN/m}^2$$

Structural design and analysis 243

Fig. 7.16 Design curves for panels with edges free to move inwards

To find the pressure at which this plate begins first to yield, try first small deflection theory:

$$\frac{a}{b} = 2.25 \quad \text{so that} \quad k_2 = 1.0 \text{ approximately}$$

Then

$$278 \text{ MN/m}^2 = \frac{p}{2}\left(\frac{0.56}{0.006}\right)^2$$

whence

$$p = 0.0638 \text{ MN/m}^2$$

Check the deflection at first yield:

$$D = \frac{Et^3}{12(1-\nu^2)} = \frac{209(6)^3 \, 10^{-6}}{12(1-0.09)} = 0.00413 \text{ MN m} \quad \text{and} \quad k_1 = 0.98$$

$$\text{deflection} = \frac{0.98 \times 0.0638(0.56)^4}{384 \times 0.00413} = 3.9 \text{ mm}$$

Small deflection theory thus gives a deflection about 65 per cent of the thickness and is probably adequate. However, let us take this example to illustrate the use of large deflection theory. Because the stress is divided into two parts, direct calculation of the pressure to cause yield is not possible, and two trial pressures must be taken: referring to Fig. 7.13,

$$\frac{\sigma}{E}\left(\frac{b}{t}\right)^2 = \frac{278}{209,000}\left(\frac{0.56}{0.006}\right)^2 = 11.6$$

Now, for

$$p = 0.06 \text{ MN/m}^2 \quad \frac{p}{E}\left(\frac{b}{t}\right)^4 = \frac{0.06}{209{,}000}\left(\frac{0.56}{0.006}\right)^4 = 21.8$$

whence, from Fig. 7.13,

$$\frac{\sigma_3}{E}\left(\frac{b}{t}\right)^2 = 1.2 \quad \text{and} \quad \frac{f_2}{E}\left(\frac{b}{t}\right)^2 = 10.1$$

thus, $\sigma_3 = 28.8$ and $\sigma_2 = 242.3$ so that the total stress is 271 MN/m². Similarly, for $p = 0.07$ MN/m².

$$\frac{p}{E}\left(\frac{b}{t}\right)^4 = \frac{0.07}{0.06} \times 21.8 = 25.4$$

$$\frac{\sigma_3}{E}\left(\frac{b}{t}\right)^2 = 1.3 \quad \text{and} \quad \frac{f_2}{E}\left(\frac{b}{t}\right)^2 = 11.2$$

so that $\sigma = 31.2 + 268.7 = 300$ MN/m²

By interpolation, the pressure first first to cause yield of 278 MN/m² is 0·062 MN/m². This example typifies the use of Fig. 7.13 for large deflection elastic theory; in this particular case, it confirms that small deflection theory was, in fact, sufficiently accurate.

BUCKLING OF PANELS

Buckling of panels in the direction of the applied lateral pressure is known as snap through buckling. In Ref. 11, it is suggested that this is likely where the initial permanent set is $1\frac{1}{2}$–3 times the thickness.

Buckling due to edge loading has been dealt with on a theoretical basis in Ref. 14 and elsewhere. For a panel simply supported at its edges, the critical buckling stress is given by

$$\sigma_c = \frac{k\pi^2 E}{12(1-\nu^2)}\left(\frac{t}{b}\right)^2$$

where k is given by Fig. 7.17. When a plate does buckle in this way, it may not

Fig. 7.17

be obvious that it has occurred; in fact, the middle part of the panel shirks its load which is thrown on to the edge stiffeners. It is common practice to examine only the buckling behaviour of these stiffeners associated with a width of plating equal to thirty times its thickness.

Buckling due to shear in the plane of the plate causes wrinkling in the plate at about 45 degrees. Such a failure has been observed in the side plating of small ships at the sections of maximum shear. The critical shear stress is given by

$$\tau_c = kE\left(\frac{t}{b}\right)^2$$

where $k = 4\cdot8 + 3\cdot6\,(b/a)^2$ for edges simply supported or $k = 8\cdot1 + 5\cdot1(b/a)^2$ for edges clamped.

Frameworks

Analysis of the three-dimensional curved shape of the hull between main bulkheads is the correct approach to the determination of its strength. Results of a generalized analysis of such a three-dimensional grillage are not yet available to the practising engineer and, when they are, may not be easy to use. The reduction of the problem to two-dimensional strips or frames therefore remains important. In reducing the problem to two-dimensional frameworks, it is necessary to be aware that approximations are being made.

There are, in general, three types of plane framework with which the ship designer is concerned:

(a) orthogonal portals
(b) ship-shape rings
(c) circular rings.

Portals arise in the consideration of deckhouses, superstructures and similar structures and may have one or more storeys. If the loading in the plane of the portal is concentrated, the effect of the structure perpendicular to the plane of the portal is likely to be one of assistance to its strength. If the loading is spread over many portals, one of which is being isolated for analysis, the effects of the structure perpendicular to its plane will be small, from considerations of symmetry unless there is sideway when the in-plane stiffness of the plating will be appreciable. Thus, the reduction of the problems to two-dimensional frameworks is, in general, pessimistic and safe, although each problem should be examined on its merits.

Ship-shape rings arise by isolating a transverse slice of the ship, comprising bottom structure, side frames and deck beams, together with their associated plating. Treatment of the complete curved shell in this manner is likely to be highly pessimistic because the effect of longitudinal structure in keeping this ring to shape must be considerable. These longitudinals connect the ring to transverse bulkheads with enormous rigidity in their own planes. The calculations are, nevertheless, performed to detect the likely bending moment distribution around the ring so that material may be distributed to meet it. Transverse strength calculations are, therefore, generally comparative in nature except, perhaps, in ships framed predominantly transversely.

Circular rings occur in submarines and other pressure vessels, such as those containing nuclear reactors.

METHODS OF ANALYSIS

There are many good textbooks available, which explain the various analytical tools suitable for frameworks in more detail than is possible here. Reference 15 gives a thorough treatment of the more common framed structures met in ship design. A brief summary of four methods of particular use to the naval architect may, however, be worthwhile. These methods are: (a) moment distribution, (b) slope-deflection, (c) energy methods, and (d) limit design methods.

(a) The *moment distribution* of Hardy Cross is particularly suitable for portal problems where members are straight and perpendicular to each other. A description occurs in Ref. 16 and other textbooks. Bending moment distribution is obtained very readily by this method but slopes and deflection are not obtained without the somewhat more general approach of Ref. 17.

The moment distribution process is one of iteration in methodical sequence as follows:

(i) all joints of the framework are assumed frozen in space, the loading affecting each beam as if it were totally encastre, with end fixing moments;
(ii) one joint is allowed to rotate, the total moment at the joint being distributed amongst all the members forming the joint according to the formula $(I/l)/(\Sigma I/l)$; the application of such a moment to a beam causes a carry-over of one-half this value (if encastre at the other end) to the far end, which is part of another joint;
(iii) this joint is then frozen and a half of the applied moment is carried over to each remote end (sometimes, the carry-over factor is less than one-half—indeed, when the remote end is pinned, it is zero);
(iv) the process is repeated at successive joints throughout the framework until the total moments at each joint are in balance.

This process prevents sidesway of the framework which occurs unless there is complete symmetry. This is detected by an out-of-balance moment on the overall framework. As a second cycle of operations therefore, sufficient side force is applied to liquidate this out-of-balance without allowing joint rotation, thus causing new fixing moments at the joints. These are then relaxed by repeating the first cycle of operations and so on. A simple example of a moment distribution is given presently, but for a full treatment, the student is referred to standard textbooks on the analysis of frameworks, such as Ref. 15.

(b) *Slope deflection analysis* is based upon the fundamental equation

$$M = EI\frac{d^2y}{dx^2}$$

Thence, the area of the M/EI-curve, $= \int \frac{M}{EI} dx$, gives the change of slope,

Structural design and analysis 247

dy/dx. Integrated between two points in a beam, $\int \frac{M}{EI} dx$ gives the difference in the slopes of the tangents at the two points. Further, $\int \frac{Mx}{EI} dx$ between A and B, i.e. the moment of the M/EI-diagram about a point A gives the distance AD between the tangent to B and the deflected shape as shown in Fig. 7.18. These two properties of the M/EI-diagram are used to determine the distribution of bending moment round a framework.

Consider the application of the second principle to a single beam AB subjected to an external loading and end fixing moments M_{AB} and M_{BA} at which the slopes are θ_{AB} and θ_{BA}, positive in the direction shown in Fig. 7.18.

Fig. 7.18

Let the first moment of the free bending moment diagram (i.e. that due to the external loading assuming the ends to be pinned) about the ends A and B be respectively m_A and m_B. Then, taking moments of the M/EI-diagram about A,

$$\frac{M_{AB}}{EI}\frac{l^2}{2} - \frac{(M_{AB}+M_{BA})}{2EI}\frac{2l^2}{3} + \frac{m_A}{EI} = -l\theta_{BA} + \delta$$

i.e.

$$\theta_{BA} = -\frac{l}{6EI}\left(M_{AB} - 2M_{BA} + \frac{6m_A}{l^2}\right) + \frac{\delta}{l}$$

Taking moments about B,

$$\frac{M_{AB}}{EI}\frac{l^2}{2} - \frac{(M_{AB}+M_{BA})}{2EI}\frac{l^2}{3} + \frac{m_B}{EI} = l\theta_{AB} - \delta$$

i.e.

$$\theta_{AB} = \frac{l}{6EI}\left(2M_{AB} - M_{BA} + \frac{6m_B}{l^2}\right) + \frac{\delta}{l}$$

These expressions are fundamental to the slope deflection analysis of frameworks. They may be applied, for example, to the simple portal ABCD of Fig. 7.19, expressions being obtained for the six slopes, two of which will be zero and two pairs of which (if C and B are rigid joints) will be equated. On eliminating all these slopes there will remain five equations from which the five unknowns, $M_{AB}, M_{BA}, M_{CD}, M_{DC}$ and δ can be found. This method has the advantage over moment distribution of supplying distortions, but it becomes arithmetically difficult when there are several bays. It is suitable for computation by computer where repetitive calculations render a program worth writing. Sign conventions are important. Reference 18 gives some applications of slope deflection analysis to transverse strength.

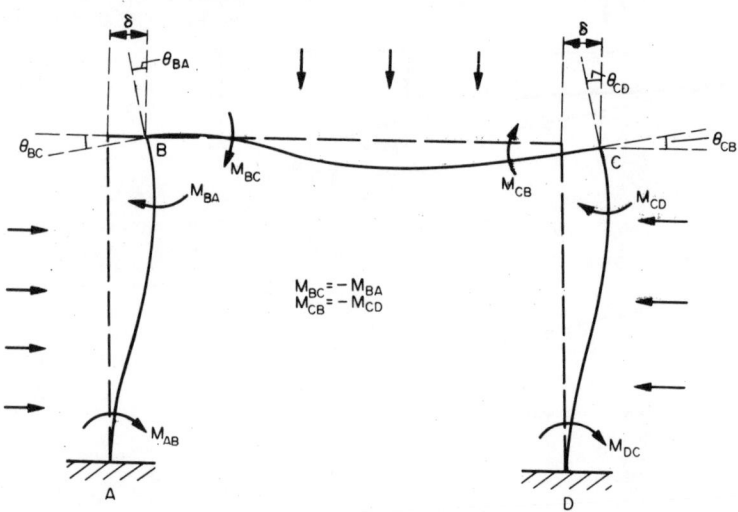

Fig. 7.19

(c) The *energy method* most useful in the context of this chapter is based on a theorem of Castigliano. This states that the partial derivative of the total strain energy U with respect to each applied load is equal to the displacement of the structure at the point of application in the direction of the load:

$$\frac{\partial U}{\partial P} = \delta_P$$

The expressions for strain energies U due to direct load, pure bending, torsion and shear are:

Direct load P, member of cross-sectional area A,

$$U = \int \frac{P^2}{2AE} dx$$

Bending moment M, curved beam of second moment I,

$$U = \int \frac{M^2}{2EI} ds$$

Torque T, member of polar second moment J,

$$U = \int \frac{T^2}{2CJ} dx$$

Shearing force S, element of cross-sectional area A, (Fig. 7.20)

$$U = \int \frac{S^2}{2AC} dx = \int \frac{\tau^2 A\, dx}{2C}$$

The strain energy in a cantilever of rectangular cross-section $a \times b$, for example, with an end load W is given by

$$U = \int_0^l \frac{M^2}{2EI} dx + \int_0^{ab} \int_0^l \frac{\tau^2}{2C} dA\, dx$$

Now shear stress τ varies over a cross-section according to the expression $\tau = (SA/Ib)\bar{y}$. For the rectangular cantilever then,

$$\tau = \frac{6W}{a^3 b}\left(\frac{a^2}{4} - y^2\right) \quad \text{and} \quad dA = b\, dy.$$

Then

$$U = \int_0^l \frac{W^2 x^2\, dx}{2EI} + 2\int_0^{a/2} \int_0^l \frac{18W^2}{a^6 bC}\left(\frac{a^4}{16} - \frac{a^2 y^2}{2} + y^4\right) dy\, dx$$

$$= \frac{W^2 l^3}{6EI} + \frac{3W^2 l}{5abC}$$

Fig. 7.20

End deflection

$$\delta = \frac{\partial U}{\partial W} = \frac{Wl^3}{3EI} + \frac{6Wl}{5abC}$$

The first expression is the bending deflection as given in Fig. 7.2, and the second expression is the shear deflection.

In applying strain energy theorems to the ring frameworks found in ship structures, it is common to ignore the effects of shear and direct load which are small in comparison with those due to bending. Confining attention to bending effects, the generalized expression becomes

$$\delta = \frac{\partial U}{\partial P} = \int \frac{M}{EI} \frac{\partial M}{\partial P} \, ds$$

Applying this, by example, to a simple ship-shape ring with a rigid centre line bulkhead which can be replaced by three unknown forces and moments, these can be found from the three expressions, since all displacements at B are zero:

$$0 = \frac{\partial U}{\partial H} = \int \frac{M}{EI} \frac{\partial M}{\partial H} \, ds$$

$$0 = \frac{\partial U}{\partial V} = \int \frac{M}{EI} \frac{\partial M}{\partial V} \, ds$$

$$0 = \frac{\partial U}{\partial M} = \int \frac{M}{EI} \frac{\partial M}{\partial M_B} \, ds,$$

summed for members BC and CDE.

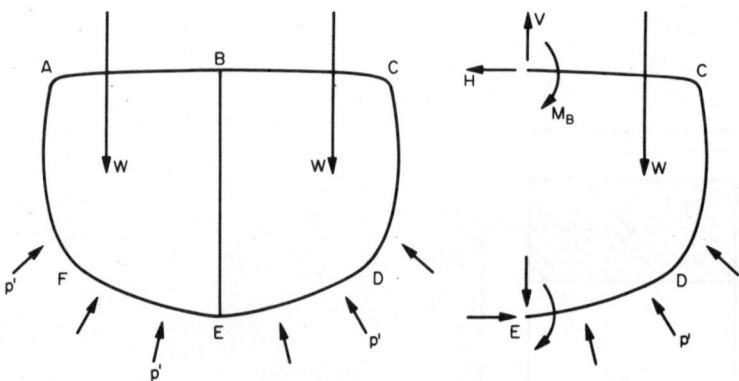

Fig. 7.21

Expressions for the bending moment M in terms of V, H, M_B and the applied load can be written down for members BC and CDE, added, and the above expressions determined. Hence V, H and M_B can be found and the bending moment diagram drawn. This method has the advantage that it deals readily with frames of varying inertia, the integrations being carried out by Simpson's rule. Like the slope deflection method, the arithmetic can become formidable.

(d) Reference 21 describes in detail the *limit design method*, called also plastic design or collapse design. This method uses knowledge of the behaviour of a ductile material in bending beyond the yield point. A beam bent by end couples M within the elastic limit has a cross-section in which the stress is proportional to the distance from the neutral axis,

$$M = \sigma Z \quad \text{where } Z = \frac{I}{y}, \quad \text{the section modulus:}$$

Fig. 7.22

Bent further, yield is reached first in the outer fibres and spreads until the whole cross-section has yielded, when the plastic moment, $M_p = \sigma_y S$ where S is the addition of the first moments of area of each side about the neutral axis and is called the plastic modulus. The ratio S/Z is called the *shape factor* which has a value 1·5 for a rectangle, about 1·2 for a rolled steel section and about 1·3 for a plating-stiffener combination. When a beam has yielded across its section, its moment of resistance is constant and the beam is said to have formed a plastic hinge.

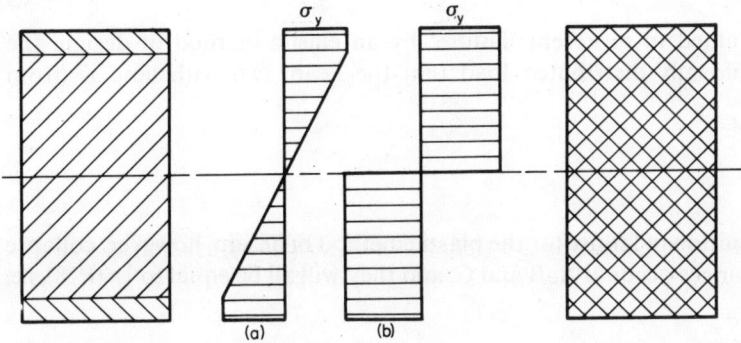

Fig. 7.23

The least load which forms sufficient plastic hinges in a framework to transform it into a mechanism is called the collapse load. A portal, for example, which has formed plastic hinges as shown in Fig. 7.24 has become a mechanism and has 'collapsed'. Let us apply this principle to an encastre beam (Fig. 7.25).

Fig. 7.24

Fig. 7.25

If yield is assumed to represent 'failure' by an elastic method of design, the maximum uniformly distributed load that the beam can withstand is (from Fig. 7.2)

$$p' = \frac{12Z\sigma_y}{l^2}$$

Using the definition of failure for the plastic method of design, however, collapse occurs when hinges occur at A, B and C, and they will all be equal to $\frac{1}{2}p'(l^2/8)$, i.e.

$$p' = \frac{16S\sigma_y}{l^2}$$

If the shape factor for the beam section is taken as 1·2, the ratio of these two maximum carrying loads is 1·6, i.e. 60 per cent more load can be carried after the onset of yield before the beam collapses.

The plastic design method is often more conveniently applied through the principle of virtual work whence the distance through which an applied load moves is equated to the work done in rotating a plastic hinge. In the simple case illustrated in Fig. 7.26, for example,

$$W \frac{l\theta}{2} = M_p\theta + M_p\theta + M_p(2\theta) = 4M_p\theta$$

i.e. collapse load, $W = 8M_p/l$. This method can be used for finding the collapse loads of grillages under concentrated load; in this case, various patterns of plastic hinges may have to be tried in order to find the least load which would cause a mechanism (Fig. 7.27).

Fig. 7.26

Fig. 7.27

Knowledge of the collapse loads of superstructures under nuclear blast or extreme winds is necessary, and the limit design method is the only way of calculating them. The method is suitable for the determination of behaviour of other parts of a ship structure subject to once-in-a-lifetime extreme loads such as bulkheads. Use of the method with a known factor of safety (or load factor), can ensure normal behaviour in the elastic range and exceptional behaviour in the plastic range—it is indeed, the only method which illustrates the real load factor over working load.

ELASTIC STABILITY OF A FRAME

The type of elastic instability of major concern to the designer of plated framed structures in a ship is that causing tripping, i.e. the torsional collapse of a stiffener sideways when the plating is under lateral load. Tripping is more likely,

(a) with unsymmetrical stiffener sections,
(b) with increasing curvature,
(c) with the free flange of the stiffener in compression, rather than in tension,
(d) at positions of maximum bending moment, especially in way of concentrated loads.

Recommended spacing, l, for tripping brackets is summarized in Fig. 7.28 for straight tee stiffeners and for curved tee stiffeners for which R/W is greater than 70.

Fig. 7.28 Spacing of tripping brackets

For curved stiffeners for which R/W is less than 70, Fig. 7.28 may be used by putting $l' = Rl/70W$. For straight unsymmetrical stiffeners l should not exceed $8W$. For curved unsymmetrical stiffeners for which R is more than $4f^2h/t^2$ (unsymmetrical stiffeners should not otherwise be used), $l = (RW/5)^{\frac{1}{2}}$ if the flange is in compression and $(2RW/5)^{\frac{1}{2}}$ if in tension.

The elastic stability of a circular ring frame under radial and end compression is the basis of important investigations in the design of submarines. Theoretically, (Ref. 14), a perfectly circular ring under radial compression will collapse in a number of circumferential corrugations or lobes. Under additional end loading, a ring stiffened cylinder may collapse by longitudinal corrugation; this load, too, alters the number of circumferential lobes due to radial pressure. Elastic instability of the whole ring stiffened cylinder between bulkheads is also possible. Finally, built-in distortions in a practical structure have an important effect on the type of collapse and the magnitude of the collapse loads. These problems involve lengthy mathematics and will not be pursued in this book (see Ref. 19). The government of the diving depth of the submarine by consideration of such elastic stability should, nevertheless, be understood.

END CONSTRAINT

The degree of rotational end constraint has more effect on deflections than it has on stresses. End constraints are shown in Ref. 20 in practical ship structures to approach the clamped condition for flexural considerations, provided that the stiffeners are properly continuous at the joint. The degree of rotational end constraint of a member is due to

(a) the stiffness of the joint itself. It is relatively simple to produce a joint which can develop the full plastic moment of the strongest of the members entering the joint; no more is necessary;
(b) the effects of the other members entering the joint. These can be calculated to give the actual rotational stiffness pertaining to the member.

Fig. 7.29

256 Basic ship theory

A square joint can provide entirely adequate stiffness and Ref. 20 gives suitable designs. Brackets may be introduced to cheapen fabrication and they also reduce, slightly, the effective span of the member. The reduction in span (Fig. 7.29) is

$$b' = \frac{b}{1+d/B}$$

EXAMPLE 2. The gantry for an overhead gravity davit comprises, essentially, a vertical deck edge stanchion 10 ft high and an overhead member 15 ft long sloping upwards at 30 degrees to the horizontal, inboard from the top of the stanchion. The two members are of the same section rigidly joined together and may be considered encastre where they join the ship.

A weight of 12 tonf acts vertically downwards in the middle of the top member. Compare the analyses of this problem by (a) arched rib analysis, (b) slope deflection, and (c) moment distribution.

Solution (a): Arched rib analysis (Castigliano's theorem)

For a point P in AB distance x from A, BM = $M_0 - Hx \sin 30 - Vx \cos 30 + 12 \cos 30[x - 7\cdot5]$, where the term [ ] is included only if positive, i.e.,

$$M = M_0 - \frac{Hx}{2} - V\frac{13x}{15} + 12 \times \frac{13}{15}\left[x - \frac{15}{2}\right]$$

$$\frac{\partial M}{\partial M_0} = 1, \quad \frac{\partial M}{\partial H} = -\frac{x}{2}, \quad \frac{\partial M}{\partial V} = -\frac{13x}{15}$$

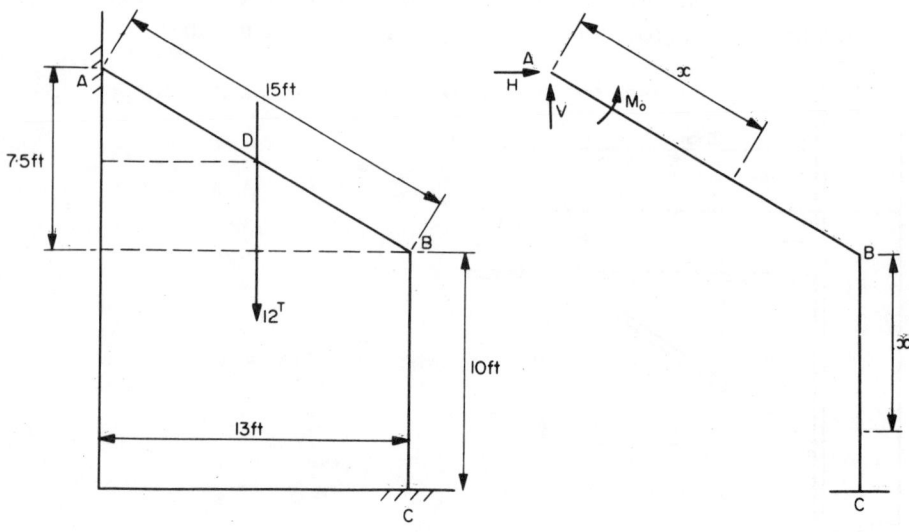

Fig. 7.30

Hence, taking care to integrate the Macaulay's brackets between the correct limits,

$$\int M \frac{\partial M}{\partial M_0} dx = 15M_0 - 56 \cdot 3H - 97 \cdot 5V + 292 \cdot 5$$

$$\int M \frac{\partial M}{\partial H} dx = -56 \cdot 3M_0 + 281 \cdot 3H + 487 \cdot 5V - 1828$$

$$\int M \frac{\partial M}{\partial V} dx = -97 \cdot 6M_0 + 487 \cdot 5H + 845 \cdot 0V - 3169$$

Similarly, for BC,

$$M = M_0 - H\frac{15}{2} - 13V + 78 - Hx$$

$$\frac{\partial M}{\partial M_0} = 1, \quad \frac{\partial M}{\partial H} = -\left(\frac{15}{2} + x\right), \quad \frac{\partial M}{\partial V} = -13$$

Hence, again, by integrating

$$\int M \frac{\partial M}{\partial M_0} dx = 10M_0 - 125H - 130V + 780$$

$$\int M \frac{\partial M}{\partial H} dx = -125M_0 + 1646H + 1625V - 9750$$

$$\int M \frac{\partial M}{\partial V} dx = -130M_0 + 1625H + 1690V - 10{,}140$$

Adding the similar expressions for AB and BC and equating to zero gives three simultaneous equations, whence

$$V = 5 \cdot 92, \quad H = 1 \cdot 71, \quad M_0 = 23 \cdot 4$$

Putting these values back into the expressions for bending moment gives

$$M_D = 21 \cdot 5, \quad M_B = 11 \cdot 6, \quad M_C = -5 \cdot 5$$

The BM diagram can thus be plotted.

A good deal of algebra has, of course, been omitted above.

Solution (b): Slope deflection (Fig. 7.31)

$$\text{Moment of free BM diagram about A or B} = \frac{1}{2} \times 39 \times \frac{15^2}{2}$$

$$= 2195 = m_A = m_B$$

258 Basic ship theory

From the slope deflection equations derived on p. 247/248

$$\theta_{AB} = 0 = \frac{15}{6EI}\left(2M_{AB} - M_{BA} + \frac{6 \times 2195}{225}\right)$$

$$\theta_{BA} = -\frac{15}{6EI}\left(M_{AB} - 2M_{BA} + \frac{6 \times 2195}{225}\right)$$

$$\theta_{BC} = \frac{10}{6EI}(2M_{BC} - M_{CB})$$

Fig. 7.31

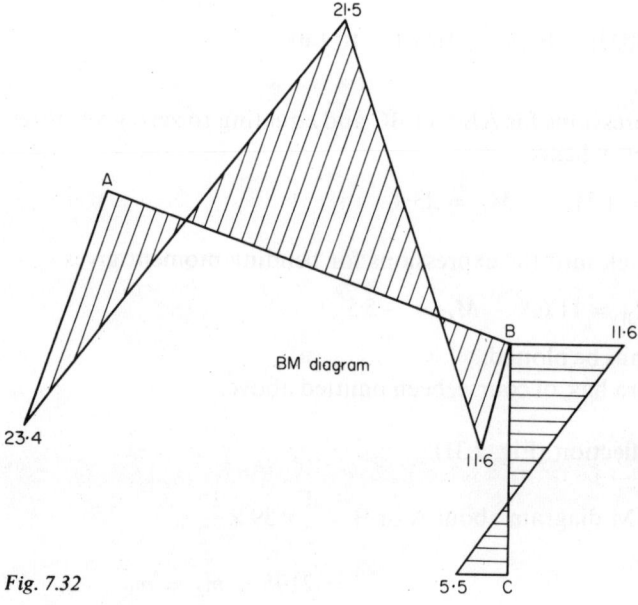

Fig. 7.32

$$\theta_{CB} = 0 = -\frac{10}{6EI}(M_{BC} - 2M_{CB})$$

Now $\theta_{BA} = \theta_{BC}$. Eliminating θ and solving the simultaneous equations gives

$M_{AB} = -23\cdot 4$

$M_{BA} = 11\cdot 7 = -M_{BC}$

$M_{CB} = -5\cdot 9$

Solution (c): Moment distribution, in the manner described in the text

	A M_{AB}	B M_{BA}	M_{BC}	C M_{CB}
Fixing moment $\frac{Wl}{8}$	19·5	−19·5	0	0
Distribution factors $\frac{I/l}{\Sigma I/l}$	—	$\frac{2}{5}$	$\frac{3}{5}$	—
Carry over factors	$\frac{1}{2}$			$\frac{1}{2}$
Fix	19·5	−19·5	0	0
Distribute		7·8	11·7	
Carry over	3·9			5·8
Totals	23·4	−11·7	11·7	5·8

From any of the above solutions the BM diagram can be sketched. (Fig. 7.32).

EXAMPLE 3. An engine room bulkhead 40 ft high is propped on one side by three equally spaced intermediate decks. Stiffeners are uni-directional and, in order to be continuous with longitudinals, must be equally spaced 2 ft 6 in. apart.

Once-in-a-lifetime loading of flooding up to 20 ft above the compartment crown is judged necessary. Top and bottom may be assumed encastre.

Compare the section moduli of stiffeners and plating thicknesses required by fully elastic and elasto-plastic analyses.

Solution: Assume, for simplicity that the hydrostatic loading is evenly distributed between each deck with a value equal to the value at mid-deck.

$$\text{Pressure A to B} = (20+5)\,\text{ft} \times \frac{64\,\text{lbf}}{\text{ft}^3} \times \frac{1\,\text{ft}^2}{144\,\text{in}^2} = 11\cdot 1\,\text{lbf/in}^2$$

$$\text{Load per foot on each stiffener A to B} = 11\cdot 1 \frac{\text{lbf}}{\text{in}^2} \times 30\,\text{in.} \times \frac{12\,\text{in.}}{1\,\text{ft}}$$

$$\times \frac{1\,\text{tonf}}{2240}\,\text{lbf} = 1\cdot 79\,\text{tonf/ft}$$

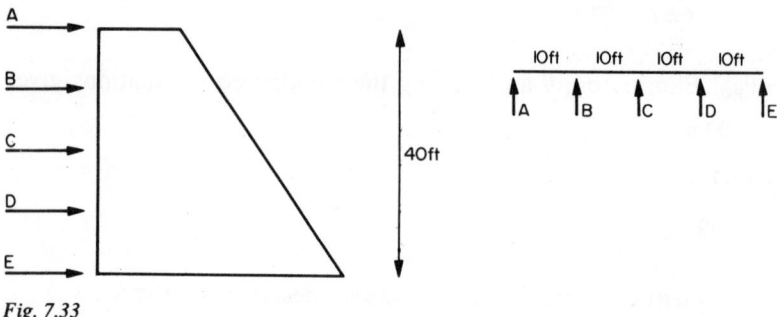

Fig. 7.33

Similarly, pressures and loads on other spans are

	AB	BC	CD	DE
p, press.	11·1	15·5	20·0	24·4 lbf/in²
p', load/ft	1·79	2·50	3·22	3·93 tonf/ft

Plating thickness: Use large deflection elastic theory, the results of which are given in Fig. 7.13. The aspect ratio $a/b = 120/30 = 4.0$ so use curves for $a/b = \infty$. Maximum stress is at the plate edge given by the addition of σ_2 and σ_3 and it is necessary to use trial values of thickness. For AB,

$$\frac{p}{E}\left(\frac{b}{t}\right)^4 = \frac{11 \cdot 1}{30 \times 10^6}\left(\frac{30}{0 \cdot 2}\right)^4 \quad \text{for trial value of } t = 0 \cdot 2 \text{ in.}$$

$$= 187 \cdot 5 \quad \text{for which, with } a/b = \infty,$$

$$\sigma = \frac{30 \times 10^6}{150^2} \times \frac{(55 \cdot 0 + 8 \cdot 0)}{2240} = 37 \cdot 5 \text{ tonf/in}^2$$

For a second trial value of $t = 0.3$ in., similarly, with $(b/t)^4 p/E = 35.8$

$$\sigma = \frac{30 \times 10^6}{100^2} \times \frac{(15 \cdot 5 + 2 \cdot 0)}{2240} = 23 \cdot 4 \text{ tonf/in}^2$$

The value of σ_3 the membrane tension, is low and is having only a small effect. Adopting small deflection theory therefore, for a yield stress of 16 tonf/in²,

$$16 \text{ tonf/in}^2 = 1 \cdot 0 \times \frac{11 \cdot 1}{2} \frac{\text{lbf}}{\text{in}^2} \times \left(\frac{30}{t}\right)^2 \times \frac{1 \text{ tonf}}{2240 \text{ lbf}}$$

$$\therefore \quad t = 30\left(\frac{11 \cdot 1}{2 \times 16 \times 2240}\right)^{\frac{1}{2}} = 0 \cdot 37 \text{ in.}$$

on small elastic theory, plating thicknesses required are

AB	BC	CD	DE
0·37	0·44	0·50	0·55 in.

Implicit in these figures is an unknown factor of safety over 'failure'. Let us now adopt the elasto-plastic definition of failure and choose, deliberately, a load factor of 2·0. Referring to Fig. 7.14 for span DE,

$$\frac{pE}{\sigma_y^2} = \frac{2 \times 24\cdot4 \times 30 \times 10^6}{(16 \times 2240)^2} = 1\cdot14$$

for which

$$\frac{b}{t}\left(\frac{\sigma_y}{E}\right)^{\frac{1}{2}} = 2\cdot95$$

so that

$$t = \frac{30}{2\cdot95}\left(\frac{16 \times 2240}{30 \times 10^6}\right)^{\frac{1}{2}} = 0\cdot35 \text{ in.}$$

Carrying out similar exercises for all bays,

Bay	AB	BC	CD	DE
$\dfrac{pE}{\sigma_y^2}$	0·52	0·72	0·93	1·14
$\dfrac{b}{t}\left(\dfrac{\sigma_y}{E}\right)^{\frac{1}{2}}$	5·00	4·10	3·40	2·95
t	0·21	0·25	0·30	0·35

A corrosion margin, say 40 per cent, now needs to be added to give thicknesses suitable for adoption. By this method, a saving has been achieved by adopting deliberate standards which are disguised by the elastic approach. Savings do not always occur, but the advantages of a rational method remain.

To determine the size of stiffeners, assumed constant for the full depth, elastic analysis is probably best carried out by moment distribution. Since the deck heights are equal at 10 ft each,

$$\text{distribution factors for B, C and D} = \frac{I/l}{\Sigma I/l} = \tfrac{1}{2}$$

The fixing moments, i.e. the residuals at the ends of AB are due to a mean uniform pressure of 11·1 lbf/in². Hence, with ends held encastre (Fig. 7.2)

$$M_{AB} = -M_{BA} = -\frac{pl^2b}{12} = -\frac{11\cdot1(120)^2(30)}{12^2\,2240} = -14\cdot9 \text{ tonf ft}$$

Similarly, due to pressures of 15·5, 20·0 and 24·4 lbf/in²

$$M_{BC} = -M_{CB} = -20\cdot8 \text{ tonf ft}$$
$$M_{CD} = -M_{DC} = -26\cdot8 \text{ tonf ft}$$
$$M_{DE} = -M_{ED} = -32\cdot7 \text{ tonf ft}$$

The resultant moments at joints B, C and D are 5·9, 6·0 and 5·9 tonf ft. Since distribution factors are $\tfrac{1}{2}$, each member takes approximately 3 tonf ft at each joint. Carry-over factors are each $\tfrac{1}{2}$ so that relaxing the 3 tonf ft moment at end

B of AB induces 1·5 tonf ft moment at A. This process is repeated for end B of BC, end C of BC, etc. The process is then repeated until the residuals at the ends of the members at each joint are substantially the same but of opposite sign, i.e. the joint as a whole is balanced. This process is worked through in the table below.

		A	B		C		D		E
		M_{AB}	M_{BA}	M_{BC}	M_{CB}	M_{CD}	M_{DC}	M_{DE}	M_{ED}
Distribution factors	$\dfrac{I/l}{\Sigma I/l}$		$\tfrac{1}{2}$	$\tfrac{1}{2}$	$\tfrac{1}{2}$	$\tfrac{1}{2}$	$\tfrac{1}{2}$	$\tfrac{1}{2}$	
Fixing moments	$\dfrac{p'l^2}{12}$	−14·9	+14·9	−20·8	20·8	−26·8	26·8	−32·8	32·8
Distribute		0	+3·0	+3·0	+3·0	+3·0	+3·0	+3·0	0
Carry over (all factors $\tfrac{1}{2}$)		+1·5	0	+1·5	+1·5	+1·5	+1·5	0	1·5
Distribute		0	−0·7	−0·7	−1·5	−1·5	−0·7	−0·7	0
Carry over		−0·4	0	−0·7	−0·4	−0·4	−0·7	0	−0·4
Totals		−13·8	17·2	−17·7	23·4	−24·2	29·9	−30·5	33·9
Distribute		0	+0·3	+0·3	+0·4	+0·4	+0·3	+0·3	0
Carry over		0·1	0	0·2	0·1	0·1	0·2	0	0·1
Totals		−13·7	17·5	−17·2	23·9	−23·7	30·4	−30·2	34·0

Maximum bending moment occurs in DE = 34·0 tonf ft.
For a maximum yield stress of 16·0 tonf/in².

$$Z = \frac{I}{y} = \frac{34 \times 12}{16} = 25\cdot5 \text{ in}^3$$

Using a plastic method of analysis, the lowest span, which must be the critical span, will become a mechanism when plastic hinges occur at D, E and near the middle of this span (Fig. 7.33). Taking a load factor of 2·0, approx.

$$M_p = \frac{\tfrac{1}{2} \times p'l^2}{12} \times 2\cdot0 = \frac{3\cdot93 \times 100}{24} \times 12 \times 2\cdot0 = 393 \text{ tonf in.}$$

$$\therefore S = \frac{393}{16\cdot0} = 24\cdot6 \text{ in}^3$$

If the shape factor is taken as 1·3, $Z = 19\cdot0$ in³. Thus, some savings occur by adopting plastic design methods for both plating and stiffeners. Because the loading is presumed to occur once in a lifetime, there is no reason why the smaller figures should not be adopted, provided that there are no other criteria of design.

While the theoretical considerations should follow, generally, the elasto-plastic and plastic methods illustrated in this example, there are other features which need to be brought out in the design of main transverse bulkheads. It will often be found economical to reduce scantlings of both stiffeners and plating towards the top, where it is warranted by the reduction in loading. Continuity of bulkhead stiffener, bottom longitudinal and deck girder is of extreme importance and will often dictate stiffener spacings. In ships designed to withstand the effects of underwater explosion, it is important to incorporate thicker plating around the edges and to permit no piercing of this area by pipes or other stress raisers; the passage of longitudinal girders must be carefully compensated; fillet connections which may fail by shear must be avoided.

Fittings

CONTROL SURFACES

Control surfaces in a ship are those which, through hydrodynamic lift and drag forces, control the motion of the ship. They include rudders, stabilizers, hydroplanes, hydrofoils and tail fins. The forces and their effects on the ship are discussed at length in other chapters. In this chapter, we are concerned with the strength of the surface itself, the spindle or stock by which it is connected to operating machinery inside the ship and the power required of that machinery.

Those control surfaces which are cantilevered from the ship's hull are the most easily calculable because they are not redundant structures. The lift and drag forces for ahead or astern motions (given in Chapter 13) produce a torque T and a bending moment M at section Z of the stock. If the polar moment of inertia of the stock is J, the maximum shear stress is given by

$$\tau_{max} = \frac{D}{2J}(M^2 + T^2)^{\frac{1}{2}}$$

Fig. 7.34 Forces and moment on a control surface

Permissible maximum stresses are usually about $3 \cdot 0$ tonf/in^2 for mild steel (45 MN/m^2) and $4 \cdot 5$ tonf/in^2 for best quality forged steel (70 MN/m^2). At section Y of the stock, torque required for the machinery to which the stock is subjected is augmented by the friction of the sleeve, whence

$$T^1 = T + P\mu\frac{D}{2}$$

The value of the coefficient of friction μ is about $0 \cdot 2$. The power required of the machinery is given by T^1 multiplied by the angular velocity of rotation of the surface: for a stabilizer fin this might be as high as 20 deg/s, while for a rudder it is, typically, 2–3 deg/s.

When there are pintle supports to the rudder, the reactions at the pintles and sleeve depend upon the wear of the bearings that is permitted before renewal is demanded. The effects of such wear may be assumed as given in Fig. 7.35.

Fig. 7.35 Forces assumed acting on rudders

Permitted bearing pressure at the sleeve which is usually about $\frac{1}{2}$ in. thick is about 1500 lbf/in² (10·3 MN/m²),

$$\frac{R}{L(D+2t)}$$ should not exceed 1500 lbf/in² (10·3 MN/m²)

At the pintles, classification societies take about the same bearing pressure. Ship department takes a somewhat larger figure.

$$\frac{Q}{ld}$$ should not exceed 5600 lbf/in² (38·6 MN/m²).

Fig. 7.36

The shearing stress in the steel pintle due to Q should not exceed the figures used for the stock itself. Structure of the rudder is analysed by conventional means, the stock continuation being regarded as a beam subject to the loads of Fig. 7.35. Because erosion can be severe the acceptable stresses are low.

SHAFT BRACKETS

A shaft bracket houses the long shaft bearing adjacent to the propeller or partway along an exposed shaft, and comprises essentially a cylinder attached to the hull by two arms of hydrofoil section. The arms may be angled slightly to the axis of the cylinder to align with the hydrodynamic flow, but it is bad practice from the point of view of strength to crank the arms so that they enter the hull normally. Shaft brackets are either fabricated or forged. Spectacle plates are forgings or castings in the shape of a pair of spectacles connecting twin shafts with a centre skeg by single arms; they generally form the extremities of the shaft swell plating.

A hydrofoil shape commonly used in warships is given in Fig. 7.37.

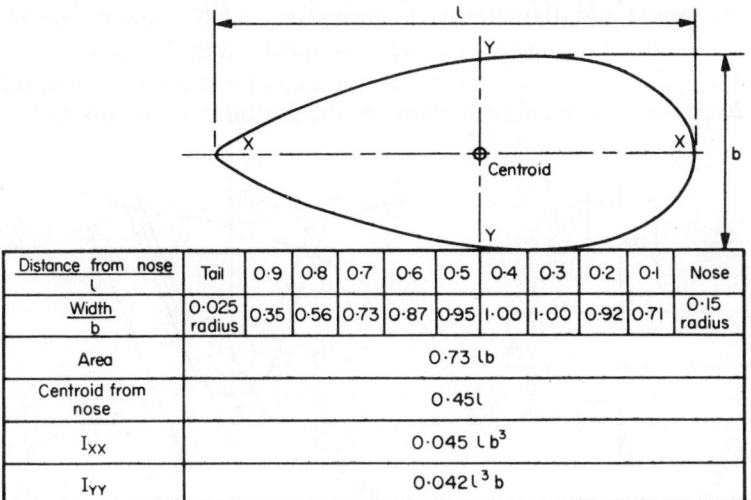

Distance from nose l	Tail	0.9	0.8	0.7	0.6	0.5	0.4	0.3	0.2	0.1	Nose
Width b	0.025 radius	0.35	0.56	0.73	0.87	0.95	1.00	1.00	0.92	0.71	0.15 radius
Area	\multicolumn{11}{c	}{$0.73\,lb$}
Centroid from nose	\multicolumn{11}{c	}{$0.45l$}
I_{XX}	\multicolumn{11}{c	}{$0.045\,lb^3$}
I_{YY}	\multicolumn{11}{c	}{$0.042\,l^3 b$}

Fig. 7.37 *Properties of hydrofoil section*

Perfect propellers in open water would not throw any load other than weight on the shaft brackets. In practice, loads may be thrown on to the brackets by,

(a) weights of propeller and shafting, accentuated by ship motion;
(b) gyroscopic effects under conditions of ship motion, including turning;
(c) variation in hydrodynamic forces on the blades;
(d) centrifugal forces when a blade is lost;
(e) whirling of the shaft.

So far as (c) is concerned, since the propeller operates in the wake of the shaft bracket, the opening between the arms should be kept as large as possible to reduce the magnitude of the wake. Also since each blade experiences a change in hydrodynamic load as it passes through the wake of each shaft bracket arm, the angle between the arms must not be equal to the angle between the propeller blades. (a) to (c) are difficult to estimate with any accuracy. Investigation of each of these effects has led to a comparative type calculation in which the largest of the following three forces is assumed to act at the centre of the propeller,

(a) F_1, based on the force needed to shear the steel propeller shaft,

$$F_1 = \frac{\pi}{10} \frac{(d_1^4 - d_2^4)}{d_1^2} \text{ tonf}$$

(b) F_2, based on the centrifugal force when a blade is lost,

$$F_2 = \frac{WN^2 D}{10^5} \text{ tonf}$$

(c) F_3, based on the accentuated weight of the propeller

$F_3 = 9W$ tonf

Where d_1 and d_2 are external and internal shaft diameters in inches, W tonf and D ft are the weight and diameter of the propeller, and N is the full power revolutions per minute of the shaft. The largest of these forces, F, is assumed to cause a rotating force in the plane of the arm axes and a moment $0.8Fh$, the reduction of 20 per cent assumed to account for the flexibility of the shaft.

Fig. 7.38

Thorough analysis of many shaft brackets has shown that three of the effects of this force are important (Fig. 7.37)

(a) longitudinal bending of an arm about YY,
(b) transverse bending of an arm about XX,
(c) axial tension or compression in an arm.

The values of these can be determined by a somewhat laborious analysis whose important results are summarized in Fig. 7.39. Maximum stress due to transverse bending will occur out of phase with those due to the longitudinal bending and the axial stress. It is not unusual to adopt the pessimistic assumption that they all occur together.

	Longitudinal bending moment M_L	Transverse bending moment M_T	Axial loading stress
Symbols	$M_1 = \pm\tfrac{1}{2}(0.8Fh)\sec\beta$ $M_2 = \pm\dfrac{u}{2}(0.8Fh)\csc\beta$ $u = \dfrac{l(a/2 + l/3)}{a^2 + al + l^2/3}$		A = arm cross-sectional area
Value	$M_1 \cos\alpha + M_2 \sin\alpha$	$\tfrac{1}{2}Fku \sin\alpha$	
Max value occurring at	$(M_1^2 + M_2^2)^{\frac{1}{2}}$ $\tan\alpha = \pm u \cot\beta$	$\tfrac{1}{2}Fku$ $\alpha = \pi/2$	$F/A \csc 2\beta$

Fig. 7.39

Although maximum stresses due to each plane of bending occur at the extremities of the neutral axes, the combined maxima occur in between these points at various points around the hydrofoil section. If σ_L and σ_T are the individual maxima due to longitudinal and transverse bending, the combined maximum stress for the hydrofoil of Fig. 7.37 is given approximately by

$$\sigma_{max} = 0{\cdot}5\sigma_L + 0{\cdot}9\sigma_T \quad \text{provided that} \quad \sigma_T > \tfrac{2}{5}\sigma_L$$

This should be augmented by that axial stress of the same sign and the total stress should not be permitted to exceed 14 tonf/in^2 if the arms are fabricated in mild steel or 18 tonf/in^2 if forged.

Finite Element Techniques

The displacement δ of a simple spring subject to a pull p at one end is given by $p = k\delta$ where k is the stiffness. Alternatively, $\delta = fp$ where f is the flexibility and $f = k^{-1}$.

If the forces and displacements are not in the line of the spring or structural member but are related to a set of Cartesian coordinates, the stiffness will differ in the three directions and, in general

$$\mathbf{p}_1 = \mathbf{k}_{11}\delta_1 + \mathbf{k}_{12}\delta_2$$
$$\text{and} \quad \mathbf{p}_2 = \mathbf{k}_{21}\delta_1 + \mathbf{k}_{22}\delta_2$$

This pair of equations is written in the language of matrix algebra

$$\mathbf{P} = \mathbf{K}\,\mathbf{d}$$

$\mathbf{P}$ is the complete set of applied loads and $\mathbf{d}$ the resulting displacements. $\mathbf{K}$ is called the stiffness matrix and is formed of such factors $\mathbf{k}_{11}$ which are called member stiffness matrices (or sub-matrices). For example, examine a simple member subject to loads p_X and p_Y and moments m at each end causing displacements δ_X, δ_Y and θ.

For equilibrium,
$$m_1 + m_2 + p_{Y_2}l = 0 = m_1 + m_2 - p_{Y_1}l$$
also $p_{X_1} + p_{X_2} = 0$

For elasticity,

$$p_{X_1} = -p_{X_2} = \frac{EA}{l}(\delta_{X_1} - \delta_{X_2})$$

From the slope deflection analysis on page 246 et seq. can be obtained

$$m_1 = \frac{6EI}{l^2}\delta_{Y_1} + \frac{4EI}{l}\theta_1 - \frac{6EI}{l^2}\delta_{Y_2} + \frac{2EI}{l}\theta_2$$

These equations may be arranged

$$\begin{bmatrix} p_{X_1} \\ p_{Y_1} \\ m_1 \end{bmatrix} = \begin{bmatrix} \dfrac{EA}{l} & 0 & 0 \\ 0 & \dfrac{12EI}{l^3} & \dfrac{6EI}{l^2} \\ 0 & \dfrac{6EI}{l^2} & \dfrac{4EI}{l} \end{bmatrix} \begin{bmatrix} \delta_{X_1} \\ \delta_{Y_1} \\ \theta_1 \end{bmatrix} + \begin{bmatrix} -\dfrac{EA}{l} & 0 & 0 \\ 0 & -\dfrac{12EI}{l^3} & \dfrac{6EI}{l^2} \\ 0 & -\dfrac{6EI}{l^2} & \dfrac{2EI}{l} \end{bmatrix} \begin{bmatrix} \delta_{X_2} \\ \delta_{Y_2} \\ \theta_2 \end{bmatrix}$$

i,e.
$$p = k_{11}\delta_1 + k_{12}\delta_2$$
This very simple example is sufficient to show that a unit problem can be expressed in matrix form. It also suggests that we are able to adopt the very powerful mathematics of matrix algebra to solve structural problems which would otherwise become impossibly complex to handle. Furthermore, computers can be quite readily programmed to deal with matrices. A fundamental problem is concerned with the inversion of the matrix to discover the displacements arising from applied loads, viz.
$$d = K^{-1}P$$
Now strains are related to displacements,
$$\epsilon = Bd$$
For plain strain for example,
$$\epsilon = \begin{bmatrix} \epsilon_x \\ \epsilon_y \\ \gamma_{zy} \end{bmatrix} = \begin{bmatrix} \dfrac{\partial u}{\partial x} \\ \dfrac{\partial v}{\partial y} \\ \dfrac{\partial u}{\partial y} + \dfrac{\partial v}{\partial x} \end{bmatrix} = Bd$$
and stress is related to strain,
$$\sigma = D\epsilon$$
D is a matrix of elastic constants which, for plane stress in an isotropic material is
$$D = \frac{E}{1-\nu^2} \begin{bmatrix} 1 & \nu & 0 \\ \nu & 1 & 0 \\ 0 & 0 & \frac{1}{2}(1-\nu) \end{bmatrix}$$
There are other relationships which are valuable such as the transformation matrix which changes reference axes. These together form the set of tools required for the solution of structural problems using finite element techniques. This brief description can do little more than explain the concept and the student must examine the references given (Refs. 15, 22, 23). Finite element analysis is approached broadly as follows:

(a) The structure is divided up by imaginary lines meeting at nodes, forming finite elements which are often triangular or rectangular and plane (but may be irregular and three-dimensional.)
(b) For each element, a displacement function is derived which relates the displacements at any point within the element to the displacements at the nodes. From the displacements strains are found and from the strains, stresses are derived.
(c) Forces at each node are determined equivalent to the forces along the boundaries of the element.
(d) Displacements of elements are rendered compatible with their neighbour's (this is not often totally possible).
(e) The whole array of applied loads and internal forces are arranged to be in equilibrium.

It is not within the scope of this book to describe how this analysis is carried out. It requires a good knowledge of the shorthand of matrix algebra and draws upon the work described in this chapter concerning various unit problems of beams, panels, grillages and frameworks and also the concepts of relaxation techniques and minimum strain energy.

It places in the hands of the structural analyst, a tool of enormous power and flexibility. There is no longer any need to make the assumption of simple beam theory for the longitudinal strength of the ship; the ship girder may now be built

Fig. 7.40 Analysis of typical derrick

Fig. 7.41

up from finite elements (Fig. 7.41) and the effects of the loads applied by sea and gravity determined. Indeed, this is now the basis for the massive suites of computer programs available for the analysis of total ship structure. The effects of the sea spectra are translated by strip theory into loads of varying probability and the effects of those loadings upon a defined structure are determined by finite element analysis. It is not yet a perfect tool. Moreover, it is a tool of analysis and not of design which is often best initiated by cruder and cheaper methods before embarking upon the expense of these programs.

Problems

1. A bottom longitudinal is in an area subject to an end compressive stress of 100 MN/m² and is at a still water draught of 4 m. With a width of steel plating of 28 cm assumed to be fully effective, estimate the maximum stress under the end load and a lateral load due to twice the draught. Spacing of longitudinals

is 36 cm and 1 m (simply supported), plating thickness is 4 mm and the T bar stiffener has the following properties

flange (cm)	depth (cm)	c.s. area (cm^2)	MI (toe) (cm^4)	MI (N.A.)(cm^4)
4	8	5·0	196·0	30·0

2. A transverse floor in a double bottom is 53 cm deep and 1·6 cm thick. Adjacent floors are 3 m apart and the outer bottom is 1·9 cm thick and the inner bottom is 0·8 cm thick. Each floor is supported by longitudinal bulkheads 4 m apart and is subjected to a uniformly distributed load from the sea.
   Calculate the effective modulus of section.
3. A tubular strut of length 3 m external diameter 8 cm cross-sectional area 16 cm^2 and moment of inertia about a diameter 150 cm^4 when designed for an axial working load of 0·1 MN may be assumed to be pin-ended. It has an initial lack of straightness in the form of a half sine wave, the maximum (central) departure from the straight being 8 mm; find (a) the ratio of the maximum working stress to the yield stress of 270 MN/m^2 and (b) the ratio of the working load to the load which would just cause yield ($E = 209$ GN/m^2). (RNC)
4. A square grillage is composed of six equally spaced beams of length 10 ft, three in each direction. The beams are fixed at their ends and are each acted on by a uniformly distributed load of 2 tonf/ft throughout the length. The central beam in each direction has a moment of inertia of 36 in^4. The others have the same moment of inertia which need not be that of the central beams; what should this moment of inertia be in order that no beam shall exert a vertical force on another? If, in fact, each of these four beams has a moment of inertia of 18 in^4, what is the central deflection? (RNC)
5. Four girders, each 12 m long, are arranged two in each of two orthogonal directions to form a square grillage of nine equal squares. The ends of all girders are rigidly fixed and the joints where the girders intersect are capable of transmitting deflection and rotation. All four members are steel tubes with polar MI of 0·02 m^4.
   Find the deflection at an intersection when a uniformly distributed load of 2 MN/m is applied along each of two parallel girders and the two other girders are unloaded. (Modulus of rigidity is $\frac{3}{8}$ of Young's modulus.) (RNC)
6. Calculate by the plastic design method, the 'collapse' load of a grillage in which all members are tubes of mean diameter 8 in., thickness $\frac{1}{8}$ in. and of steel of yield point 16 tonf/in^2. The grillage is 32 ft × 21 ft, consisting of three members 21 ft long spaced 8 ft apart in one direction, intersecting at right angles two members 32 ft long spaced 7 ft apart. The ends of all members are fixed. At each joint there is an equal concentrated load perpendicular to the plane of the grillage. Ignore torsion.
7. Three parallel members of a grillage are each 4 m long and equally spaced 2 m apart. They are intersected by a single orthogonal girder 8 m long. All ends are simply supported and each member has a second moment of area of 650 cm^4. Each member is subject to a uniformly distributed load of 15,000 N/m. Calculate the maximum deflection. Neglect torsion. $E = 20·9$ MN/cm^2.
8. A long flat panel of plating is 40 in. wide and subject to a uniform pressure of

25 lbf/in². What thickness should it be

(a) so that it nowhere yields,
(b) to permit a membrane stress of (28/3) tonf/in², $E = 13,500$ tonf/in², $\sigma = 0.3$ and yield stress $= 14$ tonf/in².

9. An alloy steel plate $1.50 \text{ m} \times 0.72 \text{ m}$ has an initial bow due to welding of 3 mm in the middle. It is 6 mm thick and made of steel with a Y.P. of 248 MN/m².

What pressure would this plate withstand without causing further permanent set? If the plate had been considered initially flat, what pressure would small deflection theory have given to have caused yield? What would have been the deflection?

10. The yield stress of an alloy plate is 30 tonf/in² and Young's modulus is 8000 tonf/in². The plate is 60 in. × 20 in. × 0·20 in. thick and its edges are constrained against rotation. Calculate the approximate values of

(a) the pressure first to cause yield;
(b) the elasto-plastic design pressure assuming edges restrained from inward movement;
(c) the design pressure assuming edges free to move in and a permanent set coefficient of 0·2;
(d) the pressure which the plate could withstand without further permanent set if bowed initially by 0·10 in., the edges assumed restrained.

11. A boat is supported from the cross bar of a portal frame at points 6 ft from each end. The vertical load at each point of support is 2 tonf. The portal is 10 ft high and 30 ft long and is made of thin steel tube 8 in. in diameter and $\frac{1}{8}$ in. thick; the steel has a yield point of 18 tonf/in².

If both feet are considered encastre, find the load factor over collapse in the plane of the portal. Ignore the effects of axial load.

Find also, by a moment distribution method, the ratio of the maximum working stress to the yield stress. (RNC)

12. When a temporary stiffener is welded diametrically across a completed ring frame of a submarine, bad fitting and welding distortion cause a total diametral shrinkage of 8 mm.

Fig. 7.42

The mean diameter of the steel ring is 6·1 m. The MI of the frame section is 5000 cm⁴ and the least section modulus of the ring is 213 cm³. What is the greatest stress induced in the frame?

13. Due to careless building, the ring frame shown in Fig. 7.42 is left unsupported while being built into a ship. The deck beam is an 8 in. T bar of 10 lbf/ft run with an MI of 34 in⁴, while the ribs are 6 in. T bars of 8 lbf/ft run with an MI of 17 in⁴. Members are straight and the ribs rigidly attached to the double bottom. The neutral axes of section for the deck beams and ribs are respectively 6 in. and 4·5 in. from the toe.

Assuming that the frame does not buckle out of its plane, find the maximum stress due to its own weight.

14. Light alloy superstructure above the strength deck of a frigate may be treated as a symmetrical two-dimensional single storey portal as shown. The MI of AD, AE and DH is 5,000 cm⁴ and of BF and CG is 2330 cm⁴ All joints are rigid except F and G where the elasticity of the deck causes carry-over factors of $\frac{1}{4}$ from B to C. Find the bending moment distribution in the structure when a load of 19,200 N/m is carried evenly along AD.

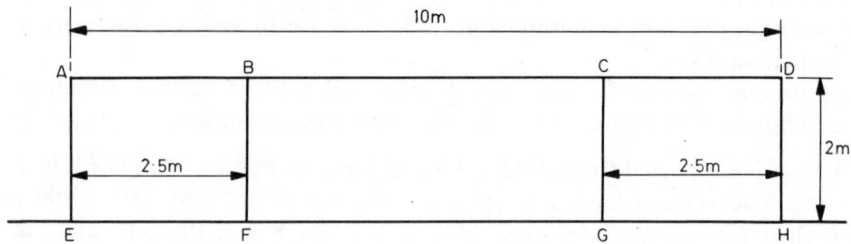

Fig. 7.43

15. The structure of a catapult trough is essentially of the shape shown. G and H are fixed rigidly but the rotary stiffnesses of A and F are such as to allow one-half of the slope which would occur were they to be pinned.

The mid-point of CD is subjected to a vertical force of 120 tonf as shown.

Fig. 7.44

(RNC)

Calculate the distribution of bending moment in the structure both by moment distribution and slope deflection analysis,

Members	AB, EF	BC, ED	CG, DH	CD
Length (ft)	3·0	2·0	6·0	4·0
I (in^4)	180	140	60	160

16. Calculate the collapse load of a rectangular portal having 3 m stanchions and a 8 m cross bar all made of tubes 20 cm in diameter, 3 mm thick and having a yield stress of 250 MN/m².

The lower feet are pinned and the upper corners rigid. Equal loads are applied horizontally inwards at the middle of each stanchion and vertically downwards at the middle of the crossbar. (Neglect the effect of end compression on the plastic moment of resistance.) (RNC)

17. The balanced rudder shown (Fig. 7.45) has a maximum turning angle of 35 degrees and is fitted immediately behind a single propeller. What torque and bending moment are applied to the rudder stock at the lower end of the sleeve bearing when the rudder is put fully over at a ship's speed of 26 knots?

In the force equation, take the constant $k = 0.100$. Also if the length of an elemental strip of the rudder surface, drawn at right angles to the centre line of the stock is l, then assume the centre of pressure of the strip to be $0.32l$ from the leading edge. (HMDTC)

18. Limiting the shear stress to 4·5 tonf/in², what should be the diameter of the stock, if solid, of the previous question? If the coefficient of friction at the sleeve is 0·20 and the rate of turn at 35 degrees is 3 degrees per second, what power is required of the steering gear?

Fig. 7.45

19. For a symmetrical shaft bracket with arms of conventional shape, $\beta = 18°$, $a = 5·2$ ft, $l = 5·9$ ft, $k = 44·0$ in., $h = 61·6$ in. The arm section is 27 in. × 4·5 in.

Find the maximum stress in each arm near the barrel for a load of 65 tonf at the propeller. (AP & S)

References

1. Schade, H. A. The effective breadth concept in ship structure design, *TSNAME*, 1953 and 1951
2. Schade, H. A. Design curves for cross stiffened plating, *TSNAME*, 1941.
3. Clarkson, J., Wilson, J. B. and McKeeman, J. L. Data sheets for the elastic design of flat grillages under uniform pressure, *European Shipbuilding*, 1959.
4. Clarkson, J. The design for minimum weight of simply-supported flat grillages to withstand a single concentrated load, *TNEC*, 1956-7.
5. Clarkson, J. *The elastic analysis of flat grillages*, Cambridge University Press, 1965.
6. Bell, A. O., Viner, A. C. and Richardson, W. S. Beam and column strength of stiffened plating, *TRINA*, 1963.
7. Smith, C. S. Compression strength of welded steel ship grillages, *TRINA*, 1975.
8. Inglis, C. E. and Bailey, F. Stresses in rectangular plates clamped at their edges and loaded with a uniformly distributed pressure, *TINA*, 1925.
9. Timoshenko, S. and Woinowsky-Krieger, S. *Theory of plates and shells*, McGraw-Hill, 1959.
10. Clarkson, J. A new approach to the design of plates to withstand lateral pressure, *TINA*, 1956.
11. Clarkson, J. The strength of approximately flat long rectangular plates under lateral pressure, *TNEC*, 1957-8.
12. Clarkson, J. Uniform pressure tests on plates with edges free to slide inwards, *TRINA*, 1962.
13. Aalami, B. and Chapman, J. H. Large deflection behaviour of ship plate panels under normal pressure and in-plane loading, *TRINA*, 1972.
14. Timoshenko, S. *Theory of elastic stability*, McGraw-Hill, 1961.
15. Gregory, M. *Linear framed structures*, Longman, 1966.
16. Wright, J. *Distribution methods of analysis*, Thames Hudson, 1963.
17. Southwell, R. *Relaxation methods in engineering sciences*, Oxford University Press, 1940.
18. Thurston, J. W. E. Transverse strength, *TINA*, 1958.
19. Kendrick, S. B. The buckling under external pressure of ring stiffened circular cylinders, *TRINA* 1965.
20. Faulkner, D. Welded connections used in warship structures, *TRINA*, 1965.
21. Neal, B. G. *The plastic methods of structural analysis*, Chapman and Hall, 1965.
22. Livesley, R. K. *Matrix methods of structural analysis*, Pergamon, 1964.
23. Zienkiewicz, O. C. *The finite element method*, McGraw-Hill, 1967.
24. Kendrick, S. B. The structural design of supertankers, *TRINA*, 1970.
25. *A guide for the analysis of ship structures*, US Dept of Commerce, 1960.

8 Launching and docking

It is probably the enormity of the problem of moving a ship into and out of the water that most catches the imagination. The majesty of a launch is hardly less awesome than the sight of a ship from the bottom of a dock. Neither operation can be achieved without sound practical knowledge guided by some basic theory. Some practical steps are discussed in Refs. 1 and 2. This chapter is concerned with some important theoretical considerations associated with launching and docking.

Launching

A ship is most advantageously built on land under cover. Save for the conveyor belt method of construction pioneered in Scandinavia and for a few covered slipways, building under cover is not common because of the high capital cost of covering so large an area. It is best built on land because of the practical difficulties of building it in the water associated with construction, quality control and transport. A dry dock can be used and flooded up when the ship is sufficiently far advanced in construction, but a dry dock is generally too valuable a capital asset to be so long engaged. Generally, therefore, whenever possible it is preferred to build a ship on a slipway. Occasionally, these are partially or wholly below high water level and the site is kept dry by doors which, on the chosen day are opened to let the water in and provide some buoyancy to the hull. More often, the hull is constructed wholly above water and slid into the water when it is ready. Very small hulls may be built on a cradle which is lowered on wheels down a ramp into the water, but ships over about 100 tonf displacement must be slid on greased ways under the action of gravity.

Usually, the ship slides stern first into the water because this part of the ship is more buoyant, but bow first launches are not unknown. The theory presently described is applicable to both. Less often, the ship is slid or tipped sideways into the water and the considerations are then rather different.

In a well ordered, stern first launch, sliding ways are built around the ship, and shortly before the launch the gap separating them from the fixed groundways is filled by a layer of grease to which the weight of the ship is transferred from the building blocks.

There may be one, two or even four ways; generally, there are two although in Holland one way with propping ways at the sides are common. The ways are inclined and, often, cambered. Movement is prevented until the desired moment by triggers which are then knocked away to allow the ship to move under gravity down the inclined ways. After it begins to enter the water, buoyancy builds up at the stern until it reaches a value sufficient to pivot the entire ship about the fore poppet (i.e. the forward end of the launching cradle). The ship continues down the ways until it is floating freely having slid away from, or dropped off the end of, the ways. If launched in a restricted waterway, its progress into the water is impeded by drags which are arranged so as to gradually bring the vessel to a stop before it strikes the far bank.

Fig. 8.1 A stern first launch

Consider what might go wrong with this procedure. The grease might be too slippery or not slippery enough. It might be squeezed out by the pressure. Instead of the stern lifting, the ship might tip the wrong way about the end of the groundways and plunge. The forefoot might be damaged by dropping off the end of the ways or it may dig into the slip when the stern has lifted. The ship might be insufficiently strong locally or longitudinally or the ways may collapse. The braking effect of the drags might be too much or too little. The ship might, at some instant, be unstable.

Calculations are carried out before arranging the launch to investigate each one of these anxieties. The calculations predict the behaviour of the ship during launch, to enable a suitable high tide to be selected and to arrange the ship and slip to be in a proper and safe condition.

LAUNCHING CURVES

A set of six curves is prepared to predict the behaviour of the ship during launch. They are curves, plotted against distance of travel down the slip, of

(i) Weight, W
(ii) Buoyancy, Δ
(iii) Moment of weight about fore poppet, Wa
(iv) Moment of buoyancy about fore poppet, Δd
(v) Moment of weight about after end of groundways, Wb
(vi) Moment of buoyancy about after end of groundways, Δc

The geometry of the ship at any position in its travel down the ways is illustrated in Fig. 8.2 for the ways in contact. A distributed load $(W-\Delta)$ along the ways is not shown; after the stern lifts this becomes concentrated all at the fore poppet. Conventionally, the moment (v) is drawn positive when anticlockwise and (vi) is drawn positive when clockwise. A typical set of launching curves is shown in Fig. 8.3.

Launching and docking 277

Fig. 8.2 Ship and way geometry

The important features of these curves are as follows:

(a) at the point at which the moment of buoyancy about the fore poppet equals the moment of weight about the fore poppet, the stern lifts;
(b) the difference between the weight and buoyancy curves at the position of stern lift, is the maximum force on the fore poppet;
(c) the curve of moment of buoyancy about the after end of the ways must lie wholly above the curve of moment of weight; the least distance between the two curves of moment about the after end of ways, gives the least moment against tipping about the end of ways;
(d) crossing of the weight and buoyancy curves before the after end of ways, indicates that the fore poppet will not drop off the end of the ways.

These curves answer some of the anxieties about the launch directly, but certain other investigations are necessary. From the difference between the

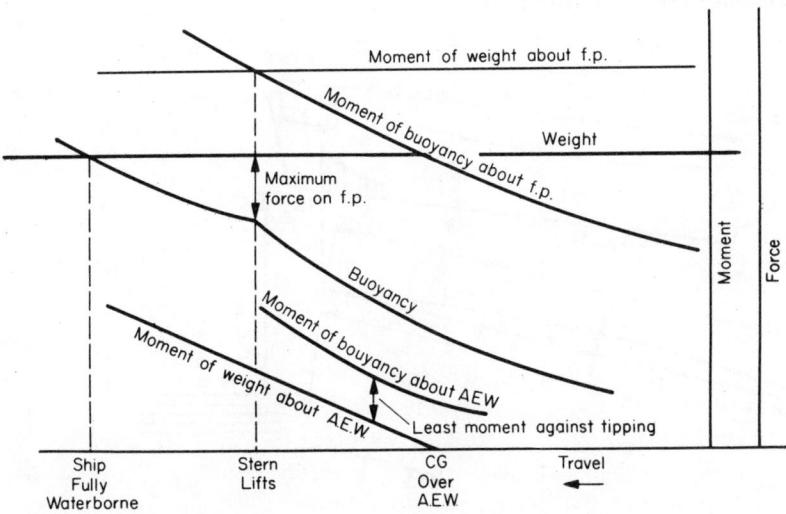

Fig. 8.3 Typical launching curves

278 Basic ship theory

weight and buoyancy curves before stern lift, the grease pressures can be determined. This difference at stern lift (and for *Queen Mary* for example, it was 8325 tonf) giving the maximum force on the fore poppet, enables the poppet and internal strengthening of the ship to be devised; it also causes a loss of stability. From all of these features is judged the adequacy of the height of tide and the length of ways. Indeed, curves are usually constructed·for more than one height of water to determine the minimum acceptable height. How are the curves constructed?

CONSTRUCTION OF LAUNCHING CURVES

The curve of weight results usually from the weights weighed into the ship plus an estimate of what remains to be built in during the period between calculation and launch. Centre of gravity position is similarly estimated and the two moment of weight curves produced.

Buoyancy and centre of buoyancy at any position of travel is determined by placing the relevant waterline over a profile of the ship with Bonjean curves drawn on and integrating in the usual fashion. For this calculation, dynamic considerations are ignored and the ship is assumed to travel very slowly. While the correct waterline can be determined by sliding a tracing of the ship over a drawing of the slip, it is more accurately found from the geometry of the situation. Let

α = the initial slope of the keel
L = length between perpendiculars
e = distance of the fore poppet abaft the FP
h = initial height of the fore poppet above water
β = declivity of groundways, i.e. slope of chord
f = camber of ways of length K
r = radius of camber
t = distance abaft the fore poppet

Fig. 8.4

From simple mensuration, the camber of an arc of a circle is given by

$$f = \frac{K^2}{8r} \quad \text{so that} \quad (f-y) = \frac{(K-2x)^2}{8r}$$

$$\therefore \quad y = \frac{K^2}{8r} - \frac{(K-2x)^2}{8r} = x\frac{(K-x)}{2r}$$

After travelling a distance x, the fore poppet is raised y above the chord and the keel has moved through an angle x/r. The height of the fore poppet above the water is now therefore, approximately

$$h - \beta x + y = h - \beta x + \frac{x}{2r}(K-x),$$

while the height above water of a point t abaft the fore poppet is

$$h - \beta x + y - t\left(\alpha + \frac{x}{r}\right) = h - \beta x + \frac{x}{2r}(K-x) - t\left(\alpha + \frac{x}{r}\right)$$

If there is no camber, r is, of course, infinite.

If, in this expression t is put equal to $-e$, it will give the height of the keel at the FP above water or, when it is negative, below water, i.e. the draught at the FP. If t is put equal to $L-e$, the expression gives the negative draught at the AP. Thus, for a given travel down the ways x, a waterline can be drawn accurately on the Bonjean profile from which buoyancy and centre of buoyancy can be determined.

This is satisfactory when the ways are fully in contact, but after stern lift, while the draught at the fore poppet can be determined in this way, trim cannot. Now at all times after stern lift the moments of weight and buoyancy about the fore poppet must be equal. For the position of travel under consideration, the fore poppet draught is found as already described; buoyancy and moment of buoyancy are then calculated for several trims about the fore poppet and a curve plotted as shown in Fig. 8.5. Where the curves of moment about fore poppet cut, there is the correct trim; buoyancy can be read off and the position of centre of buoyancy calculated. Having determined the correct trim, the passage of the forefoot to assess the clearance from the slip can be drawn.

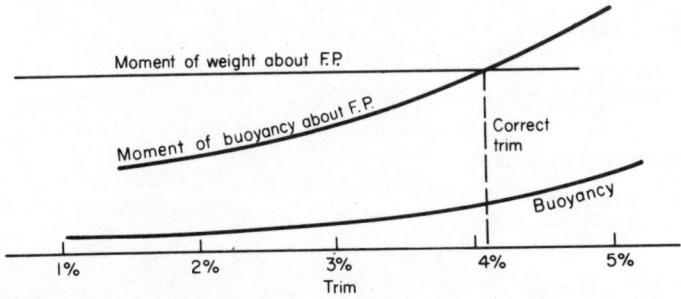

Fig. 8.5 *Determination of correct trim after stern lift*

If the launching curves indicate that the fore poppet will drop off the ways, adequate depth of water must be allowed under the forefoot for the momentum of the drop to prevent damage to the forefoot. What is adequate will depend on the amount of the excess of weight over buoyancy, the inertia of the ship and the damping effects of the water; it is best determined from an examination of previous launches.

GROUNDWAYS

Typically, the declivity of the groundways is 1 in 20 and the camber a half a metre in a groundway length of 300 m from fore poppet to after end (or 18 in. in 1000 ft). The radius corresponding to this camber is 22,500 m. Originally, camber was probably meant to offset the sinkage of the slip as the ship's weight grew. It has another important effect in rotating the ship to dip the stern deeply into the water; this increases the buoyancy force and causes an earlier stern lift than would be the case without camber. This increases the moment against tipping but also increases the load on the fore poppet.

The total load on the groundways is the difference between weight and buoyancy $W - \Delta$. Dividing by the length in contact gives a mean load per unit length and this, divided by the width of ways gives a mean pressure. The maximum total load on the ways is the initial one, W, and experience has shown that the mean pressure associated with this load should not, for many greases, exceed about 2·5 tonf/ft² (27 tonnef/m²) or the grease tends to get squeezed out. Both the ship, which has an uneven weight distribution, and the ways are elastic and they are separated by grease; what is the true distribution of pressure along the length has never been measured. Ignoring the moment causing the small angular acceleration of the ship due to camber, it is known that, before stern lift (Fig. 8.2),

(a) $W - \Delta$ = total load on ways,
(b) $Wa - \Delta d$ = moment of way load about fore poppet.

To estimate the load distribution at any instant of travel, it is customary to assume that the distribution is linear, i.e. that the curve of load per unit length p' against length is a trapezoid. If the length of ways remaining in contact is l at any instant and the loads per unit length at the fore poppet and after end of ways are, respectively, p'_f and p'_a, the conditions (a) and (b) become

(a) $W - \Delta = \frac{1}{2}l(p'_f + p'_a)$

(b) $Wa - \Delta d = p'_f \frac{l^2}{2} + \frac{1}{3}l^2(p'_a - p'_f)$

Solving these equations for p'_f and p'_a,

$$p'_f = 4\frac{W-\Delta}{l} - 6\frac{Wa-\Delta d}{l^2}$$

$$p'_a = 6\frac{Wa-\Delta d}{l^2} - 2\frac{W-\Delta}{l}$$

This is a satisfactory solution while p'_f and p'_a are positive, and the load per unit length can be represented by a trapezium. When $(Wa-\Delta d)/(W-\Delta)$ is greater than $\tfrac{2}{3}l$, p'_f becomes negative and when $(Wa-\Delta d)/(W-\Delta)$ is less than $\tfrac{1}{3}l$, p'_a becomes negative. There cannot be a negative load so for these conditions, the trapezoidal presumption is not permissible. It is assumed, instead, that the distribution is triangular whence, for

$$\frac{Wa-\Delta d}{W-\Delta} > \tfrac{2}{3}l \quad \text{then} \quad p'_a = \frac{2(W-\Delta)^2}{3l(W-\Delta)-3(Wa-\Delta d)}$$

and for

$$\frac{Wa-\Delta d}{W-\Delta} < \tfrac{1}{3}l \quad \text{then} \quad p'_f = \frac{2(W-\Delta)^2}{3(Wa-\Delta d)}$$

Fig. 8.6 *Assumed load distribution*

On these assumptions, it is possible to plot the maximum loads per foot or, divided by the width of ways, the pressure against travel down the slip. The maxima will always occur at the fore poppet or the after end of the ways and typical pressure variation in which the distribution is all trapezoidal, is shown in Fig. 8.7. Permissible end pressures so far as grease behaviour is concerned vary with the grease, temperature and the experience of different yards; 5 tonf/ft² (55 tonnef/m²) is typical but figures of 10 or even 15 are not unknown. An

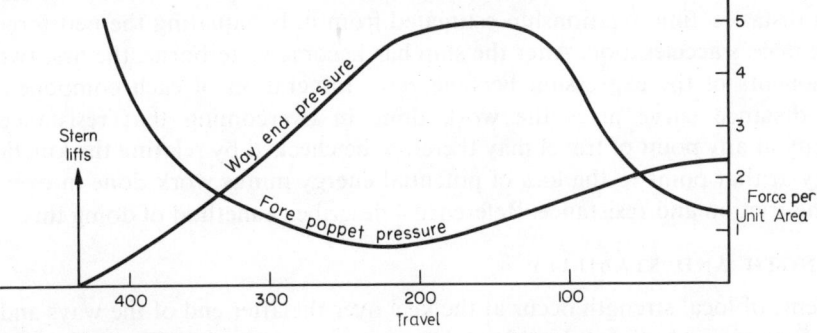

Fig. 8.7 *End pressures*

important objective of this part of the calculations is the determination of poppet strength, and the positions along the ship where internal shoring will be needed to take high loading from the way end. At the moment of stern lift, while the load on the fore poppet is known, the pressure rises to an indeterminate value since the length of ways over which the load is applied is not known.

THE DYNAMICS OF LAUNCHING

The force accelerating the ship down the groundways is, at any instant, approximately

$(W-\Delta)\theta$ – way friction – water resistance – drag forces

θ is the slope of the ways at the centre of gravity of the ship. Way friction is $\mu(W-\Delta)$; the coefficient of friction μ is usually less than 0·02, although at the commencement it can be slightly higher and tests should be conducted to establish the figures for the particular lubricant over a range of temperatures. Water resistance is due to the hull friction, the creation of the stern wave and to the resistance of locked propellers, water brakes or masks, etc., where fitted; this resistance is expressed by $K\Delta^{2/3}V^2$ where V is the velocity of travel and K is a constant determined from similar ships with similar water braking devices (for *Queen Mary* it was 0·001). Retarding forces due to chain drags are found to follow a frictional law, $\mu'w$ where w is the weight of the chains and μ' is 0·40–0·80 depending upon the state of the slipway; this figure must be determined from trials or from previous launches.

Reference 3 gives figures for a particular ship for the effects of entrained water expressed as a fraction z of the buoyancy. The equation of motion of the ship before it is waterborne is then

$$(W-\Delta)\theta - \mu(W-\Delta) - K\Delta^{\frac{2}{3}}V^2 - \mu'w = \text{nett force} = \frac{(W+z\Delta)}{g}\frac{dV}{dt}$$

This differential equation cannot, of course, be solved mathematically because of the presence of Δ.

Consideration of each of the factors at intervals of travel down the slip, however, enables a component force diagram to be built up as shown in Fig. 8.8 and a distance–time relationship estimated from it, by equating the nett force to the mass × acceleration. After the ship has become waterborne, the first two components of the expression become zero. Integration of each component force–distance curve gives the work done in overcoming that resistance. Velocity at any point of travel may therefore be checked by relating the kinetic energy at that point to the loss of potential energy minus work done in overcoming friction and resistance. Reference 4 describes a method of doing this.

STRENGTH AND STABILITY

Problems of local strength occur at the keel over the after end of the ways and at the fore poppet both for the ship and for the poppet structure. The difficulties

Fig. 8.8 Forces acting during launch

of containing the large forces at the fore poppet account for the increasing number of very large oil tankers and other bulk carriers being built in dry docks (productivity is of course high).

At the instant of stern lift, the hull girder undergoes a maximum sagging bending moment, the longitudinal strain from which in some large ships has been measured to give stresses of 5–6 tonf/in^2. The bending strain is easily found from the data already compiled to ensure a safe launch but strain measured in practice is usually somewhat below this, due probably to the effects of water resistance. Breakage is usually measured.

Stability is also at a minimum at the instant of stern lift due to the large fore poppet load at the keel. The $\overline{GM}$ is calculated by the methods described in Chapter 5 both for the ship with the concentrated load at the keel and fully afloat. While instability with the ship supported each side by the ways is unlikely, no naval architect would permit a ship to be launched with a negative virtual $\overline{GM}$ at the instant of stern lift. Any sudden sinking of the ways, for example, could be increased by an unstable ship. Ballasting is, in any case, often carried out to increase the longitudinal moment against tipping and presents no difficulty if needed for stability purposes.

SIDEWAYS LAUNCHING

When the ship is small or waterfront space is not at a great premium, ships may be built on an even keel broadside on to the water and consigned to the water sideways. There are three common methods of sideways launching:

(a) the ship slides down ways which are built well down under the water;
(b) the ship tips or drops off the end of the ways into the water, sometimes tipping a part of the ways too;
(c) the ship is built on piles which are made to collapse by a sideways push to allow the ship to fall into the water.

284 *Basic ship theory*

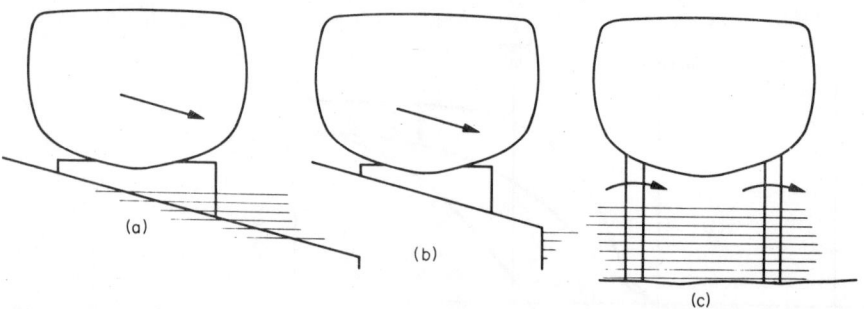

Fig. 8.9 Sideways launching

In all of these methods the ship takes to the water violently and may roll heavily—on entry, the ship may roll thirty degrees or more. Stability at large angles and watertightness are therefore important considerations. Waves may cause damage on adjacent shores (Ref. 5).

Conventional calculations are not performed. Declivity of ways is usually of the order of 1 in 8 in order to give a high speed of launch to clear the end of the ways. Grease pressures permitted, 2·5–3·0 tonf/ft^2, are somewhat higher than with end launch.

Docking

From time to time, attention is needed to the outer bottom of a ship either for regular maintenance or to effect repairs. Access to the bottom may be obtained by careening, by hauling up a slipway or by placing in a dock from which the water is removed. There are limitations to what work can be done by careening, while the magnitude of the machinery needed to haul a ship up a slipway is such that this procedure is confined to ships up to a few hundred tonf in displacement.

The practical aspects of docks and docking are discussed fully in Refs. 2 and 6. This chapter is concerned with theory which assists such a successful operation and some design features of floating docks. Features of principal concern are

(*a*) load distribution between dock and ship;
(*b*) behaviour of blocks;
(*c*) strength of floating docks;
(*d*) stability.

This list by no means exhausts the problems associated with docking and constructing docks, which include design of caissons and pumping systems and the whole field of difficulties facing civil engineers in the construction of graving docks. It does, however, embrace the major concerns of the practising naval architect. Basically, docking is the placing of an elastic ship with an uneven weight distribution on to an elastic set of blocks supported in turn by an elastic floating dock or a relatively rigid graving dock. Blocks will not be of an even height and are subject to crush, creep and instability. In many aspects of ship design, the criteria of design are based on misuse or accident; with floating docks, there is little scope for permitting maloperation because if this were a major criterion of design, the lifting capacity of the dock would be unduly penalized.

LOAD DISTRIBUTION

A theoretical analysis of the behaviour of a ship in a floating dock is given in Ref. 7, which produces the longitudinal distribution of load on the blocks. A digital computer and the time to feed it data and program it may not always be available, however, and dockmasters may have to fall back on the practices which were current before this theory was deduced.

It has been assumed in the past that the load distribution along the blocks followed the weight distribution of the ship except at the after cut up and at any other gap in the blocks. Forward of the after cut up, the weight distribution is assumed augmented by the weight abaft the cut up spread over a length equal to twice the length of the overhang, and distributed according to a parabolic law such that the moment of weight is the same as the moment of overhang about the cut up. If the weight and moment of the overhang about the cut up are respectively W and M, the augment in load per unit length at the cut up, a, is

$$a = \frac{9W^2}{16M}$$

Fig. 8.10 *Load distribution in dock*

In a floating dock, the load distribution is further affected by the buoyancy distribution along the dock which is under the control of the dockmaster. For a given buoyancy distribution, the loading in the past has been determined by a method similar to the longitudinal strength calculation for a ship. The difference between the total buoyancy and ship's weight plus weight of dock and contained water gives the net loading. As explained in Chapter 6, shearing force on a girder is obtained by integrating the nett loading, and bending moment is obtained by integrating the shearing force along the length. In the case of the docked ship, the loading and the subsequent integrations apply to the combined ship and dock. Difficulty arises in trying to separate the two because their interaction is not known. In the past, bending moment has been divided up in the ratio of their respective second moments of area of section. This is not satisfactory and, in time, the practice will be replaced by advice resulting from analysis of the type given in Ref. 7.

Floating docks are classified by their lifting capacity. Lifting capacity is the buoyancy available when the dock is floating at its working freeboard. Working freeboard is often 6 in. (0·15 m) at the pontoon deck. Buoyancy available arises from the tanks which can be emptied to provide lift to the dock without undue strain.

BLOCK BEHAVIOUR

Depending as it does on defects, age, grain, moisture content and surface condition, it is not surprising to find wide variation in the behaviour of a stack of wooden dock blocks, as experiments have shown. Provided that the blocks are cribbed to prevent instability, it is common practice not to permit block pressures in excess of 40 tonf/ft², although the ultimate load intensity of a stack of English oak blocks may be as high as 100 tonf/ft².

Experiments have shown that the crippling pressure for a stack of blocks h high and a in width is given approximately by

$$p = 40 - \frac{h^2}{a^2} \text{ tonf/ft}^2$$

or

$$p = 11 \left(40 - \frac{h^2}{a^2}\right) \text{tonnef/m}^2 = 1\cdot07 \left(40 - \frac{h^2}{a^2}\right) \times 10^5 \text{ N/m}^2$$

where p is the load divided by the total plan area of a stack of blocks, irrespective of the half siding of keel. The formula is suitable for English oak and is obviously an approximation. For a 5 ft stack of 15 in. blocks it gives a crippling load of 24 tonf/ft²; for a 6 ft stack it is 17 tonf/ft². A 2 m stack of 40 cm blocks has a crippling load of 165 tonnef/m². In practice, 6 ft stacks are rare and pressures in excess of 20 tonf/ft² for a single uncribbed stack are not permitted. It is normal good practice to crib a certain number of blocks, which increases the crippling load as well as preventing tripping due to the trim of the docking ships.

The importance of exact alignment of blocks cannot be over-emphasized. Measurements of the loads in dock blocks have shown that a stack will take many times the load of its neighbour by being only a fraction of an inch higher. A lack of fit of half an inch between adjacent blocks is not unusual at present and is responsible for wild variation in dock block loading. It is responsible, too, for the departures of the block loading curve from the ship's weight distribution in graving docks.

Reference 7 also points out that great care is needed to ensure that blocks are all of even stiffness. The number of blocks to ensure a mean deflection of stacks of x is

$$\text{Number of blocks} = \frac{2 \times \text{ship's weight}}{x \times \text{block stiffness}}$$

Launching and docking

For a mean deflection of ½ in. on blocks with a stiffness of 50 tonf/in., the minimum number of blocks required is $W/12.5$ tonf. Clearly, this limitation is impractical for ships over about 2000 tonf in displacement and, in general, the larger the ship, the larger the block deflection that must be accepted.

STRENGTH OF FLOATING DOCKS

It is clear even from a cursory examination, that a dockmaster can place severe strains on a dock by a thoughtless selection of buoyancy tanks. In the transverse direction, if the dockmaster first selects the buoyancy tanks in the dock walls to begin raising the dock, a couple will be applied to the dock as shown in Fig. 8.11 which could cause damage. Similarly, in the longitudinal direction, if a ship has much weight amidships, the use of the buoyancy tanks at the ends of the dock could break it in two. It is good practice to select those buoyancy tanks immediately beneath the heaviest weights. Dock behaviour longitudinally, if the dock is made of steel, is checked continuously during lift by measuring the breakage. A strict limit to breakage is placed by the naval architect in the instructions for use of the dock. Reinforced concrete docks do not suffer much elastic distortion and breakage is not used as a measure of behaviour; instead, strict pumping patterns are imposed.

Fig. 8.11 Strains imposed by maloperation

Analysis of the strength of a floating dock was too difficult arithmetically until computers became available. The first reasonably precise analysis was published in 1966 (Ref. 7). This treated the pontoon deck as a grillage simply supported on its two long edges by the dock walls. The lumped weights of the ship were assumed supported by three rows of blocks to each stack of which was applied a lack of fit. Analysis was performed by reducing the problem to that of an unevenly loaded beam on an elastic foundation for which the differential equations can be readily formed, although the numerical solution is formidable without a computer.

The solution given by Ref. 7 is equally applicable to graving docks by applying very high figures to the dock rigidity. Standard comparative longitudinal strength calculations to cater for transit conditions are also performed on the floating dock structure itself as described for the ship in Chapter 6.

STABILITY DURING DOCKING

Loss of stability due to grounding or docking has been discussed fully in Chapter 5. Calculation of this loss is a standard procedure before every docking, since a list developing before the ship is in contact with the blocks completely along the keel can be extremely dangerous and can dislodge the blocks.

A floating dock is trimmed approximately to the trim of the ship and large suing forces before the keel takes the blocks are thereby avoided. There is a critical stability condition when the ship is just clear of the water and the restoring waterplane for both ship and dock is provided only by the dock walls. In this condition, the dock designers normally demand a minimum $\overline{GM}$ of 5 ft (1·6 m). When the pontoon is lifted clear, the waterplane is, of course, much larger. Free surface effects in a floating dock are also large.

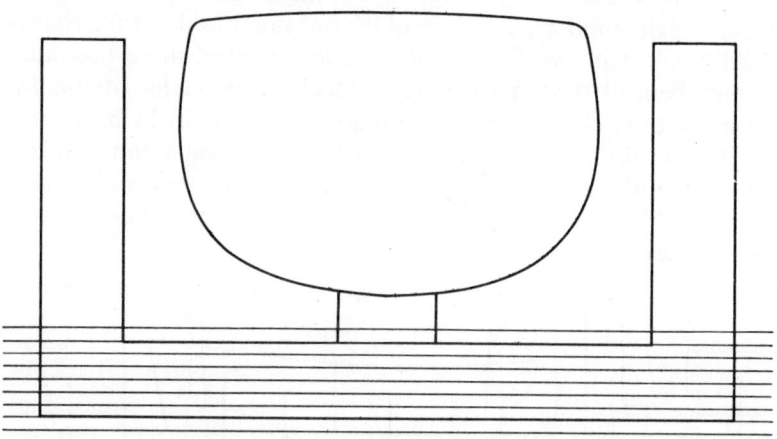

Fig. 8.12 *Critical stability condition*

Large angle stability is important not only for ocean transit conditions but for the careening which is necessary during maintenance and repair operations.

References

1. Andrews, H. B. Launching. Chapter XI of *Principles of Naval Architecture* (Ed. Comstock, J. P.), *SNAME*, 1967.
2. Newton, R. N. *Practical construction of warships*, Longman, 1970.
3. Gray, R. C. The dynamics of launching, *TNEC*, 1959–60.
4. McNeill, J. M. Launch of the quadruple screw turbine steamer, *Queen Mary*, *TINA*, 1935.
5. Todd, F. H. and Laws, E. Some model and full scale experiments on side launching, *TNEC*, 1946–7.
6. Hind, J. A. *Ship design and shipbuilding production*, Temple Press, 1965.
7. Vaughan, H. Elastic analysis of a ship in a floating dock, *TRINA*, 1966.
8. Cameron, R. R. G. The sliding of a large tanker on the slipway, *TRINA*, 1969.
9. Ractliffe. A. T. Launchway pressure, *TRINA*, 1973.
10. Potvin, A. B., Hartz, B. and Nickum, G. C. Analysis of stresses in a floating dock due to a docked ship, *TSNAME*, 1969.

Problems

1. A vessel has a launching weight of 5800 tonf, the CG being 26 ft abaft the mid-length and the fore poppet 230 ft before the mid-length. Construct a launching diagram from the following data:

Mid-length abaft AEGW, ft	0	20	40	60	80
Buoyancy, tonf	2560	3190	3840	4530	5330
CB abaft AEGW, ft	131	143	158	173	185

State:

(a) distance of mid-length abaft the after end of groundways when the stern lifts;
(b) force on fore poppets when the stern lifts;
(c) reserve moment against tipping. (AP & S)

2. A vessel whose launching weight is 25 MN with CG 5 m abaft amidships has the fore poppet positioned 50 m forward of amidships. Find the force on the fore poppet and the travel when the stern lifts from the following data:

Travel down slip, m	50	60	70	80	90
Buoyancy, MN	10·1	12·3	15·3	19·4	24·6
CB abaft amidships, m	47	40	33	26	19

Sliding ways 70 cm wide each side are proposed, with a length of 95 m. What is the mean pressure on the lubricant before motion takes place?

3. In a certain ship, the length of sliding ways was 163 m and the breadth 1·63 m. The launching weight was 9755 tonnef and c.g. estimated at 75·50 m forward of the after end of the sliding ways. Calculate the mean pressure per square foot on the ways. Assuming the pressure to vary in a linear manner from forward to the after end of ways, what is the pressure at each end? (AP & S)

4. A ship of length 500 ft between perpendiculars is built on a slip with its keel at a slope of $\frac{5}{8}$ in. to one foot. It is launched on groundways which extend to the fore poppet only and have a camber of 2 ft over their length of 600 ft and a slope of chord of $\frac{3}{4}$ in. to one foot. If the underside of keel produced at the fore perpendicular is initially 18 ft above water level and the fore poppet is 60 ft aft of the fore perpendicular, what are the draughts at the fore perpendicular and at the after perpendicular when the ship has travelled 200 ft down the slip?
(AP & S)

5. A ship is launched from ways 720 ft long, with a camber of 18 in. and a declivity of $\frac{9}{16}$ in./ft. The slope of the keel is $\frac{33}{64}$ in./ft. If the minimum height of stopping up is 2 ft 6 in., find the height of the fore poppet above the after end of the ways when the ship has travelled 200 ft down the ways. Assume the fore poppet initially at the fore end of ways. (AP & S)

6. Construct a set of launching curves from the following information:

launching weight	5230 tonnef
CG abaft midships	7 m
fore poppet before midships	69 m
after end of groundways from c.g. at rest	100 m

Travel down slip (m)	30	60	75	90	105	120	135
Buoyancy (tonnef)							
before stern lift	830	1960	2600	3350	4280	5600	
after stern lift					4050	4700	5550
Moment of buoyancy about fp before stern lift							
(1000 tonnef m)	132	219	282	356	450	585	
Moment of buoyancy about AEGW (1000 tonnef m)				42	76	160	316

(a) When does the stern lift?
(b) What is the maximum force at the fore poppet?
(c) What is the minimum moment against tipping?
(d) How does the ship leave the ways?

7. A ship weighs 28,500 tonnef at launch. The fore poppet is 72 m before the CG of the ship. The after end of the groundways is 155 m from the CG before the ship moves. The following table gives the data derived for the passage of the ship in full contact with the ways:

Travel, m	120	135	150	157·5	165
Buoyancy, tonnef	9000	15,600	24,400	29,200	35,000
CB abaft AEGW, m—		7·5	21·5	28·0	33.0

Deduce a set of launching curves and pick off the important data. (HMDTC)

8. A floating dock of rectangular bottom shape, 400 ft long and 90 ft wide floats, when empty, at a draught of 3·5 ft. It is used to dock a ship of 3600 tonf displacement, 360 ft long, which is symmetrically placed in the dock. The weight distribution of the ship is symmetrical about amidships and has the values shown in the table below:

Distance from midships, ft	0	20	40	60	80	100	120	140	160	180
Section from midships		1	2	3	4	5	6	7	8	9
Weight per section, tonf		289	284	272	252	224	191	150	101	37

Draw the curves of load, shearing force and bending moment for the dock and ship combination, in still water of 35 ft^3/tonf.

The weight of the dock may be assumed equally distributed along its length.

(HMDTC)

9 The ship environment

The designer of any engineering product, if it is to be successful, must know the conditions in which his equipment is going to exist and operate for its full life cycle. The naval architect is no exception, and for convenience the environmental conditions with which he is concerned may be divided into two categories:

(a) the environment external to the ship which affects the ship as a whole and all exposed equipment. These conditions are caused by the sea and climate. Also the ship performance can be influenced by the depth or width of water present;

(b) the internal environment which affects the personnel and the internal equipment. To some extent, this environment is controllable, e.g. the temperature and humidity can be controlled by means of an air conditioning system. The full study of this internal environment involves consideration of:

(i) ship motion effects arising from the action of the waves and wind on the ship as a whole. Some of these effects can be reduced by artificial means such as stabilizers;

(ii) temperature, humidity and freshness of the air, including freedom from odours;

(iii) vibration arising mainly from the interaction of the propeller pressure field with the hull of the ship but also arising from machinery and wave impact;

(iv) noise arising from machinery, the sea, the wind, the propellers and people. In all ships, compartment levels of noise are significant, lower levels being required in some more than others. In warships, the level of noise radiated by the ship into its environments is also important. In this case, if the noise level is too high the ship will be more easily detected by an enemy and weapons will more readily home on to it;

(v) shock arising from wave impact, collision or enemy action. Clearly, design against the effects of shock is of great importance in a warship which is expected to fight an enemy and withstand a certain amount of damage.

The external environment. The sea

WATER PROPERTIES

Certain physical properties of the sea are of considerable importance to the designer. They are:

(a) *Density*. The density of the water in which the ship floats affects her draught and trim (Chapter 3) and depends mainly upon the temperature and salinity. The standard values of density of fresh and salt water at various temperatures are given in Tables 9.1 and 9.2.

(b) *Kinematic viscosity.* This is particularly relevant to the frictional resistance experienced by a ship as it defines the Reynolds' number (Chapter 10). The standard values of the kinematic viscosity of fresh and salt water at various temperatures are given in Tables 9.3 and 9.4.

(c) *Salinity.* 'Standard' density and kinematic viscosity have been mentioned above. Values for actual samples of sea water will vary from area to area and will depend, amongst other things, upon the salinity. For instance, many objects will float in the Dead Sea, which has a very high salt content, which would sink in fresh water.

Table 9.1
Mass densities for fresh water
(last decimal figure is doubtful)

°C	ρ	°C	ρ	°C	ρ
0	999·79	10	999·59	20	998·12
1	999·79	11	999·49	21	997·92
2	999·89	12	999·40	22	997·72
3	999·89	13	999·30	23	997·43
4	999·89	14	999·10	24	997·24
5	999·89	15	999·00	25	996·94
6	999·89	16	998·91	26	996·75
7	999·79	17	998·71	27	996·45
8	999·79	18	998·51	28	996·16
9	999·69	19	998·32	29	995·87
				30	995·57

(a) Metric units; ρ in kg/m³

°F	ρ	°F	ρ	°F	ρ
32	62·414	51	62·401	70	62·295
33	62·414	52	62·398	71	62·289
34	62·417	53	62·395	72	62·282
35	62·417	54	62·392	73	62·273
36	62·421	55	62·385	74	62·263
37	62·421	56	62·382	75	62·257
38	62·421	57	62·376	76	62·247
39	62·421	58	62·373	77	62·237
40	62·421	59	62·366	78	62·231
41	62·421	60	62·363	79	62·221
42	62·421	61	62·356	80	62·212
43	62·421	62	62·350	81	62·202
44	62·417	63	62·344	82	62·192
45	62·417	64	62·337	83	62·183
46	62·414	65	62·331	84	62·173
47	62·411	66	62·324	85	62·163
48	62·411	67	62·318	86	62·151
49	62·408	68	62·311		
50	62·405	69	62·305		

(b) British units; ρ in lb/ft³

Table 9.2
Mass densities for salt water (salinity 3·5 per cent) (last decimal figure is doubtful)

°C	ρ	°C	ρ	°C	ρ
0	1028·03	10	1026·85	20	1024·70
1	1027·93	11	1026·66	21	1024·40
2	1027·83	12	1026·56	22	1024·11
3	1027·83	13	1026·27	23	1023·81
4	1027·74	14	1026·07	24	1023·52
5	1027·64	15	1025·87	25	1023·23
6	1027·44	16	1025·68	26	1022·93
7	1027·34	17	1025·38	27	1022·64
8	1027·15	18	1025·19	28	1022·25
9	1027·05	19	1024·99	29	1021·95
				30	1021·66

(a) Metric units; ρ in kg/m^3.

°F	ρ	°F	ρ	°F	ρ
32	64·177	51	64·100	70	63·949
33	64·174	52	64·094	71	63·939
34	64·174	53	64·087	72	63·930
35	64·171	54	64·081	73	63·920
36	64·168	55	64·071	74	63·910
37	64·165	56	64·065	75	63·901
38	64·161	57	64·058	76	63·891
39	64·158	58	64·052	77	63·878
40	64·155	59	64·042	78	63·869
41	64·152	60	64·036	79	63·859
42	64·145	61	64·029	80	63·846
43	64·142	62	64·020	81	63·836
44	64·136	63	64·010	82	63·824
45	64·132	64	64·004	83	63·814
46	64·126	65	63·994	84	63·801
47	64·123	66	63·988	85	63·791
48	64·116	67	63·978	86	63·779
49	64·110	68	63·968		
50	64·103	69	63·959		

(b) British units; ρ in lb/ft^3

THE SEA SURFACE

The sea presents an ever changing face to the observer. In the long term, the surface may be in any condition from a flat calm to extreme roughness. In the short term, the surface may present the appearance of a fairly steady level of roughness but the actual surface shape will be continuously varying.

Any observer is aware that a stream of air passing over a water surface causes ripples or waves to form, e.g. by blowing across the top of a cup of tea ripples are formed. The precise mechanism by which the transfer of energy takes place is not known. Nor is the minimum velocity of air necessary to generate waves known accurately, and figures between 0·6 and 6 m/s (2 and 21 ft/s) have been suggested by various workers in this field.

Table 9.3

Values of kinematic viscosity for fresh water, v, in metric units of $(m^2 s^{-1}) \times 10^6$. Temp. in degrees Celsius

Deg. C	0·0	0·1	0·2	0·3	0·4	0·5	0·6	0·7	0·8	0·9
0	1·78667	1·78056	1·77450	1·76846	1·76246	1·75648	1·75054	1·74461	1·73871	1·73285
1	1·72701	1·72121	1·71545	1·70972	1·70403	1·69836	1·69272	1·68710	1·68151	1·67594
2	1·67040	1·66489	1·65940	1·65396	1·64855	1·64316	1·63780	1·63247	1·62717	1·62190
3	1·61665	1·61142	1·60622	1·60105	1·59591	1·59079	1·58570	1·58063	1·57558	1·57057
4	1·56557	1·56060	1·55566	1·55074	1·54585	1·54098	1·53613	1·53131	1·52651	1·52173
5	1·51698	1·51225	1·50754	1·50286	1·49820	1·49356	1·48894	1·48435	1·47978	1·47523
6	1·47070	1·46619	1·46172	1·45727	1·45285	1·44844	1·44405	1·43968	1·43533	1·43099
7	1·42667	1·42238	1·41810	1·41386	1·40964	1·40543	1·40125	1·39709	1·39294	1·38882
8	1·38471	1·38063	1·37656	1·37251	1·36848	1·36445	1·36045	1·35646	1·35249	1·34855
9	1·34463	1·34073	1·33684	1·33298	1·32913	1·32530	1·32149	1·31769	1·31391	1·31015
10	1·30641	1·30268	1·29897	1·29528	1·29160	1·28794	1·28430	1·28067	1·27706	1·27346
11	1·26988	1·26632	1·26277	1·25924	1·25573	1·25223	1·24874	1·24527	1·24182	1·23838
12	1·23495	1·23154	1·22815	1·22478	1·22143	1·21809	1·21477	1·21146	1·20816	1·20487
13	1·20159	1·19832	1·19508	1·19184	1·18863	1·18543	1·18225	1·17908	1·17592	1·17278
14	1·16964	1·16651	1·16340	1·16030	1·15721	1·15414	1·15109	1·14806	1·14503	1·14202
15	1·13902	1·13603	1·13304	1·13007	1·12711	1·12417	1·12124	1·11832	1·11542	1·11254
16	1·10966	1·10680	1·10395	1·10110	1·09828	1·09546	1·09265	1·08986	1·08708	1·08431
17	1·08155	1·07880	1·07606	1·07334	1·07062	1·06792	1·06523	1·06254	1·05987	1·05721
18	1·05456	1·05193	1·04930	1·04668	1·04407	1·04148	1·03889	1·03631	1·03375	1·03119
19	1·02865	1·02611	1·02359	1·02107	1·01857	1·01607	1·01359	1·01111	1·00865	1·00619
20	1·00374	1·00131	0·99888	0·99646	0·99405	0·99165	0·98927	0·98690	0·98454	0·98218
21	0·97984	0·97750	0·97517	0·97285	0·97053	0·96822	0·96592	0·96363	0·96135	0·95908
22	0·95682	0·95456	0·95231	0·95008	0·94786	0·94565	0·94345	0·94125	0·93906	0·93688
23	0·93471	0·93255	0·93040	0·92825	0·92611	0·92397	0·92184	0·91971	0·91760	0·91549
24	0·91340	0·91132	0·90924	0·90718	0·90512	0·90306	0·90102	0·89898	0·89695	0·89493
25	0·89292	0·89090	0·88889	0·88689	0·88490	0·88291	0·88094	0·87897	0·87702	0·87507
26	0·87313	0·87119	0·86926	0·86734	0·86543	0·86352	0·86162	0·85973	0·85784	0·85596
27	0·85409	0·85222	0·85036	0·84851	0·84666	0·84482	0·84298	0·84116	0·83934	0·83752
28	0·83572	0·83391	0·83212	0·83033	0·82855	0·82677	0·82500	0·82324	0·82148	0·81973
29	0·81798	0·81625	0·81451	0·81279	0·81106	0·80935	0·80765	0·80596	0·80427	0·80258
30	0·80091	0·79923	0·79755	0·79588	0·79422	0·79256	0·79090	0·78924	0·78757	0·78592

v in English units of $(ft^2 s^{-1}) \times 10^5$. Temp. in degrees Fahrenheit

Deg. F	0·0	0·1	0·2	0·3	0·4	0·5	0·6	0·7	0·8	0·9
32	1·92314	1·91949	1·91585	1·91222	1·90860	1·90499	1·90139	1·89780	1·89422	1·89066
33	1·88710	1·88354	1·88000	1·87646	1·87294	1·86942	1·86592	1·86242	1·85894	1·85546
34	1·85200	1·84855	1·84512	1·84169	1·83828	1·83487	1·83148	1·82809	1·82471	1·82135
35	1·81799	1·81463	1·81129	1·80795	1·80462	1·80130	1·79799	1·79469	1·79140	1·78812
36	1·78485	1·78160	1·77835	1·77512	1·77189	1·76868	1·76547	1·76227	1·75908	1·75590
37	1·75273	1·74957	1·74642	1·74327	1·74014	1·73701	1·73389	1·73078	1·72768	1·72459
38	1·72150	1·71843	1·71536	1·71230	1·70926	1·70621	1·70318	1·70016	1·69714	1·69413
39	1·69114	1·68814	1·68516	1·68219	1·67922	1·67626	1·67331	1·67037	1·66744	1·66451
40	1·66160	1·65869	1·65578	1·65289	1·65000	1·64713	1·64426	1·64139	1·63854	1·63569
41	1·63285	1·63002	1·62720	1·62438	1·62157	1·61877	1·61598	1·61319	1·61042	1·60765
42	1·60488	1·60213	1·59938	1·59664	1·59390	1·59118	1·58846	1·58575	1·58304	1·58035
43	1·57766	1·57498	1·57231	1·56965	1·56700	1·56435	1·56171	1·55908	1·55646	1·55384
44	1·55123	1·54861	1·54601	1·54341	1·54082	1·53823	1·53565	1·53308	1·53052	1·52796
45	1·52541	1·52287	1·52034	1·51782	1·51530	1·51279	1·51029	1·50779	1·50530	1·50281
46	1·50034	1·49786	1·49540	1·49294	1·49049	1·48804	1·48560	1·48317	1·48074	1·47832
47	1·47591	1·47349	1·47108	1·46868	1·46628	1·46389	1·46151	1·45913	1·45675	1·45439
48	1·45203	1·44968	1·44734	1·44500	1·44268	1·44035	1·43803	1·43572	1·43342	1·43112
49	1·42882	1·42654	1·42425	1·42198	1·41971	1·41744	1·41518	1·41293	1·41068	1·40844
50	1·40620	1·40397	1·40175	1·39953	1·39731	1·39510	1·39290	1·39070	1·38851	1·38632
51	1·38414	1·38197	1·37980	1·37763	1·37547	1·37332	1·37117	1·36903	1·36689	1·36475
52	1·36263	1·36050	1·35839	1·35628	1·35417	1·35207	1·34997	1·34788	1·34579	1·34371
53	1·34164	1·33957	1·33750	1·33544	1·33338	1·33133	1·32929	1·32725	1·32521	1·32318
54	1·32116	1·31914	1·31713	1·31513	1·31313	1·31114	1·30915	1·30716	1·30518	1·30321
55	1·30124	1·29926	1·29730	1·29533	1·29337	1·29142	1·28947	1·28753	1·28559	1·28365
56	1·28172	1·27980	1·27789	1·27598	1·27408	1·27217	1·27028	1·26839	1·26650	1·26462
57	1·26274	1·26086	1·25898	1·25711	1·25524	1·25338	1·25152	1·24967	1·24782	1·24598
58	1·24414	1·24231	1·24048	1·23866	1·23684	1·23503	1·23322	1·23142	1·22962	1·22782
59	1·22603	1·22424	1·22245	1·22066	1·21888	1·21710	1·21533	1·21356	1·21180	1·21004
60	1·20828	1·20653	1·20479	1·20305	1·20132	1·19959	1·19786	1·19614	1·19442	1·19271
61	1·19100	1·18929	1·18759	1·18589	1·18420	1·18251	1·18082	1·17914	1·17746	1·17578
62	1·17411	1·17245	1·17078	1·16912	1·16747	1·16581	1·16416	1·16252	1·16088	1·15924
63	1·15761	1·15598	1·15435	1·15273	1·15111	1·14949	1·14788	1·14627	1·14467	1·14307
64	1·14147	1·13988	1·13829	1·13670	1·13512	1·13354	1·13196	1·13039	1·12882	1·12726
65	1·12570	1·12414	1·12258	1·12103	1·11948	1·11794	1·11640	1·11486	1·11333	1·11179
66	1·11027	1·10874	1·10722	1·10571	1·10419	1·10268	1·10117	1·09967	1·09817	1·09667
67	1·09518	1·09369	1·09220	1·09072	1·08923	1·08776	1·08628	1·08481	1·08334	1·08188
68	1·08042	1·07896	1·07750	1·07605	1·07460	1·07316	1·07171	1·07027	1·06884	1·06740
69	1·06597	1·06455	1·06313	1·06172	1·06031	1·05890	1·05749	1·05609	1·05469	1·05329
70	1·05190	1·05050	1·04910	1·04771	1·04633	1·04494	1·04356	1·04218	1·04081	1·03943
71	1·03806	1·03670	1·03533	1·03397	1·03261	1·03126	1·02990	1·02855	1·02721	1·02586
72	1·02452	1·02319	1·02186	1·02053	1·01921	1·01788	1·01657	1·01525	1·01394	1·01263
73	1·01132	1·01001	1·00871	1·00741	1·00611	1·00482	1·00353	1·00224	1·00095	0·99967
74	0·99839	0·99710	0·99582	0·99455	0·99327	0·99200	0·99073	0·98946	0·98820	0·98693
75	0·98567	0·98442	0·98317	0·98193	0·98068	0·97944	0·97820	0·97697	0·97573	0·97450
76	0·97327	0·97205	0·97082	0·96960	0·96838	0·96717	0·96595	0·96474	0·96353	0·96233
77	0·96112	0·95992	0·95871	0·95751	0·95631	0·95512	0·95392	0·95273	0·95154	0·95036
78	0·94917	0·94799	0·94682	0·94565	0·94448	0·94331	0·94214	0·94098	0·93982	0·93866
79	0·93751	0·93635	0·93520	0·93405	0·93291	0·93176	0·93062	0·92948	0·92834	0·92721
80	0·92608	0·92495	0·92382	0·92269	0·92157	0·92045	0·91933	0·91821	0·91709	0·91598
81	0·91487	0·91376	0·91266	0·91155	0·91045	0·90935	0·90825	0·90716	0·90607	0·90498
82	0·90389	0·90280	0·90172	0·90063	0·89955	0·89848	0·89740	0·89633	0·89525	0·89418
83	0·89312	0·89205	0·89099	0·88993	0·88887	0·88781	0·88676	0·88570	0·88465	0·88360
84	0·88256	0·88151	0·88047	0·87943	0·87839	0·87735	0·87632	0·87528	0·87425	0·87323
85	0·87220	0·87118	0·87016	0·86914	0·86813	0·86712	0·86611	0·86510	0·86409	0·86309
86	0·86208	0·86108	0·86008	0·85907	0·85807	0·85708	0·85608	0·85509	0·85410	0·85311

Table 9.4
Values of kinematic viscosity for salt water, v, in metric units of $(m^2s^{-1}) \times 10^6$. (Salinity 3.5 per cent.) Temp. in degrees Celsius

Deg. C	0.0	0.1	0.2	0.3	0.4	0.5	0.6	0.7	0.8	0.9
0	1.82844	1.82237	1.81633	1.81033	1.80436	1.79842	1.79251	1.78662	1.78077	1.77494
1	1.76915	1.76339	1.75767	1.75199	1.74634	1.74072	1.73513	1.72956	1.72403	1.71853
2	1.71306	1.70761	1.70220	1.69681	1.69145	1.68612	1.68082	1.67554	1.67030	1.66508
3	1.65988	1.65472	1.64958	1.64446	1.63938	1.63432	1.62928	1.62427	1.61929	1.61433
4	1.60940	1.60449	1.59961	1.59475	1.58992	1.58511	1.58032	1.57556	1.57082	1.56611
5	1.56142	1.55676	1.55213	1.54752	1.54294	1.53838	1.53383	1.52930	1.52479	1.52030
6	1.51584	1.51139	1.50698	1.50259	1.49823	1.49388	1.48956	1.48525	1.48095	1.47667
7	1.47242	1.46818	1.46397	1.45978	1.45562	1.45147	1.44735	1.44325	1.43916	1.43508
8	1.43102	1.42698	1.42296	1.41895	1.41498	1.41102	1.40709	1.40317	1.39927	1.39539
9	1.39152	1.38767	1.38385	1.38003	1.37624	1.37246	1.36870	1.36496	1.36123	1.35752
10	1.35383	1.35014	1.34647	1.34281	1.33917	1.33555	1.33195	1.32837	1.32481	1.32126
11	1.31773	1.31421	1.31071	1.30722	1.30375	1.30030	1.29685	1.29343	1.29002	1.28662
12	1.28324	1.27987	1.27652	1.27319	1.26988	1.26658	1.26330	1.26003	1.25677	1.25352
13	1.25028	1.24705	1.24384	1.24064	1.23745	1.23428	1.23112	1.22798	1.22484	1.22172
14	1.21862	1.21552	1.21244	1.20938	1.20632	1.20328	1.20027	1.19726	1.19426	1.19128
15	1.18831	1.18534	1.18239	1.17944	1.17651	1.17359	1.17068	1.16778	1.16490	1.16202
16	1.15916	1.15631	1.15348	1.15066	1.14786	1.14506	1.14228	1.13951	1.13674	1.13399
17	1.13125	1.12852	1.12581	1.12309	1.12038	1.11769	1.11500	1.11232	1.10966	1.10702
18	1.10438	1.10176	1.09914	1.09654	1.09394	1.09135	1.08876	1.08619	1.08363	1.08107
19	1.07854	1.07601	1.07350	1.07099	1.06850	1.06601	1.06353	1.06106	1.05861	1.05616
20	1.05372	1.05129	1.04886	1.04645	1.04405	1.04165	1.03927	1.03689	1.03452	1.03216
21	1.02981	1.02747	1.02514	1.02281	1.02050	1.01819	1.01589	1.01360	1.01132	1.00904
22	1.00678	1.00452	1.00227	1.00003	0.99780	0.99557	0.99336	0.99115	0.98895	0.98676
23	0.98457	0.98239	0.98023	0.97806	0.97591	0.97376	0.97163	0.96950	0.96737	0.96526
24	0.96315	0.96105	0.95896	0.95687	0.95479	0.95272	0.95067	0.94862	0.94658	0.94455
25	0.94252	0.94049	0.93847	0.93646	0.93445	0.93245	0.93046	0.92847	0.92649	0.92452
26	0.92255	0.92059	0.91865	0.91671	0.91478	0.91286	0.91094	0.90903	0.90711	0.90521
27	0.90331	0.90141	0.89953	0.89765	0.89579	0.89393	0.89207	0.89023	0.88838	0.88654
28	0.88470	0.88287	0.88105	0.87923	0.87742	0.87562	0.87383	0.87205	0.87027	0.86849
29	0.86671	0.86494	0.86318	0.86142	0.85966	0.85792	0.85619	0.85446	0.85274	0.85102
30	0.84931	0.84759	0.84588	0.84418	0.84248	0.84079	0.83910	0.83739	0.83570	0.83400

v in English units of $(ft^2s^{-1}) \times 10^5$. (Salinity 3.5 per cent.) Temp. in degrees Fahrenheit

Deg. F	0.0	0.1	0.2	0.3	0.4	0.5	0.6	0.7	0.8	0.9
32	1.96810	1.96447	1.96085	1.95724	1.95364	1.95005	1.94647	1.94290	1.93934	1.93580
33	1.93226	1.92873	1.92520	1.92169	1.91819	1.91470	1.91122	1.90775	1.90429	1.90084
34	1.89740	1.89398	1.89057	1.88718	1.88379	1.88041	1.87704	1.87368	1.87034	1.86700
35	1.86367	1.86035	1.85705	1.85375	1.85046	1.84718	1.84391	1.84065	1.83740	1.83416
36	1.83093	1.82771	1.82450	1.82129	1.81810	1.81492	1.81174	1.80858	1.80542	1.80227
37	1.79914	1.79601	1.79289	1.78978	1.78667	1.78358	1.78050	1.77742	1.77436	1.77130
38	1.76825	1.76521	1.76218	1.75916	1.75614	1.75314	1.75014	1.74715	1.74417	1.74120
39	1.73824	1.73528	1.73234	1.72940	1.72647	1.72355	1.72063	1.71773	1.71483	1.71194
40	1.70906	1.70619	1.70332	1.70047	1.69762	1.69478	1.69194	1.68912	1.68630	1.68349
41	1.68069	1.67790	1.67512	1.67235	1.66959	1.66684	1.66409	1.66135	1.65861	1.65589
42	1.65317	1.65045	1.64774	1.64504	1.64234	1.63965	1.63697	1.63429	1.63163	1.62897
43	1.62631	1.62367	1.62104	1.61842	1.61580	1.61319	1.61059	1.60799	1.60540	1.60282
44	1.60025	1.59767	1.59510	1.59254	1.58998	1.58743	1.58489	1.58236	1.57983	1.57730
45	1.57479	1.57229	1.56979	1.56730	1.56482	1.56235	1.55988	1.55742	1.55496	1.55251
46	1.55007	1.54763	1.54519	1.54276	1.54033	1.53791	1.53550	1.53309	1.53069	1.52830
47	1.52591	1.52353	1.52117	1.51880	1.51645	1.51410	1.51175	1.50942	1.50708	1.50476
48	1.50244	1.50012	1.49782	1.49551	1.49322	1.49093	1.48864	1.48636	1.48409	1.48182
49	1.47956	1.47730	1.47505	1.47280	1.47057	1.46833	1.46610	1.46388	1.46166	1.45945
50	1.45724	1.45504	1.45283	1.45064	1.44845	1.44626	1.44408	1.44190	1.43973	1.43757
51	1.43541	1.43326	1.43112	1.42899	1.42685	1.42473	1.42261	1.42049	1.41838	1.41628
52	1.41418	1.41208	1.40999	1.40791	1.40583	1.40375	1.40169	1.39962	1.39756	1.39551
53	1.39346	1.39141	1.38937	1.38734	1.38531	1.38328	1.38126	1.37925	1.37724	1.37523
54	1.37323	1.37124	1.36926	1.36728	1.36530	1.36333	1.36137	1.35941	1.35745	1.35550
55	1.35355	1.35160	1.34966	1.34772	1.34578	1.34385	1.34192	1.34000	1.33808	1.33617
56	1.33426	1.33236	1.33046	1.32856	1.32667	1.32479	1.32290	1.32103	1.31915	1.31728
57	1.31542	1.31356	1.31170	1.30985	1.30801	1.30616	1.30432	1.30249	1.30066	1.29883
58	1.29701	1.29520	1.29339	1.29159	1.28979	1.28800	1.28621	1.28442	1.28264	1.28086
59	1.27908	1.27731	1.27553	1.27376	1.27200	1.27024	1.26848	1.26673	1.26498	1.26324
60	1.26150	1.25976	1.25802	1.25630	1.25457	1.25285	1.25113	1.24942	1.24771	1.24600
61	1.24430	1.24261	1.24092	1.23923	1.23755	1.23587	1.23420	1.23253	1.23086	1.22920
62	1.22754	1.22589	1.22424	1.22259	1.22094	1.21930	1.21767	1.21603	1.21440	1.21278
63	1.21115	1.20953	1.20791	1.20629	1.20467	1.20306	1.20146	1.19985	1.19825	1.19665
64	1.19506	1.19348	1.19189	1.19032	1.18874	1.18717	1.18561	1.18404	1.18248	1.18092
65	1.17937	1.17781	1.17626	1.17471	1.17316	1.17162	1.17008	1.16855	1.16701	1.16548
66	1.16396	1.16244	1.16092	1.15941	1.15790	1.15640	1.15490	1.15340	1.15191	1.15041
67	1.14892	1.14744	1.14596	1.14448	1.14300	1.14153	1.14006	1.13859	1.13713	1.13566
68	1.13421	1.13275	1.13130	1.12985	1.12841	1.12696	1.12552	1.12409	1.12265	1.12122
69	1.11979	1.11837	1.11695	1.11553	1.11411	1.11270	1.11129	1.10988	1.10848	1.10708
70	1.10568	1.10428	1.10289	1.10150	1.10011	1.09873	1.09735	1.09597	1.09459	1.09322
71	1.09185	1.09048	1.08912	1.08775	1.08639	1.08504	1.08368	1.08233	1.08098	1.07964
72	1.07830	1.07696	1.07562	1.07428	1.07295	1.07162	1.07030	1.06897	1.06765	1.06633
73	1.06502	1.06370	1.06239	1.06109	1.05978	1.05848	1.05718	1.05588	1.05458	1.05329
74	1.05200	1.05071	1.04943	1.04815	1.04687	1.04559	1.04432	1.04304	1.04177	1.04051
75	1.03924	1.03798	1.03672	1.03546	1.03421	1.03296	1.03171	1.03046	1.02922	1.02797
76	1.02673	1.02550	1.02427	1.02304	1.02182	1.02060	1.01937	1.01816	1.01694	1.01573
77	1.01452	1.01330	1.01209	1.01088	1.00968	1.00847	1.00727	1.00607	1.00487	1.00368
78	1.00248	1.00129	1.00011	0.99892	0.99774	0.99655	0.99538	0.99420	0.99302	0.99185
79	0.99068	0.98952	0.98836	0.98720	0.98604	0.98489	0.98374	0.98259	0.98144	0.98029
80	0.97915	0.97801	0.97686	0.97572	0.97458	0.97344	0.97231	0.97118	0.97004	0.96892
81	0.96779	0.96667	0.96555	0.96444	0.96332	0.96221	0.96110	0.96000	0.95889	0.95779
82	0.95669	0.95558	0.95448	0.95338	0.95228	0.95119	0.95009	0.94900	0.94791	0.94683
83	0.94574	0.94466	0.94359	0.94251	0.94144	0.94037	0.93930	0.93823	0.93717	0.93611
84	0.93504	0.93398	0.93292	0.93186	0.93080	0.92975	0.92869	0.92764	0.92659	0.92554
85	0.92450	0.92346	0.92242	0.92138	0.92035	0.91932	0.91829	0.91726	0.91623	0.91521
86	0.91418	0.91316	0.91213	0.91111	0.91009	0.90907	0.90806	0.90704	0.90603	0.90502

The surface, then, is disturbed by the wind, the extent of the disturbance depending upon the strength of the wind, the time for which it acts and the length of the water surface over which it acts. These three qualities are referred to as the *strength, duration* and *fetch* of the wind, respectively. The disturbance also depends on tide, depth of water and local land contours. Wave characteristics become practically independent of fetch when the fetch is greater than about 300 miles.

Once a wave has been generated it will move away from the position at which it was generated until all its energy is spent. Waves generated by local winds are termed *sea* and those which have travelled out of their area of generation are termed *swell*. Sea waves are characterized by relatively peaky crests and the crest length seldom exceeds some two or three times the wave-length. Swell waves are generally lower with more rounded tops. The crest length is typically six or seven times the wave-length. In a swell, the variation in height between successive waves is less than is the case for sea waves.

The sea surface presents a very confused picture which defied for many years any attempts at mathematical definition. Developments in the theory of random variables since about 1940 have now made it possible to construct a mathematical model of the sea surface. The essential feature of these theories was, however, foreseen by R. E. Froude when, in 1905, (Ref. 1) he stated:

> ... irregular wave systems are only a compound of a number of regular systems (individually of comparatively small amplitude) of various periods, ranging through the whole gamut (so to speak) represented by our diagrams and more. And the effect of such a compound wave series on the models would be more or less a compound of the effects proper to the individual units composing it.

Unfortunately, at that time the mathematics needed to develop his ideas into a practical tool for the naval architect had not been developed.

Before proceeding to consider the irregular sea surface, it is first of all necessary to consider a regular wave system as this is the basic building brick from which the picture of any irregular system is built up. Such a system with crests extending to infinity in a direction normal to the direction of propagation of the wave has the appearance of a large sheet of corrugated iron. The section of the wave is regular and two cases are of particular significance. They are: (i) the trochoidal wave, and (ii) the sinusoidal wave.

The theory of these two wave forms is developed in the following paragraphs which can be omitted by the student wishing to have only a general appreciation of wave systems.

Waves

TROCHOIDAL WAVES

The trochoidal wave theory has been adopted for certain standard calculations, e.g. that for longitudinal strength. By observation, the theory appears to reflect many actual ocean wave phenomena although it can be regarded as only an approximation to the complex wave form actually existing.

The section of the trochoidal wave surface is defined mathematically as the path traced by a point fixed within a circle when that circle is rolled along and below a straight line as shown in Fig. 9.1.

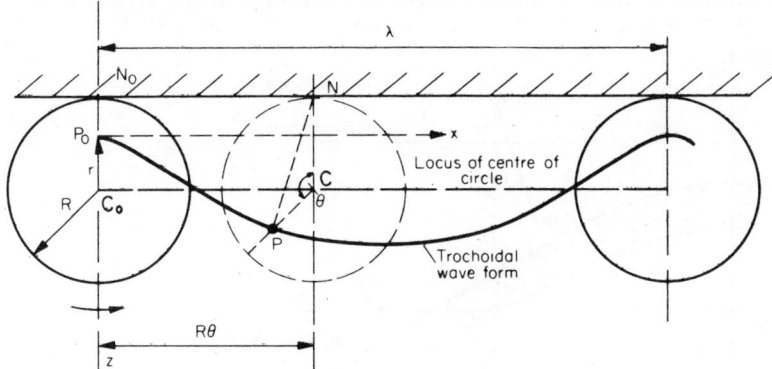

Fig. 9.1 *Generation of trochoidal wave form*

Suppose the height and length of the wave to be generated are h_w and λ respectively: then the radius of the generating circle is R, say, where

$$\lambda = 2\pi R$$

and the distance of the generating point from the centre of the circle is r, say, where

$$h_w = 2r$$

Let the centre of the generating circle start at position C_0 and let it have turned through an angle θ by the time it reaches C. Then

$$C_0 C = N_0 N = R\theta$$

Relative to the x-, z-axes shown in Fig. 9.1, the co-ordinates of P are

$$x = R\theta - r \sin \theta$$
$$= \frac{\lambda}{2\pi} \theta - \frac{h_w}{2} \sin \theta$$
$$z = r - r \cos \theta = \frac{h_w}{2}(1 - \cos \theta)$$

As the circle rolls it turns, instantaneously, about its point of contact, N, with the straight line. Hence $\overline{NP}$ is the normal to the trochoidal surface and the instantaneous velocity of P is

$$\overline{NP} \frac{d\theta}{dt} \text{ normal to } \overline{NP}$$

Surfaces of equal pressure below the water surface will also be trochoidal. Crests and troughs will lie vertically below those of the surface trochoid, i.e. the length of the trochoidal wave is the same in all cases and they are all generated by a rolling circle of the same diameter. At great depths, any surface disturbance is not felt so that the radius of the point generating the trochoidal surface must reduce with increasing depth.

Consider two trochoidal sub-surfaces close to each other as shown in Fig. 9.2.

Fig. 9.2 Sub-surface trochoids

By definition, no particles of water pass through a trochoidal surface. Hence, for continuity the space shown shaded in Fig. 9.2 must remain filled by the same volume of water.

Let t = thickness of layer at P (measured normal to the trochoidal surface).

$$\text{Velocity at P} = \overline{\text{PN}}\frac{d\theta}{dt}$$

Hence the condition of continuity implies

$$t\overline{\text{PN}}\frac{d\theta}{dt} = \text{constant for all values of } \theta$$

i.e.

$$t\overline{\text{PN}} = \text{constant for all values of } \theta$$

Now $\overline{CP}$ and $\overline{C'P'}$ are parallel and, provided δz is small, $\overline{PN}$ and $\overline{P'N'}$ are very nearly parallel. Resolving along PN

$$\overline{P'N'} + \delta z \cos\phi = \overline{PN} + t$$

$$\therefore \quad t = \delta z \cos\phi + \delta\overline{PN}, \quad \text{where} \quad \delta\overline{PN} = \overline{P'N'} - \overline{PN}$$

$$= \delta z \left(\frac{R - r\cos\theta}{\overline{PN}}\right) + \delta\overline{PN}$$

$$\therefore \quad t\overline{PN} = \delta z(R - r\cos\theta) + \overline{PN}\,\delta\overline{PN}$$

Also

$$\overline{PN}^2 = R^2 + r^2 - 2Rr\cos\theta$$

Differentiating and remembering that R and θ are constant

$$2\overline{PN}\delta\overline{PN} = 2r\delta r - 2R\cos\theta\,\delta r$$
$$\therefore t\overline{PN} = \delta z(R - r\cos\theta) + r\,\delta r - R\cos\theta\,\delta r$$
$$= R\,\delta z + r\,\delta r - \cos\theta\,(r\,\delta z + R\,\delta r)$$

Since $t\overline{PN}$ is constant for all values of θ

$$r\,\delta z + R\,\delta r = 0$$

$\therefore$ in the limit

$$\frac{1}{r}dr = -\frac{1}{R}dz$$

Integrating

$$\log_e r = c - \frac{z}{R} \text{ where } c = \text{constant}$$

If $\quad r = r_0$ at $z = 0$, $c = \log_e r_0$

$$\therefore \log_e r = \log_e r_0 - \frac{z}{R}$$

i.e.

$$r = r_0 \exp\left(-\frac{z}{R}\right)$$

That is to say, the radius of the point tracing out the sub-surface trochoid decreases exponentially with increasing depth. This exponential decay is often met within natural phenomena, and is very rapid as is illustrated in Table 9.5 for a surface wave 150 m long and 15 m high, i.e. a wave for which

$$R = \frac{\lambda}{2\pi} = \frac{75}{\pi} = 23\cdot 87\,\text{m}$$

$$r_0 = \frac{15}{2} = 7\cdot 5\,\text{m}$$

Table 9.5
Decay of orbital radius with depth

z (m)	r (m)	z (m)	r (m)
0	7·50	25	2·57
5	6·06	50	0·87
10	4·88	100	0·10
23·87	2·76		

Although it has been convenient to study the shape of the trochoidal wave using the artifice of a point within a rolling circle, a particle in the water surface itself does not trace out a trochoid. The absolute motion is circular and neglecting bodily movement of masses of water such as those due to tides, is obtained by superimposing on Fig. 9.1 an overall velocity of C from right to left such that

$$C = \frac{\lambda}{T}$$

This superposition of a constant velocity in no way invalidates the results obtained above or those which follow. The use of the 'stationary' trochoid as in Fig. 9.1 is merely one of mathematical convenience.

The magnitude of C can be expressed in terms of λ by considering the forces acting on a particle at P in Fig. 9.1. Such a particle will suffer a downward force due to gravity and a 'centrifugal force' in the line $\overline{CP}$.

If the mass of the particle is m, the gravitational force is mg and the centrifugal force $mr\omega^2$ where $\omega = d\theta/dt$.

Since the surface is one of equal pressure, the resultant of these two forces must be normal to the surface, i.e. it must lie in the direction of $\overline{NP}$.

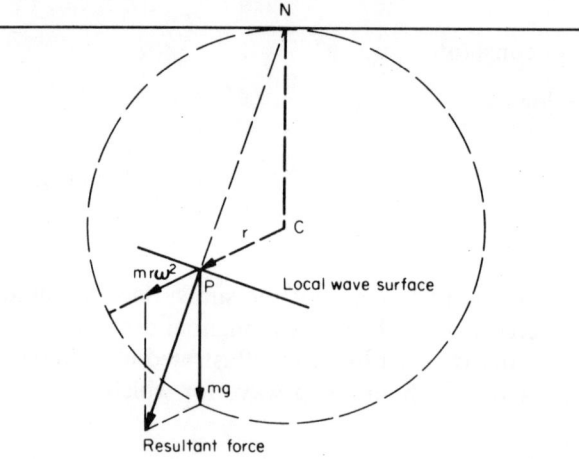

Fig. 9.3 *Forces on particle in wave surface*

Referring to Fig. 9.3,

$$\frac{mg}{\overline{NC}} = \frac{mr\omega^2}{\overline{CP}}$$

i.e.

$$\frac{mg}{R} = \frac{mr\omega^2}{r}$$

Whence

$$\omega^2 = \frac{g}{R}$$

Now $C = \lambda/T$ where T, the wave period $= 2\pi/\omega$.

$$\therefore \quad C = \lambda\omega/2\pi = \omega R$$

Hence

$$C^2 = \omega^2 R^2 = gR = \frac{g\lambda}{2\pi}$$

Relationship between line of orbit centres and the undisturbed surface

In Fig. 9.4, the trochoidal wave form is superimposed on the still water surface. It is clear that the volume of water in a crest, as measured above the

Fig. 9.4 *Line of orbit centres in relation to the still water surface*

still water level, must be equal to the volume of a trough measured below this level. Put another way, the area $P_0 \, P'_0 \, P''_0$ must equal the area of the rectangle $P_0 \, P'_0 \, L' \, L$ or, for simplification of the integration

$$\int_0^{x=\pi R} z \, dx = \pi R (r + \delta z)$$

where δz = distance of still water surface below the line of orbit centres. Since $x = R\theta - r \sin \theta$ and $z = r - r \cos \theta$, we obtain

$$\int_{\theta=0}^{\theta=\pi} (r - r \cos \theta)(R - r \cos \theta) \, d\theta = \pi R(r + \delta z)$$

$$\int_0^\pi (rR - rR \cos \theta - r^2 \cos \theta + r^2 \cos^2 \theta) \, d\theta = \pi R(r + \delta z)$$

i.e.

$$\pi R r + \frac{\pi}{2} r^2 = \pi R(r + \delta z)$$

$$\therefore \quad \delta z = \frac{r^2}{2R}$$

This property has been used in the past as a wave pressure correction in the longitudinal strength calculations.

SINUSOIDAL WAVES

Mathematically, the trochoidal wave is not easy to manipulate and the basic units from which an irregular sea is assumed to be built up are sinusoidal in profile.

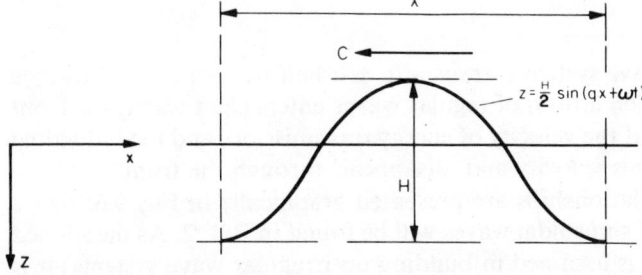

Fig. 9.5 *Profile of sinusoidal wave*

For a wave travelling with velocity C in the direction of decreasing x, Fig. 9.5, the profile of the wave can be represented by the equation

$$z = \frac{H}{2}\sin(qx+\omega t)$$

In this expression, $q = 2\pi/\lambda$ is known as the *wave number* and $\omega = 2\pi/T$ is known as the *wave frequency*. The wave velocity as in the case of the trochoidal wave, is given by

$$C = \frac{\lambda}{T} = \frac{\omega}{q}$$

Other significant features of the wave are

$$T^2 = \frac{2\pi\lambda}{g}$$
$$\omega^2 = \frac{2\pi g}{\lambda}$$
$$C^2 = \frac{g\lambda}{2\pi}$$

Water particles within the waves move in orbits which are circular, the radii of which decrease with depth in accordance with the expression

$$r = \frac{H}{2}\exp(-qz) \text{ for depth } z$$

From this it can be deduced that at a depth $z = +\lambda/2$, the orbit radius is only $0{\cdot}02H$ so that for all intents and purposes motion is negligibly small at depths equal to or greater than half the wavelength. (See Table 9.5.) The proof of this relationship is similar to that adopted for the trochoidal wave.

The hydrodynamic pressure at any point in the wave system is given by

$$p = \rho g \frac{H}{2}\exp(-qz)\sin(qx+\omega t)$$

The average potential and kinetic energies per unit area of the wave system are equal, and the average total energy per unit area is

$$\rho g \frac{H^2}{8}$$

The energy of the wave system is transmitted at half the velocity of advance of the waves. Thus, when a train of regular waves enters calm water, the front of the waves advances at the velocity of energy transmission, and the individual waves travel at twice this velocity and 'disappear' through the front.

Two of the above relationships are presented graphically in Fig. 9.6.

A fuller treatment of sinusoidal waves will be found in Ref. 2. As mentioned above, this wave form is assumed in building up irregular wave systems. It is also used in studying the response of a ship to regular waves. Differences in

Fig. 9.6

response to a trochoidal wave would be small if the waves are of the same height and length.

IRREGULAR WAVE PATTERNS

Behind the apparent confusion of the sea there is statistical order and the sea surface may be regarded as the result of superimposing a large number of regular sinusoidal waves of different, but small, heights and various lengths in random phase. An important parameter is the range of lengths, and hence frequencies, present in the system.

If all these wave components travel in the same direction, the irregular pattern will exhibit a series of straight crests extending to infinity in a direction normal to the direction of wave travel. Such a system is termed a *long-crested irregular wave system* and is referred to as *one-dimensional* (frequency). In the more general case, the individual wave components travel in different directions and the resultant wave pattern does not exhibit long crests but rather a series of humps and hollows. Such a system is termed an *irregular wave system* or *two-dimensional system* (frequency and direction). The remainder of this section is devoted to the long-crested system.

How is this irregular system to be defined? It is possible to measure the time interval between successive crests passing a fixed point and the heights between successive troughs and crests. These vary continuously and can be misleading in representing a particular sea. For instance, a part of the system in which many component waves cancelled each other out because of their particular phase relationships would appear to be less severe than was in fact the case.

Provided the record of surface elevation against time is treated carefully, however, it can yield some very useful information. If $\bar{\lambda}$ is the average distance between crests and $\bar{T}$ the average time interval in seconds, it can be shown that, approximately

$$\bar{\lambda} = \frac{2g}{3} \frac{\bar{T}^2}{2\pi} = 3\cdot41\bar{T}^2, \text{ ft}$$

$$= 1\cdot04\bar{T}^2, \text{ m}$$

This relationship between $\bar{\lambda}$ and $\bar{T}$ is represented in Fig. 9.7. Both can be related to wind speed as defined in Ref. 3 by the expression:

Average period $= 0\cdot285 V_w$, s

where $V_w =$ wind speed in knots.

Since an observer is more likely to record $\bar{T}$ using a stop watch, applying the classical relationship $\lambda = gT^2/2\pi$ would lead to an error.

In general, in this chapter record is used to refer to a record of the variation of sea surface elevation, relative to its mean level, with time. A complete record would be too difficult to analyse and a sample length is usually taken from time to time, the duration of each being such as to ensure a reasonable statistical representation of the sea surface.

The values of wave height in a sample can be arranged in descending order of magnitude and the mean height of the first third of the values obtained. This mean height of the highest one-third of the waves is termed the *significant wave height*. The height of the highest wave occurring in a given record can also be found. If a large number of wave records is so analysed for a given ocean area, it is possible to plot the probability of exceeding a given significant wave height. Results, generally based on Ref. 20, are presented in Fig. 9.8 for the North Atlantic, Northern North Atlantic and world wide. It will be noted that the Northern North Atlantic is the most severe area as would be expected from general experience.

HISTOGRAMS AND PROBABILITY DISTRIBUTIONS

The wave heights can also be arranged in groups so that the number of waves with heights falling into various intervals can be counted. These can be plotted as a histogram as in Fig. 9.9 in which the area of each rectangle represents the number of waves in that interval of wave height. In practice, it is usual to arrange scales such that the total area under the histogram is unity. The histogram shows the distribution of heights in the wave sample, but in many applications subsequent analysis is easier if a mathematical curve can be fitted to the results. Three theoretical distributions are of particular importance.

Fig. 9.7 Average period and wave-length

Fig. 9.8 Waves at OWS station India

306 Basic ship theory

The Normal or Gaussian distribution which is defined by the equation

$$p(x) = \frac{1}{\sigma\sqrt{(2\pi)}} \exp\left\{-\tfrac{1}{2}\frac{(x-\mu)^2}{\sigma^2}\right\}$$

where μ = mean of values of x, σ^2 = variance, and σ = standard deviation.

The Logarithmically Normal or Log-Normal Distribution which is defined by the equation

$$p(\log x) = \frac{1}{\sigma_1\sqrt{(2\pi)}} \exp\left\{-\tfrac{1}{2}\frac{(\log x - u)^2}{\sigma_1^2}\right\}$$

where u = mean value of $\log x$, σ_1^2 = variance, and σ_1 = standard deviation.

The Rayleigh distribution which is defined by the equation

$$p(x) = \frac{x}{a}\exp\left\{-\frac{x^2}{2a}\right\}, \quad x > 0$$

where $2a$ is the mean value of x^2.

In these expressions, $p(x)$ is a probability density. Plotted to a base of x the total area under the curve must be unity, expressing the fact that it is certain that the variable under examination will take some value of x. The area under the curve in a small interval of x, dx, is $p(x)\,dx$ and this represents the probability that the variable will take a value in the interval dx.

Integrating the curve leads to a *cumulative probability distribution* in which the ordinate at a given value of x represents the area under the probability distribution between 0 and x. The ordinate thus represents the probability that the variable will have a value less than, or equal to, x.

It will be noted that the normal and log-normal distributions as functions of x are defined by two variables, μ and σ or u and σ_1, and the Rayleigh distribution by one variable a. Hence, it is necessary to determine the values of these quantities which most closely fit the observed wave data.

EXAMPLE 1. A record contains 1000 waves with heights up to 10 m, the numbers of readings falling into various 1-m groups are

Height (m)	0–1	1–2	2–3	3–4	4–5	5–6	6–7	7–8	8–9	9–10
Number of waves	6	29	88	180	247	260	133	42	10	5

Plot a histogram for these data and derive the corresponding normal distribution.

Solution: The histogram is obtained by erecting a series of rectangles on each height band such that the area of each rectangle is proportional to the number of waves in that height band. For ease of comparison with the probability curve, the total area of all rectangles is made unity by dividing by 1000 and the histogram is plotted as in Fig. 9.9.

Fig. 9.9 Histogram and normal probability curve superimposed

The mean, μ, of the wave heights is found by summating the products of the average height in each band (x_r say) by its frequency of occurrence (F_r) and the variance follows as in the table. Using this table (Table 9.6),

$$\mu = \frac{4750}{1000} = 4\cdot 75$$

$$\sigma^2 = \frac{2282}{1000} = 2\cdot 282$$

$$\therefore \quad \sigma = 1\cdot 510$$

Hence the equation to the normal curve is

$$p(x) = \frac{1}{1\cdot 510\sqrt{(2\pi)}} \exp\left\{-\tfrac{1}{2}\left(\frac{x-4\cdot 75}{1\cdot 51}\right)^2\right\}$$

$$= \frac{1}{3\cdot 785} \exp\left\{-\left(\frac{x-4\cdot 75}{2\cdot 135}\right)^2\right\}$$

Corresponding values of x and $p(x)$ are given in the tables (Table 9.6) and these have been plotted in Fig. 9.9 superimposed on the histogram.

In applying the above techniques, it must be realized that particular sets of records are only *samples* of all possible records, known in statistics as the *population*, e.g. the wave data reproduced above for weather station India were made in one area only and for limited periods of time. When an analytical expression is fitted to the observed data, it is desirable to demonstrate that the

Table 9.6

x_r	F_r	$x_r F_r$	$x_r - \mu$	$(x_r - \mu)^2$	$F_r(x_r - \mu)^2$
0·5	6	3	−4·25	18·06	108·5
1·5	29	43·5	−3·25	10·56	306·2
2·5	88	220	−2·25	5·06	445·5
3·5	180	630	−1·25	1·56	281·3
4·5	247	1111·5	−0·25	0·06	15·5
5·5	260	1430	+0·75	0·56	146·2
6·5	133	864·5	+1·75	3·06	407·3
7·5	42	315	+2·75	7·56	317·7
8·5	10	85	+3·75	14·06	140·8
9·5	5	47·5	+4·75	22·56	112·7
	1000	4750			2281·7

x	0·5	1·5	2·5	3·5	4·5	5·5	6·5	7·5	8·5	9·5
$p(x)$	0·0050	0·0260	0·0870	0·1874	0·2606	0·2340	0·1350	0·0504	0·0120	0·0018

expression is reasonably valid. The reliability of the hypothesis can be evaluated by applying statistical tests of significance which enable estimates to be made of the expected variation of the measured data from the analytically defined data if the hypothesis is true.

WAVE SPECTRA

A very useful method of presenting data on the wave system is in the form of a wave spectrum. When there are n regular sine wave components present and n is not too large, a *line spectrum* can be drawn as Fig. 9.10 where the height of each ordinate represents the component wave amplitude or half the square of the component wave amplitude. In this latter case the ordinate is proportional to the component wave energy.

Fig. 9.10 Line spectrum

In practice, n is usually so large and the amplitude of each component so small, that the concept of a *continuous spectrum* is more convenient. In this, the area of the spectrum between frequencies f and $f+\delta f$ represents

$$\sum_{f}^{f+\delta f} \tfrac{1}{2}\zeta_A^2$$

That is, the area under the curve between frequencies f and $f+\delta f$ represents the sum of the energy of all component waves having frequencies in the band. In the limit, as δf tends to zero, the curve becomes smooth. With this type of spectrum it can be shown that

Area under spectrum = m_0 = mean square of surface elevation

Fig. 9.11 *Continuous spectrum*

Referring to Fig. 9.12, m_0 can be obtained by measuring the surface elevation ζ, relative to the mean level, at equal time intervals. If n such measurements are taken:

$$m_0 = \frac{1}{n}\sum \zeta^2$$

Fig. 9.12

For reasonable accuracy, the time interval chosen should not be greater than half the minimum time interval between successive crests and the number of readings must be large.

For waves represented by a Rayleigh distribution:

Most frequent wave amplitude = $0.707\sqrt{(2m_0)} = \sqrt{m_0}$
Average wave amplitude = $0.886 \sqrt{(2m_0)} = 1.25\sqrt{m_0}$
Average amplitude of $\frac{1}{3}$ highest waves = $1.416 \sqrt{(2m_0)} = 2\sqrt{m_0}$
Average amplitude of $\frac{1}{10}$ highest waves = $1.800 \sqrt{(2m_0)} = 2.55\sqrt{m_0}$

Note: This presentation is used as some authorities plot ζ^2 against f as the spectrum. In this case, the area under the spectrum is $2m_0$ where m_0 is defined as above.

The average amplitude of $\frac{1}{3}$ highest waves is denoted by $\zeta_{\frac{1}{3}}$ and is termed the *significant wave amplitude*.

The probability that at a random instant of time the magnitude of the wave amplitude exceeds some value ζ is given by (for a normal distribution).

$$P(\zeta) = 1 - \text{erf}\,[\zeta/\sqrt{(2m_0)}]$$

The error function (erf) is tabulated in standard mathematical tables.

The percentages of wave amplitudes exceeding certain values are shown in Fig. 9.13. It will be seen that more than 60 per cent of waves have amplitudes of $\sqrt{m_0}$ or less.

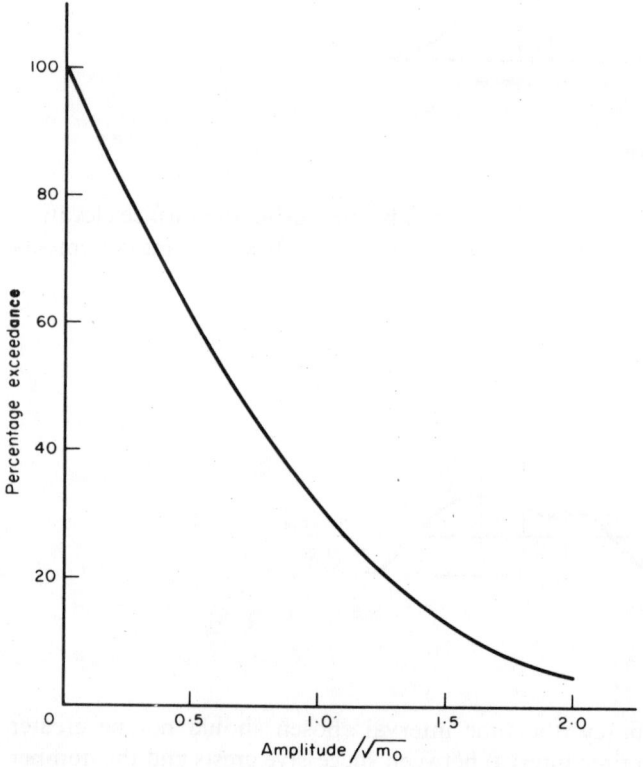

Fig. 9.13

One problem is that the waves become more severe with wind duration and fetch, i.e. the length of the sea surface exposed to the wind. Some of the differences between the spectra advanced by various authorities are probably due, therefore, to the difficulty of deciding when a sea is fully developed because a uniform wind seldom blows long enough for this to be determined. When a wind begins to blow, short, low amplitude waves are formed at first. As the wind continues to blow, larger and longer waves are formed. As the wind dies down the longer waves move out of the area by virtue of their greater velocity, leaving the shorter waves. Thus the growth and decay of wave spectra is as shown in Figs. 9.14 and 9.15.

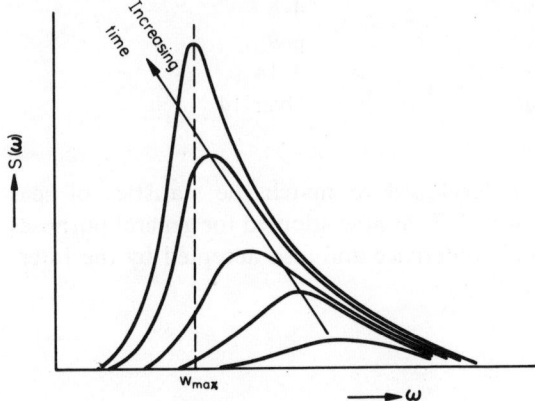

Fig. 9.14 Growth of spectra

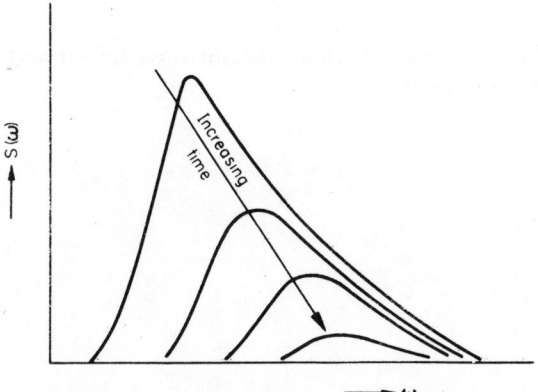

Fig. 9.15 Decay of spectra

312 Basic ship theory

SEA STATE CODE

A generally accepted description of the sea state appropriate to various significant wave heights is afforded by the sea state code.

Sea state code

Code	Description of sea	Significant wave height (m)
0	Calm (glassy)	0
1	Calm (rippled)	0–0·1
2	Smooth (wavelets)	0·1–0·5
3	Slight	0·5–1·25
4	Moderate	1·25–2·50
5	Rough	2·50–4·00
6	Very rough	4–6
7	High	6–9
8	Very high	9–14
9	Phenomenal	Over 14

ITTC SPECTRA

Various wave spectra have been developed to match the statistics of seas measured in different parts of the world. That now adopted for general purposes by the International Towing Tank Conference and also accepted by the International Ship Structures Congress is:

$$S(\omega) = \frac{A}{\omega^5} \exp(-B/\omega^4)$$

ω is the circular frequency of the waves (s^{-1}) and A and B are constants. When only the significant wave height is known,

$A = 8\cdot 10 \times 10^{-3} g^2$
$B = 3\cdot 11/\zeta^2_{\frac{1}{3}}$

ζ = significant wave height in m. When both significant wave height and the characteristic wave period, T_1, are known,

$$A = \frac{173\, \zeta^2_{\frac{1}{3}}}{T_1^4}$$
$$B = 691/T_1^4$$
$$T_1 = 2\pi \frac{m_0}{m_1}$$

A typical family of spectra for long crested seas using the single parameter formula is shown in Fig. 9.16. With this simple version the ratio between the frequency or wave length at peak energy and the significant wave height is constant for all spectra the value of the ratio being 39.2. This is not true for all ocean spectra although many have values in the range 30 to 50. Hence for general

Fig. 9.16

Fig. 9.17

purposes, such as prediction of ship motion likely to be experienced by a new design, the use of the simple formula is acceptable. Where it is necessary to vary the ratio the more elaborate formula can be used. Figure 9.17 presents a family of spectra with a significant wave height of 7·5 metres.

The ITTC spectrum is similar in form to a spectrum in use for many years known as the Pierson–Moskowitz spectrum. The Neumann spectrum has also been commonly used while many different spectra have been developed for specific purposes, particularly to represent coastal seas or seas with limited fetch (Ref. 21).

WAVE AMPLITUDES

Presented with a long record of the surface elevation as measured at a fixed point (Fig. 9.18) it is possible to establish a mean level and record the amplitudes at crests and troughs (ζ_1, ζ_2, ζ_3, etc.).

Fig. 9.18 *Wave elevation recorded at a fixed point*

The mean square crest amplitude is given by

$$\bar{\zeta}^2 = \frac{1}{n}(\zeta_1^2 + \zeta_2^2 + \ldots + \zeta_n^2)$$

When the band of frequencies present in the wave system is narrow, the statistical properties of the system approximate those of the Rayleigh distribution (Ref. 5). These include:

(a) the most frequently occurring wave amplitude, the mode, is given by:

$$\text{mode} = 0.707 \zeta_s \text{ where } \zeta_s = (\bar{\zeta}^2)^{\frac{1}{2}}$$

(b) the chance that ζ should exceed a certain value r is given by

$$\int_r^\infty p(r)\,dr = \exp(-r^2/\bar{\zeta}^2)$$

(c) if the values of ζ were to be arranged in descending order of magnitude, the mean value of the first cn of these is given by $k_1 \zeta_s$ where corresponding values of c and k_1 are given below:

Table 9.8
Corresponding values of c and k_1

c	k_1	c	k_1
0·01	2·359	0·4	1·347
0·05	1·986	0·5	1·256
0·1	1·800	0·6	1·176
0·2	1·591	0·7	1·102
0·25	1·517	0·8	1·031
0·3	1·454	0·9	0·961
0·3333	1·416	1·0	0·886

(d) the expected value of the maximum amplitude in a sample of n values is $k_2 \zeta_S$ where corresponding values of n and k_2 are given in Table 9.9.

Table 9.9
Corresponding values of n and k_2

n	k_2	n	k_2
1	0·707	500	2·509
2	1·030	1000	2·642
5	1·366	2000	2·769
10	1·583	5000	2·929
20	1·778	10,000	3·044
50	2·010	20,000	3·155
100	2·172	50,000	3·296
200	2·323	100,000	3·400

(e) in such a sample the probability that ζ will be greater than r is

$$1 - \exp[-\exp\{-(r^2 - r_0^2)/\bar{\zeta}^2\}]$$

where $r_0^2/\bar{\zeta}^2 = \log n$

Many wave systems are of this narrow frequency band type. In the more general case, a parameter ε can be used to represent the width of the frequency spectrum. The extreme values of ε are 0 and 1 representing a Rayleigh and normal distribution of wave amplitude respectively.

Then, if m_0 is the mean square value of the wave surface relative to the mean level, the variance as previously defined, it can be shown that the

mean square crest height $= (2 - \varepsilon^2) m_0$

By putting $\varepsilon = 0$, it follows that

$$\bar{\zeta}^2 = 2m_0$$

On the other hand in a very broad spectrum with $\varepsilon = 1$,

mean square crest height $= m_0$

In practice, it is possible to obtain an estimate of the value of ε by using the fact that, over a long section of wave record, the ratio of the number of zero crossings to the number of turning values (maximum or minimum) has the expectation

$$(1 - \varepsilon^2)^{\frac{1}{2}}$$

Thus, referring to Fig. 9.18 and remembering that, in practice, a much longer record would be used

Number of zero crossings $= 11$; Number of turning values $= 19$

Hence

$$(1 - \varepsilon^2)^{\frac{1}{2}} = \tfrac{11}{19} = 0.58$$

316 Basic ship theory

i.e.

$$\varepsilon = 0.815$$

Another useful relationship is that the mean crest to trough height is given by

$$2\left\{\frac{\pi}{2}(1-\varepsilon^2)m_0\right\}^{\frac{1}{2}}$$

EXTREME WAVE AMPLITUDES

The naval architect is often concerned with the extreme waves that can occur. Suppose a number of records, say M, are taken with the same significant wave amplitude and N values of wave amplitude are recorded from each record. If the greatest wave amplitude in each record is noted there will be M such maxima. Then Table 9.10 expresses the maximum wave amplitudes in terms of the significant amplitude $\zeta_{\frac{1}{3}}$ for various values of N.

Table 9.10
Exceptionally high waves

N	5% lower	Most frequent	Average	5% greater
20	0·99	1·22	1·32	1·73
50	1·19	1·40	1·50	1·86
100	1·33	1·52	1·61	1·94
200	1·45	1·63	1·72	2·03
500	1·60	1·76	1·84	2·14
1000	1·70	1·86	1·93	2·22

Thus, if each record has 200 wave amplitudes then, of the M maximum readings,

5 per cent can be expected to be lower than $1.45\zeta_{\frac{1}{3}}$
The most frequent value = $1.63\zeta_{\frac{1}{3}}$
The average value   = $1.72\zeta_{\frac{1}{3}}$
5 per cent can be expected to be greater than $2.03\zeta_{\frac{1}{3}}$

OTHER MEANS OF DEFINING AN IRREGULAR WAVE SYSTEM

For a proper study of waves, and phenomena associated with them, it is necessary to use the energy spectrum concept as described above. For many applications, however, a simpler approach will suffice. One such application was that used in Ref. 6 based on wave data given in Ref. 7. The data for North Atlantic waves are reproduced in Table 9.11 and Fig. 9.19.

Climate

THE WIND

The main influence of the wind is felt indirectly through the waves it generates on the surface of the sea. As stated above, the severity of these waves will depend upon the strength (i.e. velocity) of the wind, the time it acts (i.e. its duration) and the distance over which it acts (i.e. the fetch).

Table 9.11
North Atlantic waves. Frequency of occurrence in days per year

Wavelength (ft) ± 25 ft	Wave height (ft)								
	0–5	5–10	10–15	15–20	20–25	25–30	30–40	40–50	Total
	Frequency in days per year								
75	0.13								0.13
125	0.30								0.30
175	0.64	0.46							1.10
225	1.73	1.90	0.7	0.36					4.69
275	2.81	6.77	1.63	0.68					11.89
325	3.05	12.69	3.13	1.21	0.17				20.25
375	2.88	13.07	5.12	2.05	0.46	0.06			23.64
425	2.50	11.46	7.19	3.17	0.85	0.13			25.30
475	2.07	9.64	9.16	4.65	1.27	0.17			26.96
525	1.69	7.74	10.58	6.30	2.01	0.25	0.06		28.63
575	1.23	5.86	10.62	8.21	2.92	0.36	0.11		29.31
625	0.85	4.23	9.27	10.36	4.23	0.53	0.21		29.68
675	0.53	2.86	7.61	11.84	5.71	0.89	0.34	0.04	29.82
725	0.34	1.90	5.92	10.83	7.34	1.44	0.76	0.07	28.60
775	0.27	1.06	4.48	8.42	8.73	2.20	1.50	0.17	26.83
825	0.21	0.49	3.22	5.92	7.11	3.38	2.60	0.30	23.23
875	0.19	0.17	2.28	4.15	4.93	4.55	4.02	0.80	21.09
925	0.17		1.44	2.60	3.09	3.40	4.91	1.73	17.34
975	0.15		0.80	1.42	1.78	1.95	3.38	2.41	11.89
1025	0.13						1.90	2.03	
1075	0.10						1.23	1.33	
1125	0.08						0.59	0.67	
1175	0.06						0.17	0.23	
1225	0.04							0.04	
1275	0.02							0.02	
	22.17	80.30	83.15	82.17	50.60	19.31	17.89	9.41	365.0

Table 9.12
The Beaufort Scale

		Limits of speed		
		(Kts)	(m/s)	(ft/s)
0	Calm	1	0.3	2
1	Light air	1–3	0.3–1.5	2–5
2	Light breeze	4–6	1.6–3.3	6–11
3	Gentle breeze	7–10	3.4–5.4	12–18
4	Moderate breeze	11–16	5.5–7.9	19–27
5	Fresh breeze	17–21	8.0–10.7	28–36
6	Strong breeze	22–27	10.8–13.8	37–46
7	Near gale	28–33	13.9–17.1	47–56
8	Gale	34–40	17.2–20.7	57–68
9	Strong gale	41–47	20.8–24.4	69–80
10	Storm	48–55	24.5–28.4	81–93
11	Violent Storm	56–63	28.5–32.6	94–106
12	Hurricane	64 & over	32.7 & over	107 & over

Fig. 9.19 Occurrence in days per year of waves exceeding a particular height in the North Atlantic

The strength of the wind is broadly classified by the *Beaufort Scale*. The numbers 0 to 12 were introduced by Admiral Sir Francis Beaufort in 1806, 0 referring to a calm and force 12 to a wind of hurricane force. Originally, there were no specific wind speeds associated with these numbers but in 1939 the values shown in Table 9.12 have more recently been adopted internationally. The figures relate to an anemometer at a height of 6 m above the sea surface.

No fixed relation exists between the spectra of a sea and the speed of wind generating it. Figure 9.20 shows a relationship agreed by the ITTC but it applies only to fully developed seas where duration and fetch are large. Figure 9.21 shows the probability of exceeding a given wind speed in the North Atlantic based on Ref. 20.

The ship environment 319

Fig. 9.20

Fig. 9.21

The wind velocity varies with height. At the surface of the water, the relative velocity is zero due to a boundary layer effect. Reference 8 defines a nominal wind at 33 ft above the waterline, and the variation in wind velocity with height is assumed to be in accord with Fig. 9.22 which is based on that reference. It will be noted, that these nominal velocities will be about 6 per cent less than those defined by the Beaufort Scale at a height of 6 m above the surface. Also given in Fig. 9.22 is a curve based on this nominal height.

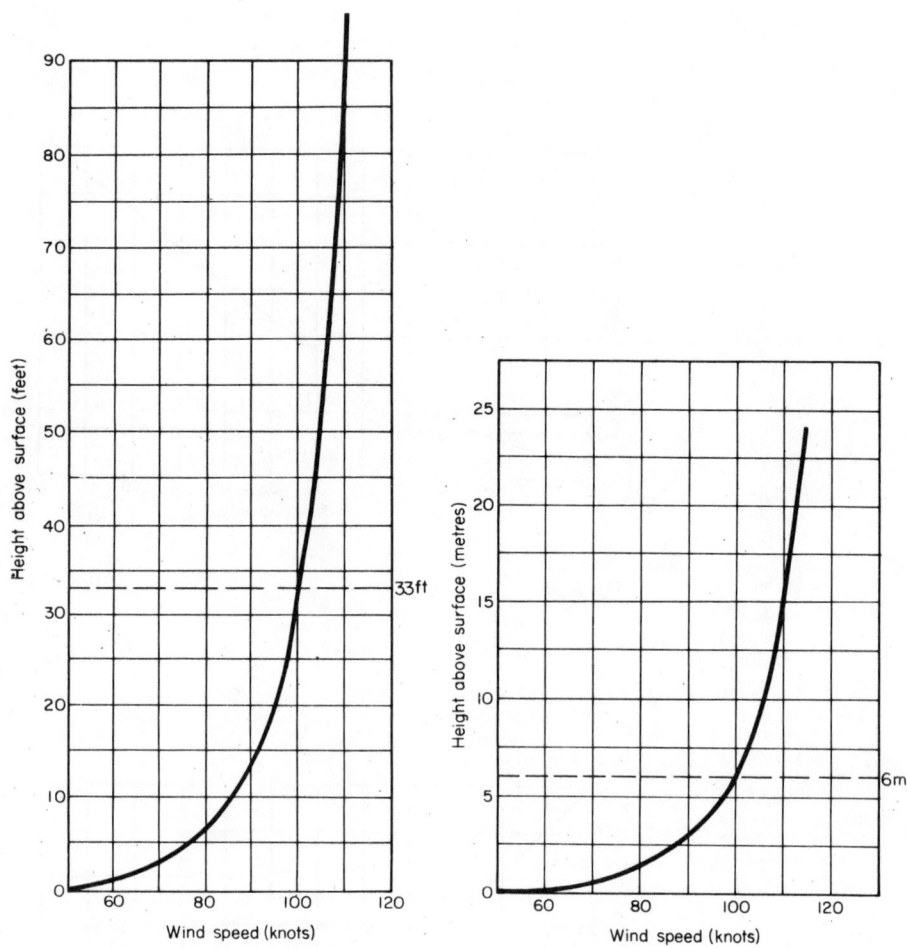

Fig. 9.22 *Variation of wind speed with height above sea surface (nominal wind speed 100 knots)*

For nominal velocities other than 100 knots, the true velocities can be scaled in direct proportion to the nominal velocities.

More direct influences of the wind are felt by the ship as forces acting on the above water portions of the hull and the superstructure. The fore and aft components of such forces will act either as a resistive or propulsive force. The lateral force will act as a heeling moment. Thus, standards of stability adopted in a given design must reflect the possible magnitude of this heeling moment, e.g. large windage area ships will require a greater stability standard as discussed in Chapter 4.

Another direct influence of the wind, including the effect of the ship's own speed, is to cause local wind velocities past the superstructure which may entrain the funnel gases and bring them down on to the after decks, or which may produce high winds across games decks to the discomfort of passengers. These effects are often studied by means of model experiments conducted in a wind tunnel, in order to obtain a suitable design of funnel and superstructure.

AMBIENT AIR

A ship is completely immersed in two fluids—air for the upper portion and water for the lower portion. Because the specific heat of water is much greater than that for air, the former suffers a much slower variation of temperature due to climatic changes. In defining the temperature environment of the ship, it is necessary to quote temperatures for both the air and water. Further, it is common experience that the humidity of air is important in determining the degree of comfort in hot climates. This idea is elaborated later in this chapter, but for the present, it is enough to know that for air it is necessary to specify the temperature that would be recorded on both a 'wet bulb' and a 'dry bulb' thermometer.

Standard temperatures considered by the Ministry of Defence as being appropriate to different regions of the world at various times of the year are given in Table 9.13. At present these are expressed in degrees Fahrenheit. The equivalent figures in degrees Celsius are given in parentheses rounded to the nearest integer.

Table 9.13
Standard climatic figures, Ministry of Defence

	Air temperatures		Relative humidity (%)	Water temperature near the surface of deep water (°F)
	Dry bulb (°F)	Wet bulb (°F)		
Av. max. Summer temps.				
Persian Gulf	94 (34)	86 (30)	72	90 (32)
Tropics	88 (31)	80 (27)	70	85 (29)
Av. min. Winter temps.				
Temperate winter	25 (−4)	—		40 (4)
Sub-Arctic winter	14 (−10)	—		35 (2)
Arctic	−20 (−29)	—		28 (−2)

Reference 9 suggests the conditions given in Table 9.14. Again figures in parentheses are the approximate values in degrees Celsius.

Table 9.14
Recommended values from Ref. 9

	Dry bulb (°F)	Wet bulb (°F)	Relative humidity (%)
Red Sea passenger vessels	90 (32)	86 (30)	85
Other passenger vessels	88 (31)	80 (27)	70
Persian Gulf cargo vessels and tankers	90 (32)	84 (29)	78

Reference 10 quotes highest recorded air temperature in the Tropics and lowest air temperatures in the Arctic. These are given in Table 9.15.

Table 9.15
Extreme recorded air temperatures

	Harbour	At sea
Tropics	125°F (52°C)	100°F (38°C)
Arctic	−40°F (−40°C)	−22°F (−30°C)

These temperatures are important to the ship design in a number of ways. The air temperature, for instance, influences:

(a) the amount of heating or cooling required for air entering the ship to maintain a given internal temperature;
(b) the amount of thermal insulation which can be economically justified;
(c) efficiency of some machinery;
(d) the amount of icing likely to occur in cold climates and thus the standard of stability required to combat this (Chapter 4), and the need to provide special de-icing facilities.

The water temperature influences:

(a) density of water and thus the draught;
(b) the efficiency of, and hence the power output from, machinery, e.g. steam machinery may suffer a loss of about 3 per cent of power in the tropics compared with temperate conditions. The effect on other machinery may be greater, but all types are affected to some degree including auxiliaries such as electrical generators, pumps, and air conditioning plant;
(c) whether ice is likely to be present and if so how thick and, thus, whether special strengthening of the ship is necessary.

Both air and water temperatures can cause expansion or contraction of materials leading to stresses where two dissimilar materials are joined together. Temperature differences between the air and water can lead to relative expansion or contraction of the upper deck relative to the keel causing the ship to hog or sag. This leads to stresses in the main hull girder and can upset the relative alignment of items some distance apart longitudinally. Similarly, if one side of the ship is in strong sunlight the main hull will tend to bend in a horizontal plane.

CLIMATIC EXTREMES

So far, only those climates likely to be met by ships in normal voyages have been considered. All would be likely to be met, for instance, by a passenger liner operating between the United Kingdom and Japan. The designer must also recognize that his ship may encounter extreme climatic conditions on a few occasions. These include:

Dust and sand. These cause abrasion of surfaces and penetrate into joints where movements due to vibration, and to changes in temperature, may bring about serious wear. Movements of particles can also set up static electrical charges. Although arising from land masses, dust and sand can be carried considerable distances by high winds. Reference 10 specifies test conditions, e.g. equipment subject to a direct current of air at the rate of 170 ft³/min (4·8 m³/min) with 0·04 g of dust/ft³ of air (1·41 g of dust/m³ of air).

Driving rain. Equipments are tested by spraying with fresh water at 30±5 psi (0·207±·034 MN/m²) using suitable spray heads each delivering 100±10 gallons per hour (0·455±0·045 m³/hr). Intensity of water applied is to be not less than the equivalent of 10 in. (0·254 m) per hour.

Driving sea-spray and snow. The designer must also cope with driving sea-spray, which has a more corrosive effect than rain, and snow or sleet which can be more abrasive.

Green sea loading. When heavy waves break over the ship exposed equipment and structure are assumed to be subject to a steady pressure of 3·5 p.s.i. (0·024 MN/m²). Mariner Class vessels have reported maximum deck pressures of 10 p.s.i. (0·069 MN/m²) when operating in a Sea State 7.

Weapon blast, etc. Warships can be subject to heavy loads when using their own armament. Guns cause deck reaction forces, missiles produce an efflux which can cause physical or chemical damage, depth charges subject the ship to underwater shock. The disposition of weapons and sensitive equipment must be such as to minimize possible damage from these effects.

High Winds. Exposed equipments are typically designed to operate efficiently in relative winds of up to 70 knots and to survive in winds of up to 120 knots.

Biological Agents. These include fungi which grow and reproduce rapidly when relative humidity is about 90 per cent and temperatures about 30°C (86°F). Fungi can be particularly damaging to optical and electrical equipment apart from causing physical blockage. The tropics provide a fine breeding ground for insects of all types. Termites are particularly damaging. In addition, bacteria cause damage to certain textiles and other cellulosic materials.

Physical Limitations

There are various physical limitations, either natural or man-made, which must be considered by the designer. They are:

(a) Depth of water available

The draught of the ship including any projections below keel level must not exceed the minimum depth of water available at any time during service. This depth may be dictated by the need to negotiate rivers, canals, harbour or dock entrances. If the vessel has to operate for any distance in shallow water, the increased resistance which occurs in these conditions must be taken into account. Various empirical formulae exist for estimating the depth of water needed to avoid loss of speed. One is:

$$\text{Depth in fathoms} > \frac{5}{3} \times \frac{VT}{(L)^{\frac{1}{2}}}$$

where T and L are in ft and V is in knots.

If T and L are in metres the expression becomes:

$$\text{Depth in fathoms} > 3 \cdot 02 \frac{VT}{(L)^{\frac{1}{2}}}$$

Allowance must be made for the sinkage and trim that will occur. For example, a large ship drawing say 25 ft of water may strike bottom in 28 ft of water if it attempts to negotiate the shallows too quickly.

(b) *Width of water available*

This is usually limited by the need to negotiate canals, harbour or dock entrances. As with shallow water the ship is acted upon by additional interference forces when negotiating narrow stretches at speed. Apart from the direct influence on beam, it may be necessary to adopt special manoeuvring devices for ships habitually operating in confined waters.

(c) *Height available above the water line*

Most ships have, at one time or another, to pass below bridges in entering ports. Unless the bridge itself can be opened, as in the case of Tower Bridge in the Pool of London, the ship must either keep masts and funnels below the level of the bridge or the uppermost sections must be capable of being lowered. In deciding the extent of the obstruction, tidal variations must be catered for.

(d) *Length*

The length of a ship may be limited by the building slips, fitting-out berths and docks available or by the length of canal lock or harbour dimensions.

The internal environment. Ship motions

The study of ship motions is considered in more detail in Chapter 12. The ship designer is concerned principally with the roll, pitch and heave motion amplitudes and their frequencies or periods which are to be used in designing structure and equipments. He normally assumes that these will not be exceeded and associates them with a factor of safety based upon previous successful design. Strictly speaking, any amplitudes of motion should be associated with the probability of their occurrence during the life of the ship.

To avoid overdesign, it is usual to consider two sets of motion figures; those under which equipment should be capable of meeting its specification fully,

Table 9.16
Motions for a ship of about 5000 tonnes

Condition	Motion	Amplitude	Period (s)
Extreme motions	Roll	$\pm 25°$	9–10
	Pitch	$\pm 7°$	6
	Heave	± 3 m	6
Moderate motions	Roll (stabilized)	$\pm 6°$	9–10
	Pitch	$\pm 5°$	6
	Heave	$\pm 1 \cdot 5$ m	6

and a second set in which the equipment must be able to function albeit with reduced performance. Again, certain equipment needs only to function in certain limited sea states, e.g. that associated with transfer of stores between two ships at sea.

Typical design figures for a warship about 160 m long are given in Table 9.16.

The air

If no action were taken to modify the air in a closed compartment within the ship, what would happen? Consider the case where people and heat producing equipment are both present. Then:

(a) due to the people and equipment the temperature within the space would rise steadily until the heat passing through the compartment boundaries matched the heat input from within;
(b) due to the moisture breathed out by the people the moisture content of the air would increase;
(c) due to the people breathing, the oxygen content would decrease and the carbon dioxide content increase;
(d) due to the movement of the people dust would be created;
(e) smells would be produced.

Put briefly, the temperature, humidity, chemical purity and physical purity are changed. Complete air conditioning therefore involves control of all these factors. Only in special cases, such as the submarine, is the chemical purity of the air controlled by using special means to produce new oxygen and absorb the carbon dioxide, although in all surface ships a certain minimum quantity of fresh air is introduced to partly control the chemical balance. This is typically about 0.3 m^3 (10 ft^3) of fresh air per man per minute. In general, the physical purity is only controlled within broad limits by filters in air distribution systems. Exceptions to these may be special 'clean' workshops or operating theatres. With only one device, namely cooling, to effect control of both temperature and humidity some compromise between the two is necessary. More precise control of both can be effected by cooling in conjunction with after-warming. This is discussed more fully in Chapter 14.

Temperature is measured by means of a thermometer in either *degrees Celsius* (*Centigrade*) (°C) or *degrees Fahrenheit* (°F). Pure water freezes at 0°C or 32°F and boils at 100°C or 212°F at sea level. To convert from one system to the other,

$$\text{Temperature in }°C = \tfrac{5}{9}(\text{temperature in }°F - 32)$$

It is a common experience, that the sunny side of a house feels warmer than the side in shade. This is because the body feels not only the warmth of the surrounding air but also the warmth of the sun's radiation. To define temperature precisely it is necessary to distinguish between these two. The *dry bulb temperature* is that measured in still air by a thermometer which is unaffected by radiated heat. To measure the effect of radiated heat a special device known as a globe thermometer is used. In this, the conventional thermometer is enclosed in a black sphere. This device records the *globe temperature*.

Another common experience is that one feels chilly in wet clothing. This is because the water, as it evaporates, absorbs heat from the body. This effect is measured by the *wet bulb temperature* which is that recorded by a thermometer with its bulb covered by wet muslin and subject to a moving air stream. It follows, that the wet bulb temperature can never be higher than the dry bulb and will, in general, be lower. Air can only hold a certain quantity of water vapour at a given temperature. The higher its moisture content the slower the rate of water evaporation from a wet body and the closer the wet bulb temperature will approach the dry bulb measurement.

Thus, the amount of water vapour present is important in relation to the maximum amount the air can contain at that temperature. This ratio is known as the *relative humidity*. The ability of air to hold water vapour increases with increasing temperature. If the temperature of a given sample of air is lowered, there comes a time when the air becomes *saturated* and further reduction leads to condensation. The temperature at which this happens is known as the *dew point* for that sample of air. If a cold water pipe has a temperature below the dew point of the air in the compartment, water will condense out on the pipe. This is why chilled waterpipes are lagged if dripping cannot be tolerated.

Since a human being's comfort depends upon temperature, humidity and air movement, it is difficult to define comfort in terms of a single parameter. For a given air state, an *effective temperature* is defined as the temperature of still, saturated air which produces the same state of comfort.

When a kettle of water is heated, the temperature rises at first and then remains constant (at 100°C) while the water is turned into steam. To distinguish between these two conditions, heat which causes only a temperature change is called *sensible heat* (i.e. it is clearly detectable) and heat which causes only a change of state is called *latent heat* (i.e. hidden heat). The sum of these two heats is known as the *total heat*.

The *British Thermal Unit*, Btu, which is the heat required to raise one pound of pure water through one degree Fahrenheit, and the *calorie*, which is the heat required to raise one gramme of pure water through one degree Celsius were the standard measurements but the basic SI unit is the joule. Some useful equivalents are:

1 Btu	= 1·05506 kJ
1 hp hr	= 2·68452 MJ
1 calorie	= 4·1868 joules (J)
1 kilowatt	= 56·869 Btu/min
	= 3412 Btu/hr
1 horsepower	= 42·407 Btu/min
	= 2544 Btu/hr
1 Btu	= 778·17 ft lbf

This section covers briefly the basic definitions associated with air conditioning comfort. These are put to use in the design of an air conditioning system in Chapter 14.

Lighting

There is a clear need for certain compartments to have a minimum level of illumination in order that work in them can be carried out efficiently.

Light is an electromagnetic radiation and the eye responds to radiation in that part of the spectrum between 7600 Å and 3800 Å. In this, Å stands for angstrom which is a wave-length of 10^{-10} m. The energy of the radiation can be expressed in terms of watts per unit area but the eye does not respond equally to all frequencies. Response is greater to greens and yellows than to reds and blues. Initially, wax candles were used as standards for illumination. A *lumen* (lm) is the amount of luminous energy falling per unit area per second on a sphere of unit radius from a point source of one candle-power situated at the centre of the sphere. The intensity of illumination is defined by either:

$$1 \text{ lm/ft}^2 = 1 \text{ foot-candle}$$

or

$$1 \text{ lm/m}^2 = 1 \text{ lux} = 1 \text{ metre-candle}$$

Reference 11 suggests standards of illumination for merchant ships and these are given in Table 9.17. Figures in parentheses are the approximate equivalents in lux.

Table 9.17
Suggested standards of illumination

Space	lm/ft²	Space	lm/ft²
Passenger cabins	7 (75)	Nursery	10 (108)
Dining rooms	10–15 (108–161)	Engine rooms	15–20 (161–215)
Lounges	7–10 (75–108)	Boiler rooms	10 (108)
Passageways	2–5 (22–54)	Galleys	15 (161)
Toilets	7 (75)	Laundries	15 (161)
Shops	20 (215)	Store-rooms	7 (75)

Standards used within the Ministry of Defence are given in Table 9.18—local figures relate to desk tops, instrument dials, etc. Special fittings are used in dangerous areas such as magazines, paint shops, etc., and an emergency system of red lighting is also provided. In darkened ship conditions, only this red lighting is used over much of the ship so as not to impair night vision.

In some ships, lighting may be regarded as merely a necessary service but in large ships and particularly in passenger liners, lighting can have a considerable influence on atmosphere. This can be especially important in the public rooms, and shipowners often enlist the services of lighting engineers and designers. Light intensity and colour is important and also the design of the light fittings themselves and their arrangement, e.g. it is essential to avoid glare.

Table 9.18
Lighting standards, RN ships

Space	Level of illumination (lux)	
	General	Local
Accommodation spaces	150	300
Machinery spaces	100	300
Galley, bakery	100	200
Workshops	150	400
Magazines	150	300
Stores, general	100	300
Switchboards	150	300
Bathrooms	100	—

Reference 11 states that, economic considerations lead to a desire to rationalize light fittings throughout the major part of the ship and suggests that a 230 volt, 60 hertz unearthed system will become standard for merchant ships. The Ministry of Defence (Navy Department) favours a three wire 115/0/115 volt, 60 hertz, unearthed system which provides a very flexible system with the choice of 115 or 230 volts to suit electrical demands of all sorts, including lighting.

In deciding upon the type of light fitting, it is necessary to consider the efficiency of the appliance, its probable life and the effect it will have on the general lighting system. Efficiency is important in air-conditioned spaces as less heat is generated in the production of a given light intensity. Efficiency is expressed in terms of lumens per watt and increases generally with increasing wattage of the fitting.

Typical values of efficiency and life are given in Table 9.19.

Table 9.19
Efficiency and life of light fittings. From Ref. 11

Type of fitting	Efficiency (lm/W)	Life (hr)
Single coil tungsten	8–20	1000
Tungsten–quartz iodine	22	2000
Fluorescent	24–66	5000
Cold cathode	10–40	30,000

Vibration and noise

Vibration theory is dealt with in many textbooks and reference should be made to Ref. 12 for an introduction to the subject. Fuller treatment is given in Ref. 13. In the present context, it is sufficient to point out that the ship is an elastic structure containing a number of discreet masses and, as such, it will vibrate when subject to a periodic force.

Vibration can lead to physical discomfort, to mechanical failure in sensitive equipment or to spurious readings due to the acceleration imparted to masses within the equipment. Vibration of visual displays can make them difficult to read. The human body responds to the acceleration rather than directly to the amplitude and frequency of the vibration. Reference 14 gives the figures reproduced in Table 9.20 as representing the general effect on human beings (all the accelerations are given in terms of the unit of gravitational acceleration g):

Table 9.20
Relation between measured acceleration and general appraisal of vibration

Vertical acceleration		Horizontal acceleration		General appraisal of vibration
At ends of ship (g)	In accommodation (g)	At ends of ship (g)	In accommodation (g)	
0·010	—	—	—	Very weak
0·010–0·025	0·010	0·010	—	Weak
0·025–0·050	0·010–0·025	0·010–0·025	0·010	Noticeable
0·050–0·120	0·025–0·050	0·025–0·050	0·010–0·025	Slightly uncomfortable
0·120–0·250	0·050–0·125	0·050–0·125	0·025–0·050	Very uncomfortable
0·250–0·500	0·125–0·250	0·125–0·250	0·050–0·120	Extremely uncomfortable
0·500–1·000	0·250–0·500	0·250–0·500	0·120–0·250	Hardly supportable
1·000	0·500	0·500	0·250	Unbearable

As with any vibratory phenomenon, the response of the ship, or part of the ship, to an exciting force depends upon the frequency of the excitation compared with the natural frequency of the structure and the damping present as indicated in Fig. 9.23.

In this figure, the magnification Q is defined as

$$Q = \frac{\text{dynamic response amplitude}}{\text{static response amplitude}}$$

and ω/ω_0 is the ratio of the frequency of the applied disturbance to the natural frequency of the structure. It should be noted, that the most serious vibrations occur when the natural frequency of the structure is close to that of the applied force, i.e. at resonance.

EXCITATION

Periodic forces causing excitation can arise from the sea or
(a) misalignment of shafts and propeller out of balance. Such forces will always be present to some extent, but they should not be unduly large unless workmanship has been poor or the propeller has been damaged. The frequency of forces arising from this source will be equal to the speed of rotation of the shaft and the magnitude of the force will increase as increasing powers are transmitted through the shaft;
(b) the fact that the propeller is rotating in a non-uniform flow. As each blade passes close to the hull there will be an interaction imparting a force to the hull. Other forces can be transmitted through the bearings and plummer blocks due to the cyclic variation in propeller thrust. These forces will have

Fig. 9.23 *Magnification factor*

a frequency given by the product of the shaft revolutions and the number of blades on the propeller and will increase with increasing thrust transmitted;

(c) any reciprocating or rotary equipment although, in general, the balancing of rotary equipment is sufficiently good to prevent such machinery being a serious problem. Large diesels or reciprocating compressors are the most likely sources of vibration, the frequency of the periodic force depending upon the running speed and number of cylinders.

RESPONSES

The ship responds to the exciting forces by vibrating as a free-free beam. In this type of vibration, certain points along the length suffer no displacement and these points are called *nodes*. The term *anti-nodes* is used for the points of maximum displacement between nodes. The hull can vibrate in different ways, or *modes*, involving 1, 2, 3, 4 or more nodes (Fig. 9.24), although the single node mode applies only to torsional vibration. The natural frequency of the vibration increases as the number of nodes increases as is discussed later.

There is nothing a designer can do to prevent this free-free vibration, and there is little he can do to alter the frequencies at which resonances occur. He can only recognize that they exist, calculate the critical frequencies and try to avoid any exciting forces at these values. For H.M. ships, the experience with many

Fig. 9.24 Modes of vertical vibration

designs has been analysed and curves produced to define the largest vibratory amplitude likely over a range of frequencies. The data are reproduced in Ref. 10 and Fig. 9.25 is the curve relating to major warships, i.e. frigates and larger ships. The ship is considered in four sections as shown in Fig. 9.26.

Fig. 9.25 Vibration tests: variation of amplitude with frequency in major warships

332 Basic ship theory

Fig. 9.26 Ship sections for DEF 133

For the forward region, amplitudes up to 5 hertz are taken as 50 per cent of those of the after region curve and above this frequency as equal to those defined by the main region curve. The curves relate specifically to the vertical vibration. Transverse vibration will generally be rather less, but for design purposes is usually assumed equal to it. Fore and aft vibration amplitudes are generally insignificant except at the masthead position, but even here they are low compared with the vertical and transverse levels. The remaining vibratory mode—the torsional—is not common and there is not a lot of available evidence on its magnitude.

The local response of the ship, due either to ship girder vibration or direct resonance with the disturbing forces, is curable and is therefore of less vital interest. A deck, bulkhead, fitting or panel of plating may vibrate. Considering all the possible vibratory systems in local structures, it is impossible to avoid some resonances with the exciting forces. Equally, it is impossible to calculate all the frequencies likely to be present. All the designer can do is select for calculation those areas where vibration would be particularly obnoxious; for the rest, troubles will be shown up on trial and can be cured by local stiffening, although this is an inconveniently late stage.

CURES

As far as possible, the structural design should be such as to avoid resonance with frequencies likely to be experienced at the usual operating speeds. Where this is not possible the level of vibration can be reduced:

(a) by reducing the exciting force. If the forces are propeller induced, the tip clearance can be increased or the propellers better balanced. Reference 15 concludes that if the propellers of a ship are to be changed, the hull vibration may be assumed to vary with:

$$\frac{Q}{Z^2 D} C_z$$

where Q = torque developed by the propeller, Z = number of blades, D = diameter of propeller, and C_z represents a hull clearance factor given by Fig. 9.27. Forces arising from machinery can be reduced by improving the balance or by mounting the machinery on special mounts.

(b) by altering the exciting frequency. If the vibration is in the blade frequency (i.e. number of propeller blades times shaft r.p.m.), then the number of

blades can be changed, but in this case resonance is likely at some other ship speed.
(c) by altering the natural frequency. Once the ship is built this is only possible for local structure. The change is usually effected by a change in stiffness but again resonance may only be shifted to another frequency.

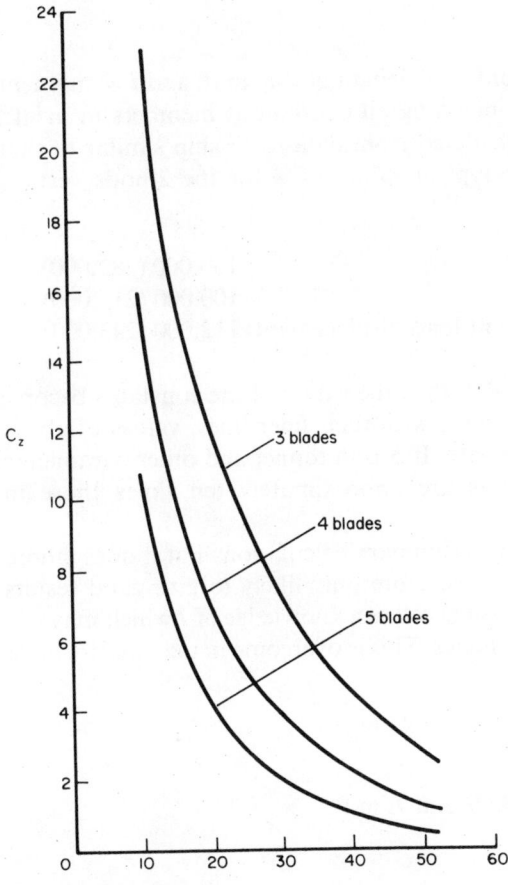

Fig. 9.27 C_z values

(d) by fitting vibration neutralizers in the form of sprung and damped weights which absorb the energy.
(e) by introducing damping into the system. The effect of damping on response is shown in Fig. 9.23.

CALCULATIONS

A number of methods are available for calculating the natural hull frequencies, most requiring the use of a computer for their ready solution. A detailed method which can be carried out by manual computation is given as an Appendix to Ref. 15 but the method is long and not within the scope of the present book. In the early design stages of a ship, it is more likely that use will be made of one of the empirical formulae available.

One of the earliest empirical formulae was proposed by *Schlick*, viz.

$$\text{Frequency} = \phi \left(\frac{I}{\Delta L^3}\right)^{\frac{1}{2}} \text{c.p.m.}$$

where Δ = ship displacement in tonf, L = length of ship in ft, and I = moment of inertia of the midship section including all continuous members in in^2 ft^2. ϕ is a coefficient which is best calculated from data for a ship similar to that being designed. In Ref. 13, some typical values of ϕ for the 2-node vertical vibration are given:

Large tankers	130,000 (282,000)
Small trunk deck tankers	100,000 (217,000)
Cargo ships at about 60 per cent load displacement	112,000 (243,000)

If I is in m^4, L is in m and Δ in MN, then the values of the constants become as shown in parentheses. For warships, with their finer lines, values of about 160,000 (347,000) are more appropriate. If Δ is in tonnef and other parameters in the metric system, the constants are approximately ten times those in parentheses.

The Schlick formula is useful for preliminary calculations but it does ignore the effects of entrained water and is therefore only likely to give good results where a similar ship is available. It also involves a knowledge of I which may not be available during the early design stages. This is overcome in the *Todd* formula which can be expressed as:

$$\text{Frequency} = \beta \left(\frac{BH^3}{\Delta L^3}\right)^{\frac{1}{2}} \text{c.p.m.}$$

where Δ is measured in tonf and B, H and L in ft.

Values of β were found to be

Large tankers	61,000 (11,000)
Small trunk deck tankers	45,000 (8150)
Cargo ships at about 60 per cent load displacement	51,000 (9200)

If Δ is expressed in MN and linear dimensions in metres the values of the constants are as in parentheses. If Δ is expressed in tonnef and linear dimensions in metres the constants, within the accuracy of the formula, can be taken as ten times those in parentheses.

To account for the entrained water, a virtual weight Δ_1 can be used instead of the displacement Δ, where

$$\Delta_1 = \Delta \left(1 \cdot 2 + \frac{1}{3}\frac{B}{T}\right)$$

A variety of other empirical formulae have been proposed by various authorities and these are reviewed in Ref. 19.

In Ref. 13 results are presented which suggest that the frequency of the 2-node horizontal vibration is likely to be of the order of 1·37 times that of the corresponding vertical mode.

Having estimated the frequency of the 2-node vibration, it is necessary to estimate the 3-node period and so on. The theory of a vibrating uniform beam predicts that the 3-node and 4-node vibrational frequencies should be 2·76 and 5·40 times those for the 2-node mode. It is found that in ships the ratios are lower and for very fine ships may be 2, 3, 4, etc. In Ref. 14, ratios of 2·15, 3·37, 4·53, 5·54, 6·42, 7·24 and 8 were measured on one ship.

Some typical natural frequencies of hull for various ship types are given in Table 9.21, most of the data being taken from Ref. 14.

Table 9.21
Natural frequencies of hull for several types of ship

Type of ship	Length (m)	Condition of loading	Frequency of vibration						
			Vertical				Horizontal		
			2-node	3-node	4-node	5-node	2-node	3-node	4-node
Cargo ship	85	Light	150	290			230		
		Loaded	135	283			200		
Cargo ship	130	Light	106	210			180	353	
		Loaded	85	168			135	262	
Passenger ship	136		104	177			155	341	
Tanker	227	Light	59	121	188	248	103	198	297
		Loaded	52	108	166	220	83	159	238
Destroyer	160	Average action	85	180	240		120	200	
G.M. Cruiser	220	Average action	70	130	200		100	180	270

NOISE

Noise surveys are becoming more common in both merchant ships and naval ships. Reference 16 reports three such surveys. The internationally agreed unit for sound intensity is 10^{-16} watts/cm² and at 1000 hertz this is close to the threshold of hearing. Due to the large range of intensity to which a human ear is sensitive a logarithmic scale is used to denote the intensity of sound and the usual unit in which noise levels are expressed is the *decibel*. If two noise intensities are w_1 and w_2 then the number of decibels, n, denoting their ratio is

$$n = 10 \log_{10} \frac{w_1}{w_2} \text{ db}$$

As a reference level, $w_2 = 10^{-16}$ watts/cm² is used.

Instruments measuring noise levels in air record sound pressure so that

$$n = 10 \log_{10} \frac{w_1}{w_2} = 10 \log_{10} \left(\frac{p_1}{p_2}\right)^2 = 20 \log_{10} \frac{p_1}{p_2}$$

where p_2 is the pressure in dynes/cm² corresponding to the threshold of hearing. This becomes $p_2 = 0{\cdot}0002$ dynes/cm².

Thus a sound pressure level of $0{\cdot}1$ N/m² (1 dyne/cm²) is represented by

Level in db $= 20 \log 1/0{\cdot}0002 = 74$ db

In the open, the sound intensity varies inversely as the square of the distance from the source. Hence halving the distance from the noise source increases the level in db by $10 \log 4 = 6$ db and doubling the distance reduces the level by 6 db. The addition of two equal sounds results in an increase of 3 db and each 10 db increase is roughly equivalent to a doubling of the subjective loudness.

A noise typically contains many components of different frequency and these varying frequencies can cause different reactions in the human being. In order to define fully a given noise it is necessary, therefore, to define the level at all frequencies and this is usually achieved by plotting results as a noise spectrum.

Noise can have a number of effects on the human being. It may:

(a) annoy;
(b) disturb sleep;
(c) interfere with conversation. Conversational speech at a distance of 1 m represents a noise level of about 60 db. The greatest interference is created by noises in the frequency range 300–5000 hertz;
(d) damage hearing. Noise levels of 130–140 db can cause pain in the ear and higher levels can cause physical damage;
(e) upset the normal senses, e.g. it can lead to a temporary disturbance of vision.

Thus noise effects can vary from mere annoyance, itself very important in passenger vessels, to interference with the human being's ability to function efficiently and eventually can cause physical damage to the body.

Reference 16 concludes that the noise sources on the ships surveyed can be divided into four types:

(a) airborne noise from ventilation system and neighbouring cabins;
(b) structure-borne noise from machinery, plumbing, footsteps, etc.;
(c) propeller-vibration induced noise in the form of low frequency 'rumble' in accommodation aft and the rattling of doors and fittings;
(d) the creaking of bulkheads due to distortion of the ship in a seaway.

Various methods are available for reducing the effect of noise, the particular method depending upon the noise source and why it is undesirable. For instance, the noise level within a communications office with many teleprinters can be reduced by treating the boundary with noise absorption material. A heavy, vibrating, machine transmitting noise through the structure can be mounted on special noise isolating mounts, care being taken to ensure that the mounts are not 'short-circuited' by pipes connected to the machine. Such pipes must include a flexible section. Where a piece of equipment produces a high level of air-borne noise in a compartment adjacent to an accommodation space the common boundary can be treated with noise insulation material. For the best results, the whole boundary of the offending compartment should be treated to reduce the level of structure borne noise which can arise from the impact of the pressure waves on, say, deck and deckhead.

As reported in Ref. 17, the positioning of machinery in the after end of the ship has simplified the noise problem in some modern passenger liners.

ICE

When the temperature falls sufficiently, ice forms on the rigging and upperworks of ships constituting a hazard, as discussed in Chapter 4. Remedial action may also be difficult because the deck machinery itself may have been rendered unusable by ice. As well as reducing stability, ice may hazard the whole ship by structural damage caused by sea ice or by the icebergs which originate in glaciers. Reference 22 discusses the formation of sea ice. While fresh water has its maximum density at 4°C sea water of salinity greater than 24·7% increases in density right down to its freezing point (which is $-1\cdot33\,°C$ at 24·7% salinity). Thus freezing does not occur at the surface until the water below is also at the freezing point. Initially individual ice crystals are formed, creating a slush. Movement of the water surface leads to the formation of flat circular discs 30 to 100 cm in diameter with upturned rims, called pancake ice. As the temperature drops further the discs become cemented together to form a continuous sheet which in a typical Arctic winter reaches an average thickness of about 3 metres. In way of pressure ridges the thickness may be much greater.

The majority of icebergs in the North Atlantic originate at the Greenland glaciers. They vary a great deal in size but whatever the size represent a formidable threat to shipping, as witnessed by the *Titanic*. Due to their porosity, their effective density may be appreciably less than that of pure ice and the depth below water can vary between three and eight times their height above water.

Problems

1. Discuss the process by which sea waves are thought to be formed and the factors on which the wave characteristics depend. What do you understand by the term *swell?*

   Describe the type of sea you would expect to be generated by a wind blowing for some time in one direction. How would you describe, quantitatively, the resulting surface characteristics? (RNC)

2. For a regular sinusoidal wave deduce expressions for speed of propagation and period.

   Calculate the speed and period of a wave 100 m long. If the surface wave height is 3 m calculate the depth at which the height of the sub-surface profile is 0·5 m.

3. A wave spectrum is defined by the following table:

ω (1/s)	0·20	0·40	0·60	0·80	1·00	1·20	1·40
$S_\zeta(\omega)$ (m² s)	0·00	7·94	11·68	5·56	2·30	0·99	0·45
ω (1/s)	1·60	1·80	2·00	2·20			
$S_\zeta(\omega)$ (m² s)	0·23	0·12	0·07	0·00			

Calculate the significant wave height, average wave height and mean of the tenth highest waves.

4. A large number of wave heights are recorded and on analysis it is found that the numbers falling in various height bands are:

wave height band (m)	0–½	½–1	1–1½	1½–2	2–2½	2½–3	3–3½	3½–4
No. of waves	5	10	20	40	55	40	25	5

Plot these as a histogram record and deduce the normal and Rayleigh distributions which most closely fit the measured data.

5. A 20 MN ship presents a profile as below

Fig. 9.28

Assuming that the force acting on area A m² due to a wind of velocity V knots is given by

Force = $0.19 V^2 A$ newtons

calculate the force due to a nominal wind of 50 knots (i.e. as measured 6 m above the water surface) allowing for the wind gradient as defined in Fig. 9.22. Deduce the effective average wind speed.

Assuming the ship has a mean draught of 6 m and a metacentric height of 1·5 m calculate the approximate angle of heel due to the wind.

6. In a given wave sample, the number of waves of various heights are:-

Wave height (m)	0·5	1·0	1·5	2·0	2·5	3·0	3·5	4·0
No. of waves	10	39	50	35	16	5	4	1

Calculate the average and significant wave height and the average of the $\frac{1}{10}$th highest waves.

7. Calculate the wave-lengths in metres and wave velocities in metres per second corresponding to wave periods of 1, 2, 4, 6, 8, 10, 14, 18 and 20 s.

8. The successive crests of the wave profile along the side of a ship at speed in calm water are observed to be about 100 m apart. What is the approximate speed of the ship in knots? If the ship speed is reduced to 10 knots what will the distance apart of the crests become? (AP & S)

9. Check the following statement:

The orbits and velocities of the particles of water are diminished by approximately one-half for each additional depth below the mid-height of the surface trochoid equal to one-ninth of a wave-length. For example:

Depth in fraction of wave-length	0	$\frac{1}{9}$	$\frac{2}{9}$	$\frac{3}{9}$	$\frac{4}{9}$
Proposed velocities and diameters	1	$\frac{1}{2}$	$\frac{1}{4}$	$\frac{1}{8}$	$\frac{1}{16}$

(AP & S)

10. Using empirical formulae, calculate the 2-node frequency of vibration of the hull of a cargo ship to which the following data relates:

Displacement 7800 tonf
Length 420 ft
Beam 60 ft
Depth 30 ft
Draught 20 ft

Allowance should be made for the entrained water.

References

1. Froude, R. E. Model experiments on hollow versus straight lines in still water and among artificial waves, *TINA*, 1905.
2. Milne-Thomson, L. M. *Theoretical hydrodynamics*, Macmillan, 1949.
3. Practical methods for observing and forecasting ocean waves. *HO Pub. No. 603*. US Navy Hydrographic Office, 1960.
4. Draper, L. and Squire, E. M. Waves at ocean weather ship *India*, *TRINA*, 1967.
5. Longuet-Higgins, M. S. On the statistical distribution of the heights of sea waves, *Journal of Marine Research*, Vol. XI, No. 3, 1952.
6. Newton, R. N. Wetness related to freeboard and flare, *TRINA*, 1960.
7. Darbyshire, J. Wave statistics in the North Atlantic ocean and on the coast of Cornwall, *The Marine Observer*, Vol. XXV, April, 1955.
8. Sarchin, T. H. and Goldberg, L. L. Stability and buoyancy criteria for US surface ships, *TSNAME*, 1962.
9. Jones, S. J. and MacVicar, J. K. W. The development of air conditioning in ships, *TINA*, 1959.
10. Defence Specification DEF-133. Climatic, shock and vibration testing of service equipment, HMSO, August, 1971.
11. Carter, G. and Fothergill, A. E. Lighting in ships, *TRINA*, 1963.
12. Morrison, J. L. M. and Crossland, B. *An introduction to the mechanics of machines*, Longman, 1964.
13. Todd, F. H. *Ship hull vibration*, Arnold, 1961.
14. Dieudonne, J. Vibration in ships, *TINA*, 1959.
15. Ramsay, J. W. Aspects of ship vibration induced by twin propellers, *TINA*, 1956.
16. Shearer, K. Ambient sound measurements on two passenger ships and an oil tanker, *TRINA*, 1964.
17. West, J. Acoustical problems in passenger ship design, *TRINA*, 1960.
18. Hadler, J. B. Coefficients for international towing tank conference 1957 model-ship correlation line, *DTMB Report 1185*, April, 1958.
19. Korvin-Kroukovsky, B. V. Theory of seakeeping, *SNAME*, Monograph, 1961.
20. Hogben, N. and Lumb, F. E. *Ocean Wave statistics*, HMSO, 1967.
21. *The dynamics of marine vehicles and structures in waves*. Symposium at University College London, Institution of Mechanical Engineers, 1974.
22. Bowden, K. F. The marine environment — some features of concern to naval architects, *TRINA*, 1970.

Answers to Problems

Chapter 2

1. 0·73, 0·80, 0·97, 3·70 m.
2. 8771 tonnef, 86·1 × 10⁶ newtons, 103 m³, 0·722.
3. 0·785, 0·333, 0·500.
4. 146·25 m², 145·69 m², 1·0039.
5. 2048 ft².
6. 1·2 per cent low, 0·46 per cent low.
7. 9·33 m³, 0·705 MN.
8. 5286 m², 1·65 m abaft 6 ord.
9. 2306 tonf, 16·92 ft above 10 ord.
10. 403 tonnes.
11. 36,717 m³, 4·85 m, 5·14 m.
12. 243,500 m⁴, 23,400 m⁴.
13. 182·2 × 10⁶ ft⁴.
14. 39·42 ft, 48·17 ft.
15. 2·48 tonf, 8·50 ft.
16. 26·3 ft.
17. (a) 539·3 (Simpson 2), 561·0 (trap).
    (b) 278·7 (Simpson 58–1), 290·0 (trap).
18. 0·41 per cent.
19. $M = \frac{1}{6}h^2(y_1 + 6y_2 + 12y_3 + 18y_4 + \ldots)$ about 1 ord.
21. (a) 2·09440, (b) 1·97714, (c) 2·00139, (d) 2·00000 correct.
22. (a) 201·06, (b) 197·33, (c) 199·75, (d) 200·59, (e) 200·51.
23. (a) 141·42, (b) 158·93, (c) 158·02, (d) 157·08 correct.
25. (a) 23·37, (b) 11·36.
26. (a) 4·37, (b) 7·23, (c) 9·3 per cent.

Chapter 3

1. (a) 146, (b) 544.
2. 4·94 m.
3. 8550 ft³, 6·82 ft³/tonf.
5. 1·2 in. below keel.
6. 9 degrees.
7. 21 m.
8. 54,018 tonf, 13·41 ft below 1 WL (1331 Rule).
9. 39,030 tonf, 14·24 ft below 1 WL.
10. 0·27 m below 2½ WL.
11. 12 ft 6¾ in., 18 ft 6¼ in.
12. 19 ft 6 in. abaft amidships, 22 ft 0¼ in.
13. 4·39 m.
14. 4·21 m forward, 4·70 m aft.
15. 37·38 ft forward, 40·43 ft aft.
16. 1·34, 1·65 m.

17. 3·704 m, 2·744 m.
18. 373 tonf, 13 ft 4 in., 16 ft 7 in.
19. 1·95 hours, 0·92 m, 3·56 m.
20. (a) 2350 tonf, 11·01 ft aft of amidships, (b) 205 tonf, 11·75 ft.
21. 3·77 m fwd, 4·33 m aft.
22. 10 ft 6¾ in., 14 ft 6¾ in.
23. 30 ft 3 in. forward, 30 ft 5½ in. aft.
24. 8847 m^3, 2·76 m.
25. 4459·2 tonf.
26. 42·2 ft before amidships, 8 ft 11·9 in., 8 ft 8·8 in.

Chapter 4

1. —.
2. —.
3. —.
4. 1·972 m, 0·536 m, 1·047 m.
5. 3875 tonnef m, 1252 tonnef m, 15·6 degrees.
6. 2·05 m, 1·99 m.
7. 2·1 m, 15·4 m.
8. 1·13 in.
9. 0·97T.
10. 1° 27'.
11. 4·388 m.
12. —.
13. 7° 7'.
14. 90 degrees.
15. 2·39 m, 27·13 m.
16. ·1·25 m.
17. 3·04 m.
18. 1·44 m.
19. 1° 22'.
20. 0·70 ft.
21. 0·28 m.
22. 3·28 m.
23. 45 degrees.
24. —.
25. 0·37 m.
26. (a) 70·4°, (b) 84·9°, (c) 87·1°, (d) 95·5°.
27. 74 MJ.
28. 2·60, 1·035 : 1.
29. 0·67 ft.
30. 1·54 ft.
31. 2·53 ft, 2·82 ft, 0·09 ft, 4·57 ft, 75·5°.
32. 0·509 m, 0·49 m.
33. −1·425 ft.
34. —.

Chapter 5

1. 1·73 m port, 2·99 m starboard.
2. 13 ft 3 in., 2 ft 11 in.
3. 288 tonnef, 4·70 m, 5·83 m; 6·23 m, 5·81 m.
4. 20,740 tonnef m, 10° 37', 93·31 m (added weight), 91·58 m (lost buoyancy).

5. (i) 167 tonf, (ii) 2·07 ft, (iii) 1·95 ft.
6. (a) 13·41 ft, 11·23 ft, (b) 2·65 ft.
7. 7·06 ft, 4·92 ft forward; 4·33 ft, 2·20 ft aft.
8. 1·70 m.
9. 9·70 ft, +0·98 ft.
10. 40 tonnef, 94 tonnef, 22 cm.
11. 10¾ degrees.
12. 1·8 degrees.
13. 53 tonnef, 1½ degrees.
14. 13·97 ft.
15. 4·63 min.
16. Starboard hit 40 per cent, 22½ per cent; Port hit 40 per cent, 10 per cent.

Chapter 6

1. 117 ft from fore end, 1569 tonf ft.
2. SF, $0·21L$ from end $= W/10·4$; BM amidships $= WL/32$.
3. Max. SF., 30·75 tonnef; max BM, 132·6 tonnef m,.
4. SF, 48 tonf. 30 ft from ends; BM 960 tonf ft amidships.
5. Max. SF, 690 tonnef; max. BM ,13,000 tonnef m.
6. 0·315 in.
7. SF, 714 tonnef at 3/4; BM 24,500 at 5/6.
8. 113·5 pascals.
9. 3·58 and 4·24 tonf/in².
10. σ_D, 6·07 tonf/in², σ_K 3·67 tonf/in².
11. 35.
12. z_D, 8090 in² ft; z_K, 6220 in² ft; σ_D, 4·62 tonf/in²; σ_K 6·00 tonf/in².
13. σ_D, 2·62 tonf/in²; σ_K 3·78 tonf/in².
14. 52 cm².
15. 57·5, 42·2, 19·7 MN/m².
16. 42·9, 42·9, 33·2 MN/m².
17. $\delta M/WL = 0·144$ and $0·115$.
18. 3·10 in².
19. 19 mm.
20. 8½ tonf/in², 0·3 degrees.
21. 590,000 in² ft still water, 266,000 in² ft wave.
22. 1910 tonnes approx.
23. 55 mm approx.

Chapter 7

1. 260 MN/m².
2. 7700 cm³, 14,800 cm³.
3. (a) 1:2·92, (b) 1:2·20.
4. (a) 64 in⁴, (b) 0·29 in.
5. 18 mm.
6. 4·38 tonf.
7. 7·4 cm.
8. (a) 0·80 in., (b) 0·33 in.
9. (a) 0·112 MN/m², (b) 0·035 MN/m², (c) 5·7 mm.
10. (a) 16·3, (b) 106, (c) 32, (d) 58 lbf/in².
11. (a) 2·0, (b) 1·15.
12. 90 MN/m².

13. 2·7 tonf/in², in rib at deck edge.
14. $M_{EA}=420, M_{AE}=840, M_{BA}=27{,}300, M_{BF}=8480, M_{BC}=35{,}760, M_{FB}=2120$ N m.
15. $M_{AB} = 2·5, M_{BC} = 9·9, M_{CB} = 39·9, M_{CG} = 6·7, M_{CD} = 46·6, M_{GC} = 3·3$ tonf ft.
16. 0·03 MN.
17. Torque, 51·4 tonf ft; BM, 764 tonf ft.
18. 21·8 in., 15·5 hp.
19. 15·4 tonf/in².

Chapter 8

1. (a) 54 ft, (b) 1500 tonf, (c) 180,000 tonf ft.
2. 75·5 m, 7·7 MN, 0·19 MN/m².
3. 18·36, 14·31 fwd, 22·41 aft tonnef/m².
4. —7·81 ft forward, 22·67 ft aft.
5. 28·5 ft.
6. (a) 97 m, (b) 1,480 tonnef, (c) 41,000 tonnef m.
7. (a) lift at 144 m (b) max. force on FP 7,950 tonnef, (c) min tip mt. 700,000 tonnef m, (d) floats off.
8. Max. BM, 55,250 tonf ft; max. SF, 432 tonf.

Chapter 9

1. —.
2. 12·5 m/s, 8·0 s, 28·5 m.
3. 4·85 m, 3·03 m, 6·19 m.
4. $p(x) = \dfrac{1}{1·925} \exp\left\{-\dfrac{(x-2·19)^2}{1·18}\right\}$,

   $p(x) = \dfrac{x}{5·38} \exp\left\{\dfrac{-x^2}{10·75}\right\}$.
5. 0·16 MN, 41 knots, 1° 35′.
6. 1·64 m, 2·40 m, 3·00 m.
7. 1·56, 1·56; 6·2, 3·1; 25, 6·2; 56, 9·4; 100, 12·5; 156, 15·6; 306, 21·8; 506, 28·1; 625, 31·2.
8. 24·3 knots, 16·96 m.
9. —.
10. 57·5 c.p.m.

Index

A brackets 264
Added weight method 149, 153
Addition of material 195
Addition of weight 69, 71
Admiralty 5
Air, internal condition 325
Albuera 207
Ambient air 321
American Bureau of Shipping 4
Amidships 9
Analogue computer 37
Anchoring 161
Angle of loll 117, 154
Angstrom 327
AP (After Perpendicular) 9
Approximate formulae,
  BM 41
  longitudinal strength 205
  stability 130
  VCB 42
  vibration 332
Approximate integration 22
Arched rib analysis 256
Archimedes of Syracuse 1
Archimedes' Principle 57
Areas, curve of 12
Armour 168
Association Technique Maritime et Aèronautique 6
Assumed neutral axis 187
Atwood's formula 107
Automated draughting equipment 40
Automatic levelling 163

Bacteria 168, 323
Balance on a wave 181
Bar xi
Barnes' method for cross curves 111
Beam, influence on stability 126
Beams 228, 230
Beaufort scale 317, 318
Bending stresses 189
Bent nail fatigue 227
Berthing 159
Bilging 146
Biological agents 168, 323
Block coefficient 12
Blue book 174
BM 20, 41
Board of Trade 5, 156
Body plan 8
Bonjean curves 12, 35, 181, 202, 278
Bouguer, Pierre 1
Box girders 200, 230
Brackets 255
British Corporation 4
British thermal unit 326
Brittle fracture 215
BSS 1991 x, 22
Buckling 207, 208, 227, 244

Built in stresses 208, 215
Bulk carriers 163
Bulkhead deck 156
Buoyancy 57, 181
Bureau Veritas 4

Cable, chain 161
Caissons 284
Calorie 326
Camber 11
Candle power 327
Capsizing 154
Captain 4
Careening 284
Castigliano's theorem 248
Celsius unit xii, 325
Centigrade 325
Centre of buoyancy 18
Centre of flotation 15, 65
Centre of gravity 18, 126
Change of density 62, 74
Chapman, Frederick 1
Chapman report ix
Clan Alpine 207
Classification societies 4, 190
Climate 316
Climatic extremes 322
Coastguards, US 5
Coefficient of fineness 12
Coefficient of midship section 12
Collapse design 251
Collision 147
Collision bulkheads 147
Compartment standard 156
Composite sections 188
Computer-aided design 40
Computers 38
Constant displacement method 154
Continuous spectrum 308
Control surfaces 263
Conventions 22, 42
Conversion British/metric 62
Coordinates of a trochoid 179
Corrosion allowance 190, 261
Corrosion fatigue 227
Corrugated plating 236
Coulomb xi
Counterflooding 163
Cracking 207, 208, 212, 215
Criterion numeral 156
Cross curves of stability 106, 109
Cumulative probability 306
Curtain bulkheads 163
Curve, metacentric 122
Curve of areas 11
Curve of buoyancy 121
Curve of flotation 123
Curve of statical stability 115
Curve, the Z 124
Cutty Sark 3

Damage control 162
Damaged stability 149, 153, 155
Damping, effect on vibration 330
Decay of wave spectrum 312
Decibel 335
Deckhouses 216
De-gaussing 167
Degrees Kelvin x
Density xi, xii, xiii, 55, 74, 291
Dept. of Trade 5, 156
Depth of water 323
Derricks 103
Design trim 73
Design waterplane 7
Dew point 326
Digital computer 39
Discontinuities 211, 216
Dispersion 168
Displacement xiii, 59, 64
Displacement, influence on stability 126
Displacement lines 9
Displacement sheet, table 77
Dock blocks 286
Docking 70, 275, 284
Double bottom 147
Draught, influence on stability 126
Drift 11
Dry bulb temperature 325
Duration, wind 296, 316
Dust 322
Dynamical stability 128
Dynamics 203
Dynamics of launching 282

Effective breadth of plating 230, 233
Effective temperature 326
Elastic stability 254
Elasto-plastic theory 237
End constraint 255
Enemy action 168
Energy methods 248
Environment, external 291
Environment, internal 324
Environment, ship 291
Environmental pollution 171
Equilibrium 93
Equilibrium conditions 94
Equivalents, metric, SI xi
Euler 1
Exaggeration factor 232
Excitation of vibration 329
Expansion joints 218
Expansion of outer bottom plating 21
Experiment, inclining 133
Explosives 163, 164
Extreme wave amplitudes 316

F curve 122
Factor of subdivision 156
Fahrenheit units xii, 325
Failure 206, 207, 208, 226, 252
Farad xi
Fatigue 199

Fetch, wind 296, 316
Finite element techniques 216, 267
Fire protection 159, 160
First rule, Simpson's 25
Flare 11
Flashpoint 164
Flexure of hull 199
Floating docks 287
Floodable length 156
Flooded $\overline{GZ}$ 154
Flooding 146, 148
Flooding board 162
Flotation 55, 148
Flotation, centre of 15
Flutter 199
Foot candle 327
Fore poppet 276
Form, influence on stability 124
Foundering 147
FP (fore perpendicular) 9
Fracture 215, 227
Frameworks 228, 245
Free flooding 150
Free surface 101, 118, 147
Freeboard 10, 156
Freely suspended weights 103
Frequency, wave 302
Froude, William 1, 2

Gas 168
Gauss rules 32
Gaussian distribution 306
Germanische Lloyd 4
Girder, ship 175
Globe temperature 326
Grain 163
Graving dock 284
Great lakes 190
Green seas 323
Grillages 175, 232
Ground effect machine 60
Grounding 70, 84, 158
Groundways 275, 280
Growth of wave spectrum 311
$\overline{GZ}$ curve 116

Half breadth plan 8
Heel 11, 94, 164
Heeling during turn 132
Heeling trial 138
Hertz xi
High rates of strain 166
Histograms 304
Hogging 176
Hole in a plate 212
Hole, ingress of water 163
Hollow box girder 200
Hollow shapes 20
Horsepower 326
Humidity, relative 326
Hydrofoil 263, 265
Hydrogen peroxide 165
Hydroplanes 263

Hydrostatic curves   76
Hydrostatic pressure   58
Hygroscopic materials   163, 165

Ice formation   337
Ice strengthening   159
Illumination standards   327
IMCO (Inter-Governmental Maritime Consultative Organization)   6, 159
Impact   216
Inclining experiment   133
Inflow through a hole   163
Influence lines   180, 192
Infra-red radiation   168
Inglis-Bailey results   239
Initial stability   95
Institution of Engineers and Shipbuilders in Scotland   6
Integraph   35
Integration   22
Integrator   36, 109
International Towing Tank Conferences   22
Irradiation   165
Irregular shapes   14
Irregular wave patterns   303
ITTC spectra   312
Izod test   21

Joint stiffness   255
Joule   xi, 326

Kelvin degrees   x, xii
Kilowatt   326
Kinematic viscosity   292
Knot   xi

Lagrange   1
Large angle stability   106
Large deflection theories   237
Latent heat   326
Launching   275
Launching curves   276
Law of flotation   57
LCB   18
LCG   18
Leclert's theorem   124
Length, influence on stability   126
Liberty ships   211
Life saving equipment   161
Lifeboats   161
Lighting   327
Limit design   251
Line spectrum   308
Lines plan   8
Liquid gas   163, 165
Lloyd, Edward   4
Lloyd's Insurance Corporation   4
Lloyd's Register of Shipping   4, 205
Load factor   254
Load waterplane   9
Loadline   157, 159
Locked up stresses   215
Log normal distribution   306

Loll   117, 154
Long crested wave pattern   303
Longitudinal strength   175
Lost buoyancy method   149, 153
Lumen   327
Lux   xi, 327

M or metacentric curve   122
Magnetic mines   167
Magnification factor   330
Margin line   156
Masks   282
Mass density   xii, xiii, 55, 99, 292
Matrix methods   267
MCT1″   xiii, 68
Mean   44
Mechanical shock   166
Median   44
Meganewton   xiii
Metacentre   19, 96
Metacentric height   96
Metacentric diagram   79, 80
Method of least squares   136
Metric equivalents   xi, xii, xiii
Metric system   x
Middle line plane   7
Midship section coefficient   12
Midships   9
Mile, nautical   xi
Minimum $\overline{GM}$ 155
Ministry of Transport   5
Minoans   187
Mode   44, 314
Model testing   113
Models, use in stability work   113
Moment distribution   246
Morrish's rule   42
Moseley's formula   129
Moulded dimensions   9
Multiples   xii
Murray's method   205

Nautical mile   xi
Navy department   5
Neumann wave spectrum   313
Neutral equilibrium   93, 127
Neverita, Newcombia   207
Newton   xi, xiii
Newton-Cotes rules   29
Newton, Isaac   1
Nippon Kaiji Kyokai   4
Noise   168, 291, 328, 335
Nomenclature   xvi
Non-contact explosion   166
Normal distribution   306, 315
Normand's formula   42
Norske Veritas det   4
North East Coast Institution of Engineers and Shipbuilders   6
Notch toughness   216
Number, wave   302

Ocean Vulcan   207

Offsets 9
Ohm xi
Oil carriage 163, 164
Oil pollution 159
One dimensional wave system 303
One metre trim moment xiii, 69
Optimum design 226
Outer bottom expansion 21

Panels of plating 228, 236
Pappus Guldinus, theorem of 49
Parallel sinkage 60
Pascal xi
Permeability 150
Permissible length 156
Petrol, carriage 164
Physical limitations of environment 323
Plane shapes 14
Planimeter 34
Plastic design, modulus 251
Plasticity 238
Plating stiffeners 228
Plunge 146, 156
Pollution 171
Population, statistics 307
Portals 245
Poundage 21
Pre-wetting 168
Preferred values xiii
Prefixes xii
Pressure in a wave 201
Pressure mines 168
Preston and *Bruce* 207
Prismatic coefficient 13
Pro-metacentre 20, 121
Probability distributions 43, 209, 304
Prohaska (stability) 113, 127
Properties of fluids 55
Protective plating 168

Radhaz 168
Radioactive material 163, 165
Rake 11
Range (statistical) 44
Range of stability 116
Rankine 2
Rankine unit xii
Rayleigh distribution 306, 314, 315
Reactor protection 148, 165
Reciprocal weight density 56
Rectangular block stability 100
Rectangular holes 214
Reech's method for cross curves 112
Reed's method 218
Register Book 5
Registro Italiano 4
Relative humidity 326
Reliability 208
Reserve of buoyancy 60
Response in vibration 330
Response operators 209
Righting lever, moment 95
Rise of floor 10

River water 74
Round down 11
Royal Corps of Naval Constructors 5
Royal George 4
Royal Institution of Naval Architects 6
Rudder 263
Rules for longitudinal strength 205

Sagging 176
Salinity 292
Sample, statistics 307
Sand 322
Sandwich protection 148
Santacilla 1
Schlick formula 334
Scope 161
Scott Russell 2
Sea 296
Sea-spray 323
Sea state code 312
Sea surface 293
Sea to river water 74
Second moment of area 188
Second rule, Simpson's 28
Section modulus 187, 195, 204
Self trimming 163
Sensible heat 326
Shaft brackets 264
Shallow water effects 323
Shape factor 251
Shear force 178, 183
Shear lag, flow, diffusion 191, 200, 217, 230
Sheer 11
Sheer drawing, draft 8
Sheer plan 7
Shear stresses 190
Shielding, reactor 165
Shifting boards 163
Ship girder 175
Ship motion 291, 324
Shock 166, 291
Shock mountings 167
SI x
Sideways launching 283
Signatures of ships 167
Significant wave height, amplitude 304, 310
Sills 147
Simpson's rules 24
Sims, Sir A. J. viii
Simulation 41
Simulator 37
Sisal 165
Slender body theory 202
Sliding ways 275
Slope deflection method 246
Slopes and deflections 199
Small deflection theories 236
Smith correction, effect 200
Society of Naval Architects and Marine Engineers 6
Spacings, Tchebycheff 31
Specialization in design 3
Specific gravity 56

Specific volume xiii, 56
Spectacle plates 264
Spectra, wave 209, 308, 311
Sprinkler systems 160
Square holes 212
Stability 93
  initial 95
  large angle 106
Stability, angle of vanishing 116
Stability assessment 130
Stability calculations, accuracy 114
Stability, dynamical 128
Stability, influence of form 96, 125
Stability of submerged body 127
Stability on grounding, docking 158, 287
Stability, range of 116
Stability standards 130
Stabilizers 263
Stable equilibrium 96, 127
Standard deviation 44, 306
Standard of stability 155
Starved horse look 237
Statical stability curve 115
Statistics 43, 209
Statutory freeboard 157
Stiffened plating 228
Still water BM 205
Strain energy 248
Strength, wind 296, 316
Stress concentrations 211
Stress raisers 216
Strip theory 202
Structural dynamics 203
Structural reliability 208
Struts 227
Superstructures 216
Surface, sea 293
Surfaces of B, M, F, Z 120
Swedged, swaged plating 236
Swell 296
Symbols xvi, 22

Table of offsets 9
Tanker explosions 164
Tchebycheff displacement sheet 78
Tchebycheff's rules 30
Temperature, ambient 291, 321, 325
Temperature, dry bulb 325
  effective 326
  globe 326
  wet bulb 326
Three, ten minus one rule 28
Tilt test 138
Todd formula 334
Tonf per inch immersion xiii, 61
Tonne, tonnef xiii, 59
Total heat 326
TPI, TPC 61
Transition temperature 216
Transverse plane 8
Trapezoidal rule 23
Tri-axial tension 216
Trial, heeling 138

Triggers 275
Trim 11, 73, 94
Trim correction 66
Tripping brackets 254
Tumble home 11
Two dimensional wave system 303

Underwater explosion 166
Uneven cooling 215
Unitized machinery 168
Units x, 22, 56
US Coastguards 5

Variance 306
Vasa, the 4
VCB 18
VCG 18
VDUs 39
Vent plates 165, 168
Vertical prismatic coefficient 14
Vibration 44, 291, 328
Vibration, cures, calculations 332
Vibration, levels, modes. 331
Virtual work 253
Viscosity, kinematic 292
Volt xi
Volume of displacement 12
Vulnerability 169

Wall-sided formula 104, 118
Water brakes 282
Water properties 291
Waterlines 8
Waterplane 8
Waterplane coefficient 12
Watertight subdivision 146, 162
Watt xi
Wave amplitudes 314
Wave frequency, number 302
Wave patterns 303
Wave pressure correction 200
Wave spectra 308, 312
Wave, standard 178
Waves 296
Waves, sinusoidal 301
Waves, trochoidal 296
Weapon blast 323
Weight 18
Weight density xiii, 55
Weight distribution 180, 205
Welding stresses 215
Wet bulb temperature 326
Wide flanged beams 229
Wind 316
Wind speed, variation with height 320
Wolf 207
Work done in heeling ship 128

Yaw 11, 94
Yielding out 209

Z curve 124